DOING A
SYSTEMATIC
REVIEW

3rd Edition

DOING A SYSTEMATIC REVIEW

A Student's Guide

M. Gemma Cherry
Angela Boland
Rumona Dickson

1 Oliver's Yard
55 City Road
London EC1Y 1SP

2455 Teller Road
Thousand Oaks
California 91320

Unit No 323-333, Third Floor, F-Block
International Trade Tower
Nehru Place, New Delhi – 110 019

8 Marina View Suite 43-053
Asia Square Tower 1
Singapore 018960

Editor: Umeeka Raichura
Assistant editor: Hannah Cavender-Deere
Production editor: Victoria Nicholas
Marketing manager: Ben Sherwood
Cover design: Shaun Mercier
Typeset by: C&M Digitals (P) Ltd, Chennai, India
Printed in the UK

Library of Congress Control Number: 2023935372

British Library Cataloguing in Publication data

A catalogue record for this book is available from the British Library

ISBN 978-1-5297-4098-1
ISBN 978-1-5297-4097-4 (pbk)

At Sage we take sustainability seriously. Most of our products are printed in the UK using responsibly sourced papers and boards. When we print overseas we ensure sustainable papers are used as measured by the Paper Chain Project grading system. We undertake an annual audit to monitor our sustainability.

Contents

List of Tables, Figures and Boxes

Tables

Figures

Boxes

Discover this textbook's online resources

Doing a Systematic Review 3e is supported by a wealth of online resources for both students and lecturers to aid study and support teaching, which are available at https://study.sagepub.com/doingasystematicreview3e

For lecturers

A detailed **Lecturer's guide** supports you to teach using the book, featuring key learning objectives, videos, weblinks, additional reading and resources for every chapter.

About the Editors

This book is largely the result of the collaboration of researchers who are, or have been, linked to the Liverpool Reviews and Implementation Group (LRiG). This research group was established in 2001 and the major focus of their work is related to conducting systematic reviews of clinical- and cost-effectiveness evidence. Members of the group also have experience in supervising and supporting students who are conducting systematic reviews as a part of their academic endeavours.

Dr M. Gemma Cherry is a lecturer in Clinical Health Psychology at the University of Liverpool and an honorary clinical psychologist at the Royal Liverpool University Hospital. Prior to qualifying as a clinical psychologist, she worked at LRiG for several years, conducting systematic reviews, particularly in the field of psychology. She was awarded her undergraduate degree in Psychology from Newcastle University in 2005, her PhD in Medical Education from the University of Liverpool in 2013 and her doctorate in Clinical Psychology from the University of Liverpool in 2016. She graduated with a Certificate in Teaching and Learning in Higher Education (Distinction) from the University of Liverpool in 2018, and uses this to guide her role as a Research Tutor on the Doctorate in Clinical Psychology programme at the University of Liverpool. Gemma is a strong believer in evidence-based practice and that primary research should be underpinned by systematic reviews.

Dr Angela Boland has worked at LRiG since it was established in 2001. During this time she has carried out many clinical- and cost-effectiveness reviews of healthcare interventions. As Director of LRiG, she has also managed and proofread many others. She has an undergraduate degree in Economics and Spanish, a master's degree and PhD in Health Economics, and a Postgraduate Certificate in Learning and Teaching in Higher Education.

Professor Rumona Dickson has been involved in the conduct of systematic reviews in healthcare for over 20 years and was the Director of LRiG from 2001 until her retirement in 2019. During that time, she was also involved in a number of master's programmes that promoted the use of systematic reviews as a learning tool to help students better understand the role of research in the evolution of health policy and practice. It was these experiences that prompted her to approach her colleagues to contribute to the first edition of this book. She is currently enjoying her retirement on the shores of Lake Winnipeg in Canada.

About the Contributors

Dr Sophie Beale joined LR*i*G in 2011 after spending 11 years at the University of York conducting economic evaluations and service reviews across a range of treatment areas for pharmaceutical, National Health Service (NHS) and government clients. She is now Director of HARE Research, an independent consultancy firm. Sophie was awarded her PhD from the University of Liverpool in 2021.

Mrs Michaela Brown has worked as a statistician at the University of Liverpool since 2009. During this time she has developed her skills in meta-analysis methods and has worked on a number of systematic reviews of healthcare interventions. Her main areas of expertise are the design, conduct and analysis of randomized controlled trials. She has an undergraduate degree in Psychology and Statistics from Newcastle University and a master's degree in Statistics from Lancaster University.

Dr Tamara Brown is Associate Professor and Theme Lead for 'Tackling Disparities' in the Obesity Institute at Leeds Beckett University. Tamara has held research posts in eight UK universities including LR*i*G (2009 to 2012). Tamara's skill set includes systematic reviews, meta-analyses, scoping reviews, mixed-methods and focus groups. Tamara is a Cochrane trained systematic reviewer and holds an honorary contract with the Office for Health Improvement and Disparities. Tamara is an active member of a large patient and public involvement group 'Obesity Voices' and champions co-production and the voice of lived experience within her research.

Dr Marty Chaplin has worked at LR*i*G and the Cochrane Infectious Diseases Group since 2013, providing statistical support to systematic reviews and meta-analyses. Marty was awarded her BSc in Mathematics in 2011 and an MSc in Statistical Epidemiology in 2012 from the University of Leeds. In 2021, Marty completed her PhD at the University of Liverpool, which focused on meta-analysis of pharmacogenetic studies.

Dr Paul Christiansen is a senior lecturer in Statistics at the University of Liverpool. He works across several fields, including forensic psychology, appetite and addiction. He has been the statistician on multiple projects validating questionnaires for use in both psychological and medical research. He received his PhD in Experimental Psychology from the University of Liverpool in 2012. Paul has presented at numerous conferences advocating best practice in statistics and measurement.

Dr Yenal Dundar is a former general practitioner and has worked as a researcher conducting systematic reviews on a wide range of topics in healthcare since 2001. During that time, he has developed particular skill in the area of systematic identification of evidence, which is an essential step in the systematic review process. He was awarded an MPhil from the Faculty of Medicine, University of Liverpool in 2006, Membership of the Royal College of Psychiatrists (MRCPsych) in 2010 and the Certificate of Completion of Training (CCT) in General Psychiatry in 2013. He became a Fellow of the Royal Australian and New Zealand College of Psychiatrists (FRANZCP) in 2021 and is working in Australia as a consultant psychiatrist.

Mr Nigel Fleeman has been a researcher at the University of Liverpool since November 1994. Originally working in public health, he conducted a number of relatively short primary and secondary research projects for local NHS bodies before he joined LRiG in October 2006. Much of his work since has been to conduct systematic reviews, on behalf of the UK HTA Programme and the Cochrane Collaboration, on a wide variety of topics. Examples include reviews to investigate the effectiveness of cancer treatments, pharmacogenetic testing, interventions aimed at reducing iron overload in patients suffering with chronic anaemia and self-management strategies for people with epilepsy. Nigel has a master's degree in Public Health from the University of Liverpool.

Dr Janette Greenhalgh is a Senior Research Fellow and has worked as a systematic reviewer at LRiG since 2006. During this time, she has conducted a wealth of systematic reviews on behalf of the UK HTA Programme and also for Cochrane on a wide variety of topics including cardiovascular disease, lung cancer, sickle cell disease and epilepsy. Janette also supervises postgraduate students who are conducting systematic reviews as part of a higher degree. Janette has a PhD in Psychology from Bangor University and a PGCE in post-compulsory education from Newport University.

Ms Juliet Hounsome worked at LRiG from 2005 to 2022 as a clinical reviewer working on both single technology assessments for NICE and health technology assessments for the HTA Programme. In addition, Juliet carried out large-scale updates of systematic reviews of prevention and intervention strategies, and of risk assessment tools for populations at high risk of engaging in violent behaviour. Juliet now carries out consultancy work for LR*i*G.

Dr Andrew Jones is a senior lecturer in Psychology at Liverpool John Moores University. Prior to this, he worked as a lecturer at the University of Liverpool. He conducts research into the factors which cause people to engage in unhealthy behaviours. He has conducted several systematic reviews, meta-analyses and umbrella reviews on these topics. He has received funding to conduct evidence syntheses for Public Health England and the World Health Organization. He received his PhD in Experimental Psychology from the University of Liverpool in 2012.

Dr Michelle Maden joined LR*i*G in 2015 to undertake her PhD at the University of Liverpool examining approaches to the incorporation of health inequalities in evidence synthesis. Since 2018, she has worked as a post-doctorate research associate in Evidence Synthesis within LR*i*G. A qualified information specialist by background with an MA in Information and Library Management, Michelle undertook a postgraduate certificate in International HTA with a focus on systematic review methods. She has expanded her role in evidence synthesis and is now involved in all aspects of reviewing, most recently for the NIHR and the World Health Organization.

Professor Elizabeth Perkins is Director of the Applied Research, Implementation and Service Evaluation (ARISE) research group and William Rathbone VI Chair of Community Nursing Research at the University of Liverpool. She has spent 20 years undertaking research studies in the field of health and social care policy. Before working at the University of Liverpool, Elizabeth worked at the Policy Studies Institute, undertaking large-scale surveys and small-scale in-depth qualitative studies for a range of funders including the Department of Health. She took up the post of Director of the Health and Community Care Research Unit (HaCCRU, now ARISE) in 1997 and has since specialized in undertaking qualitative studies, often using grounded theory, in the fields of mental health, ageing and addiction.

Gerlinde Pilkington worked as a researcher in LR*i*G from 2009 to 2016 and is now a research associate in Applied Realist Methodology within the School of Health and Related Research at the University of Sheffield. She has a background in History and Classics, and an MA in Research Methodology, focusing on social policy. She has worked on systematic reviews covering a wide range of topics including mental health, cancer treatments (focusing on treatment for older people), community wellbeing and dentistry, and really enjoys the challenges and diversity each project brings. Gerlinde has also contributed to the organization and delivery of systematic review teaching workshops and is building university-wide networks to support colleagues undertaking evidence synthesis.

Dr Helen Smith is Chief Executive Officer at Anthrologica, a leading research-based specialist in applied anthropology in global health. She is a social scientist with a disciplinary background in demography and human geography. Early in her career, she authored systematic reviews with the Cochrane Infectious Diseases and Pregnancy and Childbirth groups. Helen then became interested in how review evidence was being used in policy and practice, which led to her PhD, which explored evidence-led obstetric care in South Africa (University of Liverpool, 2002). She has authored several systematic reviews of qualitative research relating to health problems in low- and middle-income countries and has led qualitative evidence syntheses commissioned by the World Health Organization for use in guideline development.

Foreword

One of the unheralded consequences of the global pandemic has been an unparalleled growth in evidence synthesis – put simply, the science of 'doing a systematic review'. The demands of seeking answers from the literature, away from primary research and fieldwork, coupled with the need to deliver results in a timely and efficient manner have placed a premium on good advice from people who know what they are doing. The authors and editors of this welcome text definitely know what they are doing!

Of course, the pandemic had any number of unwelcome consequences – one of which is openly acknowledged by the editors – namely the understandable delay of this eagerly awaited third edition. Doing a systematic review is essentially a social exercise, typically involving a review team, advisors, stakeholders and potential users, among others. For a student, supported by one or even two supervisors, it is challenging to replicate the dynamic interactions that form the 'systematic review experience'. This groundbreaking text meets this need in at least two distinct ways.

First, you do not need to travel alone – at every stage of the review process, and for all the main types of review, you are accompanied by this experienced team of advisors to steer you along your way. Indeed, each author, a true 'guide from the side', offers essential information, practical tips and shares the benefit of their considerable experience. Such guidance has been fortified by two additional chapters, both well chosen, of which Chapter 4 on *Writing a Protocol* will prove most welcome for anyone producing a systematic review. While directed primarily at students, this text also forms an invaluable resource for supervisors, for whom each systematic review can prove a slightly different journey.

Second, this text remains both readable and practical, seen particularly in the 'Frequently Asked Questions' with answers throughout the book. These interactions stem directly from a myriad of past supervision encounters over the years and strengthen the convivial dialogue. Even as someone who has been 'doing systematic reviews' for over 25 years, I continually welcome hearing the new perspectives and alternative ideas from the authors of this essential textbook.

Those of you who simply want to blaze a straight path from A through to Z will find this an immensely practical guide to direct your first, and possibly only, systematic review. But, for others of you who, like me, intend to savour the journey, pausing along the way to reflect on available options and choices, I would encourage you to take full advantage of the authors' unique and accessible approach. When you come back to this book to guide further systematic reviews, you will find yourself with even more to appreciate. Either way, place yourself in the capable hands of this trusted guide and you will be sure to make steady progress to successfully complete your personal, unique review journey!

Professor Andrew Booth

Professor in Evidence Synthesis

School of Health and Related Research (ScHARR)

University of Sheffield

10 STEP roadmap to your systematic review

Step 1 Planning your review

Step 2 Performing scoping searches, identifying the review question and writing your protocol

Step 3 Literature searching

Step 4 Screening titles and abstracts

Step 5 Obtaining papers

Step 6 Selecting full-text papers

Step 7 Data extraction

Step 8 Quality assessment

Step 9 Analysis and synthesis

Step 10 Writing up, editing and disseminating

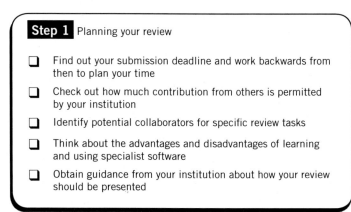

Step 1 Planning your review

- ❏ Find out your submission deadline and work backwards from then to plan your time
- ❏ Check out how much contribution from others is permitted by your institution
- ❏ Identify potential collaborators for specific review tasks
- ❏ Think about the advantages and disadvantages of learning and using specialist software
- ❏ Obtain guidance from your institution about how your review should be presented

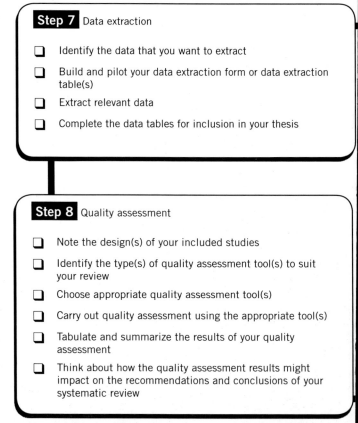

Step 7 Data extraction

- ❏ Identify the data that you want to extract
- ❏ Build and pilot your data extraction form or data extraction table(s)
- ❏ Extract relevant data
- ❏ Complete the data tables for inclusion in your thesis

Step 8 Quality assessment

- ❏ Note the design(s) of your included studies
- ❏ Identify the type(s) of quality assessment tool(s) to suit your review
- ❏ Choose appropriate quality assessment tool(s)
- ❏ Carry out quality assessment using the appropriate tool(s)
- ❏ Tabulate and summarize the results of your quality assessment
- ❏ Think about how the quality assessment results might impact on the recommendations and conclusions of your systematic review

Step 2 Performing scoping searches, identifying the review question and writing your protocol

- ❏ Identify a topic area of interest to you
- ❏ Carry out early scoping searches
- ❏ Focus your ideas to define the scope of the review
- ❏ Finalize your review question and develop your inclusion and exclusion criteria
- ❏ Consider contacting experts in the topic area
- ❏ Write a review protocol

Step 5 Obtaining papers

- ❏ Obtain the full-text papers of all potentially eligible references

Step 6 Selecting full-text papers

- ❏ Use your screening and selection tool to help you identify full-text papers for inclusion in review

Step 9 Analysis and synthesis

- ❏ Report your extracted data in your thesis
- ❏ Choose an appropriate method of analysis/synthesis
- ❏ Combine data narratively or statistically in line with your chosen method of analysis/synthesis
- ❏ Present the results of your chosen method of analysis/synthesis

Step 3 Literature searching

- ❏ Think about how comprehensive your search needs to be
- ❏ Consider the different types of evidence available to you
- ❏ Identify the specific bibliographic databases that you will search for evidence
- ❏ Identify and refine your key search terms
- ❏ Search bibliographic databases using your final search strategies and collate citations
- ❏ Consider complementary searching activities

Step 4 Screening titles and abstracts

- ❏ De-duplicate references
- ❏ Develop and pilot your screening and selection tool
- ❏ Screen all of your titles and abstracts identified via searches against your inclusion and exclusion criteria

Step 10 Writing up, editing and disseminating

- ❏ Ensure that you adhere to institutional guidelines regarding presentation and content
- ❏ Be consistent in use of language and abbreviations, and in reporting and referencing styles
- ❏ Ensure sufficient time for write-up and dissemination

Preface

Welcome to the third edition of *Doing a Systematic Review: A Student's Guide*. As with the first two editions, we want to start by welcoming you and to give you a bit of history about the book.

Why did we write this book?

There are a variety of excellent books written by systematic review experts that provide the 'How to...' of conducting a systematic review. Why, then, in 2013, did we think it was necessary to write a new one for students? Well, we wrote the first edition of this book for two reasons.

First, we have long held a strong conviction that conducting a systematic review as a postgraduate research project can yield excellent learning opportunities for students. Increasingly, academic and scientific communities are also acknowledging the value of this research activity. Conducting a systematic review requires insight into the fundamentals of research. Students learn to develop research questions, critique research findings and, most importantly, synthesize findings and make recommendations about how their results could be used to shape or guide professional practice. These are valuable skills for students to learn, no matter what their academic or professional discipline.

Second, we wanted to reflect on the systematic review process from the viewpoint of a student working independently (most likely at master's level, but perhaps at undergraduate or doctoral level) to undertake a systematic review as part of their academic programme. Even though the 'How to...' books are useful to students, they frequently don't focus on the 'But what do I do when...?' type questions that so often arise during the review process. These are the questions that students need to know the answers to more or less immediately so that they can move forward with their theses. While we wanted the first edition of our book to provide a comprehensive guide to conducting a systematic review, we decided to focus more on the *practicalities* of systematic reviewing rather than on the theory underpinning it. We pitched the first edition of this book at students conducting systematic reviews, not simply learning about them.

Understandably, we were a bit nervous about how the first edition of this book would be received. Luckily, there was no need for nerves. Responses proved what we believed: that there was a need for an easy-to-read handbook to guide students through their systematic review journey. Fortunately, our publishers agreed, and, in 2017, the second edition of our book was published. We began work on the third edition of our book in 2020 but – you guessed it – the world had other plans! With the spread of the COVID-19 pandemic and subsequent lockdowns, we had to reprioritize and instead focused our efforts on balancing work with caring for ourselves, our families and those closest to us. The publication of the third edition of our book is therefore three years later than planned, but brimming with new material to help students smoothly navigate their systematic review journey.

What does the third edition of this book contain?

This book retains our tried-and-tested stepwise approach to supporting students who are conducting a systematic review as part of their postgraduate studies. It's laid out in the same way as our previous editions, except that the book now contains 14 chapters. The first chapter explains why we think systematic reviews are important, how they came about and why they provide an excellent learning opportunity for students. The remaining chapters focus on the systematic review process and offer methodological and practical advice about how to conduct and report this type of research within the format of a postgraduate thesis. As in the previous editions, each chapter ends with a 'Frequently Asked Questions' section. These questions have been taken from student supervision meetings and highlight common challenges encountered during the review process. They include not only 'What do I do?' questions but also 'Why do I do this?' and 'What are my options?' questions. Our answers set out practical approaches to help students deal with these issues. In addition, we have included supporting web links throughout. Common sense tells you that these links have a tendency to go out of date quickly – we have tried to reference only well-established organizations, pages and resources, so that if the links no longer work, they can still be accessed via a quick Internet search.

In each edition of the book, we have drawn on our own extensive experiences of conducting systematic reviews of healthcare interventions using quantitative methods. However, the principles covered are also relevant to students in other disciplines, such as social work and education, where there is encouragement to systematically review current research or practice. We know that there are more than quantitative data to review so the book also contains introductions to reviewing qualitative data and health economics data, both of which are currently exciting, controversial and evolving areas of research. We acknowledge that these two chapters only offer students a starting point for their review journey but hope they will inspire students to read more widely around these methodological areas.

We have kept the tone informal, that of a friendly advisor, and have retained the Glossary to give the reader a more in-depth explanation of terms as they arise. As in the second edition, Glossary terms appear in bold type at first mention in the text. If you are unfamiliar with the vocabulary of systematic reviewing, then we encourage you to consult this Glossary frequently until you feel able to fully engage with the content of each chapter.

What does this book have to offer you?

We had to make some general assumptions regarding the typical reader of this book. We thought long and hard about the research skills and resources postgraduate students might have at this point in their academic journey. Based on this, we have assumed that you, the typical reader of this book, will:

- be conducting a systematic review as part of your postgraduate studies
- have access to a computer
- be able to search the Internet
- have word-processing skills and not be afraid to use them
- have your own learning objectives relating to professional practice and/or to the research process
- have a specific research area in mind
- be working (mainly) independently
- need to meet a set-in-stone deadline

As with previous editions, we've tried to make the book useful and easy to read. We've assumed that you want a no-frills approach, and each chapter is written with this in mind. The basics of systematic review methodology are delivered in bite-sized chunks so that you are not overwhelmed by the enormity of your project. Students tell us that they are happiest (and most productive) when they are in control of their own research and are not reliant on others for data or direction. This book is therefore written to guide you as you take control of your systematic review. We are confident that it will help you move forward at your own pace. We know that you will want to excel in your studies so, at the end of most chapters, we have also set out a section detailing what an examiner might be looking for in the final thesis.

What's new in this third edition?

When planning this edition, we listened to feedback from reviewers and readers of our previous editions; in response, all chapters have been updated to increase their applicability and breadth, and to reflect new directions and advances in the field of systematic reviewing. We also reflected on *who* used our book and *why* and *how* they found it useful. We found out about the different courses and disciplines that had already adopted the book as recommended or essential reading. We asked our publishers for sales and readership statistics. We read through every online review that we could find (thank you). Finally, we spent a happy few hours perusing the hashtag #systematicreview on Instagram and noting the ways in which our book was being used. We were delighted to realize that our book was not just useful to master's students but had also become key reading for doctoral students. It made sense to broaden the focus of this edition to include all postgraduate students conducting a systematic review in part or total fulfilment of their academic degree. Beyond the new front cover, this is the first obvious change to this edition.

The second notable addition to this edition is two new chapters. We recognized that, in our earlier editions, we did not spend enough time discussing *how* to write and register a review protocol. We also placed too much emphasis on analysing data from interventions studies without also telling our readers how to understand and synthesize data from correlational and experimental studies. Students told us that these were important information gaps, particularly for systematic reviews in social sciences, education or broader fields. We therefore included two new chapters: Chapter 4 (Writing a Protocol) and Chapter 9 (Understanding and Critically Appraising Data from Experimental and Correlational Studies).

Our eagle-eyed readers might also notice two final changes. First, we have repackaged our online resources into a Teaching Guide for supervisors and lecturers. We still signpost readers to further reading and resources at the end of each chapter, however, and encourage you to engage with these materials until you feel confident to tackle each step of your review. Second, you may have noticed that Gemma is now the lead editor (congratulations, Gemma). In recent years, Gemma's extensive postgraduate supervisory experience has benefited the book in many ways and brought contemporaneous student voices into the editorial process – because of this, we are confident that the book continues to address issues commonly faced by students during the review process. But don't worry, Angela and Rumona are still fully committed to the book and the author team remains intact and has, in fact, expanded – welcome, Paul and Andy.

Final thoughts

In 2020, the COVID-19 pandemic shifted the research landscape and disrupted primary research agendas and plans worldwide. Throughout the pandemic, academic institutions worked hard to support their postgraduate students (especially Health Sciences students, for obvious reasons) to complete their studies at distance. Consequently, researchers and students changed their plans and many carried out systematic reviews instead of primary research. This has led to an influx of published systematic reviews and increased attention on the importance and benefits of evidence synthesis methods. We therefore have included 'Alternative Routes' sections in some chapters which discuss the changing landscape of systematic review methodology and resources and direct the reader to alternative ways to approach aspects of their systematic review journey. We hope that you have as much fun reading this book as we have had writing and editing it. Please continue to engage with the book and with us through email, social media, reviews and word of mouth – it makes our day to know that students have found this resource helpful.

With best wishes

Gemma, Angela and Rumona

1

What is a Systematic Review?

Rumona Dickson, Gerlinde Pilkington, M. Gemma Cherry and Angela Boland

This chapter will help you to...

- Understand the term 'systematic review'

- Gain an awareness of the historical context and development of the systematic review research process

- Appreciate the learning experience provided by conducting a systematic review

- Familiarize yourself with the methods involved in conducting a systematic review

Introduction

In this chapter, we introduce you to the concept of systematically reviewing literature. First, we discuss what **systematic reviews** are and give you an overview of the evolution of systematic review methodology. Second, we outline why we think conducting a systematic review is an excellent way to gain an understanding of the process of conducting research. Third, we introduce the key steps in the systematic review process and signpost where in the book these are discussed. Finally, we highlight how systematic reviews differ from other types of **literature review**. By the end of the chapter, we hope that you will be confident that you have made the right decision to carry out a systematic review and that you are looking forward to starting your research.

What is a systematic review?

A systematic review is a literature review that is designed to locate, appraise and synthesize the best available evidence relating to a specific **research question** to provide informative and **evidence-based** answers. This information can then be used in a variety of ways. For example, in addition to advancing the field and informing future practice or research, the information can be combined with professional judgement to make decisions about how to deliver interventions or to make changes to policy. Systematic reviews are considered the best (**gold standard**) way to synthesize the findings of several studies reporting data that allow you to answer the same question, whether the evidence comes from healthcare, education, business or another discipline. Systematic reviews follow well-defined and transparent steps and require the following: definition of the research question or problem, identification and **critical appraisal** of the available evidence, synthesis of the findings and the drawing of relevant conclusions.

Evolution of the systematic review process

There are some common misconceptions about systematic reviewing. Some students (and supervisors) choose **primary research** projects over systematic reviews because they worry that systematic reviews are not 'proper research', that systematic reviews can only be conducted in the field of health or that a systematic review always includes a **meta-analysis.** If you are considering conducting a systematic review as part of your academic thesis, we think that it will set your mind at ease to know a little bit about the history and evolution of the systematic review process.

It might surprise you to know that the systematic review of **published evidence** is not new. As early as 1753, James Lind brought together data relating to the prevention of scurvy experienced by sailors (Chalmers et al., 2002).

From Lind's farsightedness we move to the 1970s. Two important events took place that laid the foundations for a revolution in the way that evidence could be used to inform practice in healthcare and other areas. In the United Kingdom (UK), a tuberculosis specialist named Archie Cochrane had recognized that healthcare resources would always be finite. To maximize health benefits, Cochrane proposed that any form of healthcare used in the UK National Health Service (NHS) must be properly evaluated and shown to be clinically effective before use (Cochrane, 1972). He stressed the importance of using evidence from **randomized controlled trials** (RCTs) to inform the allocation of scarce healthcare resources. At around the same time, in the United States of America, work by Gene Glass (1976) had led to the development of statistical procedures for combining the results of independent studies. The term 'meta-analysis' was formally coined to refer to the statistical combination of data from individual studies using a process that allows researchers to draw practical conclusions about **clinical effectiveness** or objectivity of research findings. In years to come, outputs of both research communities would combine to form the basic tenets of systematic review methodology.

In 1979, Archie Cochrane lamented:

> It is surely a great criticism of our profession that we have not organized a critical summary, by specialty or subspecialty, adapted periodically, of all relevant randomized controlled trials. (Cochrane, 1979, pp. 1–11)

In response, a group of UK and Canadian clinicians working in perinatal medicine made every effort to identify all RCTs relating to pregnancy and childbirth. They categorized the studies that they found and then synthesized the evidence from these studies. This work led to the development of the Oxford Database of Perinatal Trials (Chalmers et al., 1986). This work was instrumental in laying the foundations for significant developments in systematic review methodology (Chalmers et al., 1989), including the establishment of **Cochrane** (formally called the Cochrane Collaboration) in 1992. Cochrane is an international network of researchers from over 130 countries who work together to help healthcare providers, policy makers, and patients and their advocates make evidence-based decisions about healthcare. Since the development of Cochrane, other collaboratives have been formed. The **Campbell Collaboration** was established in 2000 and focuses on reviewing literature to demonstrate the effects of social interventions, particularly in the areas of education, crime and justice (Campbell Collaboration, 2012). More recently, the Foreign, Commonwealth and Development Office (formerly the Department for International

Development [DfID]) has used the results of systematic reviews to develop national and international policy in countries worldwide (DfID, 2012).

Why have people spent so much time developing a systematic review process and why do they continue to refine and improve methods? The answer is quite simple. Given time constraints, the amount and complexity of available information, there has been a need to develop a process that summarizes the results of research findings. Most notably, the significant increase in the amount of accessible research today makes it impossible for decision makers, policy makers and professionals to keep up to date with advances in their field. The COVID-19 pandemic has highlighted the importance of being able to bring together relevant research findings quickly and rigorously from multiple sources to guide policy making and clinical practice worldwide. A systematic review allows concise synthesis of a large body of research and therefore addresses some of these issues.

Why are we telling you all of this? Well, there are two important points to take away from this historical background. First, we want to convince you that systematic review methodology is accepted as a research methodology in its own right; in light of this, we use the terms '**review question**' and 'research question' interchangeably throughout the book. In fact, most funding bodies require a systematic review of the literature to be performed before they will fund a primary research project. In the UK, systematic reviews form the basis for the **National Institute for Health and Care Excellence** (NICE) guidelines for treatment and clinical practice (NICE, 2023) and, more recently, the **National Institute for Health and Care Research** (NIHR) has developed a national Evidence Synthesis Programme aimed at building and enhancing world knowledge through **evidence synthesis**. Throughout the world, Cochrane and Campbell Collaboration publications are viewed as gold standard systematic reviews. While you wouldn't necessarily be expected to produce a review as detailed or as comprehensive as a Cochrane or Campbell Collaboration review for your thesis, if you follow the systematic review methodology outlined in this book, you can be confident that you are conducting high-quality research.

Second, we want to show you that although the systematic review process began, and is common, in the field of healthcare, systematic reviews are being carried out and used to inform decision making in a variety of disciplines and professions. In fact, if you conduct a quick Internet search combining the terms 'systematic review' with 'education', 'business', 'social work' or 'veterinary medicine' (or almost any other professional field), you will become aware of the widespread application of systematic review methodology. Irrespective of the field in which you study, the basic tenets of systematically reviewing the evidence are the same. When a researcher or **practitioner** is faced with a problem, they aim to identify, assess and bring together the evidence relating to that problem. This information can then be used to inform changes to policy and/or professional practice.

A systematic review: a research option for postgraduate students

There are very good reasons why you are asked to carry out a research project as part of your studies, the most important being that conducting a research project enables you to both understand the research process and gain research skills. As a postgraduate student (at master's or doctoral level), you may have to choose between collecting **primary data** (e.g. conducting an **observational study**) and/or analysing **secondary data** (e.g. conducting a systematic review) as part of your academic accreditation.

Many academic programmes offer instruction in systematic review methods and encourage students to conduct systematic reviews as part of their postgraduate study and assessment. It is widely acknowledged that this approach allows students to gain an understanding of different research methods and develop skills in formulating research questions as well as identifying, appraising and synthesizing research findings to address their research questions.

Every postgraduate course and every academic institution is different. For you, this means that the presentation of your thesis must follow the accepted guidelines of the department or university where your thesis is due to be submitted. Your thesis must be an independent and self-directed piece of academic work; it should clearly address a specific research question (or questions) using detailed and original arguments. We recognize that there are lots of different types of postgraduate programmes and therefore lots of different types of theses. A systematic review may represent an entire thesis in one discipline/qualification or represent a small part of a larger body of work in another discipline/qualification. Make sure that you interpret our advice and recommendations for conducting a systematic review in light of your institution's specific requirements.

Doing a systematic review as a master's thesis

Let's assume that you are interested in studying issues related to unintended teenage pregnancy. As a master's student, you have a variety of investigational methods open to you. However, the likelihood of being able to use these may be impeded by time and resource constraints and the specific requirements of your academic institution.

Table 1.1 illustrates possible project options that may be open to you and the likelihood of you being able to successfully complete your chosen project as part of your postgraduate studies.

TABLE 1.1   Example project options for master's students interested in unintended teenage pregnancy

Question	Research options	Type of research	Risk* of not being able to complete this as an academic exercise
Relationship questions			
What is the incidence of unintended teenage pregnancy in my practice or region?	**Epidemiological survey**	Primary	Low
What programmes are available in my practice or region for reducing teenage pregnancy rates?	Survey	Primary	Low
What are the most commonly reported methods used to decrease rates of teenage pregnancy?	Systematic review	Secondary	Low
Correlation questions			
Is there a relationship between education levels and rates of teenage pregnancy in my practice or region?	Secondary analysis of existing dataset	Primary	Moderate
What is the reported relationship between education level and rates of teenage pregnancy?	Systematic review	Secondary	Low
Causation questions			
Does the provision of emergency contraception in schools decrease teenage pregnancy rates?	Intervention study	Primary	High
What impact do one-to-one counselling and group meetings have on rates of abortion for teenagers experiencing unintended pregnancy?	Randomized controlled trial	Primary	Very high
What have been shown to be the most effective programmes for decreasing teenage pregnancy rates?	Systematic review	Secondary	Low
Qualitative questions			
What are the views of teenagers on the reasons for high teenage pregnancy rates?	**Focus groups**	Primary	Moderate, with small sample size
What are pregnant teenagers' views on the importance of sex education?	Semi-structured interviews	Primary	Low, with small sample size
What are the reported views of teenagers on the reasons for high teenage pregnancy rates?	Systematic review	Secondary	Low

*Low = you are in control or have unlimited access to the data that you need; moderate = you may or may not have to go through an **ethics committee**, you are dependent on other people to give you data or you need to recruit participants; high = your study is likely to be expensive, time consuming and/or dependent on the interest and participation of others.

In our experience, master's students who opt for primary research mainly explore questions relating to associations between variables or people's experiences. The main problem with this kind of research is that its **generalizability** or **transferability** is often hampered by small sample sizes and time constraints. Although conducting a systematic review can be just as time consuming as undertaking primary research, students who form questions that can be addressed using systematic review methodology have the opportunity to work with a variety of study designs and populations without needing to worry about the issues commonly faced by researchers conducting large-scale primary research. Due to the very nature of a systematic review, students can work with existing research findings while developing critical appraisal and research synthesis skills. Conducting a systematic review provides an excellent learning opportunity and allows students to identify and set their own learning objectives.

Good research is rarely carried out on an ad hoc basis. From the outset, you need to be clear about why you are conducting your systematic review. For example, you may want to evaluate the current state of knowledge or belief about a particular topic of interest, contribute to the development of specific theories or the establishment of a new evidence base, and/or make recommendations for future research (or you might just want to carry out your review as quickly and as effortlessly as possible to gain your qualification). You need to consider what you want to learn from your master's studies. You will find that balancing your learning objectives with the objectives of your review may be challenging at times; this is most likely to be true if you are reviewing a topic of interest in your professional field (as we suggest you do). Discussing your learning objectives with your supervisor(s) and exploring alternatives with your classmates or colleagues can often help you to clarify these objectives. Box 1.1 outlines some of the advantages and disadvantages of conducting a systematic review as part of a master's thesis.

Box 1.1

A systematic review as a master's thesis: advantages and disadvantages

Advantages

- You are in control of your learning objectives and your project
- You can focus on a topic that you're interested in
- You usually don't have to gain formal ethical approval for your review before you begin

(Continued)

- You don't have to recruit participants
- You can gain understanding of a number of different research methodologies
- You can gain insight into the strengths and limitations of **published evidence**
- You can develop your **critical appraisal** skills
- The research can fit in, and around, your family (or social) life

Disadvantages

- You usually don't experience preparing and defending an ethics application
- It can be isolating as you are likely to be primarily working on your own
- It can be time consuming to find a body of research mature enough for review
- You don't face the challenges of recruiting participants
- You are reliant on the quality and quantity of available published information to address your research question
- You may find the process dull or boring at times
- There are no shortcuts and the process is time consuming

Doing a systematic review as part of a doctoral thesis

As a doctoral student, you may find you have more time and resources available to you and therefore you can plan more ambitious primary research studies than if you were a master's student. A systematic review is an excellent way of demonstrating that your empirical research is novel, methodologically sound and needed. For this reason, examiners in some disciplines view a systematic review as an integral component of a high-quality doctoral thesis.

Master's students typically need to answer a single specific question, but doctoral students tend to use systematic review methodology to describe the literature and/or theory base that informs their primary research. If you are planning to carry out a systematic review as part of your doctorate, you may well find yourself conducting a series of mini systematic reviews rather than one single review. Alternatively, you might conduct a single systematic review on a very tightly defined topic and go on to conduct a wide-ranging **narrative review** to situate the results of your systematic review and set up your empirical work in current policy and practice.

What are the basic steps in the systematic review process and how can this book help me to follow them?

We consider there to be ten basic steps involved in a systematic review. These are presented in Box 1.2 along with signposts to the chapters in which they are discussed in more detail. These steps are continually referred to and explored throughout the book, so don't worry if you don't recognize all the terms at this stage. Use the Glossary to help you to become familiar with key terms; we expect that you'll quickly start to understand their relevance to the systematic review process as you read through the book. The authors of a good quality systematic review will transparently report the methods that were used so that the reader has sufficient information to be able to replicate the review. Additionally, providing details about each step makes it easy for the reader to assess the **validity** of the review's findings. The remainder of this book provides you with a pragmatic yet detailed approach to carrying out each of these ten steps and we focus our attention on the research activities that are essential for the successful completion of your review as part of a postgraduate thesis.

Box 1.2

Ten steps in the systematic review process

Step 1: Planning your review (Chapter 2)

The first step is to plan your review by thinking about how best to use the time and resources available to you.

Step 2: Performing scoping searches, identifying the review question and writing your protocol (Chapters 3 and 4)

In this step, you carry out **scoping searches** to help you identify background litera-ture that will allow you to define and refine your review question and to set your **inclusion** and **exclusion criteria**. You also write a **protocol**. The protocol is a written plan (a 'map' of your journey) that enables you to set out the approach you will use to answer the review question.

(Continued)

Step 3: Literature searching (Chapter 5)

The aim of this step is to identify evidence (published and unpublished), using bibliographic databases and other evidence sources that you can use to address your review question.

Step 4: Screening titles and abstracts (Chapter 6)

In this step, you read the titles and abstracts of the studies identified by your searches and discard the ones that aren't at all relevant to your review question and keep the ones that may be relevant.

Step 5: Obtaining papers (Chapter 6)

This step involves obtaining the full-text papers that you identified in Step 4.

Step 6: Selecting full-text papers (Chapter 6)

This is when you apply your inclusion and exclusion criteria to your full-text papers and ruthlessly exclude ones that don't fit the criteria.

Step 7: Data extraction (Chapter 7)

This is when you identify relevant data from each paper and summarize these data using forms or tables.

Step 8: Quality assessment (Chapter 8)

In this step, you assess each included full-text paper for **methodological quality** using an appropriate **quality assessment tool**.

Step 9: Analysis and synthesis (Chapters 7–12)

This is where you scrutinize and synthesize your data, either narratively or through meta-analysis, taking into account the methodological quality of your included studies (Chapter 8). We discuss how to do this step in Chapter 7 and Chapter 9 (if you want to undertake a **narrative synthesis**) and Chapter 10 (for those who have appropriate data for meta-analysing). We also discuss how to analyse **qualitative data** in Chapter 11 and **health economics** data in Chapter 12.

Step 10: Writing up, editing and disseminating (Chapters 2 and 10–14)

This is where you bring all your hard work together. Step 10 involves writing up your background, methods and results, discussing your findings, drawing conclusions from your review and disseminating your findings. We discuss how to carry out this step in Chapters 2, 13 and 14, and touch upon it in Chapters 11 and 12 for those looking at qualitative evidence and **economic evaluations** respectively.

But don't all types of literature review follow these steps?

In this book, when we say that we've carried out a systematic review of the literature, this means that we have clearly planned and fully described the review steps that we've taken to answer the review question(s); all our actions are transparent, all the key methodological decisions have been informed by theory and/or pragmatism, and all are explicitly set out for the reader to judge. Unfortunately, not all reviews that are published have been written with this definition of 'systematic' in mind. You may be familiar with the terms 'literature review', 'systematic review' and 'narrative review', but you might not know exactly what the different terms mean. To complicate matters, in the published literature, these terms are frequently used interchangeably. Furthermore, researchers are increasingly using adapted systematic review methodology to perform other types of review, such as **rapid review** and **scoping review** or **evidence map**.

Here we outline some of the different review methods that you may come across. Some of the inherent differences between review methods are presented in Table 1.2.

Literature reviews

The term 'literature review' is often a catch-all term for any study that assimilates and synthesizes or describes the findings of more than one study. Literature reviews may or may not use a systematic approach.

Narrative reviews

Narrative literature reviews were (historically) and are (currently) typically prepared by 'experts' to provide an overview of a specific topic, to raise overlooked issues and/or identify information gaps, or to encourage new research. Authors of narrative reviews do not usually claim that their reviews are comprehensive and/or systematic.

Rapid reviews

Rapid reviews have emerged due to an ever-increasing need for information within a short time frame. Although their exact methods and approaches are loosely defined, these reviews are primarily systematic reviews in which researchers take pre-agreed shortcuts to deliver findings rapidly. These shortcuts should always be explicitly stated and justified in the write-up of the review.

Scoping reviews and evidence maps

Scoping reviews also differ from systematic reviews, though again the precise definitions and methods are still developing. Having said that, most definitions of scoping reviews include the concept of mapping out the evidence base pertaining to a particular research question or topic area (Arksey & O'Malley, 2005; Levac et al., 2010). Scoping reviews can be performed to outline the breadth and type of literature available relating to a specific topic, or to identify any gaps in the literature in question. In some cases, a scoping review can be performed to assess the feasibility of conducting a systematic review on a topic. Scoping reviews follow a similar process to systematic reviews, though the methods employed at each stage vary slightly (Munn et al., 2018). Specifically, researchers conducting scoping reviews often adopt an iterative approach, and place greater emphasis on consultation with consumers and stakeholders than those conducting systematic reviews.

Evidence mapping is an emerging method of evidence synthesis that has some commonalities with scoping reviews and the terms are often used interchangeably in guidance and published papers. Miake-Lye and colleagues (2016) concluded, from a systematic review of self-styled evidence maps, that 'the implied decision (...) of what constitutes an evidence map is a systematic search of a broad field to identify gaps in knowledge and/or future research needs that presents results in a user-friendly format, often a visual figure or graph, or a searchable database' (p. 18). As with **mixed-methods reviews**, this approach is new and methods for its use will likely evolve as further research is published. If you are planning to carry out this type of review as part of your academic thesis, you need to make sure you or your supervisor(s) are familiar with this approach.

A simple way to illustrate the difference between narrative reviews, systematic reviews, rapid reviews and scoping reviews is also presented in Figure 1.1. Essentially, a narrative review considers great breadth of information but may be limited in depth. A systematic review is usually narrow in the breadth of information considered but it looks at the data in great depth. A rapid review is also narrow, or may be narrower, than a systematic review and, due to time constraints, does not look at the evidence in as much depth. Scoping reviews/evidence maps are broader in scope than rapid reviews but do not go into as much detail as systematic reviews.

TABLE 1.2 Differences in review processes

	Narrative reviews	Systematic reviews	Rapid reviews	Scoping reviews/evidence maps
Defining a question	May or may not be clearly defined	Clearly defined and well focused Always required	Clearly defined and well focused Always required	Clearly defined Broader in focus Always required
Writing a protocol	Not usually required	Recommended/essential	Recommended	Recommended
Methodology	Does not follow explicit or rigorous methodology	Follows explicit and rigorous methodology	Follows explicit and rigorous methodology	Follows explicit and rigorous methodology but can be iterative
Searching	No predefined search strategy Not necessarily comprehensive Generally relies only on published literature Search strategies may be based on expert experience	Exhaustive and with an appropriate balance of sensitivity and specificity Carried out across a number of bibliographic databases, hand searching of reference lists from relevant papers and high-yield journals and documents/reports Grey (unpublished) literature sometimes searched Comprehensive and explicit searching methods used and reported	Predefined and explicitly stated Possibly limited by: • Search of only one database • Narrow time frame • Reliance on published literature only • No hand searching	Breadth balanced with resource availability Iterative, with additional terms added as a result of identifying key papers (use of citation chaining)
Definition of inclusion and exclusion criteria	Not essential No selection of studies based on study design	Essential Study design can be selected (e.g. only include qualitative data, RCTs or both)	Essential More exclusive than in systematic review	Essential Can be defined post hoc if rationale is reported
Screening titles and abstracts; selecting full-text papers	Generally carried out by one researcher by reading through relevant papers and based on their own experience	Explicit and systematic screening and selection, using predefined method Usually **cross-checked** by another researcher	Explicit and systematic screening and selection, using predefined method Possibly limited by: • Single person screening • Single person selection	Explicit and systematic screening and selection, using predefined method Usually cross-checked by another researcher

(Continued)

TABLE 1.2 (Continued)

	Narrative reviews	Systematic reviews	Rapid reviews	Scoping reviews/evidence maps
Quality assessment	Not necessarily	Yes	Unlikely	Unlikely
Data extraction	Yes	Yes	Yes Possibly limited by: • Single person extraction • Cross-checked by one person • Limited data extracted	Yes, though can be more iterative
Analysis and synthesis	No clear method of synthesis	Can involve meta-analysis, narrative or qualitative synthesis	Narrative synthesis only	Numerical analysis of extent and nature of studies An analytical framework or qualitative analysis can be used to provide an overview of breadth
Application	Any field	Any field	Any field	Any field
Timescale	May be carried out relatively quickly	Can be time consuming due to rigour required	Variable but usually shorter than full systematic review	Variable but usually shorter than full systematic review
Replication	Not easily replicable	Explicit methods and therefore replicable	Explicit methods and therefore replicable	Iterative process but explicit methods and therefore replicable

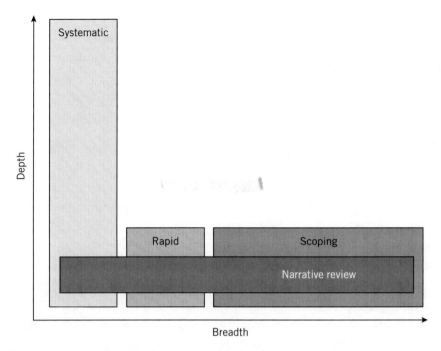

FIGURE 1.1   Depth and breadth of different types of reviews

Other types of review

Mixed-methods reviews

You might find yourself tackling a systematic review where you need to work with, and interpret, both quantitative and qualitative data to answer your research question. These types of reviews are sometimes called mixed-methods reviews (see Hong et al. [2020] and Harden et al. [2018] for a summary of different mixed-methods review approaches). You might also see the term 'mixed-methods review' used to describe reviews in which the authors have synthesized qualitative and **quantitative data** separately to answer separate sub-questions. When *we* talk about mixed-methods reviews, we mean reviews that combine the two data types to answer a single question (for instance, by qualitizing quantitative data, or vice versa). It's important not to underestimate how challenging conducting these reviews can be. Researchers conducting mixed-methods reviews need to be clear about why they are taking this approach and set out what prompted them to combine the two types of data to answer a single review question – was it to gain as comprehensive an understanding of a particular topic as possible or was it to generate new insights into a specific phenomenon? Sandelowski et al. (2007) make a distinction between 'assimilation', where the findings are incorporated into each other, and 'configuration', where the findings are used to generate new, or modify existing, theoretical or narrative accounts. Other authors use terms such as 'aggregation' and 'integration' to reflect the different types of activity associated with systematically reviewing qualitative and quantitative studies.

Realist reviews

This approach is often called realist synthesis and was developed by Pawson and colleagues (2005) as a means of determining what works for whom, in what circumstances, in what respects and how. **Realist reviews** differ from systematic reviews in a number of ways. Notably, realist reviewers aim to use existing theory to understand and explain how and why different outcomes were observed in a sample of empirical studies. Reviewers first develop a set of 'programme theories' by making assumptions about how an intervention is expected to work and the impact that it is expected to have. Relevant empirical data are then systematically (but not always exhaustively) identified and used to populate the theoretical framework. By considering the context in which an intervention is delivered, the mechanisms by which change occurs (or not), and the outcomes of the intervention, programme theories are supported, refuted or modified until a final theory, or set of theories, is identified. Realist reviews can be especially useful for policy makers and decision makers, as their findings are rich and detailed and can be used to further our understanding of complex interventions in a way that systematic review methodology may not permit. A good example of this is a realist review (Greenhalgh et al., 2007) conducted to supplement a Cochrane review on school feeding programmes (Kristjansson et al., 2007). The Cochrane review found some small benefits for disadvantaged children while the realist review revealed the contexts in which the programmes were more likely to be effective. Realist reviews can be complicated to carry out, and we wouldn't recommend this type of review as an option for postgraduate students new to systematic reviewing unless supported by an experienced supervisor.

Living reviews

Living reviews are reviews that are updated regularly (often monthly) to reflect the latest research evidence available on a specific topic (Cochrane, 2019). New information technologies and approaches (e.g. **text mining** and linked data) and continual active monitoring of evidence sources mean that the findings of high-quality living reviews are always up to date. This type of review is typically published online, and readers can sign up to receive notifications when newer versions of living reviews are made available to ensure that they always access the latest version of each review.

Complex systematic reviews

Complex systematic reviews (which are not to be confused with reviews of complex interventions) usually bring together multiple different sources of data and use advanced methods of evidence synthesis to answer an often multi-faceted and interdisciplinary review question. Complex systematic reviews bring different elements together and are often carried out in several stages. For example, a complex systematic review could be done in three stages: 1) map the evidence; 2) synthesize quantitative data, qualitative data, economic data and policy; and 3) use all the available information to create a new conceptual framework. In the UK, the NIHR and Cochrane have collaborated to develop a specific team to support researchers undertaking complex systematic reviews (see www.nihrcrsu.org for more resources). It goes without saying that we wouldn't recommend this type of review as an option for postgraduate students new to systematic reviewing unless supported by an experienced supervisor.

Umbrella reviews

Umbrella reviews are 'reviews of reviews' – that is, systematic reviews of previously published systematic reviews and/or meta-analyses (Fusar-Poli & Radua, 2018). Umbrella reviews are important as they allow researchers to quickly assess a large volume of evidence and compare and contrast the findings of previously published systematic reviews on a specific topic. This type of review is becoming increasingly popular in biomedical literature.

A few thoughts before you begin your systematic review

We like to think of the systematic review process as a journey. Experience has taught us that systematic reviewing can be challenging – especially when we don't have a good plan (protocol) to guide us. We know that untoward conditions mean that you might have to divert from your chosen route (e.g. uncommunicative authors, missing papers or poor-quality studies). Experienced systematic reviewers learn to anticipate what is going to happen next. Whether you are travelling on a busy motorway or on a rural lane, it is a good idea to pay attention to your environment (the review context) and journey time (time management) and plan what to do if your vehicle breaks down (contact your supervisor(s)). Collective experience has taught us how to overcome the most common hazards and we'd like to share our knowledge with you. In this book, we offer a broad range of tips and strategies to help you begin your journey and reach your final destination.

This chapter has introduced you to the notion of conducting a systematic review as part of your academic thesis. In the next chapter, we discuss practical tips to help you plan and manage your review. Chapters 3 to 6 will help you to get started and identify evidence, and Chapters 7 to 12 will guide you through the process of critically engaging with different types of data, including numerical data from correlational, experimental and **intervention studies** (Chapters 9 and 10), qualitative data (Chapter 11), and data from economic evaluations (Chapter 12). In Chapters 13 and 14, we lead you through ways to write up and disseminate your review to wider audiences. We recognize that systematic reviews can be bitty in that you might start a new step before the current one is fully finished; this might occur, for example, if you are waiting for papers to arrive in the post or for input from others. As such, the advantage of this book is that it hasn't been set out like a novel (i.e. written for you to read cover to cover once). Instead, each chapter is designed to stand alone. We hope that you will start by reading the whole book in chapter order, but we expect that you will then dip in and out of chapters at appropriate points in your research journey. As we mentioned earlier, some of the concepts explored in the book will seem unfamiliar to you on first reading, which is why we have included a Glossary of key terms for you to refer to as and when needed.

Frequently Asked Questions

Question 1: Is a systematic review 'real research'?

This is a valid and common question posed by students. There are some researchers and academics who argue that a systematic review is not 'real research'. We believe that they are wrong. Submitting a systematic review as part or all of an academic qualification has become commonplace in many universities worldwide and across a variety of disciplines. We believe that the many learning opportunities that are derived from the systematic review process can help students to achieve academic goals and can equip them with the skills that are required to meet the needs of research communities and to enhance their continuing professional development and practice.

Question 2: Am I taking the easy option by conducting a systematic review?

No, definitely not. Systematic reviewing can be a difficult, time-consuming and solitary activity. It's not for the faint-hearted. While you don't (usually) have to go through the ethics process (which can take time and be fraught with difficulties), there are other challenges to face, such as coping with thousands of possible research reports or government documents or, worse yet, finding none. However, the rewards, in terms of outputs and learning opportunities, make conducting a systematic review an excellent choice of project for your thesis and this methodology offers you an opportunity to display rigorous and reflective practice in your write-up. Your examiner(s) should acknowledge this effort when examining your thesis.

Question 3: Should I conduct a systematic or a narrative review for my thesis?

We are often asked this question by students who believe that narrative reviews are somehow easier or less time consuming than systematic reviews, and our answer is always the same: we advocate that students should, where possible, conduct a systematic rather than a narrative review. Students are often surprised when we tell them that many of the steps involved in systematic and narrative reviews overlap, so there isn't usually much difference in workload between the two methods. However, systematic reviews have a number of advantages over narrative reviews. For example, systematic reviews are less open to **bias** than narrative reviews, as they represent a synthesis of the available evidence pertaining to a specific review question. They can help to advance knowledge and can be easier to publish than narrative reviews. Students often find the transparent and rigorous nature of systematic review methodology helpful too, as it gives structure to the review process and minimizes the chances of missing any potentially relevant papers. Students also tell us that it can be reassuring to be able to 'check' the quality of their review against a **standardized systematic review checklist** (see Chapter 8). Having said that, some topics lend themselves better to narrative rather than systematic reviews (e.g. reviews of conceptual issues or reviews in which the primary aim is to give a broad overview of a diverse topic area). We recommend that you speak to your supervisor(s) and choose the most appropriate methodological approach for your topic area.

Question 4: I'm studying a non-health discipline – can I still conduct a systematic review?

The short answer is: yes, you can! Although the process of systematically reviewing the literature is often linked to healthcare, systematic reviews are now considered best practice across a range of disciplines and topic areas, including criminology, business, transport, housing, environment, politics and history. A high-quality systematic review has the potential to advance a field of enquiry regardless of discipline, so don't rule out conducting a systematic review solely because you are studying a non-health discipline. To further illustrate the widespread application and value of systematic review methodology, we have tried to use examples from systematic reviews conducted across a range of disciplines throughout this book.

Question 5: Are there any ethical considerations that I need to think about if I decide to conduct a systematic review for my thesis?

This is a good question, and one that is commonly overlooked by postgraduate students. It's rare to have to seek ethical approval to conduct a systematic review. However, that does not mean that there aren't potential ethical issues that may arise during the conduct of a systematic review (Vergnes et al., 2010). For example, using systematic review methodology does not explicitly prevent the inclusion of 'unethical' studies, although this is something that would likely be picked up on during **quality assessment** (see Chapter 8). Furthermore, if participants have given informed consent for their data to be included in the primary research studies included in the review, this consent may not stretch to secondary analysis of these data in the form of a systematic review or meta-analysis. It's unlikely that these issues will arise (unless you plan to use **individual patient data** to inform a meta-analysis), but it's important to be mindful of the potential for this, and to discuss these issues with your supervisor(s) if and when you come across them.

Question 6: Can I ask other people to help me with review activities or do I need to work on my own?

We strongly believe that the best way to conduct a high-quality systematic review is through teamwork, as working independently can be viewed as a limitation of the review process. In particular, if you are planning on publishing your work (see Chapter 14) collaboration on some specific review activities is essential (e.g. **searching, screening** and selecting studies, **data extraction** and quality assessment). However, you must be aware that, as with any assessed assignment, your review is expected to be your own work. Make sure that you check your institution's guidelines and take advice from your supervisor(s) *before* involving anyone else in any part of your review. If this isn't permitted by your institution, it's important to ensure that your work is thorough and that you act as your own colleague (e.g. by cross-checking your own data extraction or quality assessment results – see Chapters 7 and 8 for more information). We also believe that you should acknowledge lone working as a limitation when writing up your work. If your final review is good enough, you always have the option of asking a potential co-author to perform any cross-checking necessary for publication after your review has been examined (see Chapter 14).

Question 7: Where do systematic reviews fit in the wider context of research and policy?

Systematic reviews are often used to inform research and policy, as discussed earlier in this chapter. As shown in Table 1.3, depending on the policy need, research question(s) posed and urgency, different methods of evidence synthesis might be used. As a well-rounded student, it is a good idea to make yourself aware of where and how systematic review findings can inform decision making. This will help you to understand the broader research context and the process by which evidence synthesis can facilitate the pathway from individual research studies to changes in policy and practice.

TABLE 1.3 Examples of how evidence synthesis can inform policy or decision needs

Policy or decision need	Method(s) of synthesis
Require an overview of the extent and nature of evidence on a broad topic	Scoping review – will provide a broad overview of research that has been undertaken in a particular field or area
Need evidence to inform policy or practice quickly	Rapid review – aims to be systematic, but steps in the review process are expedited to provide a quicker output
Need evidence to routinely inform or update policy or practice	Umbrella review or systematic review – may take the form of single or multiple reviews commissioned to answer a specific question or questions
Review policy in light of recently published research (e.g. COVID-19)	Living review – a systematic review which is continually updated to incorporate new evidence as it emerges
Need a summary of complex issues and interventions	Realist review – a systematic review that addresses what works for whom and under what circumstances

Further Reading and Resources

Aromataris, E., & Munn, Z. (Eds) (2020). *JBI manual for evidence synthesis*. https://synthesismanual.jbi.global

Booth, A., Sutton, A., Clowes, M., & Martyn-St James, M. (Eds) (2021). *Systematic approaches to a successful literature review* (3rd ed.). SAGE Publications.

Gough, D., Oliver, S., & Thomas, J. (Eds) (2017). *An introduction to systematic reviews* (2nd ed.). SAGE Publications.

Higgins, J.P.T., Thomas, J., Chandler, J., Cumpston, M., Li, T., Page, M.J., & Welch, V.A. (Eds) (2022). *Cochrane handbook for systematic reviews of interventions* (version 6.3, updated February 2022). https://training.cochrane.org/handbook/current

Hutton, B., Salanti, G., Caldwell, D.M., Chaimani, A., Schmid, C.H., Cameron, C., Ioannidis, J.P., Straus, S., Thorlund, K., Jansen, J.P., Mulrow, C., Catalá-López, F., Gøtzsche, P.C., Dickersin, K., Boutron, I., Altman, D.G., & Moher, D. (2015). The PRISMA extension statement for reporting of systematic reviews incorporating network meta-analyses of health care interventions: checklist and explanations. *Annals of Internal Medicine, 162*(11), 777–84.

Page, M.J., McKenzie, J.E., Bossuyt, P.M., Boutron, I., Hoffmann, T.C., Mulrow, C.D., Shamseer, L., Tetzlaff, J.M., Aki, E.A., Brennan, S.E., Chou, R., Glanville, J., Grimshaw, J.M., Hróbjartsson, A., Lalu, M.M., Tianjing, L., Loder, E.W., Mayo-Wilson, E., McDonald, S., ... Moher, D. (2021a). The PRISMA 2020 statement: an updated guideline for reporting systematic reviews. *British Medical Journal, 372*, n71.

Page, M.J., Moher, D., Bossuyt, P.M., Boutron, I., Hoffmann, T.C., Mulrow, C.D., Shamseer, L., Tetzlaff, J.M., Aki, E.A., Brennan, S.E., Chou, R., Glanville, J., Grimshaw, J.M., Hróbjartsson, A., Lalu, M.M., Tianjing, L., Loder, E.W., Mayo-Wilson, E., McDonald, S., ... McKenzie, J.E. (2021b). PRISMA 2020 explanation and elaboration: updated guidance and exemplars for reporting systematic reviews. *British Medical Journal, 372*, n160.

Pickering, C., & Byrne, J. (2014). The benefits of publishing systematic quantitative literature reviews for PhD candidates and other early-career researchers. *Higher Education Research and Development, 33*(3), 534–48.

Pluye, P., & Hong, Q.N. (2014). Combining the power of stories and the power of numbers: mixed methods research and mixed studies reviews. *Annual Review of Public Health, 35,* 29–45.

Pooley, N., Olariu, E., & Floyd, D. (2016). When is the use of a systematic literature review appropriate? A comparison of systematic, rapid, and scoping reviews and their application to the HTA process. *Value in Health, 19*(7), A396.

Porritt, K., McArthur, A., Lockwood, C., & Munn, Z. (Eds) (2020). *JBI handbook for evidence implementation.* https://implementationmanual.jbi.global

Stewart, L.A., Clarke, M., Rovers, M., Riley, R.D., Simmonds, M., Stewart, G., Tierney, J.F., & PRISMA-IPD Development Group. (2015). Preferred reporting items for systematic review and meta-analyses of individual participant data: the PRISMA-IPD statement. *Journal of the American Medical Association, 313*(16), 1657–65.

2

Planning and Managing
My Review

Gerlinde Pilkington and Juliet Hounsome

This chapter will help you to...

- Co-ordinate your research activities

- Plan and make appropriate use of the resources available to you

- Feel confident managing all aspects of your systematic review from start to finish

- Complete your review on time

Introduction

This chapter focuses on how you can co-ordinate your review activities and suggests how you can employ the resources at your disposal to maximize the chances that your review will progress smoothly. We start by helping you to consider the key resources available to you before you start your review. We then discuss hints and tips for successful time and resource management that you can use as your review progresses. Some of the points considered in this chapter are also addressed in other chapters, but we feel it's necessary to highlight their importance in this chapter too. There are concepts that we talk about here that you might not have heard of – but rest assured that they are covered in the remaining chapters. You might want to treat this chapter as an overview chapter and come back to it again when you've read the rest of the book.

Help: where do I start?

Welcome to the world of systematic reviewing. You may be feeling both apprehensive and excited, and you may have many questions about the research process and be wondering what lies ahead. Be assured that you are not alone! This chapter has been designed to help by offering you advice on how to successfully manage each stage of your systematic review.

Don't just think of the review process as one distinct entity; break it down into bite-sized chunks – macro-managing the whole journey and micro-managing the individual stops along the way. Planning ahead and thinking about each stage at the outset can help save time later. Organization and planning are the key factors to successfully completing a systematic review, so take a deep breath, get out your pen and paper (or tablet, laptop or smartphone) and get started. Put a plan in place now for the research activities you need to undertake. However, be aware that plans don't always go as intended, and as a researcher you need to learn to be pragmatic and flexible, and to adjust your timetable as necessary.

The first thing that you need to think about is the submission deadline for the completed review. As a master's student, it is likely that you will be working to a tight time schedule. Think about when your thesis is due to be submitted and plan backwards from then. Whether you are looking at months or weeks or years, you will find that the review process will expand to fill the time that you have available. Doctoral students often complete their systematic reviews early in their research journey to inform the remainder of their doctoral work, so may not face the same time pressures as master's students. Nonetheless, if you are a doctoral student, it's important for you to also carefully plan your timelines to ensure that you are able to submit your completed thesis on time.

The next step that we recommend you take is to write a review protocol (a summary of the methods that you are planning to follow during the review process). Students often worry about how to do this, but don't panic, we discuss this fully in Chapter 4 and most of the chapters in this book also contain a list of points to consider when you are writing your protocol. Writing a review protocol makes you think about the overall review process and therefore allows realistic goals to be set at the start. You don't have to write a protocol, but we encourage you to do so.

You also need to consider the potential scale of your review. You probably won't know this yet, but you should have a better idea once you have completed your scoping searches and formulated a protocol (see Chapters 3 and 4). The results of your scoping searches should give you an idea of the volume and type of relevant studies available. If your review is likely to include a small number of studies (i.e. fewer than five), spending time setting up systems and learning how to use new software may not be time well spent. However, if you are likely to include more than five studies in your review, as we would anticipate, using **reference management software** may save you time and effort in the long run. The design of your included studies also affects how you manage your review. For example, quantitative and qualitative studies are likely to require different analysis packages. Having a clear idea, from the outset, of the direction of your review allows you plenty of time to investigate the data management and analysis options available to you.

If we liken the systematic review process to a journey, planning the route is essential. You need to know how long you have to reach your destination (when do you submit?), what type of route you are going to take (qualitative/quantitative?) and what to pack for your journey (what resources?). The rest of this chapter focuses on how you can co-ordinate your activities. We suggest how you can use the resources at your disposal to ensure that your review continues moving forward without too many disruptions.

What types of resources are available?
Time

As a student you will be very aware that you have a deadline – an often inflexible one that is set by your academic institution. Careful planning, efficient project management and realistic expectations of what is achievable will enable you to make the most of your time. You can make life much easier for yourself if you overestimate, rather than underestimate, the time it takes to complete key tasks.

People

During the review process, other people (e.g. supervisor(s), colleagues and peers) may be available to contribute to review activities. These activities include cross-checking your extracted data (Chapter 7) and quality assessment results (Chapter 8), and/or proofreading text (Chapters 13 and 14). More importantly, don't forget to call on the help of other reviewers, **information specialists** and/or statisticians if you need them – they can help you to choose the most effective review methods, search for evidence, locate references and analyse your data appropriately. Throughout the book, we highlight areas where we feel your review may benefit from the help of others. A word of warning though: you need to speak to your supervisor(s) to find out how much of a contribution from others is allowed, as some academic courses demand that every piece of work that is produced is entirely the student's own. In our view, having somebody to assist you with, for example, study selection does not violate this principle any more than asking your supervisor(s) for guidance. However, you must check before asking others for help with your review.

Tools

We assume that, as a student, you are using a computer and have Internet access. We also assume that you are using a word-processing package to write up the different stages of your review. There is an array of tools available to help you manage your research. These include software that can assist with data management, data storage and structured document template examples. In particular, think about the advantages and disadvantages of using a reference management software package to manage your studies (e.g. EndNote, RefWorks or Mendeley). Be creative. Look for technology that can help you conduct your review, chat to other students about the tools that they have used, or will be using, and listen to the advice of your supervisor(s). Also, check what resources are available to you via your institution as they are likely to be free (or discounted) and may come with additional support that explains how to use the software/application appropriately. If using software that is new to you, check out any instructional videos that may be available online.

Managing your time and co-ordinating activities

Figure 2.1 lists all the steps in the systematic review process that are discussed throughout this book, which should soon become familiar to you. It can be used as a checklist of the different stages that you will inevitably go through when completing your review. You can use it as you make plans to start your journey, building in some scheduled stops before arriving on time at your final destination.

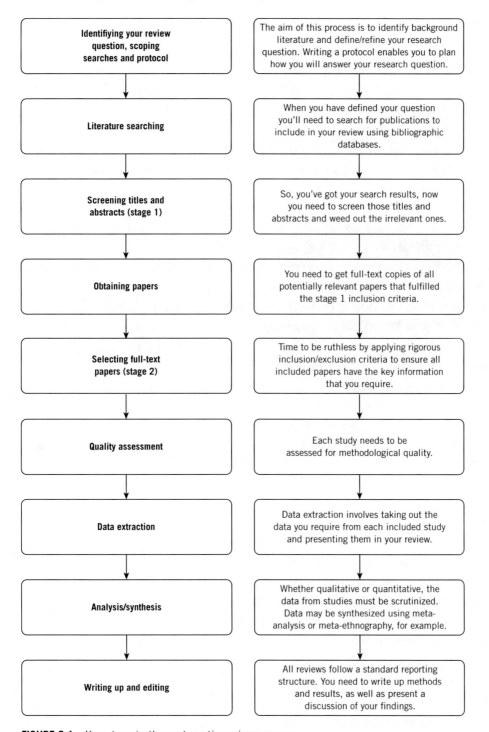

| Identifiying your review question, scoping searches and protocol | The aim of this process is to identify background literature and define/refine your research question. Writing a protocol enables you to plan how you will answer your research question. |

| Literature searching | When you have defined your question you'll need to search for publications to include in your review using bibliographic databases. |

| Screening titles and abstracts (stage 1) | So, you've got your search results, now you need to screen those titles and abstracts and weed out the irrelevant ones. |

| Obtaining papers | You need to get full-text copies of all potentially relevant papers that fulfilled the stage 1 inclusion criteria. |

| Selecting full-text papers (stage 2) | Time to be ruthless by applying rigorous inclusion/exclusion criteria to ensure all included papers have the key information that you require. |

| Quality assessment | Each study needs to be assessed for methodological quality. |

| Data extraction | Data extraction involves taking out the data you require from each included study and presenting them in your review. |

| Analysis/synthesis | Whether qualitative or quantitative, the data from studies must be scrutinized. Data may be synthesized using meta-analysis or meta-ethnography, for example. |

| Writing up and editing | All reviews follow a standard reporting structure. You need to write up methods and results, as well as present a discussion of your findings. |

FIGURE 2.1   Key steps in the systematic review process

Time is probably the most crucial resource you have so it's a good idea to plan now for what lies ahead. You need to make sure you meet your deadlines, whether self-imposed or supervisor driven. Start by managing your review as you mean to go on. Be calm, organized and efficient. Unfortunately, we can't tell you how much time to allocate to the individual stages of your review. In our experience, data extraction almost always takes more time than you anticipate, and almost everyone under-estimates how long it takes to reflect on their results and write up the discussion. Furthermore, systematic reviews of qualitative evidence tend to be more iterative than reviews of quantitative evidence, and so the processes of extracting and syn-thesizing data may be more time consuming. Having said that, each review (and reviewer) is different and, with so many unforeseeable factors at play, the best advice we can give you is that, inevitably, some deadlines will be missed. Just make sure that you know your final submission deadline and that you meet it.

When it comes to systematic reviewing, you will never find that you have spare time on your hands – even if you might want (need) some. While some tasks may seem tedious (or perhaps you may just put off doing a task because you don't think you have time to complete it before you have to be somewhere), you can always find a different task to be getting on with. You'll soon learn that you can start a task and then put it on hold while you make progress with another task. As you get on with your review you will be working on distinct yet overlapping activities. You might find that while some tasks are ongoing (such as waiting for the arrival of the full-text papers that you have ordered), you can get on with something else (such as reading the papers that you already have).

Peers and colleagues are often quite willing to help out with some basic tasks. For example, when screening and applying **inclusion criteria** (Chapter 6), your supervisor(s) or peers could cross-check all or some of your decisions (e.g. 10 per cent). This helps to ensure you are not dismissing potentially relevant studies. From an editing perspective, your supervisor(s) should take a periodic look at drafts of your work and provide feedback. How this will be done, and when, needs to be negotiated in advance with your supervisor(s) to ensure that you are both aware of when you will send drafts and receive feedback. We all have friends or family who are great at spotting mistakes; you can ask them to read chapters of your work and to do their best to find typing errors or half-written sentences. Just make sure you (and your collaborator(s)) are clear on expectations and timelines before you begin, particularly if you plan to publish your review (more about this in Chapter 14).

Another way to make best use of your time is to ensure that your work, from initial drafting of your protocol to final editing of your thesis, is consistent. Establishing consistency across all aspects of the review process (e.g. formatting, data extraction, analysis) early on can save precious time and effort later. You might wonder why this is important at such an early stage and perhaps you are thinking, 'Surely I can go back and change minor things later?' The short answer to this is that 'minor' things can end up as 'major' things. It is likely that you will end up spending hours and hours editing sections of text in your document because you didn't carefully consider consistency at the beginning of your research. We suggest that you bear in mind the following advice as you conduct your review:

- Be consistent with use of terminology throughout. For example, some authors will discuss health status, treatments and patient groups, while other authors will talk about health outcomes, interventions and populations. Some user groups may prefer certain terms over others (e.g. autistic people may prefer to be called autistic, rather than people with autism). You need to choose the terms that you want to use and stick with them.
- If your review topic refers to terms or concepts that are interchangeable, it's often useful to pick those that are most commonly used or preferred and stick with them to avoid confusion for the reader; for example, 'social interactions' and 'social relations' could be interchangeable, but can also mean different things in different contexts. *and always select abbrev. starting point!*
- If using abbreviations, be consistent; for example, if you want to abbreviate the phrase 'cardiovascular disease' don't use both CD and CVD.
- It will save time if you're consistent with how you spell words or phrases. Think about capitalization and hyphenation; for example, would you use Actor-Network Theory or actor network theory?
- Always list the included studies in your tables in the same way (alphabetically or chronologically) – be consistent throughout your document.

Managing your review: employing the right resources for the job

Now that we've discussed time-saving tips and highlighted potential pitfalls, it's time to consider how other resources can be used to make the review process easier for you to manage.

Managing your record keeping

Make record keeping a priority. Record keeping is a basic and required step in project management and allows you to keep an up-to-date and accurate account of what you have achieved at different stages of the review. It also helps you to outline and plan future activities. Unfortunately, it is an activity that is all too often neglected during the review process. Inevitably, the reviewer ends up questioning their own actions: Why did I leave out that study? Did I search that bibliographic database? How many duplicate references did I have? The best way to avoid this unnecessary stress is to take note of everything you do as you carry out day-to-day review activities. There are many ways to keep records, from pen-and-paper notes written chronologically to the use of electronic database systems tailored to suit your review. Choose the method that you prefer. From our experience, electronic record keeping is more efficient than the pen-and-paper method, especially when it comes to searching for information, and it is satisfyingly time saving if you are dealing with a large number of included studies.

Table 2.1 gives an example of record keeping. Keeping thorough and accurate records in this way allows you to review the decisions you have made and having this information to hand can help you to defend and justify your decision making. For example, if you are asked why a specific paper was not included in your review, you can easily check your records and determine whether it was included in your search results and, if it was, the reason for its subsequent exclusion (Chapter 6).

TABLE 2.1   Example of record keeping

Reference	Included at screening?	Obtained paper	Included at selection?	Reason for exclusion
Anderton (2002)	Yes	Electronic	No	Inappropriate population
Apple (2013)	Yes	Paper	Yes	Not applicable
Brent (2002)	Yes	Still to get		
Bryan (2002)	No	Not applicable		
Clyde (2003)	Yes	Paper	Yes	Not applicable

In addition, we suggest that you keep a research activity journal (again, electronic or paper) on a daily or weekly (as appropriate) basis. The purpose of this journal is to allow you to look back and reflect, at regular intervals, on your more general research activities. This will enable you to monitor progress and highlight issues that you might want to return to later. Often, conducting a systematic review involves a steep learning curve during which time you will be developing and refining many new skills, so it's a good plan to keep track – especially for your curriculum vitae and when preparing for your *viva voce* examination (if applicable).

Managing your files (paper or electronic)

The term 'managing files' (electronic and/or paper) relates to systems for storing information, backing up information and organizing files so that you are always working on the most up-to-date version of your document.

Storing information

During the review process, organized storage of information is essential. The storage of information is comparable to packing for a journey: you need to have more than enough space in your car as you know that you will be picking up more passengers along the way.

However small you think your review is, you will soon be engulfed in piles of papers, information, data and different versions of reports and tables. Before you even start your review, you need to think about how you will keep track and store your electronic and non-electronic data. Clearly ordered information storage systems accompanied by good record keeping and unique labelling of studies will help you to quickly access information as and when required by your review.

When storing files electronically, the use of folders and subfolders can be a considerable help. It is a good idea to set up folders to allow you to save files in a logical manner. An example of how to organize the information and data you might gather during the review process is shown in Figure 2.2.

This organizational system is by no means exhaustive, and perhaps small reviews might adopt a simpler system. However, note how many of the folders and subfolders match with the key stages of the review process shown in Figure 2.1.

Backing up information

The ideal electronic system has automatic, built-in backup facilities but if this isn't a feature of your computer, make sure you back up your work regularly. You could use a memory stick, external hard drive or cloud-based storage to keep copies – get into good habits early on and it will save you time and effort later in the review. For example, make sure that, on a regular basis, you back up your work to your computer, leave an electronic copy with a friend or colleague, send the latest version to yourself via email and save to your academic institution's file storage or your own cloud storage (so long as this is permitted, ethically). This might sound a little excessive, but you can never have too many backups.

Keeping files in order

You should also consider version control. You need to make sure that you are always working on the most up-to-date copy of your work, be it **data extraction tables**, report writing or referencing. One way of managing this is to include the date in the name of a file (e.g. introduction_25_nov_2022). It is then important to change the date with each substantive update of your work. As can be seen in Figure 2.2, to avoid confusion, older versions of your files can be moved into an archive folder.

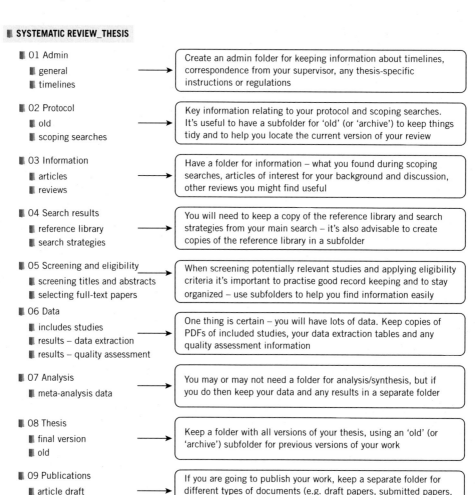

SYSTEMATIC REVIEW_THESIS

- 01 Admin
  - general
  - timelines

  → Create an admin folder for keeping information about timelines, correspondence from your supervisor, any thesis-specific instructions or regulations

- 02 Protocol
  - old
  - scoping searches

  → Key information relating to your protocol and scoping searches. It's useful to have a subfolder for 'old' (or 'archive') to keep things tidy and to help you locate the current version of your review

- 03 Information
  - articles
  - reviews

  → Have a folder for information – what you found during scoping searches, articles of interest for your background and discussion, other reviews you might find useful

- 04 Search results
  - reference library
  - search strategies

  → You will need to keep a copy of the reference library and search strategies from your main search – it's also advisable to create copies of the reference library in a subfolder

- 05 Screening and eligibility
  - screening titles and abstracts
  - selecting full-text papers

  → When screening potentially relevant studies and applying eligibility criteria it's important to practise good record keeping and to stay organized – use subfolders to help you find information easily

- 06 Data
  - includes studies
  - results – data extraction
  - results – quality assessment

  → One thing is certain – you will have lots of data. Keep copies of PDFs of included studies, your data extraction tables and any quality assessment information

- 07 Analysis
  - meta-analysis data

  → You may or may not need a folder for analysis/synthesis, but if you do then keep your data and any results in a separate folder

- 08 Thesis
  - final version
  - old

  → Keep a folder with all versions of your thesis, using an 'old' (or 'archive') subfolder for previous versions of your work

- 09 Publications
  - article draft
  - old

  → If you are going to publish your work, keep a separate folder for different types of documents (e.g. draft papers, submitted papers, published articles)

FIGURE 2.2   Useful folder and subfolder headings

Unique labelling of studies used in your thesis (e.g. as part of background information or included studies) should be assigned consistently. For example, use of first author and year of publication (e.g. Brown_2022) is a simple way to identify studies and is easy to remember; if the author has published multiple studies in a single year, include the journal title as well (e.g. Brown_BMJ_2022) or add 'a', 'b', and so on to the year (e.g. Brown_2022a).

Managing your data extraction (Chapter 7)

Planning how you are going to manage your data is critical to the quality of your review; it is important that you are clear about the data you need, how you are going to use the data and what format the data need to be in. Furthermore, you need to know all of this before you begin to extract data from your included studies.

Not all study authors will report the data that interest you in the same way. You need to try to make the data that you are extracting as uniform as possible so that they can be used as planned when it comes to **data synthesis**. For example, when extracting data on participant characteristics, authors can choose to record age as a mean value (65 years of age), median value (62 years of age) or present a range of ages (58 to 70 years of age). For your review, you should extract data on participant age in such a way that you can compare age across your included studies. Designing and piloting a structured **data extraction form** or data extraction table(s) and thinking carefully about how each required field should be completed (and therefore reported in your thesis) will go a long way to ensuring that the data you extract can be used as you had originally planned (see Chapter 7). The content of the data extraction form must always be considered in relation to the **data tables** that you plan to use in your thesis (e.g. participant characteristics, study characteristics and study results tables).

Managing your references

We recommend that students use some form of reference management software package to facilitate storage and use of references. If you do not have access to such a program through your academic institution there are several open-access (free) programs available on the Internet.

The main purpose of reference management software is to help you to organize, annotate and integrate required references into your work. As a systematic reviewer, this type of software offers you the following benefits:

- automatic download of reference details (titles, abstracts, **keywords**, etc.) from bibliographic databases (e.g. Web of Science, formerly known as Web of Knowledge)
- electronic storage of all reference information, including notes, images and PDFs
- ability to group and organize studies using keywords (e.g. background, included studies, excluded studies)
- the function of adding and formatting in-text **citations** and bibliographies (e.g. **Harvard** or **Vancouver referencing style**)

Although extremely useful, reference management software is not infallible. It is necessary to check that automatically downloaded references have been imported correctly from each bibliographic database. It is also important to check for spelling mistakes and capitalization, particularly if you have entered references by hand, and that in-text citations and bibliographies are formatted correctly. Remember, if you are manually typing references into your reference library, each field (such as 'journal title' or 'authors') may have to be entered in a specific way.

It is worth noting that examiners often check the accuracy of the referencing in a thesis to allow them to form an overall assessment of the student's attention to detail. Reference management software, appropriately used, saves time and makes it easier for students to be consistent when formatting and citing references.

Practical applications: choosing the right software

Table 2.2 lists different types of software packages that you might think about using during your systematic review and contains practical advice on how and when you might use these packages. Our view of the pros and cons of the different packages should help you to make an informed choice when it comes to identifying the most appropriate software package(s) for your review. The right tools for the right job make everything go smoothly – why walk to the next town when you can hitch a ride with a friend?

Remember, the Internet can help you to decide which software to use, how to get the best from it and how it can benefit you. For example, http://systematicreviewtools. com is a web-based catalogue of tools that supports various tasks within the systematic review and wider evidence synthesis process. Search for instructional **blogs**, video tutorials and 'how to' guides. Audio-visual material (with step-by-step software instructions) can be a fantastic help, especially if you learn by watching and doing rather than reading. Ask your supervisor(s) if there are staff or students who are experienced software users within your institution, ask the librarian for help with reference management software and check your institution's web pages for resources that may be useful. You never know, there may be a free course or workshop that has all the right answers.

Writing your thesis

You will need to obtain (and follow) a copy of your academic institution's thesis submission guidelines. Read this document thoroughly, boring as this may be, before you even begin your systematic review. Key things to look for are required thesis structure and length, and recommended referencing system. What we present here stems from our experiences of building documents that require consistent presentation of text, headings, tables, figures and references. Remember, word-processing packages make it easy for you when it comes to writing up your thesis. Not only do they have set styles for headings, subheadings, regular text and bullet lists, they can even create your table of contents. As you become familiar with the software, you will find all sorts of helpful features that will allow you to manage your review efficiently and effectively. Don't forget to make full use of the search facility and the electronic thesaurus. Take time to 'play' around with the programs you have chosen and discover the useful functions they offer.

TABLE 2.2 Software packages available and their pros and cons

Software package	What can I do with it?	Advantages	Disadvantages
Word-processing software	Keep records of: Time management Progress made Search results Reference lists and unique identifiers Which studies are included Create forms for: Inclusion/exclusion Data extraction Quality assessment Writing up and editing Also: Create templates and use pre-set styles	A word-processing package is very useful for all stages of the review, not just writing up. You will be able to look back and reflect on decisions made – justification and accountability are crucial in a *viva voce* situation.	Compared with spreadsheets and database software, word-processing packages have less functionality when it comes to creating and manipulating tables. Additionally, they are not always the best choice when dealing with complex numeric data – they are more suited to text.
Spreadsheet software	Keep records of: Time management Progress made Reference lists and unique identifiers Which studies are included Create forms for: Inclusion/exclusion Data extraction Quality assessment Manipulation of numerical data Also: Create tables, graphs and charts	Excellent for numerical data and can be used throughout the review process. Better than a word-processing package for creating tables through use of filter and sort tools. Each workbook can contain multiple sheets. Most packages have a function that allows data to be imported and exported (e.g. into a word-processing or statistical package), the same data can then be presented in different formats.	Not so useful if most data are qualitative in nature. Make sure you know the basics before setting something up. Spreadsheets are often misused or data are entered incorrectly into inconsistently formatted cells. This can alter values and skew results.
Database software	Keep records of: Time management Progress made Search results Reference lists and unique identifiers Which studies are included Create forms for: Inclusion/exclusion Data extraction Quality assessment	Excellent for use in reviews with vast quantities of data. Can be used for everything other than statistical analysis, referencing and writing up your report. Databases are usually intuitive and user-friendly with lots of useful functions. Each database has the capability to store multiple forms and tables that can be interlinked, and this avoids having several documents clogging up your folders.	If you have never used a database before you might find it time-consuming to learn. If you have fewer than five studies included, setting up a database probably isn't worthwhile. A few hours spent learning how to get the best from software is time well spent in a bigger or more complex review.

(Continued)

TABLE 2.2 (Continued)

Software package	What can I do with it?	Advantages	Disadvantages
	Also: Create tables, charts and graphs	Most packages have the function to import/export data (e.g. to word processor, spreadsheet or statistical package), which enables the same data to be presented in different formats and ensures that the data are entered accurately.	
Specialist software (e.g. statistical, qualitative)	Conduct statistical analyses Directly extract data into the package Create graphs and charts Code data Prepare data for analysis	Can perform analyses for you and produce graphs, tables and figures.	If you don't know very much about statistics, you might be analysing your data inappropriately. If you are keen to use a statistical package, we suggest you take some time to look at the different packages available and, in consultation with an expert, decide how you might utilize them. It can take a significant period of time to learn how to use specialist packages.
Reviewing software	Conduct some or all stages of the review using just one package	There are numerous systematic review software packages (some of which are free) which cover all aspects of the review process from screening titles and abstracts, data extraction, producing tables and forest plots, to writing up. Some allow web-based functionality so that you can use technology other than a computer (e.g. a mobile phone) and allow collaboration with other reviewers as files can be accessed by multiple people at the same time.	As they are designed for generic reviews and have predefined functions, they may not allow enough flexibility for certain reviews. The free packages often limit the size of a review that can be done and may only be available for a set amount of time.
Reference management software	Store references De-duplicate multiple references Generate unique identifier for individual studies Use custom fields and grouping feature Insert references in-text and create bibliographies Attach PDFs and images to the correct reference	Most online databases allow you to save references to a reference management software package. Use this software to create bibliographies and insert the correct references into a document – this function can save a significant amount of time. Multiple fields allow for adding notes, grouping and organizing references (e.g. background, included studies, excluded studies).	Software may not be freely available via your institution; however, you can access free/online versions. It can be time-consuming to learn to use. However, the likelihood is that you will spend more time referencing manually. You must check that the word-processing package and reference management software that you choose are compatible; otherwise you will not be able to insert in-text citations.

Write as you go along, or at the very least keep bullet points that you can expand on later. We suggest that you structure your review as soon as you can so that you can write the straightforward sections, such as background information or research rationale, long before you start to write up your results. For information, we have included a suggested document structure (Box 2.1). This structure has generic headings that you might find helpful as you plan how to write up your review and suggests subheadings to indicate what you may wish to report in your methods section. It would also be useful to look at other published systematic reviews or theses for inspiration – indeed, some academic institutions recommend that you write up your review as if you were submitting it for publication (that is, identify a 'target' academic journal and structure your write-up according to their author guidelines, which you can find on most journal webpages; see Chapter 14). Don't forget to also mention your protocol (Chapter 4) and, if possible, include it in an appendix to your thesis.

Box 2.1

Suggested document structure

- Title page and preface (don't forget to include your name, date and acknowledgements, etc.)
- Glossary and definitions
- Table of contents
- Abstract or summary (a brief synopsis of all included chapters or sections)
- Background
- Research question
- Methods
- Search strategy
- Inclusion and exclusion criteria
- Screening and selection
- Data extraction and quality assessment
- Methods of synthesis/analysis
- Results
- Discussion (including principal findings, strengths and limitations, and relevant factors)
- Conclusion
- References
- Appendices

Importantly, it's all an issue of style. Does your institution have a set format for word-processed documents? Will you lose marks if you use the wrong style? For example, you could be asked to write using the Times New Roman typeface with the font size at 11 pts and the spacing set to double, perhaps with a large margin. Does your subject area or institution have preferred styles of writing? Can you use abbreviations? How should you reference? We always recommend starting as you mean to go on by using the correct styles from day one.

As soon as you start to write up your review, you will realize that it is extremely important for you to manage your references appropriately. You could find yourself writing text such as 'Three studies were set in Japan' or '16 studies used valid outcome measures'. You need to make sure that the reader can identify the studies to which you refer. To do this, you must add references to your text. This also helps to ensure that you give credit where credit is due, and that you are not inadvertently plagiarizing and/or misrepresenting others' work. You need to plan ahead and think about how to make your review clear and easy to read. Take, for example, the sentence: 'Three studies were set in Japan.' Using Vancouver formatting, this sentence would look like this: 'Three studies[1,2,6] were set in Japan.' Using Harvard formatting, the same sentence would look like this: 'Three studies (Brown, 1999; Jones, 2012; Smith, 2000) were set in Japan.' Some reference formats are more conducive than others to the reporting of systematic reviews. However, you must follow the reporting guidelines set by your institution. Referencing is made easier with reference management software because it allows for the formatting of in-text references and bibliographies in a variety of predefined styles at the touch of a button. This comes in handy if you want to publish your review in a **peer-reviewed academic journal** that requires a different referencing style (Chapter 14).

Also, as we mention in Chapter 8, don't forget that you can check the quality of your review by using a systematic review quality assessment checklist on your own review. Using a checklist is a win–win situation. You can identify areas where you think your write-up is weak (and you can make changes before submission) or, more likely, you can reassure yourself that you have done a good job.

If you feel that you need additional support with conducting and/or writing up your work, discuss this with your academic advisor or supervisor(s) as soon as you can. They may be able to co-ordinate a support plan to make conducting your review and/or writing your thesis easier for you (e.g. proofreading support or extensions to the deadline).

Final thoughts

So, now you have a better idea about how to make use of your time and how to co-ordinate your research activities using the appropriate resources for each job. But we know that you're a beginner, and that this all might still seem very bewildering. We think it is a good idea for you to keep the lessons you've learnt from this chapter at the back of your mind as you work through your review – treat this chapter as a practical guide that you have to hand.

Here are our key messages:

- Organization is key to a successful review
- Plan ahead but be prepared to be flexible
- Identify the resources you have available to you
- Plan your file storage system at the start so you know where information is to be stored
- Back up files regularly
- Keep detailed records of the tasks that you've completed
- Use a reference management software package
- Check institution style guides for thesis submission
- Larger or more complex reviews may benefit from the use of specialist software packages
- Speak to your supervisor(s) and/or experts for help and advice

---

Key points to think about when writing your protocol

Well-designed protocols reflect most of the headings in Box 2.1 with the exception of results and discussion. Protocols usually include a section on review timelines – use the information in this chapter to help plan your time.

What an examiner is looking for in your thesis

- A well-structured document that adheres to institutional submission guidelines
- Academic style with appropriate use of language and with no (or very few) spelling mistakes and typing errors – if this is an area where you are weak (e.g. if English is not your first language), seek assistance
- Appropriately formatted (and correct) in-text references and a similarly correct **reference list** – don't throw away marks or irritate your examiner(s) by skimping on this aspect of your thesis

Frequently Asked Questions

Question 1: I work full-time. How can I manage my time?

Many of the tasks, such as Stage 1 screening (Chapter 6) and data extraction (Chapter 7), can be carried out in short time slots. Make the most of the time that you do have available. For example, if you have an hour free, scan-read some titles. An important thing to remember is that, with certain non-critical tasks, it is OK to start a new task before you have completed a current one. Be flexible, co-ordinate your activities to reflect the time available on any given day but remember that you need to block out some dedicated time for writing up (and **dissemination**).

Question 2: What do I do if an article that I ordered arrives later than planned?

It depends. If the article arrives on the day that you are due to submit your thesis, you can acknowledge its existence without incorporating it into your review. You might state, 'The following study was received too late for incorporation in the review. However, future updates should examine its eligibility and implications.' If it arrives the week before you are due to submit, and you are confident that inclusion will not change your conclusions, you could state, 'The following study was received too late for incorporation in the review; however, a cursory examination suggests that the results of the current review would not be sensitive to its findings.' If it arrives the week before you are due to submit, and you believe that inclusion will change your review findings, you need to discuss what to do about it with your supervisor(s) and make a pragmatic decision based on what you can realistically achieve during the week before submission.

Question 3: I don't know what to do about the statistical aspects of my review – what are statistical software packages, and will they help me?

Statistical software packages are specialized computer programs for combining numerical data. It is possible that, at some point in your review, you will need to use a statistical package to conduct statistical analyses and/or produce graphs and tables. If you are not familiar with statistical software packages, you are probably not very familiar with statistics either. This means that you really should seek statistical advice from an expert.

Question 4: Should I use a spreadsheet (e.g. Microsoft Excel) or a database (e.g. Microsoft Access) to help me manage my review?

The tasks that can be achieved using spreadsheets and databases are similar – both systems use tables to store data. However, while there is an overlap in functionality, they are designed to carry out different jobs. In short, spreadsheets are essentially large tables (or several tables) that have the ability to run formulae and analyses; they also have the functionality to produce summaries and reports of data. Databases are large tables that can store vast amounts of data in various formats; tables can be interlinked and manipulated. There isn't a right or wrong choice; your choice will be based on what software you think best fits the needs of your review.

Question 5: How can I get the most out of my chosen software?

If you know what you want to achieve with specific software, but don't quite know what steps you need to take, we recommend that you take advantage of all that the Internet has to offer. Part of the research journey (for us at least) is often figuring out how to do something new or how to solve a problem; this might include conducting multiple Internet searches for inspiration, followed by a bit of trial and error, and the joy of walking into a colleague's office and celebrating success (and then sharing the new-found knowledge).

Question 6: Are there any checklists available to help me structure my write-up?

Yes, there are many checklists available to help you structure your write-up. Looking at other systematic reviews, you will find that a common feature is the inclusion of a PRISMA flow diagram. PRISMA stands for **Preferred Reporting Items for Systematic Reviews and Meta-Analyses** (Page et al., 2021a; 2021b). The PRISMA flow diagram represents a standardized approach to reporting how many studies were identified for inclusion in your review, and what happened to these studies as your review progressed (i.e. how many were excluded from your review, why and when). There are several templates on the PRISMA website (http://prisma-statement.org) depending on the sources of information you have searched, and there is also the function to create your own flow diagram. You can also visit the EQUATOR Network (www.equator-network.org) for information about reporting guidelines (and more) for systematic reviews.

Further Reading and Resources

Aromataris, E., & Munn, Z. (Eds) (2020). *JBI manual for evidence synthesis.* https://synthesismanual.jbi.global

Booth, A., Sutton, A., Clowes, M., & Martyn-St James, M. (Eds) (2021). *Systematic approaches to a successful literature review* (3rd ed.). SAGE Publications.

Gough, D., Oliver, S., & Thomas, J. (Eds) (2017). *An introduction to systematic reviews* (2nd ed.). SAGE Publications.

Higgins, J.P.T., Thomas, J., Chandler, J., Cumpston, M., Li, T., Page, M.J., & Welch, V.A. (Eds) (2022). *Cochrane handbook for systematic reviews of interventions* (version 6.3, updated February 2022). https://training.cochrane.org/handbook/current

Pears, R., & Shields, G. (Eds) (2022). *Cite them right: The essential referencing guide.* Palgrave Macmillan.

Porritt, K., McArthur, A., Lockwood, C., & Munn, Z. (Eds) (2020). *JBI handbook for evidence implementation.* https://implementationmanual.jbi.global

step 2

3

Defining My Review Question and Identifying Inclusion and Exclusion Criteria

M. Gemma Cherry and Rumona Dickson

This chapter will help you to...

- Understand the importance of taking the time to develop, refine and clarify your review question

- Become aware of the pitfalls and challenges related to the development of a good review question

- Identify inclusion and exclusion criteria

- Deal with challenges (e.g. what to do if your review question or inclusion and exclusion criteria need to change during the review process)

Introduction

In this chapter, we lead you through the process of formulating a clearly structured review question using five practical steps. These steps will help you to focus your systematic review topic. We introduce the role of scoping searches and highlight the importance of discussing your topic with others. The chapter then provides guidance on translating your chosen topic area into a valid and manageable review question and a set of inclusion and exclusion criteria.

Be prepared: good preparation leads to good performance

When embarking upon a research project, two key components are required to ensure a successful and smooth journey: your review question (which tells you your destination) and your review protocol (which details your proposed route and research activities). In this chapter we deal with your review question; the protocol is discussed in more detail in Chapter 4.

The development and refinement of the question is the most important phase of any research project. When conducting a systematic review, the review question and the review protocol are what you come back to when you are in the middle of the research and feel a bit overwhelmed or confused – which you almost certainly will be at some point during your systematic review journey. The review question, therefore, needs to be clear, well defined, appropriate, manageable and relevant to the outcomes that you are seeking. Be aware that defining your review question and writing your review protocol may take longer than you think. However, we can assure you that it is a vital investment on your part, as it will save you time and energy as your project proceeds. We recommend that you follow five steps when developing your review question. These five steps are presented in Box 3.1.

Box 3.1

Developing a review question

Step 1: Identify a topic area of interest to you

Step 2: Carry out early scoping searches

Step 3: Focus your ideas to define the scope of the review

Step 4: Finalize your review question and develop your inclusion and exclusion criteria

Step 5: Consider contacting experts in the topic area

How do I develop my review question?

Step 1: Identify a topic area of interest to you

It is important to identify a review question in a topic area that interests you. You will be working on your review for some time and you will need this interest to help you maintain motivation for the duration of the project. Your topic may be informed by external factors (e.g. requirements of your professional practice or research interests of your supervisor(s)); however, the specifics of your research question are likely to be under your control.

Unfortunately, you might have your heart set on addressing a review question only to encounter unexpected challenges. For example, someone else may have already published a review addressing your specific question, there may be very limited research available on your chosen topic, or there may already be a massive amount of published research. To overcome these hurdles, we recommend that you keep your topic area broad and remain open-minded when initially looking at the available evidence.

Step 2: Carry out early scoping searches

Once you have identified your potential topic area(s), the next step is to conduct preliminary literature searches. These are frequently called scoping searches and are discussed more fully in Chapter 5. They are not as comprehensive as the **main search** that you will use later to identify studies, reports or documents for inclusion in your review, but rather are performed to determine whether your topic area is suitable for a review by giving you a snapshot of the volume and type of evidence available for synthesis. You can choose to search a range of bibliographic databases (see Table 5.2, which shows many of the most searched databases available), including Google Scholar. Don't forget to also search **PROSPERO**, an international prospective register of systematic reviews held by the University of York's **Centre for Reviews and Dissemination** (CRD), to check what reviews are currently underway in your topic area. More detail about the breadth and scope of PROSPERO can be found in Chapter 4.

The results of your scoping searches and search of PROSPERO will quickly let you know if the review that you want to carry out has already been published. If this is the case, don't panic, just be glad that you have discovered it at this early stage rather than midway through your write-up. Look closely at the published review that you have found to check what question was actually addressed. Is it exactly the same as your question and did the authors use appropriate systematic review methods? When was it published? Has there been research published on the topic since it was published? If you were to update the review, could you provide a clear rationale as to why an update is needed (e.g. addition of a meta-analysis; synthesis of new or more complex data that may change the conclusions of the earlier review)? Could you clearly demonstrate independence of thought and highlight your unique contribution? If so, there may be a rationale for updating the existing published review. If not or you see too much overlap, you will need to reformulate or adapt your review question. Think of it like planning an alternative route because of a road closure – it's a nuisance but far better to re-route at this early stage in your research.

Scoping searches also allow you to identify the individuals or groups of researchers who are leaders in your topic area. The results may also highlight a variety of (perhaps disparate) viewpoints. Published research studies frequently contain a section that outlines future research directions; it can be useful to read these to see if your proposed review question is mentioned or if authors have called for a synthesis of available evidence before more primary research is conducted. If this is the case, it is a good sign that there is a gap in the research evidence that your review could fill.

The results of scoping searches also tell you how much published literature and information are available in your topic area. For example, from the results of your scoping searches you will know whether there is little or no published research in your topic area, a common fear raised by many of the students we supervise. When we are asked, 'How little is too little?' the answer that we give is that this depends on the purpose of your review. For example, if the purpose of your review is to demonstrate to your examiner(s) that you are able to identify, critically appraise and synthesize literature, including zero papers in your review would be inappropriate. You might then think about expanding your review question to include wider groups of participants, more interventions or different outcomes (see Frequently Asked Questions at the end of this chapter). However, if you are conducting a review to inform subsequent empirical work or your own professional practice, you may want to continue with your original question, particularly if you are also thinking of applying for a grant to fund primary research. Many funders make it a requirement that a systematic review is carried out to show that there is a need for the research prior to funding subsequent work in the area. If there is no published evidence, it is generally appropriate to use results of the (rather thin) review to demonstrate that your research has identified a gap in knowledge.

In contrast, we are often asked, 'How much is too much?' Some students find that their scoping searches end up returning hundreds of published papers or documents. If this happens, you might want to think about narrowing your review question or changing the focus of your review. For example, perhaps choose a more specific population, comparator, intervention, phenomenon, **perspective**, outcome or setting. You can look at some of the published papers in the topic area to get a sense of how to narrow your review question. For example, if you are interested in teenage pregnancy, you may want to consider the lived experiences of pregnant teenagers. Are you interested in the experiences of teenagers whose pregnancies were unplanned? Are you only interested in pregnant teenagers in a specific country? Considering different perspectives will help you to focus your question and will yield a more manageable and **homogeneous** set of evidence.

Do not be disheartened if, at this stage, you have to modify, expand or reject a topic area or review question because your scoping searches identify an evidence base that is different to the one that you expected (or hoped) to find – this is very common. Conducting scoping searches will give you an idea of the current state of knowledge relating to your topic. It is like studying a map before starting a journey so that you get the lay of the land and are able to explore different travel options.

Step 3: Focus your ideas to define the scope of the review

Once you have identified a topic area and conducted early scoping searches to determine the volume and type of literature available and the important current issues, the next stage is to focus on the direction that you want your review to take. At this stage, it is important to produce a short summary of your ideas (no more than one side of A4 paper) and explore these ideas with your supervisor(s) and/or peers to solicit their views. If possible, it may also be worthwhile attending a live or online conference in the topic area to get a sense of the current research issues relating to your chosen topic. A **mind map** of the results of your earlier scoping searches can be a useful way to summarize your ideas and may highlight key issues that you had not previously considered. You can either draw a mind map by hand or take advantage of the many free mind-mapping websites available on the Internet.

Figure 3.1 provides an example of how mind mapping can help to focus a topic area. The example shown in Figure 3.1 is typical of the refinement of a research question relating to fever in children. You can see that there are a number of different ways to approach such a broad topic area, and that there are also a number of potential review questions. For example, you could consider current guidelines for treating fever in children and systematically review them; you could take a qualitative approach and systematically review research reporting parents' views on treating fever in children; or you could consider the best method or time to treat fever (e.g. when first presented or after 12 hours). Each review question requires its own specific methods of searching for evidence and synthesizing data (see Chapter 5) so it's important to consider all the options before finalizing your review question (see Box 3.2 for more detail).

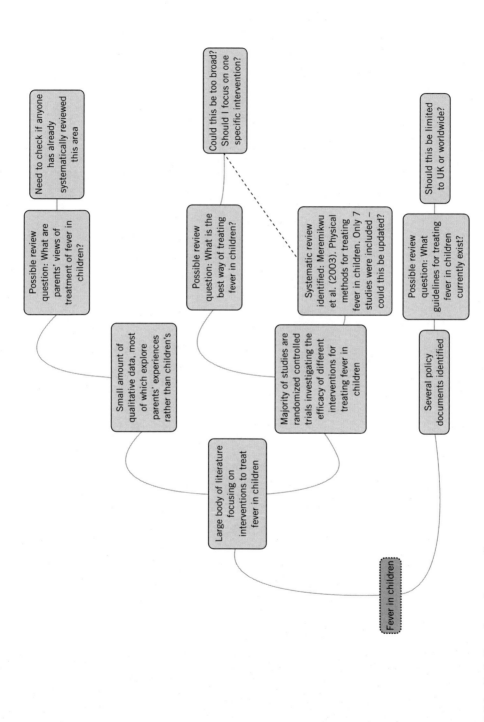

FIGURE 3.1 Evolution of a review question

Box 3.2

Evolution from general idea to final review question

Qualitative or quantitative evidence?

Students often ask, 'Should my systematic review include qualitative or quantitative evidence, or both?' The answer to this lies with your review question. You must choose the evidence that best helps you to answer that question. Consider again the fever in children example. Figure 3.1 displayed a number of possible ways that you could choose to systematically review the research in this area.

1. When is the best time to treat fever in children?

This approach lends itself best to quantitative evidence. The variable of interest is a quantifiable concept (time) and therefore the outcome that you are interested in would be efficacy of treatment at a certain time point after the initial onset of fever. Doctors' or parents' views on the best time to treat fever would not be very useful in this case.

2. What is the best way of treating fever in children?

This is a quantitative question. You may be interested in the clinical effectiveness of a new drug for lowering fever. Does it work quickly? Does it have side effects?

3. What are parents' views on treatment of fever in children?

In this case, if you are interested in considering parents' views on the best way to treat fever in children, qualitative research findings would provide a rich source of data.

4. What guidelines for treating fever in children currently exist?

This question can only be answered using quantitative evidence and can be addressed through a review of existing guidelines for, perhaps, healthcare workers or parents.

By this stage, you may have spent lots of time and energy on your chosen topic area and the thought of starting again or changing your approach might not be welcome. However, it is important to consult and consider the views of others, especially your supervisor(s). It is far better for your topic area to change or evolve at this stage rather than after the review is under way. It might require a little more reading or literature searching, but consideration of the opinions and ideas raised in your discussions with your supervisor(s), peers and/or professional colleagues is time well spent.

Step 4: Finalize your review question and develop your inclusion and exclusion criteria

Now it is time to finalize your review question and develop your inclusion and exclusion criteria. By now, you will have identified a topic area that interests you and will have begun to focus your ideas. It is only now that this abstract concept will begin to take shape as a review question. Your review question is a formal statement of the intention of your systematic review. It is a statement that develops from what you know (as identified through the examination of available evidence) to what it is that you want to know, or know more, about. A good systematic review question should be answerable, motivating and spark your own thoughts and interests, be researchable (i.e. can be completed to a high standard within the timelines set and resources available), be neither too broad nor too narrow, and have a focus on information that is both available (i.e. published or **grey literature**) and accessible (i.e. available to you).

A review question is different from a hypothesis because a hypothesis states the probable direction of a relationship between variables, whereas a systematic review question always ends with a question mark and is always connected to a body of existing knowledge. A systematic review question can be descriptive (presenting a concept), normative (exploring preferences about what should happen), observational or relational (investigating a relationship between two or more variables), causal (investigating the effect of one or more **independent variables** on one or more outcome variables) or theoretical (exploring factors that cause a condition, event or process). Examples of review questions relating to infection control in hospitals are displayed in Table 3.1.

Inclusion and exclusion criteria

At this stage, it's also important to define your inclusion and exclusion criteria. Inclusion criteria describe the specific attributes that a study must have if it is to be included in your review; they are sometimes known as eligibility criteria. Exclusion criteria describe the specific attributes that *disqualify* a study from inclusion in your review. Inclusion and exclusion criteria are always mutually exclusive, but not always mutually stated. For example, study design, date of publication, language of publication and publication type may all form exclusion criteria but may not be explicitly stated in your inclusion criteria.

TABLE 3.1 Different types of review question

Type	Example review question
Descriptive	What are the trends in canine cognitive dysfunction syndrome over the past ten years in the UK?
Normative	How do veterinarians perceive the service delivery issues relating to care for dogs with canine cognitive dysfunction syndrome?
Observational/relational	Is there a relationship between owner anxiety and canine cognitive dysfunction syndrome?
Causal	Does cannabidiol have an impact on the intensity and severity of symptoms of canine cognitive dysfunction syndrome?
Theoretical	What are the facilitators and barriers reported by veterinarians that are most likely to influence owner help-seeking for symptoms of canine cognitive dysfunction syndrome?

Inclusion and exclusion criteria should clearly map onto your review question and contain sufficient detail and clarity to enable you to include and exclude studies from your review accurately and appropriately. Development of your inclusion/exclusion criteria and review question often occur in parallel and should be seen as complementary rather than separate tasks; to some extent your review question defines your inclusion/exclusion criteria but thinking specifically about inclusion/exclusion criteria can also help you to identify review questions that are ambiguous or too specific, broad or narrow, and can help you to focus your review question accordingly.

There are several ways to define your inclusion and exclusion criteria. One way to develop inclusion criteria, used predominantly in systematic reviews of effectiveness, is to generate a **PICO** table. PICO stands for Population, Intervention, Comparator and Outcome. Occasionally people also include Study design and Setting, therefore turning PICO into **PICOSS**. An example of a PICOSS table assessing the evidence for reading as an intervention is shown in Table 3.2.

TABLE 3.2 Example of a comprehensive PICOSS table

Review question	What is the evidence for reading aloud and group reading as therapeutic interventions to improve the health and wellbeing of patients with neurological disorders in clinical and long-term care settings?
Population	Adults and children with any neurological disease or insult, progressive or traumatic
Intervention	Individual reading; reading aloud; reading in groups
	Any form of reading used either as a therapeutic intervention or as an activity to identify therapeutic benefit and/or improve health or wellbeing
Comparator	The stated interventions compared with each other or no intervention

(Continued)

TABLE 3.2   (Continued)

Outcomes	Any positive or adverse health-based outcome, any objective health-based clinical outcome measure
	Any subjective outcome, whether it be identified through qualitative or quantitative data collection methods
Study design	All
Setting	Hospital wards, rehabilitation centres, nursing and residential homes, respite centres and hospices. Outpatient and community settings

The PICOSS table shown in Table 3.2 is detailed and clearly states relevant inclusion criteria pertaining to the key components of the research question. However, some people find it helpful to replace PICO/PICOSS with PECO (Population, Exposure, Comparator, Outcomes), or a more general table or summary paragraph outlining the key parameters and variables of interest, particularly if they aren't focusing on intervention research. An example of a detailed summary paragraph is presented in Box 3.3. If you plan to systematically review qualitative evidence, see Chapter 11 for further guidance.

Box 3.3

A comprehensive summary paragraph detailing inclusion/exclusion criteria

Review question

'Is there a relationship between shame and criticism in family carers of people with long-term mental health difficulties?'

Inclusion/exclusion criteria

Studies will be included if they: a) are published in English or have an English-language abstract available; b) report data from family carers aged 18 years or over who provide at least ten hours of face-to-face care to relative(s) aged 18 years or over with long-term mental health difficulties; and c) report quantitative data sufficient for computation of **effect size**(s) regarding the relationship between shame and criticism. In keeping with relevant literature in this area, the term 'long-term mental health difficulty' will be defined as any non-organic mental health difficulty of ≥ 6 months' duration. Studies will be excluded if they are published prior to 1975.

Irrespective of *how* you define your inclusion and exclusion criteria, and regardless of whether the evidence considered as part of your review will be qualitative, quantitative or both, it's important to pay careful consideration to this step. This will help you to avoid nasty surprises later on in the review process.

It's also important to think about what bias you will introduce into your review by stipulating specific inclusion and exclusion criteria (e.g. by only including studies published in a certain language). We recommend that you pay attention to **language bias**, **publication bias** and bias that may arise as a result of only including studies reported in a particular format (e.g. by only including full-text publications). Language bias occurs because studies that report positive findings are most likely to be published in English-language journals, and studies with null or negative findings are more likely to be published in non-English-language journals. You therefore need to consider the implications of including only English-language papers in your review. Publication bias occurs because studies that report positive findings are more likely to be submitted and selected for publication in a peer-reviewed academic journal than studies that report null findings. It's important to bear this in mind when deciding what type of evidence you plan to search for (see Chapter 5). If you choose to only include evidence that is reported in full-text format, you may miss out on the most up-to-date evidence. An example of this would be the results of studies that have recently been reported at a conference, which may be available in abstract format only. However, if you do include abstract-only evidence, you need to acknowledge the limitations of this type of evidence in your thesis (e.g. limited information available and the fact that early results do not always match final results).

Finally, it's important to think about the *people* whose voices may or may not be heard in the research included in your systematic review, and the impact that some of your decisions may have on this. For example, if you choose only to include quantitative studies using self-report questionnaires, will you inadvertently exclude people who aren't proficient enough in spoken or written English to participate? If you include only research that focuses on children and parent dyads, will you hear the voices of children who do not have contact with their parents? This may not be problematic, but it's important to think through these decisions, and associated implications for equality, diversity and inclusion (EDI), as you develop your review question and finalize your inclusion and exclusion criteria. The National Institute for Health and Care Research (NIHR) **INCLUDE** (Innovations in Clinical Trial Design and Delivery for the Under-Served) frameworks may help you to reflect on EDI as it relates to research during this important step.

You may, at this stage, realize that you need to carry out further work before you can finalize your review question and/or inclusion and exclusion criteria. If this is the case, don't be disheartened – it's essential to get this right before progressing to the next stage.

Step 5: Consider contacting experts in the topic area

When you have a well-developed and well-defined review question and inclusion and exclusion criteria, and you are confident that your review question is unique and has not previously been considered, you may wish to contact experts in your topic area for reassurance. The purpose of the contact would be to ensure that your question is relevant and that you are indeed on the right track in relation to currently accepted practice. If you choose to contact experts, we suggest you should be well versed in your topic area before you approach them and be very clear about what it is you want from them. As you would expect, a generic email saying you are a postgraduate student doing a review and want their help is unlikely to receive a response. However, a well-thought-out email (as shown in Box 3.4), explaining your review question and its importance to your professional practice, and containing a set of well-defined questions, has a good chance of receiving a response.

Box 3.4

Example of a well-thought-out email to a topic area expert

Dear Professor Cooter

Re: Systematic review of online educational interventions to improve the reading skills of Key Stage One pupils

I would be very grateful if you could advise me on an aspect of the review that I am currently conducting as part of my master's studies at the University of Liverpool. The preliminary aim of the review is to examine the efficacy of online educational interventions to improve the reading skills of Key Stage One pupils. I've completed my scoping searches and have identified several relevant systematic reviews in the area (see attached). As a published expert in this pedagogical area, please could you examine this list and let me know if you are aware of any other pertinent systematic reviews that I may have missed during my searches and/or if you know of any ongoing reviews that are due to be published in the next three months? This will help me to ensure that I am addressing a novel question, which has not previously been addressed.

Thank you very much for your help.

Yours sincerely

Felicity Rigby

If you are conducting the review to inform your professional practice, you may also wish to consider key stakeholders' perspectives, a process which in health-care is commonly referred to as '**patient and public involvement and engagement**' or PPIE. To ensure that PPIE is meaningful rather than tokenistic, it's important to build effective partnerships so that people who are affected by (or interested in) your review question can have a voice and influence, or co-develop, some of the components of your review process. For example, if you are interested in investigating the effectiveness of interventions designed to target chronic pain, changes in pain levels may seem an appropriate outcome from a clinical point of view. However, people living with chronic pain may view this differently, and may instead consider psychological wellbeing, irrespective of pain levels, to be a more appropriate outcome. Consideration of the views of patients and the public may therefore help to ensure that your review question has both practical and theoretical relevance.

Final thoughts

Good news – you are almost ready to begin your review! You have a review question (the destination) and if you take our advice, this question will be well focused and accompanied by clearly stated inclusion and exclusion criteria. However, before you go any further, you need to write a review protocol (which explains how you will get to your destination). This is a very important stage and should not be skipped. It is so important that we have added a new chapter to this book (Chapter 4) that talks you through how to write a protocol. Don't forget, most of the chapters in this book also contain a list of points to consider when writing your protocol.

Key points to think about when writing your protocol

- Results of scoping searches can help you to describe the quality and quantity of the relevant evidence available
- It is important to make a case for why your review question is important and needs to be addressed
- Clearly stated inclusion and exclusion criteria are essential to the successful completion of your review
- Consider what is important to the people who are directly affected by your research topic when devising your review question and inclusion and exclusion criteria

What an examiner is looking for in your thesis

- Evidence of scoping searches
- A well-set-out systematic review question – this lets the examiner know you have carefully considered the different components of the question
- An explicit statement of your inclusion and exclusion criteria

Frequently Asked Questions

Question 1: How long will it take to develop my review question and inclusion and exclusion criteria?

This is a valid and common question asked by students and unfortunately the answer is, 'How long is a piece of string?' It will depend on the topic area, your experience in the topic area, the amount of published research available, the clarity of the original idea, the length of time it takes to hear back from your supervisor(s) and others involved in your review, the amount of time you can dedicate to it (i.e. will you be studying full-time or part-time?) and many other variables. At this point, you will likely consider different options, and this will take time, but remember 'failing to prepare means preparing to fail'. Whatever time is spent on this activity will be time saved later because you will have a clear question and a plan that you will be able to use to guide your review.

Question 2: What if I am struggling to define my inclusion and exclusion criteria?

It is our experience that students often fail to clearly define aspects of their inclusion and exclusion criteria. For example, the population might be very broad – such as adults with diabetes. It might be necessary to define the population more specifically as 'adults with newly diagnosed diabetes' – which would identify a population that is totally different from people diagnosed with diabetes in childhood. If you are finding it difficult to define your inclusion and exclusion criteria at an early stage, you will most definitely struggle when it comes to putting searches together and/or deciding which papers are relevant. Clearly defined inclusion and exclusion criteria will save you time and reduce stress later in the review process. If you're struggling to define yours, we recommend that you revisit your review question to see whether it requires some modification. It may also be helpful to discuss this with your supervisor(s), who may be able to provide a more objective viewpoint.

Question 3: What if I lose interest in the topic halfway through the review?

Unfortunately, this is something that sometimes happens to students and often can't be helped, particularly as you will be investing lots of time and energy on the review. This is why we strongly encourage you to pick a topic area that interests you. However, as you will likely be conducting a relatively short-term research project, we hope that you will stay motivated throughout the research process. It is worth knowing that all researchers, at some point in a research project, will wonder why they ever began the project.

Question 4: Can I refine or change my review question?

This is a question that is commonly asked by students at various points in their systematic review journey. In our experience, students' most commonly cited reasons for wanting to refine or change their review questions relate to boredom or lack of interest, having an unrealistic initial topic idea or question, and/or being faced with unforeseen developments in the field (such as someone publishing a very similar review). We tell students that, unfortunately, losing interest in a topic is not a good reason to refine or change a review question. However, if, after conducting your scoping searches, you realize that your initial review question is too broad, narrow or unrealistic, by all means refine or change it. Again, if a very similar review to yours is published while you are still in the planning stages, it might be advisable to refine or alter your review question to avoid duplication. If this happens much later in the review process, however, we would advise you to think carefully before abandoning your review question completely. Can you reflect upon the published review in your discussion? Is your review exactly the same, or can the results of your review still make a contribution to your discipline? Try to view this challenge as a learning opportunity rather than a barrier to your success. If you do change your review question, ensure that you update your protocol to reflect this, as outlined in Chapter 4.

Further Reading and Resources

Aromataris, E., & Munn, Z. (Eds) (2020). *JBI manual for evidence synthesis*. https://synthesismanual.jbi.global

Booth, A., Sutton, A., Clowes, M., & Martyn-St James, M. (Eds) (2021). *Systematic approaches to a successful literature review* (3rd ed.). SAGE Publications.

Gough, D., Oliver, S., & Thomas, J. (Eds) (2017). *An introduction to systematic reviews* (2nd ed.). SAGE Publications.

Higgins, J.P.T., Thomas, J., Chandler, J., Cumpston, M., Li, T., Page, M.J., & Welch, V.A. (Eds) (2022). *Cochrane handbook for systematic reviews of interventions* (version 6.3, updated February 2022). https://training.cochrane.org/handbook/current

Porritt, K., McArthur, A., Lockwood, C., & Munn, Z. (Eds) (2020). *JBI handbook for evidence implementation.* https://implementationmanual.jbi.global

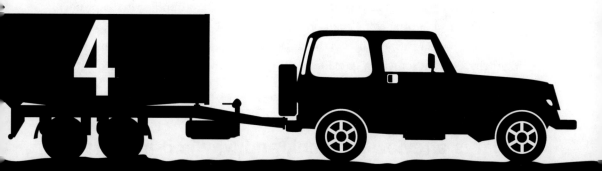

4

Writing a Protocol

M. Gemma Cherry and Angela Boland

This chapter will help you to...

- Understand the importance of writing a review protocol

- Decide when and how to write your review protocol

- Register or publish your review protocol

- Think about how to deal with review protocol deviations

Introduction

Good news – you are almost ready to begin your review! The only thing left to do is write a protocol. As we explained in Chapter 3, writing a protocol is an important step for any researcher. No researcher would consider conducting a randomized controlled trial (RCT), for example, without first writing a protocol, and your systematic review is an important piece of research which deserves to have an overall plan.

This chapter guides you through the process of writing (and registering or publishing, where applicable) your review protocol. We begin by outlining what a protocol is and why it's important. We then provide a practical step-by-step guide to writing a protocol. Within this, we discuss the sections you may want to consider including, highlight different sources of guidance that may help you when you come to write it, and outline what to do afterwards.

What is a review protocol, and why is it important?

A review protocol is a written summary of the methods that you plan to use in your systematic review, together with the rationale for choosing these methods. Your protocol (or 'map' of your journey) enables you to set out the approach you will use to answer the review question. Students often worry about how to do this, but don't panic – this chapter is designed to guide you through the process. In addition, most of the chapters in this book contain a list of important points for you to consider when writing your review protocol. The aim is to provide you with key information that you can use to guide its development.

There are several benefits to writing a protocol. First, and perhaps most importantly, a well-written protocol can help to defend against arbitrary decision making further on in the review process. This is essential because, as we discussed in Chapter 1, systematic reviews use transparent, rigorous, trustworthy and replicable methods, and thus, in theory, reduce the potential for bias. Before you start searching for evidence, it's important to clearly state what you plan to do and why, and to justify any deviation from your plans. Otherwise, you risk making later decisions in an ad hoc rather than systematic way.

This may sound obvious, and you may be thinking, 'I know what I want to do, so why do I need to waste time writing it down, especially when I'm on a tight schedule anyway?' Our answer is, 'Because it's very easy to deviate from your plans without meaning to'. Published studies can't always be neatly judged against a priori inclusion and exclusion criteria, and we have learned the hard way that you often have to make difficult decisions during the course of a systematic review. For example, what do you do if you're interested in the experiences of adults with a cancer diagnosis, but a published paper has included both adult and adolescent participants? A review protocol makes it much easier to deal with these sorts of questions because it sets out exactly what you have planned to do at each stage of the review, and therefore guards against subjectivity and bias creeping into your review. Although writing a review protocol isn't mandatory, it is good practice, and failure to do so could cost you time and effort, as demonstrated by the example in Box 4.1.

Box 4.1

Potential pitfalls of not writing a protocol

Jason planned to conduct a systematic review to examine predictors of post-natal depression and/or anxiety in primiparous women. He specified the following a priori inclusion and exclusion criteria: i) longitudinal peer-reviewed studies, which ii) reported quantitative data regarding the relationship between variables measured within four weeks of birth and iii) depression or anxiety measured at least three months later using a validated measure or subscale, iv) presented results for adult women aged 18 years and over who had just given birth to their first child and v) were written in English. Jason was in a rush so he didn't write a protocol because his supervisors said it was an optional step. He decided instead to choose his quality assessment tool and select which data to extract as soon as he had a good idea of the papers he would include in his review. He combined synonyms for 'first-time mother' with 'anxiety' and 'depression' and completed his searches. He began to screen his search results. He initially thought that he had found 12 papers to include in his review, which he was pleased about. However, when he looked in more detail, three papers reported a composite score of general emotional distress rather than anxiety or depression. A further two papers assessed outcomes at eight weeks post-birth, whilst two papers included women regardless of how many children they had given birth to. This meant that only five of Jason's papers met his inclusion criteria. Jason decided to include all of the studies anyway, because he didn't have time to re-do the searches. He figured that, as no-one knew what he had initially planned, it wouldn't be a problem. He hastily re-wrote his inclusion and exclusion criteria and submitted his systematic review for examination. However, the examiners questioned why he had only searched for depression or anxiety rather than for other psychological outcomes given that he had extracted data on a range of outcomes. They also questioned his rationale for limiting searches to 'new mothers'. They were surprised to see that no-one else had dual screened Jason's studies and asked to see his protocol. Jason had to admit that he hadn't actually written a protocol, and had conducted his review in a rather ad hoc manner. He was asked to re-run his searches to ensure that no relevant papers were missed before his review could be passed.

Second, a protocol acts as a benchmark against which the quality of your final systematic review can be judged. Readers can easily compare what you actually did with what you said you would do. Making your review protocol publicly available means that your readers can check against **selective reporting bias** – bias that occurs when you don't report certain components of your systematic review if they don't fit with the direction or nature of your results. You might be tempted not to report, for example, associations that run counter to your expectations, or non-significant results of interventions that contradicted what you had hoped to find. Selective reporting introduces bias into your review and is a real problem. Writing a protocol helps to safeguard against this becoming a tempting option.

Third, a protocol allows you to expand on your planned methodology and rationale, and you can save space in your final write-up, if needed, by signposting to your protocol. It also allows readers to understand and replicate your methodology and provides essential detail that is often missing from final reports or publications (Allers et al., 2018).

Finally, a protocol can reduce duplication of effort among researchers and students alike. Systematic reviews are becoming more commonplace and, as we outlined in Chapter 1, are increasingly mandated or encouraged at master's or doctoral level. There is nothing more frustrating than conducting a good quality review as part of your studies only to find that someone published the same review just before you were due to submit. As we outlined previously, we recommend that before starting your review you search for published protocols to check that no-one else has 'claimed' your review. It's good practice to return the favour and make your protocol publicly available (more on this later). This can also promote collaboration amongst reviewers.

Writing a review protocol

Step 1: Scope out what kind of protocol is recommended or is good practice in your field

Some organizations, such as Cochrane, the Campbell Collaboration and the **JBI**, mandate publication of a protocol before a systematic review can start. It is unlikely that you, as a student, will need to adhere to these requirements. However, the first thing that we suggest is that you check what is recommended or is good practice with regard to protocols in your field. A good way to do this is to search for published review protocols in your topic area. As well as demystifying the process, this will give you a sense of how much detail is required and help you to identify different ways to make your protocol publicly available. This approach will help you to structure your protocol and write for the appropriate audience(s).

If your review is within health and social care, registering your review protocol with PROSPERO (an international prospective register of systematic reviews; www.crd.york.ac.uk/prospero) is the most common (and quickest) means of making it publicly available. Hosted by the Centre for Reviews and Dissemination at the University of York and funded by the National Institute for Health and Care Research:

> [PROSPERO] includes details of any ongoing systematic review that has a health-related outcome in the broadest sense. Reviews may be of interventions, diagnosis, service delivery, prognostic factors, risk factors, genetic associations, and epidemiological reviews relevant to health and social care, welfare, public health, education, crime, justice and international development, as long as there is a health-related outcome. Systematic review protocols registered on PROSPERO can include studies of any design. (Centre for Reviews and Dissemination, 2016, p. 3)

PROSPERO was launched in 2011 in response to the need for improved documentation and availability of systematic review protocols. At the time of writing, over 150,000 systematic review protocols have been registered with PROSPERO. If your topic falls outside of the scope of PROSPERO, check to see if there is a similar register within your field.

Some peer-reviewed academic journals also publish review protocols. Publishing your protocol is an optional step, but one worth considering – Allers et al. (2018) found that the methodological and reporting quality of systematic reviews with published protocols was better than those without published protocols. In 2012, the journal *Systematic Reviews* was the first open-access peer-reviewed academic journal to exclusively publish systematic reviews, including systematic review protocols, but other journals have now followed suit. It is a good idea to do an Internet search to identify potential target journals in your field early on in the review process. Publishing your review protocol in a peer-reviewed academic journal does not preclude registration with PROSPERO; you can do both. In fact, almost 90 per cent of protocols published in *Systematic Reviews* between 2012 and 2017 were also registered with PROSPERO (Rombey et al., 2019).

Step 2: Write your protocol

The next step is to actually write your protocol. The structure will differ depending on your topic, type of review and dissemination choices. Regardless of specifics, a well-thought-out protocol describes the current evidence base, identifies your review question and outlines your review methods.

You may find specific guidance helpful – or necessary – when writing your protocol. For instance, if you plan to register your protocol with PROSPERO, it is essential to follow their guidance. This can be found at www.crd.york.ac.uk/prospero/#guidancenotes and comprises 40 sections which must be completed prior to submission. This might sound a lot but students find the comprehensive structure and guidance really helpful, as it leaves little room for interpretation and encourages (or forces) them to think about issues that they may not have considered until later. PROSPERO guidance is organised into: Review Title and Timescale (five items); Review Team Details (nine items); Review Methods (15 items); and General Information (11 items). There are also plenty of example protocols on the PROSPERO website.

The Preferred Reporting Items for Systematic Reviews and Meta-Analyses (PRISMA) protocol (PRISMA-P) checklist is also helpful, particularly for systematic reviews of the effectiveness of an intervention. The PRISMA-P checklist, an extension of the original PRISMA statement (Moher et al., 2015; Shamseer et al., 2015), was designed to guide the development of systematic review and meta-analysis protocols examining the effectiveness of therapeutic interventions; researchers conducting other types of review are also encouraged to broadly follow this guidance. The PRISMA-P checklist is widely used by journal reviewers and editors to guide judgements about the quality and thoroughness of a review. The PRISMA-P checklist combines elements from PROSPERO guidance, the main PRISMA checklist (Liberati et al., 2009; Moher et al., 2009) and other key checklists for ensuring the quality of systematic reviews, and was developed and refined through expert consensus. The PRISMA-P checklist contains 17 items organised into three sections: Administrative Information (five items), Introduction (two items) and Methods (ten items). These represent the minimum standard of reporting; additional details can be found in Moher et al. (2015) and Shamseer et al. (2015).

Journals usually also have specific instructions for authors who are submitting a protocol for publication, so it's essential to ensure that your protocol adheres to journal requirements at this stage – it's much easier to meet editorial requirements as you go along rather than to rewrite lots of text later. These instructions are normally stylistic rather than content specific but some journals mandate that you follow published guidance such as PRISMA-P when preparing a protocol for submission.

Table 4.1 provides a guide to the sections you may want to consider including in your review protocol as a minimum. We've also linked these sections with the corresponding sections in the PROSPERO guidance and PRISMA-P checklist. These steps or terms may seem unfamiliar to you right now – don't worry, you'll soon be on solid ground. You may also find the Glossary, at the end of the book, useful. We also cover all of these points in the next chapters, so it's worth reading the book cover to cover before sitting down to write your protocol. We specifically recommend that you make use of the 'Key points to think about when writing your protocol' and 'What an examiner is looking for in your thesis' sections at the end of most chapters.

TABLE 4.1 Broad overview of a protocol structure

Title	Content	Corresponding PROSPERO section	Corresponding PRISMA-P section
Title	This should clearly set out the aim of your review and should ideally contain the words 'systematic review' to make it easy to identify.	Items 1 and 2	Items 1a and 1b
General information	This section should summarize the study team, roles within the team, sources of support and funding, and any conflicts of interest.	Items 6 to 14	Items 3a, 3b, 5a, 5b and 5c
Background, including summary of existing literature	This section can be developed from the results of your scoping search. It should provide a context for your review and should include a discussion of relevant literature. However, it should generally not make specific reference to any of the studies that you are likely to include in your review. This section should end with a rationale explaining why your review question is important and why it needs to be addressed. This text can eventually form the background section of your thesis.	Not required, but best practice to summarize for your own records at this stage	Item 6
Research question	You should present your research question in as much detail as possible.	Item 15	Item 7
Methods *Search strategy* *Inclusion/exclusion criteria* *Screening and selection* *Data extraction* *Quality assessment* *Data analysis* *PPIE* *Dissemination plan*	This is the section where you detail what you will do during the review process and how long you think each task will take. Under the heading of search strategy, we recommend that you describe the resources that you want to search and give summary details of how you will look for published literature (e.g. journal articles and conference proceedings) and, if appropriate, unpublished or grey literature (e.g. registry data and government reports). In a protocol, you don't have to list all the specific search terms you used; however, it is good practice to provide one example search in an appendix. It should then clearly state your inclusion and exclusion criteria; it can also be helpful to reproduce your PICO/PICOSS table, if appropriate, in your protocol. Finally, this section should go on to describe what data will be extracted, how data will be quality assessed, who will do each task and how the data will be analysed. If you plan to carry out a meta-analysis, you need to think about subgroups and **heterogeneity** in advance. It's also helpful to outline your plans for PPIE (if relevant), together with details of how you plan to disseminate the findings of your review.	Items 16 to 29, item 35	Items 8 to 17
Time frame and current review status	You should include a plan of how long you anticipate that each important review activity will take. The tips discussed in Chapter 2 may help you to set realistic timelines for your review. You should also explicitly state where you are up to with the review (e.g. searches not yet completed).	Items 3, 4, 38 and 40	Not required, but best practice to summarize for your own records at this stage

PICO = population, intervention, comparator and outcome; PICOSS = population, intervention, comparator, outcome, study design and setting; PPIE = patient and public involvement and engagement

Step 3: Make your protocol publicly available

By this stage, you will have an idea of where you plan to register or publish your protocol, and you will have written your protocol according to the relevant guidance. The final step is to make your protocol publicly available. The amount of time it can take to make your protocol publicly available varies depending on where you plan to register or publish your review and the time point at which you can submit your protocol may also vary.

The PROSPERO team advises that you submit your protocol for registration when you have committed to conducting your review because they ask for an estimated time frame for completion at the point of registration. This approach safeguards against registering reviews that are never started or completed. However, you are not permitted to register your review if you have already completed data extraction. Ideally, your protocol should be submitted to PROSPERO before you start to screen studies against inclusion and exclusion criteria, so make sure that you register your review no later than this point (and ideally sooner). Protocols are reviewed by the PROSPERO team before approval for inclusion in the database; this process is designed to check that all relevant areas of the template have been completed. Feedback is given on certain areas if required but methodological or topic-specific feedback is not usually provided. Make sure you factor in some time to ensure you are able to adequately respond to any queries.

Publishing your protocol in a peer-reviewed academic journal can take time, as all submissions are independently peer reviewed (as you may expect from the name) by experts in the field. You can expect to wait a little while before receiving reviewer comments, and then expect to have to make changes to your protocol in line with reviewers' suggestions. This may feel like time you don't have, but seeking peer review of your final protocol can be very valuable as it can help to strengthen the quality and feasibility of your protocol (and therefore completed review), and can highlight issues that you may not have thought about but which may require addressing at an early stage. You will also be able to include any peer-reviewed publications on your curriculum vitae, which can be very helpful when it comes to applying for jobs or professional training later on. Of course, you must balance the decision to publish your protocol in a peer-reviewed academic journal with the time that you have available to complete your academic degree before deciding whether to pursue this option. More information about publishing, including the peer-review process, can be found in Chapter 14.

Final thoughts

If you've taken our advice, your review question will be well focused, and you will have clearly stated inclusion and exclusion criteria and a clearly written protocol. You are now ready to begin searching for evidence.

Key points to think about when writing your protocol

- Ensure that you follow guidance, where appropriate, and complete all sections relevant to your review
- Pay careful attention to protocol amendments or deviations (see Frequently Asked Question 2)
- Ensure that you make your protocol publicly available at an early stage

What an examiner is looking for in your thesis

- A clear, well-written and comprehensive protocol
- Consideration and discussion of any protocol amendments or deviations, and the potential impact they may have on results

Frequently Asked Questions

Question 1: Should I write a review protocol?

Simply put, it is good practice to write, and then refer to, a review protocol. Having a protocol makes your research journey easier and will help you to plan research activities, guide your decision making, reduce the risk of bias, and show what progress you have made. Writing a review protocol makes you think about the overall review process and therefore allows realistic goals to be set at the start of the project. However, it is not essential.

Question 2: What happens if I decide to change my review methods mid-way through my review?

Your next steps depend on why and at what stage of the review process you decided to change your methods. If you haven't found enough studies or found too many, you may wish to narrow or refine your question – this is OK provided you include enough studies to satisfy the requirements of your degree programme. Ideally, you should plan for this possibility in your protocol (e.g. 'We plan to include studies that fulfil the following criteria... If we do not find enough studies (i.e. $n < 5$), we will widen these to include...'). If you find a different quality assessment tool and want to use it, or if your supervisory team changes, this is OK too – just add this to your list of protocol deviations.

However, a protocol is not only designed to keep your review on track, but also to help ensure the rigour of your research. Quality assessment tools usually assess whether analyses were appropriate and reported adequately – this is to safeguard against researchers only reporting statistically significant findings, for example. It's the same with your review. Changing your protocol because your included studies found both statistically significant results and those that were not statistically significant, which made it difficult for you to draw clear conclusions, is not a good enough reason to do so.

If you make changes to a protocol that you have also registered in PROSPERO, you need to make the same changes and edits to your registered version. PROSPERO is set up to display the most recent record with previous versions and dates also available. The PROSPERO team adopts a pragmatic approach to determining whether revisions constitute an amended protocol or a new review. If changes to the review question or inclusion criteria are so substantial that they require the protocol to be revised throughout, the PROSPERO team classes this as a new review. It's more difficult to make changes to a protocol published in a peer-reviewed academic journal; changes would normally appear as an erratum rather than a revision. In this case, it is important to clearly state and discuss any protocol deviations in your thesis and any subsequent publications.

Question 3: What if I don't know what I'm going to do yet?

By the time you start your review, you should have a clear idea of what you plan to do and why. If you don't, you're not ready to start your review. Do some more reading and have a good chat with your supervisor(s). Sometimes it's difficult to specify exactly what you plan to do because it may change depending on the nature of your included studies. For example, if you plan to include all study designs as long as they meet your inclusion criteria, it may be difficult to specify which quality assessment tool(s) you plan to use. In this case, we recommend that you plan for every eventuality (e.g. 'Quality of RCTs will be assessed using X. Quality of **non-randomized studies** will be assessed using Y. Quality of observational studies will be assessed using Z'). Similarly, you may not know if you will be able to meta-analyse your data just yet. That's OK – set out all of the conditions that you consider will need to be met in order for meta-analysis to be possible, and then describe your analysis plan (including any planned **sensitivity analyses**).

Question 4: How late is too late to write a protocol?

Ideally, you should start to write your protocol as soon as you can, but not so soon that you haven't thought through all of what you will do or are not committed to an idea or question. Conversely, there is no point publishing a protocol as you are writing up your review, because that would defeat the object. PROSPERO guidance states that you should submit your protocol no later than the point of starting data extraction, and ideally sooner. We agree with this; ideally, you should submit your protocol before you conduct your searches, but certainly no later than when you plan to start data extraction or quality assessment, whichever comes first.

Further Reading and Resources

Centre for Reviews and Dissemination, University of York. (2016). *Guidance notes for registering a systematic review protocol with PROSPERO.* www.crd.york.ac.uk/prospero/documents/Registering%20a%20review%20on%20PROSPERO.pdf

Moher, D., Shamseer L., Clarke, M., Ghersi, D., Liberati, A., Petticrew, M., Shekelle, P., Stewart, L.A., & the PRISMA-P Group. (2015). Preferred reporting items for systematic review and meta-analysis protocols (PRISMA-P) 2015 statement. *Systematic Reviews, 4*(1), 1.

Shamseer, L., Moher, D., Clarke. M., Ghersi, D., Liberati, A., Petticrew, M., Shekelle, P., Stewart, L.A., & the PRISMA-P Group. (2015). Preferred reporting items for systematic review and meta-analysis protocols (PRISMA-P) 2015: elaboration and explanation. *British Medical Journal, 349*, g7647.

Developing My Search Strategy

Yenal Dundar, Nigel Fleeman and Michelle Maden

This chapter will help you to...

- Understand the difference between scoping searches and a main search for evidence

- Judge the most appropriate bibliographic databases to search

- Design your search strategy

- Report the methods of your search for evidence

Introduction

This chapter guides you through the process of identifying evidence that will allow you to answer your review question. We begin by discussing scoping searches and then provide guidance on how to plan your **search strategy** and carry out individual searches for evidence. Finally, we discuss how best to report these methods in your protocol and thesis.

What is meant by searching and where do I start?

Searching is an umbrella term that describes the many methods for identifying evidence that is relevant to your review question. Potential sources of relevant evidence include bibliographic databases, volumes of specialist journals, reference lists from retrieved articles, research registers, government databases, newspapers and experts in your field. In this chapter, we focus on two related yet distinct methods of searching: scoping searches and your main search for evidence. As discussed in Chapter 3, scoping searches are used to inform the development and refinement of your review question and inclusion/exclusion criteria. In contrast, your main search for evidence is the one that identifies relevant evidence for inclusion in your review. We explain how you might carry out these searches in more detail later in this chapter. However, before you start, it's important to remember that, no matter what you are doing, it is always good to have help. We recommend that you take ample time to think about the resources/expertise available to you before you begin to search for evidence. This advice might feel frustrating, particularly if you are keen to start searching immediately. However, seeking help at this stage may save you time in the long run, so it's time well spent.

When it comes to searching, a helping hand can come from an information specialist or librarian who is used to searching bibliographic databases (more on these later). These experts have professional knowledge of the information that is kept and indexed electronically and have a good idea of how to interrogate specialist bibliographic databases efficiently. When you show your preliminary or final review question to specialists, you may be surprised (pleasantly, we hope) when they are able to offer a different perspective and suggest ways to help you to explore your question more fully. We are often amazed at the different perspectives brought by colleagues who see things through a different kaleidoscope from our own.

As discussed in Chapter 2, help can also come in the form of reference management software packages such as EndNote, RefWorks or Mendeley. These software packages not only allow for direct exportation of references (and their abstracts) from the Internet and bibliographic databases, they also have tools that enable you to easily identify (and then delete) duplicate records (see Chapter 6). Reference management software packages are also useful when it is time to extract data, synthesize results and write up your thesis. These allow you to sort references into relevant groups, e.g. all included studies or all studies with the same endpoint and to directly insert references into your thesis using your preferred referencing style (e.g. Harvard or Vancouver).

Finally, your supervisor(s) can be a valuable source of help and advice. They may be able to quickly identify key papers in your topic area that you can use as a starting point when planning your search strategy. They will also be able to advise you about how much evidence you need to find, where to search for it and who may be able to help you carry out this important task. We recommend that you speak to your supervisor(s) before you begin your scoping searches and main search for evidence.

Scoping searches

As discussed in Chapter 3, scoping searches should be the first searches that you conduct. Scoping searches differ from your main search as they use simple **search terms** and are designed to provide an overview of the literature that is relevant to your review question or topic. Scoping searches can help you to locate a sufficient number of key references quickly (e.g. studies and other reviews published on your broad research topic), give you a clear understanding of the key issues related to your topic area and provide an estimate of how many studies you are likely to find when you carry out your main search. The results of scoping searches can therefore help you to determine the direction of your review, develop and refine your review question and build your main search.

Scoping searches need to be carried out early on, prior to finalizing your review question and writing your review protocol. You may, or may not, need to report the details of your scoping searches in your thesis. Ask your supervisor(s) if there is a departmental preference or, to be on the safe side, include details in an appendix. Scoping searches may sound time-consuming, but it's time well spent. When conducting scoping searches, you don't need to search every available resource – a couple of relevant and up-to-date data sources will likely suffice (e.g. MEDLINE). Similarly, you don't need to read through hundreds of full-text papers at this stage – the titles and abstracts of potentially relevant studies will give you an idea of the type and breadth of available evidence.

Planning your search strategy and designing your searches

Once you have carried out your scoping searches, focused your review question and inclusion/exclusion criteria, and written your protocol, the next step is to plan your search strategy and design your searches. For clarity, we use the terms 'main search' and 'search strategy' interchangeably throughout this book to refer to a global approach to searching, and the term 'search' to refer to specific searches designed for individual bibliographic databases.

Box 5.1 summarizes the key steps to consider when planning your search strategy. Although we present these as sequential steps, we often find that searching is an iterative process and therefore you may find that you work through these steps in a non-linear fashion, returning to a step more than once.

Box 5.1

Key steps to consider when planning your main search

Step 1: Think about how comprehensive your main search needs to be

Step 2: Consider the different types of evidence available to you

Step 3: Identify the specific bibliographic databases that you will search for evidence

Step 4: Identify and refine your key search terms

Step 5: Search bibliographic databases and collate references

Step 6: Consider complementary searching activities

Step 1: Think about how comprehensive your search needs to be

First, think about how comprehensive your search needs to be, considering your review question and your topic area. Some argue that you must find all the available evidence relevant to your review question, no matter how long it takes. The counterargument is that it is not worth spending a long time conducting lots of different searches that only find one additional obscure piece of evidence which includes information that will not, in all probability, change the overall results of the review. As a student, you will likely have time and resource constraints placed upon you and, therefore, we recommend a pragmatic approach to searching. That's not to say that we discourage thoroughness (quite the opposite!), but we recommend that your main search is adequately balanced in terms of specificity (it identifies the relevant evidence) and sensitivity (it does not identify too many irrelevant sources or pieces of evidence).

Step 2: Consider the different types of evidence available to you

Once you have reflected on how comprehensive your search needs to be, it is important to consider the different types of evidence available to you. Broadly speaking, there are two main types of evidence. Evidence from commercial publishers is commonly referred to as 'published literature'. Common examples of published literature include peer-reviewed academic journal articles and academic books. The main sources of published literature are bibliographic databases, volumes of specialist journals, reference lists from already retrieved articles and newspaper archives. In contrast, the term 'grey literature' (also known as unpublished literature) is commonly used to refer to the vast array of evidence *not* controlled by commercial publishers. Common sources of grey literature include legislation, government documents or databases, annual reports, bulletins, statistics, dissertations or theses, **conference proceedings** and research registers of ongoing or unpublished studies. Both types of evidence can be found by searching the Internet.

TABLE 5.1 Strengths and limitations of searching for published and grey literature

	Published literature	Grey literature
Pros	• Easier to locate • Easier to search systematically and transparently • Easier to clearly report results in thesis • Easier to transfer results of search to reference management software • Usually peer-reviewed	• Allows access to diverse evidence sources • Reduces risk of publication bias • Often not limited by restricted word count • Searches can identify ongoing or unpublished studies
Cons	• Data might be limited • Risk of publication bias	• Harder to locate • Peer-review status is often unclear, and therefore evidence may be more likely to be biased • Harder to search systematically and transparently • Harder to store results of searches • Harder to clearly report methods in thesis

It is a common misconception that systematic reviews should only include published literature. While it is true that some topics (such as systematic reviews of clinical effectiveness of healthcare interventions) lend themselves more to the inclusion of published literature, others (such as systematic reviews of changes in governmental legislation) do not. When choosing what type of evidence to search for, our advice is to think carefully about where you may find the most relevant evidence for your review question, together with the pros and cons of searching for published and grey literature (see Table 5.1).

Step 3: Identify the specific bibliographic databases that you will search for evidence

Once you have decided whether to search for published and/or grey literature, you must next identify how you plan to search for this evidence. Most systematic reviews rely on bibliographic databases as their primary data source. Bibliographic databases are available electronically and contain records of published and grey literature (in some cases). These records, as a minimum, include a title, author(s) and a source (e.g. journal article). The structure via which these databases are accessed is commonly referred to as a platform or **interface**. Most bibliographic databases relate to a specific discipline, although some are multidisciplinary in content. While some bibliographic databases can be accessed without charge by the public via the Internet, the majority are available on a subscription-only basis. Your institution should have access to a range of bibliographic databases. If, however, you cannot access a specific bibliographic database through your institution, speak to an information specialist or librarian who might be able to give you temporary access. They may also be able to give advice about the most relevant databases to search.

Examples of some common databases are presented (by discipline) in Table 5.2; this list is not exhaustive but is intended as a guide. It is likely that you will need to search more than one bibliographic database to identify sufficient relevant evidence for inclusion in your review. However, make sure that you search only those that are most relevant to your review question and topic area. For example, if the aim of your research is to synthesize participants' experiences of a particular phenomenon, you will need to consider data from studies that use a range of qualitative research methods (e.g. **grounded theory**), and you will require a wide range of evidence. A broad search across several bibliographic databases is therefore likely to be needed. However, if, for example, the aim of your review is to examine the clinical effectiveness of a specific healthcare intervention, your search would likely be focused on a smaller number of particular healthcare databases. You can also look at the search strategies of topic-relevant systematic reviews for ideas about which databases to search.

TABLE 5.2 Databases and other sources of information by discipline

Database and URL	Coverage
Multidisciplinary	
Library Hub Discover https://discover.libraryhub.jisc.ac.uk	Holdings of United Kingdom (UK) National Libraries, university libraries and specialist research libraries
Google Scholar* https://scholar.google.com	Scholarly literature (including articles, theses, books and abstracts)
JSTOR (Journal Storage) www.jstor.org	Academic journal articles (humanities, social sciences, and sciences), books and primary sources
Library of Congress Catalogue* https://catalog.loc.gov/vwebv/searchBrowse	Books, periodicals, manuscripts, maps, music, recordings, images and electronic resources
ProQuest Dissertations & Theses Global https://about.proquest.com/en/products-services/pqdtglobal	Dissertations and theses
Scopus www.scopus.com/standard/marketing.uri	Abstracts and references of journal articles, books, trade publications, conference papers, articles in press and patents covering multiple disciplines
Web of Science (formerly Web of Knowledge) https://clarivate.com/webofsciencegroup/solutions/web-of-science	Abstracts and references of journal articles, books, conference proceedings, patents and datasets covering multiple disciplines
Criminal justice	
The Home Office (UK Government)* www.gov.uk/government/organisations/home-office	UK government and policy documents
Criminal Justice Abstracts www.ebsco.com/products/research-databases/criminal-justice-abstracts	Abstracts and references of journal articles on topics including forensic science, policing, corrections, criminal law and investigations
Index to Legal Periodicals and Books Full Text (H.W. Wilson) www.hwwilsoninprint.com/index_legal.php	Indexes legal journals, law reviews and books published in Great Britain, Ireland, the United States, Canada, Australia and New Zealand
Economics	
EconLit www.aeaweb.org/econlit www.ebsco.com/products/research-databases/econlit	Abstracts and references of all types of economic research, including capital markets, econometrics, economic forecasting, environmental economics and government regulations
Research Papers in Economics (RePEc) http://repec.org	Abstracts and references of journal articles, working papers, books and book chapters
Education	
EPPI Centre (Evidence for Policy & Practice Information Centre)* https://eppi.ioe.ac.uk	Systematic reviews covering education and initial teacher training (also health promotion, public health, social welfare and international development)
ERIC (Education Resources Information Center) https://eric.ed.gov	Abstracts and references of journal articles, research reports, curriculum and teaching guides, conference papers, dissertations and theses and books on all aspects of education

(Continued)

TABLE 5.2   (Continued)

Database and URL	Coverage
Educational Research Abstracts Online www.tandfonline.com/db/era	Abstracts and references of educational research articles
Health	
CINAHL (Cumulative Index to Nursing and Allied Health Literature) www.ebsco.com/products/research-databases/cinahl-database	Abstracts and references of journal articles, books, dissertations, conference proceedings, standards of practice and book chapters covering nursing, biomedicine, health sciences librarianship, alternative/complementary medicine, consumer health and 17 allied health disciplines
ClinicalTrials.gov* https://clinicaltrials.gov	Clinical trials registry and results database including publicly and privately supported worldwide clinical trials
Cochrane Library* www.cochranelibrary.com	Access to the Cochrane Database of Systematic Reviews (CDSR) including full-text Cochrane Reviews (and protocols) and Cochrane Central Register of Controlled Trials (CENTRAL) Bibliographic details of randomized controlled trials (RCTs) and quasi-RCTs
Embase® www.embase.com	Abstracts and references of journal articles and conference proceedings covering biomedicine and pharmacology
EU Clinical Trials Register* www.clinicaltrialsregister.eu	Clinical trial protocol and results of studies conducted in the European Union (EU) and the European Economic Area (EEA) or conducted outside the EU/EEA that are linked to European paediatric-medicine development
International HTA (Health Technology Assessment) database* https://database.inahta.org	Bibliographic details for ongoing and published health technology assessments by international HTA organizations
UK HTA (Health Technology Assessment) database* www.journalslibrary.nihr.ac.uk/programmes/hta	Bibliographic details for ongoing and published health technology assessments by UK HTA organizations
MEDLINE® www.nlm.nih.gov/medline/index.html	Abstracts and references of journal articles, covering biomedicine and health, life sciences, behavioural sciences, chemical sciences and bioengineering
PROSPERO* www.crd.york.ac.uk/prospero	A register of systematic review protocols in health and social care, welfare and public health (also education, crime, justice and international development)
PubMed®* https://pubmed.ncbi.nlm.nih.gov	Abstracts and references of journal articles, covering biomedicine and health, life sciences, behavioural sciences, chemical sciences and bioengineering
History and humanities	
America: History and Life www.ebsco.com/products/research-databases/america-history-life-full-text	Abstracts and references of journal articles covering the history and culture of the United States and Canada

Database and URL	Coverage
Humanities Index https://about.proquest.com/en/products-services/bhi-set-c	Abstracts and references of humanities journals and weekly magazines published in the UK and other English-speaking countries
British Periodicals https://about.proquest.com/en/products-services/british_periodicals	Facsimile page images and searchable full text of periodicals from the late 17th century through to the early 21st
ProQuest Historical Newspapers https://about.proquest.com/en/products-services/pq-hist-news	Archives (full page images) of historical titles including *The Guardian* and *The Observer*, *The Irish Times* and *The Weekly Irish Times*, *The New York Times*, *The Times of India*, *The Baltimore Afro-American*, *The New York Amsterdam News* and *The Washington Post*
Social sciences	
ASSIA (Applied Social Sciences Index & Abstracts) https://proquest.libguides.com/assia	Abstracts and references of journal articles, covering health, social services, psychology, sociology, economics, politics, race relations and education
Campbell Collaboration Library of Systematic Reviews* www.campbellcollaboration.org	Systematic reviews and evidence gap maps covering business and management, crime and justice, disability, education, international development, knowledge translation and implementation and social welfare
CORDIS* (Community Research and Development Information Service) https://cordis.europa.eu	Project reports funded by the EU framework programmes for research and innovation (Framework Programmes 1 to Horizon 2020) held by the European Commission
PsycINFO www.apa.org/pubs/databases/psycinfo	Abstracts of and references to book chapters, technical reports and dissertations in psychology and psychological aspects of related disciplines
Sociological Abstracts https://about.proquest.com/en/products-services/socioabs-set-c	Abstracts of and references to international literature in sociology and related disciplines in the social and behavioural sciences
Web of Science www.webofscience.com	Abstracts of and references to journal articles from across the social sciences

*Free to access without the need for a paid subscription

Step 4: Identify and refine your key search terms

Once you have identified which bibliographic databases you plan to search, you need to choose key search terms and refine them until you have a final search for each database. This may sound easy, as no doubt you are familiar with searching the Internet via search engines such as Google or Google Scholar, where you type in a number of search terms relevant to whatever it is you are trying to find. However, you are probably less familiar with searching specialist bibliographic databases, which can make devising search strategies more challenging. Indeed, we must stress that designing an optimal search for a specific bibliographic database can take time and is likely to be an iterative process. It is highly unlikely that you will identify the optimal search terms to use on your first attempt (and if you think you have, it may be worth double-checking your terms with an information specialist or librarian).

Most bibliographic databases allow you to be more precise and use more advanced and complex searches than those you would use when searching the Internet. This is because most bibliographic databases have more than just one field (i.e. box) in which to add text terms. You can also combine the terms entered in each box by using 'AND', 'OR' and 'NOT', also known as **Boolean operators** (see Table 5.3).

TABLE 5.3   Use of Boolean operators when searching for evidence

Boolean operator	Function	Examples
AND	Combines terms and therefore narrows the search and identifies records containing all of the words entered	(education AND university) This search retrieves records containing both the words 'education' and 'university'
OR	Broadens the search and identifies records containing *any* of the words entered	(education OR university) This search retrieves records containing either the word 'education' or the word 'university'
NOT	Used to exclude something and therefore narrows the search and identifies records that *do not* contain the term following it	(education NOT university) This search retrieves records containing the word 'education' but excludes those which also contain the word 'university'

Most bibliographic databases also allow you to search specific fields, such as author, title or year of publication, to limit your searches and to specify search parameters – for example, by year or language. Furthermore, most bibliographic databases allow you to search for and combine both **free-text words**, and **subject headings/ index terms** (also known as **thesaurus terms** or controlled vocabulary). Free-text words are words located anywhere in the title, abstract or main text of the article. In addition to whole words such as 'cancer', most bibliographic databases offer you the option of using 'wildcards' (commonly a question mark (?), an asterisk (*) or a symbol such as '$') when searching for free-text words. These enable you to:

- Search for part of a word (e.g. 'wom?n' will find 'woman' and 'women'; 'psychi-atr*' will find 'psychiatrist', 'psychiatry' or 'psychiatric')
- Search for a whole word that may have different spellings (e.g. 'behavi*r' will find 'behavior' and 'behaviour')
- Include a search term and its plural (e.g. 'trial$' will identify 'trial' and 'trials')

Subject headings/index terms are words assigned to publications to highlight the important topics or subjects being discussed (e.g. a randomized controlled trial, a specific type of exposure or particular group of participants), and they appear in a separate field in the database. Most databases have their own list of specific subject headings/index terms. For example, **Medical Subject Headings (MeSH terms)** are subject headings used for indexing articles for MEDLINE and PubMed. MeSH terms allow you to consistently retrieve information even when authors use different terms to refer to the same concept. To illustrate, all qualitative research articles should be indexed in MEDLINE and PubMed under the term 'Qualitative Research', even if they use different methodologies (e.g. **interpretative phenomenological analysis** or grounded theory), and therefore using the MeSH term 'Qualitative Research' may help to improve the accuracy of your search. When conducting a MEDLINE search via PubMed, free-text words are automatically mapped to the corresponding MeSH terms, making the searching of databases easier. You can refer to the United States National Library of Medicine website for further information on MeSH terms (www.nlm.nih.gov/mesh). Using the advanced search feature in PubMed to restrict your free-text terms to the title and abstract field will help you to focus your search results.

When searching a specific bibliographic database, students often tell us that it can be difficult to decide how many free-text words or subject headings/index terms to use and are unsure about how best to combine them. In our opinion, using a combination of free-text words and appropriate subject headings/index terms in your search is considered good practice and should improve the accuracy of your search results. However, the exact number of terms to use depends on your review question and inclusion and exclusion criteria.

When deciding on your search terms, it is often helpful to identify the database record for a study that meets your inclusion criteria, check what subject headings/index terms were used to index it and then use the same subject headings/index terms to begin putting your search together. Looking at the subject headings/index terms of a number of relevant pre-identified references can help you to build up the key terms for your search and can be a useful starting point when building a search. It may also be helpful to revisit your inclusion and exclusion criteria at this point as they may provide some direction (e.g. if you plan to only include studies that focus on people with psychosis, the term 'psychosis' may be a useful starting point). Don't forget that there are often differences between UK and US spellings of the same word (e.g. tumour and tumor), as well as differences between technical terms and lay terms (e.g. neoplasm and cancer). Don't worry if you need to include multiple search terms for one concept – it's better to be comprehensive than to miss potentially relevant studies. Box 5.2 shows an example of a comprehensive MEDLINE search strategy.

Box 5.2

Example of a MEDLINE (Ovid) search on the use of smartphones in people with cognitive impairment

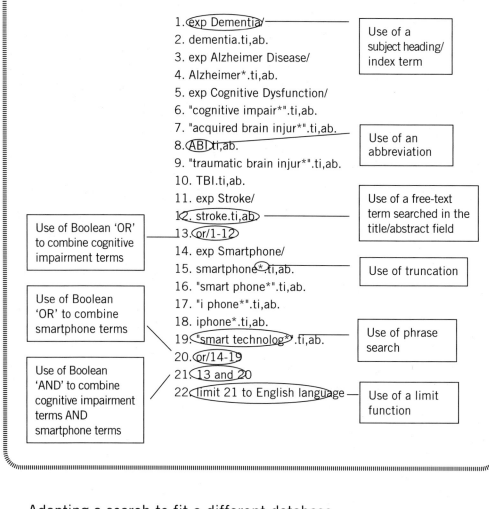

1. exp Dementia/
2. dementia.ti,ab.
3. exp Alzheimer Disease/
4. Alzheimer*.ti,ab.
5. exp Cognitive Dysfunction/
6. "cognitive impair*".ti,ab.
7. "acquired brain injur*".ti,ab.
8. ABI.ti,ab.
9. "traumatic brain injur*".ti,ab.
10. TBI.ti,ab.
11. exp Stroke/
12. stroke.ti,ab.
13. or/1-12
14. exp Smartphone/
15. smartphone*.ti,ab.
16. "smart phone*".ti,ab.
17. "i phone*".ti,ab.
18. iphone*.ti,ab.
19. "smart technolog*".ti,ab.
20. or/14-19
21. 13 and 20
22. limit 21 to English language

Use of a subject heading/ index term

Use of an abbreviation

Use of a free-text term searched in the title/abstract field

Use of truncation

Use of phrase search

Use of a limit function

Use of Boolean 'OR' to combine cognitive impairment terms

Use of Boolean 'OR' to combine smartphone terms

Use of Boolean 'AND' to combine cognitive impairment terms AND smartphone terms

Adapting a search to fit a different database

It is likely that you will need to search more than one bibliographic database. Remember, one size does not fit all when it comes to searching and you may need to adapt elements of your search depending on the database being searched. Most databases offer online user guides, which contain all the information that you need to tailor your search strategy to a specific database. Don't be afraid to use these guides. When searching several resources, information specialists can also advise you on how to tweak your key search terms to ensure that your searches can identify the data that you need. This is one of the reasons that we recommend that you work with information specialists – they are familiar with the unique features of different databases and can help you to identify appropriate search terms for each database. We recommend that you carefully check all your searches for errors or omissions before you run them in the databases.

Step 5: Search bibliographic databases and collate references

Once you think that you have finalized your search terms and identified relevant databases to search, the next step is to run your searches. Remember to check that the key studies you identified from your scoping searches are among the results – if not, go back and revise your search terms and/or choice of databases until these studies are identified. When you are satisfied with your final search strategy, it's time to search your chosen databases and collate all the identified references. As previously stated, most bibliographic databases allow you to export references directly into reference management software packages (revisit Chapter 2 for more information). We recommend that you take advantage of this facility where possible as it can save time and effort. However, ensure that you make a note of the number of references retrieved for each database before exporting them to your reference management software package, as you will need to report this information in the 'Results' section of your thesis. We often advise students to begin to populate their PRISMA (Preferred Reporting Items for Systematic Reviews and Meta-Analyses) flow diagram when searching (more on this in Chapter 6) – it is much easier than trying to do this after the fact. It's also a good idea at this stage to copy and paste your individual searches into a separate electronic file so that you know exactly how your searches were configured for each database as you'll need to include these details in the 'Methods' section of your thesis (and/or your appendices). Some platforms will also allow you to save your search strategies so that you can re-run them later to check for newly published evidence (see the Frequently Asked Questions at the end of this chapter). We recommend that you take advantage of this facility when time allows.

Step 6: Consider complementary searching activities

In addition to searching bibliographic databases, you may also wish to consider complementary searching activities such as **hand searching**, **citation chaining** and contacting relevant researchers in the field. If these activities result in the identification of new references, make sure that, where applicable, you add these to your reference management software package and PRISMA flow diagram.

Hand searching

The concept of hand searching has evolved over time. In the early days of systematic reviews (before the 1990s), researchers did not have access to an extensive range of online bibliographic databases that listed both past, current and upcoming publications. It was therefore necessary to go to the library and literally hand search the sources (e.g. journals of interest) to identify relevant studies (and then make photocopies of potentially eligible papers).

While literal hand searches may still be undertaken, the term is increasingly used to refer to searches of electronic tables of contents of key journals or conference proceedings to identify potential articles of interest. Hand searches of this nature are often carried out to supplement bibliographic database searches but can be time-consuming, so it's important to reflect on the potential added value of this approach before beginning.

In contrast, literal hand searching might be of particular value if your review takes a historical perspective and you need to examine specific documents held in specialist libraries or document storage areas. Having said this, resources that are available electronically change almost daily. For example, the British Library (British Library Archives, 2013) and the Library of Congress (Library of Congress, 2013) now have excellent online archives of British and US newspapers, so it's worth seeing what is available electronically before considering literal hand searching.

Citation chaining

Citation chaining, sometimes referred to as snowballing, is the practice of looking at the **bibliography** of one article to find other, related articles. The effectiveness of citation chaining at identifying citations makes it best practice in systematic reviews despite this being a time-consuming task. There are two main types of citation chaining. If you have a key publication, you can look at its bibliography to find other relevant studies that your search may have missed – this process is known as **backward searching**. Alternatively, you can see which papers have subsequently cited your key publication by using a database such as Web of Science (using the 'Cited Reference Search') or a search engine such as Google Scholar (using the 'Cited By [# results]' link) – this process is known as **forward searching**.

Contacting relevant researchers

If you plan to include grey literature in your review, including studies in progress, it is also good practice to contact relevant researchers in the field (e.g. people who publish widely in your topic area) to see whether they are aware of any unpublished or recently submitted data that are relevant to your review question.

Reporting the methods of your search for evidence

It is important to keep detailed records of the methods that you used to search for studies. Having this information available means that you (and others) can re-run and update the searches later if you need to. It should also make life easier for you when it comes to writing the 'Methods' section (i.e. how you searched for studies) of your thesis. You therefore need to make sure that you record the following information as you go along, and then include it in the 'Methods' section of your thesis:

- The date that each search was carried out (including scoping searches, if any)
- The version of each bibliographic database searched (e.g. MEDLINE 1946 to Present)
- The interface used for each bibliographic database searched (e.g. Ovid or Dialog, which can both be used to access MEDLINE)
- All of the search terms used for each specific search (Note that your institution may require you to report only your search for one bibliographic database in your 'Methods' section, and include the remainder in an appendix, so it's best to check)
- Any complementary search activities, such as contacting experts or performing hand searching or citation chaining
- The reference management software that was used to store and manage the results of your searches

The PRISMA-S extension for searching (Rethlefsen et al., 2021) provides guidance on how to report the details of your search for evidence (see https://osf.io/sfc38). We also recommend that you consult Box 5.3 as it contains an example of how to write up the conduct of your search strategy in the 'Methods' section of your thesis.

Box 5.3

How to report your search strategy in your 'Methods' section

This case study illustrates the search strategy used in a published systematic review by Wilson and colleagues (2022) which examined the use of smartphones by people with cognitive impairment.

(Continued)

Search strategy

The following bibliographic databases were searched: MEDLINE, CINAHL, PsycINFO, The Cochrane Library and Scopus from their inception until 31 October 2020. Searches were devised with the help of an information specialist and were limited to English-language publications. Table 5.4 details the search strategy used across each database. The Alzheimer's Society (www.alzheimers.org.uk) and Age UK (www.ageuk.org.uk) websites were scanned for grey literature. References of included studies were searched and citation chaining was conducted on all included studies. Where appropriate, corresponding authors of the included studies and other experts were contacted for information on additional published and unpublished studies and a call for evidence was submitted via Twitter. Searches were limited to English-language publications.

TABLE 5.4 Search strategy

Database (platform)	Search
MEDLINE (Ovid)	(exp Dementia/ or dementia.ti,ab. or exp Alzheimer Disease/ or Alzheimer*.ti,ab. or exp Cognitive Dysfunction/ or "cognitive impair*".ti,ab. or "acquired brain injur*".ti,ab. or ABI.ti,ab. or "traumatic brain injur*".ti,ab. or TBI.ti,ab. or exp Stroke/ or stroke.ti,ab.) and (exp Smartphone/ or smartphone*.ti,ab. or "smart phone*".ti,ab. or "i phone*".ti,ab. or iphone*.ti,ab. or "smart technolog*".ti,ab.) Limit to English language
CINAHL (EbscoHost)	(MH "Dementia+" or MH "Alzheimer's Disease" or Alzheimer* or MH "Cognition Disorders+" or "cognitive impair*" or "acquired brain injur*" or ABI or "traumatic brain injur*" or TBI or MH "Stroke+" or stroke) and (MH "Smartphone" or smartphone* or "smart phone*" or i phone* or "iphone*" or "smart technolog*")
PsycINFO (EbscoHost)	(DE "Dementia" or dementia or DE "Alzheimer's Disease" or Alzheimer* or DE "Cognitive Impairment" or "cognitive impair*" or "acquired brain injur*" or ABI or DE "Traumatic Brain Injury" OR DE "Brain Concussion" or "traumatic brain injur*" or TBI or DE "Cerebrovascular Accidents" or stroke) and (DE "Smartphone Use" OR DE "Smartphones" or smartphone* or "smart phone*" or ipad* or "i pad*" or i phone* or "iphone*" or "smart technolog*")
The Cochrane Library	MeSH descriptor: [Dementia] explode all trees or (dementia):ti,ab or MeSH descriptor: [Alzheimer Disease] explode all trees or (Alzheimer*):ti,ab or MeSH descriptor: [Cognitive Dysfunction] explode all trees or (cognitive NEXT impair*):ti,ab or (acquired NEXT brain NEXT injur*):ti,ab or (ABI):ti,ab or (traumatic NEXT brain NEXT injur*):ti,ab or (TBI):ti,ab or MeSH descriptor: [Stroke] explode all trees or (stroke):ti,ab) and (MeSH descriptor: [Smartphone] explode all trees or (smartphone*):ti,ab or (smart NEXT phone*):ti,ab or (ipad*):ti,ab or (i NEXT pad*):ti,ab or (iphone*):ti,ab or (i NEXT phone*):ti,ab or (smart NEXT technolog*):ti,ab
Scopus	TITLE-ABS-KEY (dementia or alzheimer* or "cognitive impair*" or "acquired brain injur*" or ABI or "traumatic brain injur*" or TBI or stroke) and TITLE-ABS-KEY (smartphone* or "smart phone*" or ipad* or "i pad*" or iphone* or "i phone*" or "smart technolog*")

Alternative routes

It's important to note that there are other searching techniques which you may wish to use that can optimize the results of your systematic review searches. Search **filters** (or methodological filters) are parameters that you can apply to limit your search results to specific types of study designs (e.g. RCTs or systematic reviews), outcomes (e.g. economic costs), populations (e.g. specific age groups) or studies conducted in specific geographic areas (e.g. low- and middle-income countries). The InterTASC Information Specialists' Sub-Group Search Filter Resource (https://sites.google.com/a/york.ac.uk/issg-search-filters-resource/home) provides access to published and unpublished search filters.

Complementary search techniques are also available to support specific types of reviews. For example, the **CLUSTER approach** (Booth et al., 2013) uses a key relevant paper as a starting point for identifying other studies by searching for studies that cite the key paper, studies written by the same author or related studies on the same project. The CLUSTER approach is particularly useful for realist reviews.

Text mining, also referred to as text data mining, is the computational analysis of words within documents and can also be used to identify relevant search terms. While it is beyond the scope of this book to examine text mining in great detail, the PubMed PubReMiner tool (https://hgserver2.amc.nl/cgi-bin/miner/miner2.cgi) is one example of a tool which analyses terms appearing in PubMed documents on a specific topic and identifies the most frequently occurring free-text terms, subject headings/index terms, authors and journal titles. More information on text mining in the development of search strategies and the tools available can be found at the UK's National Centre for Text Mining (NaCTeM; www.nactem.ac.uk) and OpenMinTeD (www.openminted.eu).

Final thoughts

We hope that, after reading this chapter, you understand the difference between scoping searches and your main search for evidence, feel sufficiently confident to be able to plan, execute and report the methods of your search for evidence, and know who to ask for help with these tasks. It's now time to see what you've found.

Key points to think about when writing your protocol

- Summary details of your scoping searches and results are useful to the reader
- List the databases (and any other resources) you plan to use for your main search, together with any complementary searching activities
- A sample search strategy in an appendix to your protocol is helpful; for example, you could outline the search terms you plan to use for a particular database

---

What an examiner is looking for in your thesis

- A clear, comprehensive and well-planned search, which has an adequate balance of sensitivity and specificity
- Sufficient detail about your search so that it could, at least in theory, be replicated by another person (see Box 5.3)

Frequently Asked Questions

Question 1: What if I don't have access to a librarian or information specialist?

Input from a librarian or information specialist will help you to identify which resources to search and how you can most effectively search them. If you do not have access to experts, do not panic. You may find you already have sufficient experience of using the bibliographic database that you plan to use and your supervisor(s) may also be able to help. It is also useful to identify systematic reviews in similar topic areas so that you can determine which sources of data the authors searched and the search terms that they used. Also, there are many educational resources that can help you with your searching – from online tutorials to library information sheets.

Question 2: Can I search multiple bibliographic databases in the same interface?

The short answer is yes. In an interface such as Ovid you can search multiple bibliographic databases separately or simultaneously by selecting the bibliographic databases that you wish to search. However, your search strategies will likely differ slightly between bibliographic databases (e.g. different subject headings/index terms), so it is advisable to search each bibliographic database separately.

Question 3: What is the difference between MEDLINE and PubMed?

The MEDLINE database can be searched directly from the National Library of Medicine as a subset of the PubMed database, or through other numerous search services that license the data (such as Ovid). Perhaps the main advantage of MEDLINE over PubMed is that it is easier to build a search strategy in steps, using multiple combinations of MeSH terms and free-text terms. However, you may find PubMed more user friendly, particularly when you want quick results (e.g. scoping searches). PubMed is also useful when you are looking for articles that have been recently published but have not yet been indexed with MeSH terms, and/or articles submitted by publishers ahead of print.

Question 4: Do I need to re-run my searches prior to submitting my thesis? If so, is it easy to do?

It's best practice to re-run your electronic searches prior to submitting your thesis, particularly if several months have passed since the searches were originally conducted. It's possible to create accounts and update your search strategies with some interfaces (e.g. Ovid). You may find this useful when you are near the end of your thesis, as this will enable you to easily check for relevant papers that may have been recently published in the period after running your searches. It will be harder to update searches of other sources of information, such as grey literature, as you will need to manually re-run your searches to be certain that no additional relevant evidence has been recently published. This final step may not be compulsory for a master's thesis, but may be required for a doctorate or if you choose to publish your review at a later date (see Chapter 14).

Question 5: What if I miss relevant papers or don't have time to conduct complementary searching activities?

This is a common worry faced by most students given the time pressures that they are often under. It is likely that, in the time you have available, you may not be able to be exhaustive in your searching, and even if you are, it's impossible to be 100 per cent certain that you have identified all the relevant papers. The important thing is that you can demonstrate that you have searched the key resources, used appropriate methods to identify relevant studies and consulted with others who can help, such as an information specialist, librarian or your supervisor(s). If you realize that you have missed a key study later on (e.g. when you are writing your 'Discussion' section), you must address the fact that your review may not include all available information, and outline how this might affect the conclusions that you draw and the recommendations that you make (discussed further in Chapter 13).

Question 6: Should my bibliographic database search find all of the available evidence?

Not necessarily. When devising your bibliographic database search strategies, you should strive for an adequate balance of sensitivity and specificity – you don't want to have to trawl through thousands of irrelevant references but equally you don't want your bibliographic database searches to return only 25 papers either. We can't advise on the optimum number of references to aim for, but we advise you to be comprehensive rather than exhaustive when searching bibliographic databases. If you are concerned that your electronic bibliographic database search is missing potentially relevant papers, speak to an information specialist and/or revisit the steps outlined in this chapter.

Further Reading and Resources

Booth, A., & Carroll, C. (2015). Systematic searching for theory to inform systematic reviews: Is it feasible? Is it desirable? *Health Information & Libraries Journal*, *32*, 220–35.

Booth, A., Harris, J., Croot, E., Springett, J., Campbell, F., & Wilkins, E. (2013). Towards a methodology for cluster searching to provide conceptual and contextual 'richness' for systematic reviews of complex interventions: case study (CLUSTER). *BMC Medical Research Methodology*, *13,* 118.

Booth, A., Sutton, A., Clowes, M., & Martyn-St James, M. (2021). Chapter 5: Searching the literature. In Booth, A., Sutton, A., Clowes, M., & Martyn-St James, M. (Eds) (2021). *Systematic approaches to a successful literature review* (3rd ed.). SAGE Publications.

Brunton, G., Stansfield, C., Caird, J., & Thomas, J. (2017). Chapter 5: Finding relevant studies. In Gough, D., Oliver, S., & Thomas, J. (Eds) (2017). *An introduction to systematic reviews* (2nd ed.). SAGE Publications.

Canadian Agency for Drugs and Technologies in Health (CADTH). (2018). *Grey matters: A practical tool for searching health-related grey literature*. Ottawa: CADTH. www.cadth.ca/resources/finding-evidence/grey-matters

Centre for Reviews and Dissemination. (2010). *Systematic reviews: CRD's guidance for undertaking reviews in health care*. www.york.ac.uk/inst/crd/SysRev/!SSL!/WebHelp/SysRev3.htm

Cooper, C., Booth, A., Varley-Campbell, J., Britten, M., & Garside, R. (2018). Defining the process to literature searching in systematic reviews: a literature review of guidance and supporting studies. *BMC Medical Research Methodology, 18*(1), 85.

Eriksen, M.B., & Frandsen, T.F. (2018). The impact of patient, intervention, comparison, outcome (PICO) as a search strategy tool on literature search quality: a systematic review. *Journal of the Medical Library Association: JMLA, 106*(4), 420.

Glanville, J., Bayliss, S., Booth, A., Dundar, Y., Fernandes, H., Fleeman, N.D., Foster, L., Fraser, C., Fry-Smith, A., Golder, S., Lefebvre, C., Miller, C., Paisley, S., Payne, L., Price, A., & Welch, K. (2008). So many filters, so little time: the development of a search filter appraisal checklist. *Journal of the Medical Library Association, 96*(4), 356–61.

InterTASC Information Specialists' Sub-Group Search Filter Resource. https://sites.google.com/a/york.ac.uk/issg-search-filters-resource/home

Lefebvre, C., Glanville, J., Briscoe, S., Littlewood, A., Marshall, C., Metzendorf, M-I., Noel-Storr, A., Rader, T., Shokraneh, F., Thomas, J., & Wieland, L.S. (2022). Chapter 4: Searching for and selecting studies. In Higgins, J.P.T., Thomas, J., Chandler, J., Cumpston, M., Li, T., Page, M.J., & Welch, V.A. (Eds) (2022). *Cochrane handbook for systematic reviews of interventions* (version 6.3, updated February 2022). https://training.cochrane.org/handbook/current

Rethlefsen, M., Kirtley, S., Waffenschmidt, S., Ayala, A.P., Moher, D., Page, M.J., Koffel, J.B., & PRISMA-S Group. (2021). PRISMA-S: an extension to the PRISMA Statement for Reporting Literature Searches in Systematic Reviews. *Systematic Reviews, 10*(1), 39.

6

Applying Inclusion and Exclusion Criteria

Yenal Dundar and Nigel Fleeman

This chapter will help you to...

- Screen the titles and abstracts of potentially eligible studies against your inclusion and exclusion criteria

- Select full-text papers for inclusion in your review

- Report the results of your search for evidence

Introduction

This chapter guides you through the processes of screening and selecting studies for inclusion in your review. First, we provide guidance on how the results of your search should be screened against your inclusion and exclusion criteria, and how to determine whether individual papers should be included in your systematic review. We then suggest different options for reporting the results of these activities in the 'Results' section of your thesis.

Choosing your included studies

Congratulations – by now, you should have finalized your search strategy and conducted your searches (Chapter 5) and be ready to press ahead and screen studies against your inclusion and exclusion criteria to determine their eligibility for inclusion in your review. This whole process is commonly referred to as 'screening and selection' and is usually conducted in two stages (Stage 1 = screening titles and abstracts; Stage 2 = screening and selecting full-text papers). Box 6.1 outlines the key steps involved in screening and selection. You'll note that we use the terms 'references', 'papers' and 'studies' interchangeably throughout this chapter to refer to the results of your searches, because we appreciate that not every student will search only for published peer-reviewed academic journal articles for inclusion in their review. If you do some wider reading, you may also see the term 'citation' used to refer to an individual record; don't let this confuse you. These terms all broadly refer to individual results identified by one or more search.

Box 6.1

Key steps to consider when choosing your included studies

Step 1: **De-duplicate** references

Step 2: Develop and pilot your **screening and selection tool**

Step 3: Screen all titles and abstracts identified via searches against your inclusion and exclusion criteria (Stage 1)

Step 4: Obtain the full-text papers of all potentially eligible studies

Step 5: Use your screening and selection tool to help you identify full-text papers for inclusion in your review (Stage 2)

Step 1: De-duplicate references

Before you apply your inclusion and exclusion criteria to your long list of potentially relevant studies, you first need to de-duplicate your references. This simply
involves identifying and deleting any duplicate references from your main search
results. Duplicates are almost inevitable if you have searched more than one
resource. If you have stored your references using a reference management software
package, it should be possible to merge search results from different databases and
then easily remove any duplicates automatically. However, you may also need to
remove some duplicate references one by one, because minor differences in how
a reference is indexed in different databases will result in some duplicates being
missed (e.g. an author could be indexed as J.W. Rigby in one database and J Rigby in
another). It is important to stress that duplicates are the only references you should
ever delete from your reference library. You should always know how many references your individual searches identified and, once merged, how many references
were duplicates.

Step 2: Develop and pilot your screening and selection tool

Up to this point, your inclusion and exclusion criteria (the criteria against which you
judge the relevance and suitability of studies for inclusion in your review) will have
been used to refine and shape your review question and will probably have taken the
form of a series of statements or bullet points in your protocol. We now recommend
that you use these criteria to create an electronic or paper screening and selection
'tool'. This tool will allow you to easily screen potentially relevant full-text papers
against your inclusion and exclusion criteria (more on this later), and ultimately
means you can select only those that are of relevance to your review question. An
example of a screening and selection tool is shown in Table 6.1.

It is a good idea to pilot your tool before going any further. Ideally, you and a fellow researcher (maybe your supervisor(s) or a fellow student, if permitted by your
institution) should independently screen a few of the titles and abstracts of the studies identified by your main search, and then meet up to compare and discuss the
references that each of you has identified as being relevant to the review question.
This is to ensure that you both fully understand which studies should be included
in the review. If there are discrepancies in your results, you should meet to discuss
them and identify the reasons they may have occurred. This pilot testing reduces the
chances of regular disagreements later in the review about which studies should or
should not be included and allows you to quickly identify and correct any problems

with your screening and selection tool. As for the number of references you choose to look at during the pilot exercise, this will depend on the number of references you have identified. It is not uncommon for your search strategy to identify hundreds, if not thousands, of references, particularly in the early stages of searching. It may therefore be sensible to pilot your screening and selection tool on a small proportion of titles and abstracts.

TABLE 6.1 An example of a bespoke screening and selection tool

---

Review question: What is the clinical effectiveness of different regimens of first-line chemotherapy in addition to radiotherapy for adult patients with locally advanced non-small cell lung cancer?

Inclusion criteria (based on PICOS):
Population = adult patients aged 18 years or over) with non-small cell lung cancer
Intervention = any chemotherapy + radiotherapy regimen
Comparator = any other chemotherapy + radiotherapy regimen
Outcomes = overall survival, progression-free survival, time to progression, death, adverse events and/or quality of life
Study design = randomized controlled trials (RCTs) only

CHEMOTHERAPY + RADIOTHERAPY SCREENING AND SELECTION TOOL

Reviewer name:		**Date:**
Author name/Study ID:		**Year:**
Title:		**Journal:**

Patient population	**Include** ☐ Adult patients aged 18 years or over with non-small cell lung cancer	**Exclude** ☐ Patients with other cancers ☐ Patients aged under 18 years
Interventions	**Include** ☐ Chemotherapy + radiotherapy regimen	**Exclude** ☐ Chemotherapy only ☐ Radiotherapy only
Comparators	**Include** ☐ Chemotherapy + radiotherapy regimen	**Exclude** ☐ Chemotherapy only ☐ Radiotherapy only
Outcomes	**Include if one or more of:** ☐ Overall survival ☐ Progression-free survival ☐ Time to progression ☐ Death ☐ Adverse events ☐ Quality of life	**Exclude** ☐ Does not report any outcome specified in inclusion criteria
Study design	**Include** ☐ RCT	**Exclude** ☐ Any study design other than RCT
Overall decision	☐ INCLUDED	☐ EXCLUDED
Notes		

PICOS = participants, intervention, comparator and study design; RCT = randomized controlled trial

Box 6.2

'Top tips' for designing and applying your screening and selection tool

- The inclusion and exclusion criteria should be the same as stated in your protocol, but you can add explanatory notes to your tool to aid your decision making, which may be helpful if you are finding it difficult to decide if a study meets certain criteria
- Even if you don't want to complete the tool for the papers that you look at during Stage 1 screening, it's useful to have the tool to hand so that you don't risk including papers that are interesting to you but are not relevant to the aims of your review or, conversely, excluding papers that should progress to Stage 2. During Stage 2, we would expect you to complete your tool for every full-text paper so that you have a paper trail of the decisions you've made and why you've made them – this will make your life much easier if you need to resolve disagreements between reviewers

Step 3: Screen all titles and abstracts identified via searches against your inclusion and exclusion criteria (Stage 1)

The next step is to screen the titles and abstracts of all the studies identified via your searches against your inclusion and exclusion criteria, using your screening and selection tool to guide your decision making. This is often referred to as Stage 1 and simply entails applying your inclusion and exclusion criteria to the title (and ideally to the abstract) of every potentially relevant paper to determine whether the study is relevant to your review question and fits your inclusion criteria. For example, you might decide to include only studies examining sustainable housing policies and so you may look for keywords, or related synonyms, in the title and abstract. You need to scan every reference identified by your searches and this task can be time-consuming; it can take days or even weeks if you have hundreds or thousands to look at. However, although it's a good idea to have your screening and selection tool to hand as you read through titles and abstracts and make decisions about the potential eligibility of individual studies, it's not necessary at this stage to complete the form for each reference. If you have any doubts about whether a reference should be included at this stage (in particular, if it is unclear whether the study meets all your inclusion criteria), it is always safest to include it.

If you are working electronically, you can export your titles and abstracts into a word-processing package and then use the 'find' function to highlight relevant keywords (as bold text and/or in a different colour). For example, if you are only looking for **cohort studies**, you can find and highlight 'cohort' (or 'observational' or 'longitudinal', etc.) or if you are only looking for studies that include patients with low self-esteem, you can find and highlight 'self-esteem' (or 'self esteem'); this simple activity makes potentially relevant studies easier to spot. However, you will need to be creative and think outside the box about how these concepts may be described in the text to reduce the chance of excluding relevant articles by accident – electronic scanning (i.e. using electronic methods to identify potentially relevant studies) may speed up the screening process but should never take the place of manual scanning of titles and abstracts (i.e. reading them yourself and judging their relevance).

During this process, it is worthwhile making a note of any references that are useful and that could be used to inform the 'Introduction' or 'Discussion' sections of your write-up. If there has been some delay between your scoping searches and your main search, then, before you start to scan your references, it may also be prudent to check whether your main search results include any recently published relevant systematic reviews that have addressed your review question. An easy way to check is to search for the words 'systematic review' in your main search results and then scan all of the titles and abstracts where this term appears. Such a search may be possible within your reference management software package or by exporting all the titles and abstracts into a word-processing package (and again searching for the term 'systematic review'). If you are extremely unlucky and a review addressing your review question has just been published, revisit Chapter 3 for tips on what to do next.

A word of caution before you begin. Ideally, each reference should be dual screened – that is, you and a fellow researcher should each independently consider the suitability of each record for inclusion in your review, discussing and resolving any discordant opinions as they arise. This reduces the risk of bias (e.g. misapplying your inclusion and exclusion criteria, or accidentally excluding a relevant study) and helps to make your review more robust. However, don't worry if this isn't possible or permitted. If you are working alone, simply screen your titles and abstracts, put the results to one side and repeat this process a few days (or weeks) later, reflecting upon and resolving any discrepancies. Alternatively, check whether a peer or your supervisor(s) may be willing to screen a random sample (say, 10 per cent) of your identified references, or 'cross-check' all or some of your screening (i.e. check whether they agree with the decisions that you have made). This may be a more practical solution, particularly if your search has retrieved a large number of references.

Step 4: Obtain the full-text papers of all potentially eligible studies

Once you have finished screening your titles and abstracts, you should obtain copies of the papers you marked for possible inclusion in the review. You need to have the full-text of each potentially eligible study in front of you – either electronically or in paper format. While an increasing number of full-text papers are available online, it is likely that some potentially relevant papers may not be. Your institution is likely to have an inter-library loans system and, if so, this is an obvious route for obtaining your selected papers when they are not available electronically or held in your institution's libraries. This option costs money though, so make sure that the cost is covered by your institution's budget before ordering papers. Alternatively, you can try to contact authors and ask them to send or email you a copy of their publication or search the Internet to see whether the authors have made their publication freely available via, for example, **institutional repositories** or academic social media. If, having tried all these routes, you have been unable to obtain the full-text papers that you need, then, when you write your thesis (and draft a manuscript for publication), you should clearly state any papers that you have been unable to obtain, as this is a limitation of your review (see Chapters 13 and 14).

Step 5: Use your screening and selection tool to help you identify full-text papers for inclusion in the review (Stage 2)

Having obtained the full-text papers, the next step is to determine whether these papers really do meet your inclusion criteria. You should carefully read each full-text paper and complete your screening and selection tool for each. If you decide that a study is not eligible for inclusion in your review, it is important to note the reason you excluded it at this stage. You should keep a record of which studies are included or excluded using a database (e.g. the reference management software package in which your references are stored), word-processing package or spreadsheet (see Chapter 2). When you produce your full list of included studies you may find it helpful to also list all the references that you excluded at Stage 2, together with reasons for exclusion, in a table that can be placed in an appendix to your thesis.

At this stage, you will likely be grateful for your exclusion criteria, as they may provide you with a speedy way to exclude records without having to review the papers in detail. For example, you might decide to exclude all studies that include only pharmaceutical interventions and include studies only looking at public health interventions. If use of pharmaceutical interventions is listed as an exclusion criterion, you can exclude these types of papers immediately without reading through the text looking for public health interventions.

Ideally, you should collaborate with a peer, colleague or supervisor(s) on this exercise, and meet up to discuss your findings. However, if you are working alone follow the same procedure as you did when screening titles and abstracts. When you think that you have a 'final' set of included studies, it may be worth emailing topic experts to check that you haven't missed any relevant studies. We recommend that you are very clear in your email about what you want from them and include a set of well-defined questions to maximize your chances of a response (see Box 6.3).

Box 6.3

Example of a well-thought-out email to confirm your 'final' included studies

Dear Dr Paton

Re: Systematic review of barriers and facilitators to compliance with high rise safety management systems

I am currently conducting a systematic review as part of my postgraduate studies at the University of Liverpool. I have attached my protocol to this email, which contains more information about the aims of this review and the planned methodology. After completing my searching and applying my inclusion and exclusion criteria, I have identified several studies for inclusion in my review (please see attached). I would be grateful if, after having a quick read through this list, you could let me know of any other relevant studies that I may have missed during my searches and/or of any ongoing studies that are due to be published in the next three months.

Thank you very much for your help.

Yours sincerely

Margaret Drugan

How to report the results of your searching, screening and selection exercises

The methods that you used to screen and select studies should be reported in the 'Methods' section of your thesis, just after the text that reports the methods that you used to search for evidence. In this section, you should report the following information:

- Inclusion and exclusion criteria
- Description of how these criteria were used to screen and select studies for inclusion, and by whom
- Detail on how disagreements, if any, were resolved between reviewers

In contrast, the results of your searching, screening and selection should be reported in the 'Results' section of your thesis. In this section, you need to make sure that you record the following information:

- Number of references identified by each search
- Number of duplicates removed
- Number of references you looked at when screening titles and abstracts
- Number of full-text papers you looked at
- Number of full-text papers you excluded at Stage 2 and the reasons for exclusion

An example of how you might report the methods and results of your searching, screening and selection in the 'Methods' and 'Results' sections of your thesis is provided in Box 6.4. As discussed in Chapters 2 and 4, you may find it useful to consult the PRISMA (Preferred Reporting Items for Systematic Reviews and Meta-Analyses) statement (Page et al., 2021a; 2021b) before you start writing up the 'Results' section of your review as forewarned is forearmed. PRISMA is an evidence-based minimum set of items that can help reviewers improve the reporting of systematic reviews and meta-analyses. The main PRISMA tool is a 27-item checklist and a four-phase flow diagram that outlines all aspects of the conduct of a systematic review. As mentioned in Chapter 5, PRISMA-S (an extension to the PRISMA Statement for Reporting Literature Searches in Systematic Reviews; Rethlefsen et al., 2021) is available to help you record your search details. Take a look at the PRISMA website (www.prisma-statement.org); you'll find discussion documents and the current version of the PRISMA statement. A template of the PRISMA flow diagram, which maps out the number of records identified, included and excluded, and the reasons for exclusion, is available from the website as a PDF and also as a word-processing document. A flow diagram similar to the PRISMA flow diagram shown in Chapter 2 should be included in the 'Results' section of your thesis and is essential if you plan to publish your review in a peer-reviewed academic journal (see Chapter 14).

Box 6.4

How to report the application of your inclusion and exclusion criteria in your 'Methods' and 'Results' sections

In the 'Methods' section of your thesis, a description of how you applied your inclusion and exclusion criteria comes immediately after a description of your search methods (see Chapter 5).

Methods
Inclusion and exclusion criteria

Two reviewers independently screened all titles and abstracts. Full-text papers of any titles and abstracts that were considered relevant by either reviewer were obtained where possible. The relevance of each study was assessed according to the inclusion and exclusion criteria stated in Table 6.2. Studies that did not meet the criteria were excluded and their bibliographic details were listed in an appendix alongside the reason(s) for their exclusion. Any discrepancies were resolved by consensus.

TABLE 6.2　Inclusion and exclusion criteria

	Inclusion criteria	Exclusion criteria
Population(s)	Participants 18 years or over with a diagnosis of post-natal depression	Participants with self-reported post-natal depression; studies in which data from participants aged 18 years or over cannot be separated from those aged under 18 years
Intervention(s)	Cognitive behavioural therapy (CBT)	Pharmacological interventions and/or other non-CBT psychological intervention(s)
Comparators	Wait-list control	None and/or other active treatment
Outcomes	Any validated self-report measure of psychological distress (including post-natal depression) and/or wellbeing	Clinician-reported distress and/or general wellbeing measures
Study design	Any comparative study	Non-comparative studies
Setting	Any	No exclusion
Other	English-language full-text available	Non-English-language full-text; abstract available only

Results

Quantity of research available

Electronic and hand searches identified 2228 citations; 1824 citations were identified from electronic databases and registers and 404 references were identified from other sources. One additional reference was identified following communication with an expert in the field, yielding 2229 references in total (see Figure 6.1). Once duplicates were automatically removed, there were 2001 unique references considered for inclusion. Their titles and abstracts were assessed for their relevance to the review (Stage 1). After applying inclusion criteria to the remaining 17 full-text papers (Stage 2), 12 references were excluded; four did not examine the appropriate intervention and eight reported data from the wrong patient population. As such, five references, reporting four separate studies, were included in the systematic review.

Alternative routes

There is now an increasing number of **systematic review software packages** (e.g. Rayyan, Covidence, DistillerSR) that are designed to help you to manage key aspects of the systematic review process – for example, screening and selection. Some of these packages are free (but require registration) and others you have to pay to use. These packages enable you to import your search results directly from bibliographic databases or from reference management software packages, such as EndNote. In addition to de-duplicating references automatically (although as with all reference management software packages, you may also need to remove some duplicate references by hand), these systematic review software packages contain functions that allow you to highlight key text in titles/abstracts, make notes and to upload full-text copies of your studies, which can aid the screening and selection process at Stage 1 and Stage 2 respectively. Systematic review software packages can be very useful as they normally allow more than one reviewer to screen or select studies at any given time, thus speeding up the review process.

Final thoughts

We hope that, after reading this chapter, you feel sufficiently confident to be able to de-duplicate the results of your main search for evidence, develop and pilot a

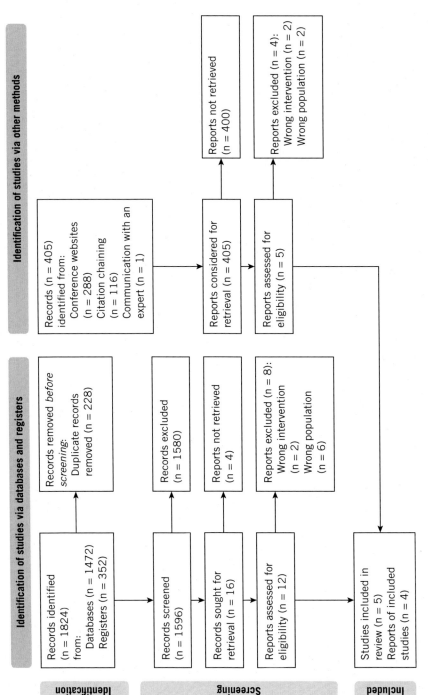

FIGURE 6.1 Identification of included studies in a systematic review

screening and selection tool, screen titles and abstracts, and select the final papers for inclusion in your review. You should now have the studies that will help you to answer your review question and feel more than ready to take the next step – extracting relevant data from these studies.

Key points to think about when writing your protocol

- Clearly report how you plan to include or exclude studies – that is, how you will screen and select the studies (and how many people will conduct these tasks). It is helpful for you to state whether you will use specific software packages for these tasks (see Chapter 2)
- Importantly, you should include a table detailing your inclusion and exclusion criteria
- Set a deadline for obtaining the full-text papers of potentially relevant studies
- Present a clear plan for how you will report your methods and results

What an examiner is looking for in your thesis

- Clear reporting of your methods and results
- Inclusion of a flow diagram like the PRISMA diagram in your 'Results' section
- A brief explanation of the reason(s) why you excluded studies at Stage 2

Frequently Asked Questions

Question 1: What if there are too many or too few studies that match my inclusion criteria?

If you think that too many studies match your inclusion criteria, you may want to refine your inclusion and exclusion criteria and/or your review question. You may also wish to consider how you can limit your search results further – for example by year, language or publication type (e.g. include only peer-reviewed academic journal articles, books or letters and/or studies published after a specific year). In contrast, if you have only identified a small number of studies that meet your inclusion criteria, your search terms may be too specific and you may wish to expand them. Alternatively, you may be able to determine, from the reasons you listed when you excluded studies, whether you need to change your inclusion and exclusion criteria (e.g. were most studies excluded because of study design? If so, do you want to broaden your inclusion criterion relating to study design?).

Many credible systematic reviews have included only one study and it may be that only one study really does address your review question. Often, the lack of studies can be considered an important finding in itself, as it means that you've identified an important gap in the evidence base where further research is required. However, identifying only one study may not allow you to fully demonstrate your systematic review skills to your examiner(s) and you may wish to broaden your review question. If you do not identify any studies at all, we suggest that you go back and modify your review question; you might also find it helpful to re-read Chapter 3. Don't forget to update your protocol if you make any methodological changes (see Chapter 4).

Question 2: What happens if I find a useful paper that has an English abstract but the full-text paper is written in a different language?

The first step is to determine whether the useful paper meets your inclusion criteria – typically you would look for any relevant information that is stated in the abstract. You might also think about using translation software to help you understand the 'Methods' section and any tables and figures. If the abstract contains potentially relevant information, you have three possible options. The first is to find somebody who can translate the paper or, at the very least, can extract the data that you need (perhaps a fellow student). The second is to use the data from the abstract and any tables and figures that you can, noting this approach as a limitation when writing up your review. The third is to exclude this paper altogether and acknowledge this when writing the limitations of your systematic review. This last option may not be ideal, especially if you had not stated 'not English language' as an exclusion criterion in your review protocol.

Question 3: My friend included 40 papers in their review but I've only found five of relevance to my review question – am I doing something wrong?

This is a difficult question to answer. There is no 'perfect' number of papers to include in your systematic review (although we discuss the potential difficulties associated with having very few relevant papers, or none, in Chapter 3, and in Question 1 in this chapter). If your searching, screening and selection processes have been sufficiently rigorous, you should feel confident that you have identified all relevant evidence for inclusion in your review. Try not to compare your review with others as every review is different.

Further Reading and Resources

Centre for Reviews and Dissemination. (2010). *Systematic reviews: CRD's guidance for undertaking reviews in health care.* www.york.ac.uk/inst/crd/SysRev/!SSL!/WebHelp/SysRev3.htm

Lefebvre, C., Glanville, J., Briscoe, S., Littlewood, A., Marshall, C., Metzendorf, M-I., Noel-Storr, A., Rader, T., Shokraneh, F., Thomas, J., & Wieland, L.S. (2022). Chapter 4: Searching for and selecting studies. In Higgins, J.P.T., Thomas, J., Chandler, J., Cumpston, M., Li, T., Page, M.J., & Welch, V.A. (Eds) (2022). *Cochrane handbook for systematic reviews of interventions* (version 6.3, updated February 2022). https://training.cochrane.org/handbook/current

Rethlefsen, M., Kirtley, S., Waffenschmidt, S., Ayala, A.P., Moher, D., Page, M.J., Koffel, J.B., & PRISMA-S Group. (2021). PRISMA-S: an extension to the PRISMA Statement for Reporting Literature Searches in Systematic Reviews. *Systematic Reviews, 10*(1), 39.

7

Data Extraction: Where Do I Begin?

Nigel Fleeman and Yenal Dundar

This chapter will help you to...

- Understand the purpose of data extraction

- Decide when and how to undertake your data extraction

- Store the data you have extracted

- Feel confident about reporting the results of your data extraction

Introduction

This chapter has been written to guide you through the process of data extraction and to encourage you to think about the links between data extraction, data presentation and data synthesis. We've focused this chapter on extracting quantitative data; to help you to understand more about quantitative data, see Chapters 9 and 10. Whilst the principles in this chapter also apply to qualitative data, if you are planning on conducting a review of qualitative evidence, read Chapter 11 before you start to extract your data.

In this chapter, we provide guidance about which data to extract, and how and where data can be stored. We discuss the best time to complete the data extraction exercise, and we conclude the chapter by describing how to report the results of your data extraction exercise in your thesis.

What do we mean by data extraction?

By this stage in the review process, you will already have identified which papers contain evidence to help you answer your review question, and, as a result of the screening and selection process, you are probably becoming familiar with the data within your included studies. Your next step is to identify, and then extract, relevant data from each study. Data extraction is the process whereby relevant data are taken from your included papers and stored in a single format – usually a data extraction form or data extraction table (see Box 7.1). Data are then presented in data tables in your thesis. The process of extracting and presenting relevant data allows you (and the reader of your thesis) to make sense of the data, both descriptively and analytically.

Box 7.1

What are the differences between data extraction forms, data extraction tables and data tables?

A data extraction form is a form into which you can extract and record relevant data from a study. You will therefore have one form for each study included in your review. You would normally include a blank copy of this form in your appendix.

Data extraction tables are tables which allow you to store extracted data from one or all of your studies in one place. These are not normally included in your thesis.

Data tables are tables that describe and summarize your extracted data in your thesis.

Before you start...

Whether or not you extract data before, during or after quality assessment (see Chapter 8) is up to you – as is the order in which you describe what you have done in the 'Methods' section of your thesis. It is sometimes recommended that data extraction takes place after the methodological quality assessment of your included studies has been carried out; this is imperative if you are planning to exclude poor-quality studies from your review. We talk about this further in Chapters 8 and 11 and discuss it in relation to meta-analysis in Chapter 10. Not only does this save time by preventing needless extraction of data you do not require but it can also reduce bias, since having extracted data, you may be more or less inclined to include or exclude a particular study if it contains data that appear to support or refute your initial hypothesis. However, some people prefer to extract data before they assess the quality of their included studies. The choice is yours.

Extracting and reporting data from included studies

Box 7.2 outlines the key steps involved in extracting and reporting data from your included studies.

Box 7.2

Key steps to consider when extracting and reporting data from studies

Step 1: Identify the data that you want to extract

Step 2: Build and pilot your data extraction form or data extraction table(s)

Step 3: Extract relevant data

Step 4: Populate the data tables for inclusion in your thesis

Step 5: Report your extracted data in your thesis

Step 1: Identify the data that you want to extract

The first thing to consider is *which* data to extract. When conducting a systematic review you are primarily interested in two types of data: **descriptive data** (e.g. study characteristics) and **analytical data** (e.g. outcomes). Each of your included studies will contain relevant descriptive and analytical data. However, it is likely that each paper will also contain *irrelevant* data. It's important to ensure that you only extract data that are likely to be useful and will help you to address your review question. For example, while data on the biological sex of the participants in a study may be useful to answer some review questions (such as 'What factors explain differences in educational attainment in 16- to 18-year-olds?'), such data may not be relevant to other review questions (such as 'Are there differences in health outcomes for pregnant people who have hospital or home births?').

We recommend that you compile a list of all of the data that you *think* will help you to summarize, describe and interpret the results of your included studies, both as individual studies and as a collection of studies. When doing so, it may be helpful to re-read your review question and protocol and re-familiarize yourself with the data extraction plan included in your protocol, as you should already have given data extraction some thought earlier in the review process. It's also a good idea to skim-read all of your included papers at this stage, as this will allow you to gain a sense of the data within the studies. You might also want to have a look at published studies or reviews in the same topic area as your review to help you identify specific data that you want to extract. Don't worry if your final list is extensive – it's a good idea to err on the side of caution and plan to extract more potentially relevant data rather than fewer. It's far easier to delete data than go back to studies later to collect more data.

If you are planning to extract and analyse qualitative data, then a more iterative approach to data extraction and analysis may be required. It may then be necessary to keep revisiting the source studies. Further information on extracting and analysing qualitative data is provided in Chapter 11.

Step 2: Build and pilot your data extraction form or data extraction table(s)

Once you have decided on the data that you want to extract, you can start to put together your data extraction form or data extraction table(s). We use the word 'or' because some people prefer to record their extracted data on a series of forms (usually one per study), which they can then collate. Others prefer to store their extracted data by entering them straight into a table or series of tables. The choice is yours. Similarly, whether you choose to complete your data extraction form/table(s) using a software package or plain, old-fashioned paper is up to you. However, using a software package can be more convenient when it comes to producing the final data tables for your thesis and may reduce the risk of data-entry errors.

If you have a well-designed data extraction form/table(s), then you are less likely to have to keep returning to the source paper(s) of each individual study during the review process, which will save you valuable time and energy. 'Top tips' for designing your data extraction form/table(s) are presented in Box 7.3.

Box 7.3

'Top tips' for designing your data extraction form/table(s)

- As a minimum, record the study's author(s) (e.g. the first named author) and year of publication
- If the study has been published in a peer-reviewed academic journal, you should record whether it has been published as a full-text paper or only as an abstract (if applicable)
- Having a unique identification number for each study and paper is a good idea, especially where there are many studies by the same authors
- If a study has linked publications, record information about these (e.g. study author, year of publication, journal or other source where published), even if you do not extract data from these papers
- Extract study characteristics data, including, where appropriate:
  o study design
  o where and when the study was conducted
  o number of participants (including any dropouts)
  o intervention(s) and comparator(s), if appropriate
  o study outcomes (including which were primary outcomes and which were secondary outcomes, and which were pre-specified)
  o analyses conducted, and main results (applicable to your review question)
  o number of participants included in analyses
  o length of follow-up (if appropriate)
  o study sponsorship
- Extract participants' demographic information. This may vary depending on your review question, but should usually include, as a minimum, participants' age, gender and ethnicity. Specific demographic characteristics may also be required – for example, participants' religion, educational level, socio-economic status or mental or physical health diagnoses
- For certain study designs (such as randomized controlled trials), you should extract baseline participant data (e.g. if your review investigates the effects of an educational intervention on participants' reading ability, then it will be important to know pre-intervention reading proficiency)
- Leave plenty of space to make additional notes

It's a good idea to pilot your data extraction form/table(s) using at least two or three of your included studies. As with other stages in the systematic review process, piloting your data extraction form/table(s) can save time and energy if done early on. The aims of the pilot exercise are twofold: first, to ascertain how easy it is to extract the data and second, to check whether all the necessary data are being captured. Piloting should prevent problems such as making the late discovery that important data have not been extracted. You may find that, at the pilot stage, you need to add or remove variables from your form/table(s). You may also find, at this stage, that having started to pilot data extraction with a form, the use of tables is going to be better for your purposes, or vice versa.

If more than one person is extracting data (more on this later), then piloting your data extraction form/table(s) should include a check on whether both reviewers share the same understanding of both the form/table(s) and the data that need to be collected. For example, age is likely to be an important variable for most studies; when extracting data on age, you need to ensure that you explicitly state whether you are referring to mean or median, **standard deviation** (SD) or range, and so on. You can either state this explicitly on your form/table(s) or design an accompanying crib sheet with detailed instructions. Even if you are not working with another person, a crib sheet can be useful to ensure consistency across your own data extraction, particularly if you don't complete your data extraction in one sitting or within a short time window.

Step 3: Extract relevant data

The next step is to extract relevant data. You can do this electronically, or you can extract data by hand. If you are extracting data from an electronic copy of a study (such as a PDF), then it is likely that you will simply copy and paste relevant sections or chunks of data into your data extraction tables. This approach not only saves time but reduces the chances of making data-entry errors. In addition, storing data electronically enables you to make, and save, backups of your work and may also make your life simpler when it comes to data synthesis. For example, some software packages enable you to analyse your data quantitatively (e.g. the use of a spreadsheet or statistical package to carry out mathematical and statistical tasks) or qualitatively (e.g. the use of a word processor or specialist software such as **NVivo** to move and code data). Chapter 2 outlines the advantages and disadvantages of using different software packages for storing data. Your choice will depend, to some extent, on the amount of data you need and on your own competence and familiarity with different software packages. Whether you extract data electronically or by hand, it's a good idea to record where in the full-text paper the extracted data are located. One way to do this is to highlight the extracted data in the original study (electronic or paper version). It's also important to be aware of potential stylistic differences between papers. For example, a mean and SD may be presented as '64 (12)' in one paper and '64 ± 12' in another. You need to decide how you want to record these data in your data extraction form/table(s), as you can save yourself a great deal of time and effort by being stylistically consistent from the outset.

Ideally, two people would independently carry out data extraction, and then meet to discuss any discordant opinions. This is generally considered to be the most robust approach, as it can help to minimize data extraction errors. Alternatively, you may ask a second person to cross-check all or some of your extracted data. There may be occasions when you do not agree about the data you have extracted. Most disagreements can be resolved through discussion. Most simply, you may find one of you has made a transcription error (data-entry error) when extracting the data. You may, however, disagree because the data in the original study are misleading; for example, data contained in a figure or table do not appear to match the data quoted in the text. If this is the case, then we recommend that you contact authors for clarity.

Where similar issues recur for the same variable in more than one study, the disagreement may highlight issues about your review question or inclusion and exclusion criteria that need addressing; for example, are your aims and objectives clear? Alternatively, disagreement may occur simply because a poorly designed data extraction form/table(s) results in a lack of clarity about which data need to be extracted, therefore indicating the need for further piloting. In some situations, you and the second reviewer may not be able to agree on which data should be extracted from the paper. In this case, we recommend that you obtain the opinion of a third person (perhaps your supervisor(s), if they are not your second reviewer), who is familiar with systematic reviews and is fully aware of the aims of your review.

If you are working independently, you need to be creative and identify ways to ensure that the data you have extracted are accurate and complete. For example, you could ask your supervisor(s) to cross-check a random sample (as opposed to all) of your extracted data. Or you could put your data aside for a week or so and then redo your data extraction, cross-checking that both sets of extracted data are the same. The latter approach can be tedious but can help you to identify data extraction errors or inconsistencies.

Whether you are working with others or working independently, we hope you'll be thankful that you took our advice and highlighted data in your source papers as it should be easy to identify precisely where you took your extracted data from. This will allow minor discrepancies to be quickly and easily rectified.

Contacting study authors for missing or additional data

Where appropriate, contacting authors for further information and clarification can improve the quality of your review. However, you should check that there are no other publications that might have been missed during your search, and which might contain the data you are looking for – perhaps, for example, a study was published after your search was completed. When requesting data from authors, it is important to be as clear as possible about which data you require. For example, is it a mean or median value you need? Or is it both? It is a good idea to send the relevant part(s) of the data extraction form/table(s) to the author for them to complete. Finally, you should prepare yourself for the fact that not all authors will respond to your data requests. It is acceptable to re-contact authors who do not respond to your first contact. It is also a good idea to log all correspondence so that when you are writing up your review, you can state whether you contacted an author but did not receive a response.

Step 4: Populate the data tables for inclusion in your thesis

After you have extracted your data, you need to think about how you will describe and summarize your extracted data in your thesis. Most of the data discussed in your thesis should also be presented in tables. To avoid confusion with data extraction tables, we refer to the tables within your thesis as 'data tables'. We cannot tell you exactly how to build your data tables, but we can suggest that you try to include tables with the following headings and variables:

- 'Study Characteristics' table (e.g. study name, date of publication, study design, study population, country, follow-up, outcomes, study sponsorship/funder)
- 'Participant Characteristics' table (e.g. mean age, sex, specific participant characteristics of interest)
- 'Study Results' table (e.g. primary outcomes, secondary outcomes and statistical analyses; see Chapters 9 and 10 for a more detailed discussion of the use of numerical data in your review)

Remember, a well-designed data extraction form/table(s) will make it easy to produce these final data tables. Again, it's a good idea to look at published systematic reviews in a similar topic area for ideas about what you should include in your data tables.

Step 5: Report your extracted data in your thesis

Having extracted your data and built your data tables, the next task is to report and make sense of the data. You need to report data in such a way that the reader can easily understand and follow your train of thought. The term 'narrative synthesis' is used to describe this process. Narrative synthesis simply refers to any presentation of results using words only (with reference to your data tables). However, there is no point in simply repeating the data from your data tables in your text – don't waste your words, and more importantly, don't annoy your examiner(s) by repeating data. Always use the data tables to present data from individual studies and use the text to report the overall findings. All discussion and interpretation of the data (including links to wider literature) should take place in the 'Discussion' and 'Conclusions' sections of your review. Don't feel that you have to comment on everything; data tables may include data not described in the accompanying text, but which nevertheless help the reader to interpret individual study results and compare and contrast the included studies.

It is common practice to begin by presenting a summary of descriptive data for all the included studies in a series of tables. As mentioned previously, the usual practice is to split the descriptive data over two data tables: the 'Study Characteristics' table and the 'Participant Characteristics' table. However, to some extent, this will depend on the number of variables that are relevant to the review question; some reviews amalgamate this information in one table, whereas others present it in three or four separate tables. You can then go on to present the results of your included studies (e.g. in a 'Study Results' table).

All data presented in your data tables should be accompanied by explanatory summary text. It is important to check that what you write in the text corresponds exactly with the information that you present in the tables. Let's assume that Table 7.1 shows the study characteristics of five hypothetical studies that can be used to assess the impact of a new fast-food restaurant (belonging to the hypothetical Acme Corporation) on the local economy.

TABLE 7.1 Example of a 'Study Characteristics' table

Study	When study conducted	Country	General study focus	Source of funding for study
Clarke (2007)	2006	USA	Local workforce	Funded by Acme Corporation
Jones (2021)	2019–2020	France	Local economy in general	Grant from European Union
Radebe (2005)	2001–2002	UK	Local workforce	Not stated
Strummer (2016)	2013–2014	France	Local restaurants	Not stated
Yeboah (1998)	1995–1996	UK	Local workforce	Funded by Acme Corporation

The study characteristics data table might be accompanied by the following explanatory summary text:

> The five studies were carried out between 1995 and 2020. The publication dates ranged from 1998 to 2021. The studies were conducted in various countries: one in the USA, two in France and two in the UK. Three studies focused on the impact of the new Acme Corporation restaurant on the local workforce, one focused on the impact on local restaurants, and the other on the impact on the local economy in general (i.e. taking into account the impact on both the local workforce and local restaurants). The source of funding for the study was acknowledged in three of the five studies; in two instances the studies were sponsored by Acme Corporation.

Let's assume that Table 7.2 presents the results of four hypothetical studies that assessed the clinical effectiveness of different chemotherapy treatments (Treatments X and Y) for patients with non-small cell lung cancer.

TABLE 7.2   Example of a 'Study Results' table

Study	Outcome (survival)	Treatments	Summary of findings (adjusted HR)
Bremner (2010)	Time from registration to death from any cause	X vs Y	HR = 1.15; 95% CI: 0.78 to 1.61; $p = .32$
Longworth (2005)	Time from surgery to death from any cause	X vs Y	HR = 1.75; 95% CI: 0.78 to 3.51; $p = .11$
Springsteen (2021)	Time from registration to death from any cause	X vs Y	HR = 1.39; 95% CI: 0.93 to 2.26; $p = .22$
Strachan (2018)	Time from diagnosis to death or last contact	X vs Y	HR = 0.79; 95% CI: 0.42 to 1.71; $p = .51$

HR = hazard ratio; CI = confidence interval; vs = versus

In this instance, results are presented as **hazard ratios** (HRs) with upper and lower **confidence intervals**. Don't worry if you don't understand what these terms mean just yet – Chapters 9 and 10 are written to help you to understand, critically appraise and synthesize numerical data. The purpose of this example is to illustrate how to summarize these data. Your explanatory text should highlight any key differences in the values reported by different studies; this will entail examining your data tables for similarities and differences, both descriptive (e.g. similar proportions of males and females) and analytical (e.g. differences in magnitude or direction of reported outcomes). Thus, the data presented in Table 7.2 might be accompanied by the following explanatory text:

None of the studies reported statistically significant differences in survival between treatments. However, while three of the studies presented a hazard ratio suggesting a slight numerical increase in survival for those treated with Y when compared with X (Bremner, 2010; Longworth, 2005; Springsteen, 2021), the remaining study suggested an improved outcome for X when compared with Y (Strachan, 2018). All studies had similar cohort characteristics in terms of median age, the proportion of males and previous treatment received.

Beyond narrative synthesis

As previously mentioned, narrative synthesis refers to any write-up of results using words only (with reference to data in data tables). However, after examining your data, you might also want to investigate your data using quantitative synthesis (e.g. meta-analysis, which in the example cited in Table 7.2 could be considered for the Bremner [2010] and Strachan [2018] studies); if so, see Chapter 10. It is important to remember that a narrative synthesis of data is often sufficient. Although we encourage you to consider whether your data lend themselves to meta-analysis, a systematic review does not require one. Don't be concerned if it is not appropriate to combine your data in a meta-analysis; just include an explanation in your thesis that justifies your approach.

Alternative routes

As highlighted in Chapters 2 and 6, there is now an increasing number of systematic review software packages that are designed to help you to manage key aspects of the systematic review process – for example, screening and selection. In addition to helping you to screen titles/abstracts and full-text papers, these packages allow you to create and/or modify your data extraction (and quality assessment) form/table(s). Examples include Rayyan and Covidence; we recommend you conduct an Internet search to find the right package for you.

Final thoughts

After you have narratively synthesized your data, you should have an idea of the similarities and differences in the results of your included studies and should feel confident about discussing the implications of these results in your 'Discussion' and 'Conclusions' sections. To round off the chapter, we considered it appropriate to give you a few pointers on how to discuss your results in your 'Discussion' section. You may wish to consider one or several of the following questions:

- Were you surprised by the results of the data extraction exercise? Did you find any specific elements of the exercise noteworthy?
- Did any of the results from a single study appear to be different from most other results and, if so, did you explain why this might have occurred?
- How did you synthesize your study results? Did you carry out a meta-analysis? What were your reasons for or against this approach?
- Were you able to answer your review question? Were the data from your included studies relevant to your target audience?
- Were you able to offer recommendations for future research?

For other ideas on how to integrate and discuss the findings of your review, look at published reviews in your topic area and read Chapter 13.

Key points to think about when writing your protocol

- State how many people will undertake data extraction
- Where more than one person will undertake data extraction, describe how disagreements will be resolved
- State the types of data you plan to extract
- Outline your plans for piloting your data extraction form/table(s)
- Discuss your plans for narrative synthesis and, if appropriate, meta-analysis

---

What an examiner is looking for in your thesis

- Expansion of the data extraction methods described in your protocol
- Inclusion of your blank data extraction form in an appendix
- Clearly presented data tables describing key data, including consistent use of headings and informative legends
- Succinct reporting of data from your included studies

Frequently Asked Questions

Question 1: When should I design and pilot my data extraction form/table(s)?

Data extraction can only take place after you have applied your inclusion and exclusion criteria. However, a draft of your data extraction form/table(s) can be designed very early in the review process. In fact, this may be done in parallel with writing your protocol. You can begin the process by looking at a key study that you have already identified for inclusion and thinking about the types of data you would extract from this study. However, you will likely need to revisit and amend this form before extracting any data from your included studies.

Question 2: How many studies should I use when piloting my data extraction form/table(s)?

This will depend on the number of studies you have identified. For example, your searches may only have identified four or five studies, in which case you could pilot the data extraction form/table(s) on two studies. However, if you have 15 included studies, you might want to pilot your form/table(s) on four or five studies.

Question 3: When is it too late to modify my data extraction form/table(s)?

It is *never* too late to modify your data extraction form/table(s). If you discover that, after completing your data extraction, important data have not been extracted, you can go back and extract these data from all your studies. Some analytic approaches will necessitate an iterative approach to data extraction (see Chapter 11) and this should be clearly stated in your protocol; however, most, if not all, quantitative approaches do not. Therefore, it is preferable not to find yourself in this situation if you can avoid it as it can be time-consuming to revisit individual studies (remember, you may also want somebody to cross-check all of your additional extraction).

Question 4: What should I do if a study is reported in more than one publication?

It is common to discover that a study has been published in multiple publications, often with different outcomes reported in each, or with the same outcomes reported at different time points. When this is the case, it is best practice to consider all the different sources as one paper and to extract all the data on the same form or in the same tables. Where the data differ across publications, this should be noted and, if possible, investigated (e.g. by contacting the author(s) for more information).

Question 5: Can I copy text verbatim from included studies?

Most academic institutions have clear rules about academic integrity and use **academic integrity software** packages (such as TurnItIn) to ensure that any work submitted in partial or total fulfilment of a postgraduate degree is the student's own work, i.e. it is not plagiarized from any other source. This means that you must ensure that all extracted data are rephrased or summarized, where possible. We appreciate that this is difficult to do and there will be some data that cannot be rephrased (e.g. numerical data). However, we have also supervised and marked lots of theses in which students have copied text verbatim rather than writing this in their own words – for example, copying text from the participant characteristics sections of included studies into their data tables. This is problematic and, in the worst case, may result in your academic integrity being questioned.

Further Reading and Resources

Centre for Reviews and Dissemination. (2010). *Systematic reviews: CRD's guidance for undertaking reviews in health care.* www.york.ac.uk/inst/crd/SysRev/!SSL!/WebHelp/SysRev3.htm

Duke University Medical Center Library & Archives. (2023). *Systematic reviews. Steps in a systematic review: extract the data.* https://guides.mclibrary.duke.edu/sysreview/extract

Steingart, K. (2010). *Data extraction and quality assessment.* www.teachepi.org/wp-content/uploads/OldTE/documents/courses/berlin/Steingart_Data_extraction_critical_appraisal_FINAL_12_Nov_2010.pdf

Tianjing, L., Higgins, J.P.T., & Deeks, J.J. (2022). Chapter 5: Collecting data. In Higgins, J.P.T., Thomas, J., Chandler, J., Cumpston, M., Li, T., Page, M.J., & Welch, V.A. (Eds) (2022). *Cochrane handbook for systematic reviews of interventions* (version 6.3, updated February 2022). https://training.cochrane.org/handbook/current

University of Wisconsin. (2010). *Systematic reviews, a guide: Data extraction.* https://researchguides.ebling.library.wisc.edu/systematic-reviews/author/data

8

Quality Assessment: Where Do I Begin?

Janette Greenhalgh and Tamara Brown

This chapter will help you to...

- Identify quality assessment tool(s) that suit your review

- Carry out quality assessment of individual studies

- Tabulate and summarize the results of your quality assessment

- Think about how your quality assessment results might impact on the conclusions and recommendations of your systematic review

Introduction

This chapter guides you as you set out to assess the quality of the studies included in your systematic review. First, we explore what we mean by quality and discuss the fundamentals of 'quality' common to all studies, regardless of study type, design or topic area. Second, we encourage you to think about the different types of study that you might come across during your review by, for example, differentiating between randomized studies and non-randomized studies. Third, we emphasize how important it is to allow sufficient time to rigorously assess the quality of your included studies and discuss how the conclusions of your systematic review might be shaped by the findings of the quality assessment exercise. Finally, we encourage you to critically appraise your own systematic review using one of the many validated systematic review checklists that are available.

Before you read any further, it's important to note that this chapter is largely focused on the quality assessment of quantitative evidence. If your systematic review is of qualitative or economic evidence, we encourage you to also refer to Chapters 11 and 12 respectively. For practical guidance on managing the review process, including quality assessment, revisit Chapter 2.

The examples we provide in this chapter are derived from our own experiences of conducting systematic reviews in a healthcare context. However, the key steps involved in conducting a systematic review (including quality assessment) are also applicable to non-healthcare contexts. We suggest that you find reviews or guidelines for reviews in your topic area and look at the quality assessment methods that were used or are recommended. The information from reviews and guidelines in your topic area together with the guidance in this chapter will help guide you through your review journey.

What is quality assessment and why do I need to do it?

By the time you reach this stage of your review you will have already identified the full set of relevant studies for inclusion in your review and you may or may not have extracted data from these studies. It's now important to examine the quality of each of these studies. You need to assess whether the studies have been designed, conducted and reported in such a way that they can be considered reliable (i.e. have rigour) and whether or not they provide meaningful answers to your research question (i.e. have relevance).

The meaning of 'quality' depends on the context in which it is used. When it comes to systematic reviewing, we need to distinguish between the quality of each of the included studies and the quality of the systematic review itself. The latter is discussed at the end of this chapter. When used to describe a study included in a systematic review, the term 'quality' refers to 'the degree to which a study employs measures to minimize bias and error in its design, conduct and analysis' (Khan et al., 2003, p. 39).

In other words, the content of the publication gives you confidence that both its design and conduct are sufficiently robust for the results to be trustworthy and generalizable. For example, when considering intervention studies, you need to be sure that the study included participants who were relevant to the aims of the study and that enough participants remained in the study to its end. To illustrate, if a study was designed to assess the effects of bibliotherapy on the psychological wellbeing of adults with anxiety, the results would be of little use if the participants in the study were adults with depression. Similarly, if only 30 out of 100 participants in the study were followed up and only their data were included in the results, only uncertain conclusions could be reached about the effectiveness (or otherwise) of bibliotherapeutic approaches.

If you have assessed a study as being of good or high quality, then this is the same as saying that you are confident that the findings of the study are credible and are highly likely to be a true representation of the results of the intervention, phenomenon or exposure that is being tested or explored. Remember, it is likely that your included studies will vary in quality. It is often mistakenly assumed that if a study has been published in a peer-reviewed academic journal, then it must be of good quality; this is not always true. Do not take published studies at face value; always delve deeper and investigate your studies for flaws and inherent weaknesses. Don't be lulled into a false sense of security by a journal's reputation. To illustrate, in our review of chemotherapy treatments for patients with non-small cell lung cancer (Brown et al., 2013), we concluded that the overall quality of the 23 included studies was poor and yet these studies were all randomized controlled trials (RCTs) published in highly regarded journals. Similarly, one of the key points arising from our review of biofeedback for the treatment of hypertension (Greenhalgh et al., 2009) was that most of the 36 included RCTs were of such poor quality that we were unable to synthesize the results or draw any firm conclusions from the data available.

The advantages of quality assessing your included studies are numerous. You develop a greater understanding of your studies and their results and learn to distinguish between good-quality and poor-quality studies. Your review also benefits as you are more likely to draw meaningful conclusions from the data. On a personal development level, the quality assessment exercise offers you the opportunity to acquire skills in critical appraisal.

When should I assess the quality of the studies in my review?

Before going any further, it's important to stress again that in the context of your review, it is up to you *when* you carry out the quality assessment exercise; you can do it before, during or after data extraction (see Chapter 7). If you extract study data before you carry out your quality assessment, you will be unaware of study quality and your reporting is less likely to be biased. Furthermore, if you choose to assess study quality after you have extracted your data, being more familiar with the study may help you to better answer the quality assessment questions.

What are the main elements of quality assessment and what do they mean?

Quality assessment is normally guided by a tool. A single quality assessment tool asks a series of questions about bias and rigour. To be able to answer the questions posed by the tool, you need to think very carefully about the methods used in the studies and how the results have been reported. You must be confident that the quality assessment tool you are using measures what it purports to measure (that it is 'valid') and provides consistent results (that it is 'reliable'). Examples of bias in studies might include **selection**, **allocation**, **performance**, **detection**, **attrition**, **reporting** and **funding bias**. Common sources of bias, what bias means and the significance of each type of bias in relation to the precision of the results of a study are shown in Table 8.1.

TABLE 8.1   Key elements of bias in healthcare intervention studies

Element	What does this mean?	Significance
Selection bias	Were the individuals selected to participate in the study likely to be representative of the target population? How were the participants selected?	You need to be able to assess how generalizable and transferable the study results are to the target population.
Allocation bias	How were participants allocated to the treatment groups? Could anyone in the study predict or control allocation to treatment groups?	The type of study design determines how participants are allocated to treatment groups; generally, the 'stronger' the study design, the lower the risk of bias from allocation to treatment.
Performance bias	Were the participants, providers of the intervention or the study investigators aware of the treatment that participants received, or were they blinded?	You need to be able to assess whether there was awareness of treatment received by certain study personnel and whether this could bias study results.

Element	What does this mean?	Significance
Detection bias	Were the people who measured the study outcomes aware of what treatment participants received or were they blinded?	You need to be able to assess whether there was awareness of treatment received by study personnel and whether this could bias study results.
Attrition bias	What proportion of participants in each group stopped having the treatment? Did they stop by themselves (dropouts) or were they stopped by study personnel (withdrawal) for whatever reason (e.g. adverse event, non-compliance, did not meet inclusion criteria)?	If a relatively large proportion of dropouts occurred, this could weaken the generalizability of the study and it might also reflect that the intervention is hard to 'stick to' (it might not 'work' or it might have unpleasant side effects in the target/general population). Attrition rates can also give the reader an insight into compliance rates; if withdrawal/dropout rates were unequal between treatment groups, then this may bias the results in favour of one group.
Reporting bias	Were all outcomes stated to be measured actually reported or did the study authors fail to report outcomes that showed no (or a negative) effect? Were some results measured post hoc, that is, was an outcome measured and reported because there seemed to be a beneficial effect or perhaps the data were trawled for an 'effective' outcome?	What reasons were given to explain the failure to report all stated outcomes? The treatment may appear more favourable than it really is if negative results from other outcomes are not reported within the paper.
Confounders	At baseline, were the participant characteristics, such as age, sex or health status, similar across all treatments?	Participants should be equally balanced in terms of variables considered important to study outcomes (e.g. sex, age, health status) – otherwise there is a risk that results will be biased in favour of one group/intervention.
Concurrent/ subsequent intervention	Did any of the participants receive other treatments that could have influenced the study outcomes?	Confidence that the study intervention did/did not have an effect is weakened if participants were not all treated in the same way (except for study intervention).
Analysis	Were the data for all participants included in the final analysis (even those participants who dropped out or withdrew)?	If there are data missing for a number of participants and these are not accounted for, published results will not properly reflect the results of the study.
Funding bias	Who funded the study?	Funders may have a vested interest in demonstrating positive outcomes for one group/intervention.

Assessing bias is a key element of determining study quality, but there are also other important issues that are linked to study quality. For example, possible issues might relate to the outcome measure employed in the study or to the intervention itself. A number of key questions could be considered regarding the outcome measure. Is the outcome measure appropriate for the study? Is it a valid and validated measure? Is it reliable? Does it measure something that is important to the people that matter (e.g. does the study use a **patient-reported outcome measure** [PROM] that was co-developed with patient and public involvement and engagement [PPIE])? When assessing study quality, it is important to consider whether the intervention was standardized across all study participants. A quality assessment tool might question this or ask whether the intervention was properly defined or described, and whether it was delivered as intended. Were those responsible for implementing the intervention appropriately trained? It's also important to consider how data were analysed, and whether statistical methods were appropriate and undertaken correctly (which we discuss in more detail in Chapters 9 and 10). Finally, it might be important to assess how far the study reflects the realities of the practice being evaluated (generalizability). Issues about implementation and generalizability are important points to consider; if you write up your review for submission to a peer-reviewed academic journal (see Chapter 14), policy makers, practitioners and researchers will be interested in how the findings could be used to change policy or practice, or guide further research.

Are any 'off-the-shelf' quality assessment tools available?

Don't worry, there are many quality assessment tools available – you don't have to design your own. There are tools that have been designed solely for the quality assessment of specific types of study (e.g. RCTs, cohort and **cross-sectional studies**) and some of them are discussed later in this chapter. There are also quality assessment tools that are designed for use with more than one study type, which can be useful if your review includes a variety of study types. If you can't find a suitable tool to quality assess your studies, you could consider modifying an existing tool. Bear in mind that formal quality assessment tools have already been through a validation process and any modifications that you make could affect the validity of the tool. If you choose to customize an existing tool, we advise you to make sure that you discuss any modifications and justify them in your review.

Where do I start? What are the key quality assessment steps?

We consider there to be six key steps involved in quality assessment, which are summarized in Box 8.1. We now guide you through each step in detail.

Box 8.1

Key steps involved in quality assessment

Step 1: Note what type(s) of study you have included

Step 2: Identify the type(s) of quality assessment tool(s) to suit your review

Step 3: Choose the appropriate quality assessment tool(s)

Step 4: Carry out quality assessment using the appropriate tool(s)

Step 5: Tabulate and summarize the results of your quality assessment

Step 6: Think about how the results of your quality assessment exercise might impact on the conclusions and recommendations of your systematic review

Step 1: Note what type(s) of study you have included

Quality assessment tools were initially developed for use in systematic reviews in medicine and healthcare; however, they are now used (sometimes with modifications) in systematic reviews across many other disciplines. This means that study type, rather than the review topic area, should guide your choice of quality assessment tool. The first step in quality assessment is to identify the type(s) of studies you have included so that you can choose the most appropriate quality assessment tool(s) to use. Often, study types are labelled inconsistently (see Chapter 9) and so it is important to focus on the study design features rather than what the study is called. The National Institute for Health and Care Excellence (NICE) has published a useful algorithm to help you classify study types and understand the different features of different study types (NICE, 2012).

There are numerous quality assessment tools available for assessing each study type. In an RCT, participants are randomly assigned to intervention groups. In non-randomized studies, participants might be assigned to different groups but not in a random manner, or the study might describe a group (or groups) of people who are either followed up over a period of time or examined at one specific point in time. Table 8.2 provides a guide to the more common study types that you might encounter when conducting your systematic review; also see Chapter 9 if you plan to synthesize data from experimental and correlational studies, because often a range of additional terms are used to describe these studies and their designs. For more information on how to quality assess qualitative and economic evidence, see Chapters 11 and 12 respectively.

TABLE 8.2 Common types of study

Study type	Description	Example
RCT	Participants are randomized to two or more treatment groups using robust methods of randomization. Can include cluster RCTs (the unit of randomization is the cluster – e.g. household, community, clinic) and cross-over designs (where participants are allocated to a sequence of interventions).	The study is designed to compare the effectiveness of a new drug treatment for breast cancer with an existing drug treatment. Participants are randomized to receive their treatment via computer-generated random numbers.
Quasi-experimental trial (also called non-RCTs)	Participants are assigned to two or more treatment groups, but randomization methods are not used in the process or the method of allocation used is not strictly random (these are sometimes called quasi-RCTs).	Participants take part in a study to assess whether cognitive behavioural therapy is more effective than drug therapy to treat anxiety. Each new participant is assigned to a treatment based on the assignment of the previous participant.
Cohort study (prospective or retrospective study) May or may not include a control group	A group of participants is identified and followed over time to assess specific outcomes. There may, or may not, be a concurrent control group.	A study to assess the effects of anti-epileptic drugs on the pregnancy outcomes of women with epilepsy includes a sample of women (via ante-natal clinics) with epilepsy who are taking anti-epileptic medication during pregnancy. A control group might be made up of women from an ante-natal clinic who have epilepsy but who are not taking anti-epileptic medication.
Case–control study	A group of participants with a particular condition are matched for age and other characteristics with a control group of participants who do not have the condition.	A group of children with asthma are compared with a group of children who don't have asthma. The two groups are compared in terms of birth weight to examine the influence of birth weight on the development of the condition.
Case series	People (or a series of individuals) who have been given similar treatments are followed for a specific time period.	First-time mothers with a diagnosis of post-natal depression are followed up for six months after a course of cognitive behavioural therapy.
Cross-sectional	Data are collected from a number of people or other sources (e.g. a database) at one point in time.	The relationship between intelligence and scientific reasoning in children is examined using questionnaires completed at one time point.

Step 2: Identify the type(s) of quality assessment tool(s) to suit your review

Once you have identified your included study type(s), you are ready to identify the appropriate quality assessment tool(s) to suit your review. Does your systematic review include only studies of a single design, or does it include a mix of designs? If you only include one type of study, then you can use a study-specific assessment tool.

If you include a range of types, you need to decide whether to use an assessment tool for each type or an all-inclusive tool that can be used across a range of studies. Quality assessment tools can be scales that give a numerical value of the 'quality' of a study, or they can be checklists that generate an overall picture of quality. We prefer to use a checklist rather than a scoring system as we think that a checklist provides more useful information about the quality of a study; a total quality score for a study does not provide any detail about the individual elements of the quality assessment, and some individual elements of quality assessment may be more 'important' than other elements. However, there are no hard and fast rules, and the choice is yours. To read about the advantages and disadvantages of the most commonly used tools, consult published guidance for undertaking reviews in healthcare (Centre for Reviews and Dissemination, 2010), or the **Cochrane Handbook for Systematic Reviews of Interventions** (Higgins et al., 2022).

We cannot advise here on specific tools – you will need to choose the most appropriate tool for your own review. Remember, you will need to make it clear in your protocol and thesis why you have selected the tool that you have used. When making your decision, you might want to consider several factors:

- Has the tool been used in similar reviews in your topic area?
- A tool is often (but not always) designed and then piloted by a number of different people to test whether it measures what it is designed to measure. Has the tool been validated?
- How lengthy is the tool and how many studies do you have to quality assess? Some tools contain a considerable number of items. Are all of the items relevant to your studies? If you have included a large number of studies in your review, will you have time to use the tool on all of them?
- It can be difficult to present and succinctly discuss findings if you are using tools with a long list of items, or ones that contain items requiring detailed textual responses. Is the design of the tool such that all the results are easily tabulated and simple to summarize? Will the tabulated results convey your findings efficiently?

Step 3: Choose the appropriate quality assessment tool(s)

Take a look at other systematic reviews in the same topic area as your review to see which quality assessment tools the authors of these reviews have used. Having found some useful examples, you might then ask your supervisor(s) if they can help you to determine which tool(s) would be appropriate to use in your review.

In Table 8.3 we list several web-accessible sources of quality assessment tools. This list is not exhaustive, but it is enough to help you get started.

TABLE 8.3   Selected sources of quality assessment tools

Source	Contents	Our thoughts
Health Technology Assessment (HTA) report (Deeks et al., 2003).	A systematic review of quality assessment tools for non-randomized intervention studies. Six tools were considered suitable for use in systematic reviews of non-randomized intervention studies.	These six tools were considered suitable for use in systematic reviews of non-randomized intervention studies by the authors of the HTA report.
	Cowley (1995) – comparative and uncontrolled **case series**. 13-item checklist.	The authors of the review did not consider any specific tool to be 'perfect'.
	Downs and Black (1998) – randomized and non-randomized studies. 27-item checklist.	
	Newcastle–Ottawa Scale (Wells et al., 2012) – cohort and case–control studies. 8-item checklist.	
	Reisch et al. (1989) – any study type. 34-'key' item checklist.	
	Thomas et al. (2004) – any study type. 21-item checklist.	
	Zaza et al. (2000) – any study type. 22-item checklist.	
Critical Appraisal Skills Programme (CASP, 2018).	Critical appraisal checklists for RCTs, systematic reviews, cohort studies, case–control studies.	These checklists were designed to help clinicians assess evidence and so some items may not be relevant to your systematic review.
The Cochrane Handbook for Systematic Reviews of Interventions (Higgins et al., 2022).	The 'risk of bias' (ROB2) tool used for RCTs in Cochrane reviews.	Detailed approach to quality assessment; time-consuming to use but very informative if applied conscientiously.
	The Risk of Bias in Non-randomized Studies of Interventions (ROBINS-I) tool for use with non-randomized intervention studies (Sterne et al., 2016).	
	The Risk of Bias in Systematic Reviews (ROBIS) tool for use with systematic reviews.	
Centre for Reviews and Dissemination (CRD) guidance (2010).	Guidance for conducting systematic reviews in healthcare.	Contains guides to criteria important in the assessment of studies. We use a slightly modified version of this guidance in many of our reviews.
The JBI (Aromataris & Munn, 2020, https://jbi.global/critical-appraisal-tools).	Guidance for conducting systematic reviews in healthcare.	Contains a set of critical appraisal tools applicable to a range of study types.

Source	Contents	Our thoughts
Social Care Institute for Excellence (SCIE, 2010).	Guidelines for conducting systematic reviews in social care.	Offers guidelines on the minimum generic criteria for assessing quality of primary research.
U.S. Department of Health & Human Services, National Heart, Lung and Blood Institute (NHLBI, 2021).	Study quality assessment tools.	Offers a suite of tools for use with a range of study types.
LATITUDES network www.latitudes-network.org	A searchable library of quality assessment tools. Also includes links to training guides.	As of September 2023, this resource is still undergoing development. However, we think that it has the potential to become a useful 'one-stop shop' for quality assessment tools.

Quality assessment of randomized controlled trials

The RCT is considered to be at the top of the evidence hierarchy in terms of study quality. Table 8.4 shows a tool that can be used to quality assess RCTs. We have based this tool on the quality assessment criteria for RCTs recommended by the Centre for Reviews and Dissemination (CRD, 2010) but have modified it slightly. Note that the list includes questions relating to the quality criteria previously described in Table 8.1. When using this tool you should complete the checklist for each included study. The responses are limited to *Yes*, *No*, *Partially*, *Not stated* and *Not applicable*. You can add further columns to the right-hand side to allow space for all studies included in your review. At the end of the exercise, you will be able to visually compare the studies by each item or component of the assessment.

However, as we noted earlier (and will become apparent later in this chapter), RCTs can be poorly executed and open to the influence of bias. Many areas of research do not lend themselves well to being examined using RCT methodology due to the nature of the research question and/or the intervention of interest. In addition, ethical and/or financial reasons can make it problematic or inappropriate to carry out an RCT.

TABLE 8.4 Example tool for quality assessment of RCTs

Reviewer name:

Author name/Study ID:

Quality item

Randomization (check for allocation bias)

Was the method used to assign participants to the treatment groups truly random?

Was the allocation of treatment concealed?

*Was the number of participants randomized stated?

(Continued)

TABLE 8.4 (Continued)

Comparability (check for confounding)

*Were details of baseline comparability presented?

Was baseline comparability achieved?

Eligibility (check for selection bias)

*Were eligibility criteria for study entry specified?

*Were there any co-interventions that may influence outcomes for each group?

Blinding (check for detection bias)

Were outcome assessors blinded to treatment allocation?

Were the individuals who administered the intervention blinded to treatment allocation?

Were participants blinded to treatment allocation?

*Was the success of the blinding procedures assessed?

Withdrawals (check for attrition bias)

*Were ≥ 80% of participants randomized included in the final analysis?

*Were reasons for participant withdrawals stated?

Were there any unexpected dropouts in either group?

Was an intention-to-treat analysis included?

Outcomes (check for outcome reporting bias)

Is there evidence that more outcomes were measured than were reported?

---

* Indicates where modifications were made to the original CRD (2010) checklist

If your review includes cluster RCTs or cross-over RCTs, it might be important to use a quality assessment tool that directly assesses these specific elements of the study design. For example, there is a Cochrane Risk of Bias tool for cluster RCTs which allows researchers to assess how and when participants are recruited to clusters and whether the study has accounted for the cluster in the analysis of outcomes (Higgins et al., 2022).

Quality assessment of non-randomized studies

As noted earlier, many elements of quality assessment are common to all types of study. Studies other than RCTs are also open to specific types of bias, and so the measure of quality assessment for your review needs to include items to account for these additional specific concerns. Concerns may include, but are not limited to, questions about:

- Relevance of the research design to the research question
- Representativeness of the study participants to the research question
- How participants were recruited
- Whether any comparison groups were utilized
- How many people started the study and how many remained at the end
- Whether the measurement tools used in the study were valid, reliable and relevant
- Appropriateness (or otherwise) of statistical analyses (see Chapter 9)

In this section we present the Newcastle–Ottawa Scale (NOS) for assessing cohort studies (Box 8.2) (Wells et al., 2012). There are also tailored versions of the NOS for **case–control studies**, intervention studies and **cross-sectional studies**. We also really like the tool that Williams and colleagues (2010) developed for assessing the quality of observational studies because it can be adapted to suit specific review questions and takes into account appropriateness of statistical analyses.

Box 8.2

Newcastle–Ottawa Quality Assessment Scale: Cohort studies

Note: The tool uses a 'star system' by which a study is judged on three broad perspectives: the selection of the study groups; the comparability of the groups; and the ascertainment of either the exposure or outcome of interest for case–control or cohort studies, respectively. Stars are pre-awarded in the NOS and are used to indicate quality elements. A study can be awarded a maximum of one star for each numbered item within the Selection and Outcome categories. A maximum of two stars can be given for Comparability. The handbook for interpretation of the NOS is available at www.ohri.ca/programs/clinical_epidemiology/oxford.asp

Selection

1) Representativeness of the exposed cohort

    a) truly representative of the average _____ (describe) in the community*

    b) somewhat representative of the average _____ in the community*

    c) selected group of users, for example, nurses, volunteers

    d) no description of the derivation of the cohort

2) Selection of the non-exposed cohort

    a) drawn from the same community as the exposed cohort*

    b) drawn from a different source

    c) no description of the derivation of the non-exposed cohort

3) Ascertainment of exposure

    a) secure record (e.g. surgical records)*

    b) structured interview*

    c) written self-report

    d) no description

(Continued)

4) Demonstration that outcome of interest was not present at start of study

    a) yes*

    b) no

Comparability

1) Comparability of cohorts on the basis of the design or analysis

    a) study controls for _____ (select the most important factor)*

    b) study controls for any additional factor* (this criterion could be modified to indicate specific control for a second important factor)

Outcome

1) Assessment of outcome

    a) independent **blind assessment***

    b) record linkage*

    c) self-report

    d) no description

2) Was follow-up long enough for outcomes to occur?

    a) yes (select an adequate follow-up period for outcome of interest)*

    b) no

3) Adequacy of follow-up of cohorts

    a) complete follow-up – all subjects accounted for*

    b) subjects lost to follow-up unlikely to introduce bias – small number lost – > ____ % (select an adequate %) follow-up, or description provided of those lost)*

    c) follow-up rate < ____% (select an adequate %) and no description of those lost

    d) no statement

Reproduced with permission from Professor George A. Wells, University of Ottawa Heart Institute

Sometimes quality assessment tools need to be modified to suit the specific purpose of a review. For example, in a systematic review of the equity impact of interventions and policies to reduce smoking (Brown et al., 2014), a criterion of 'generalizability' was added to a validated checklist (Thomas et al., 2004) because, for the purpose of the review, it was important to assess whether study findings were likely to be transferable at a regional or national level. Depending on your review topic or question, you may feel it necessary to include an additional criterion to an existing quality assessment tool to suit your needs (e.g. if an existing tool does not consider the appropriateness of statistical analyses). This approach is OK, but we would strongly advise you to reflect on all additions (and their implications) in the 'Discussion' section of your review.

Step 4: Carry out quality assessment using the appropriate tool(s)

Once you have chosen an appropriate quality assessment tool, it is time to pilot the tool. Piloting in this context just means testing the tool to see if it works by taking one or two studies and seeing whether you can answer the quality assessment questions. If you are working with someone else (e.g. a fellow student or supervisor), you can both be involved in piloting the tool. You must use the quality assessment tool in a consistent way: that is, treat all the studies the same way when assessing quality. When you are confident that you are both using the tool consistently, and in the same way, then you should both (independently) answer the quality assessment questions for each of the studies. Alternatively, one of you can cross-check the quality assessment responses of the other reviewer. We recommend that you keep careful notes about your decisions, and consistently mark up the text of the papers where you found information – marking can be carried out on paper or electronically (see Chapter 2). After completing the quality assessment exercise, you need to compare your responses and discuss any discordant opinions. If any issues remain unresolved (despite several cups of coffee!), try to find a third person to resolve the outstanding issues.

As with screening and selection (Chapter 6), and data extraction (Chapter 7), working with a partner on this task is essential if you are planning to publish your review (see Chapter 14). However, should you find yourself working on your own, it might be useful to compare your quality assessment results with any published critiques of your included studies that are available in the public domain. However, be sure to do this *after* completing the results of your quality assessment exercise to make sure you aren't introducing bias into your results. Do also be sure to note in your 'Discussion' section why and how the absence of a second reviewer to quality assess your included studies could be viewed as a limitation of your systematic review. Chapter 13 provides more guidance on this topic.

Step 5: Tabulate and summarize the results of your quality assessment

Now is the time to summarize your quality assessment findings by tabulating the results and describing them in your text. The quality assessment section is typically presented within the 'Results' section of a review, immediately after the text describing the results of your searching, screening and selection, and immediately before data tables that describe study characteristics and participant characteristics.

In Table 8.5 we present an example of a quality assessment table that appears in our systematic review of first-line chemotherapy treatments for non-small cell lung cancer (Brown et al., 2013). The review included 23 RCTs but here, for brevity, we only show the results for the first 15 studies. We order the studies in the table alphabetically by first author, but you can order them in other ways – for example, by publication date. No matter how you plan to order your studies in your tables, remember to use this order consistently in all of the tables throughout your review.

The information in Table 8.5 shows that the studies differ in terms of their quality. Even though these studies are all RCTs published in peer-reviewed academic journals, nine of the 15 studies failed to report important information describing the details of the methods used to randomize participants to treatment arms. In addition, in ten of the studies, the authors did not state whether the participants in each treatment arm were balanced in terms of their personal characteristics (e.g. similar numbers of males and females in each arm, participants of a similar age). In the overall summary of the quality of the 23 studies included in our review, we concluded that:

> Overall methodological quality of included studies was poor. Only six of the 23 included studies reported sufficient information for them to be assessed as adequately randomized and with adequate concealment of allocation. All studies clearly reported the number of participants randomized. All studies reported inclusion criteria and, except for four studies, all reported details about co-interventions, for example palliative radiotherapy and/or second-line chemotherapy. Six studies were reported as 'open'. Blinding of participants, investigators or outcome assessors was considered to be not stated in 16 out of the 23 included studies. The outcomes of over 80 per cent of patients were assessed in all studies and all studies reported reasons for dropout; 10 trials used an intention to treat approach to assess overall survival. Five of the studies appeared to report fewer outcomes than initially stated. (Brown et al., 2013, p. 25)

Step 6: Think about how the results of your quality assessment exercise might impact on the conclusions and recommendations of your systematic review

Now that you have tabulated and summarized the results of the quality assessment exercise, you should have a good overview of your included studies. You should now be starting to think about how the methodological quality of your studies might

TABLE 8.5 Example of quality assessment table of RCTs

Trial	Randomization – Truly random	Randomization – Allocation concealment	Randomization – Number stated	Baseline comparability – Presented	Baseline comparability – Achieved	Inclusion criteria specified	Co-interventions identified	Blinding – Assessors	Blinding – Administration	Blinding – Participants	Blinding – Procedure assessed	Withdrawals – <80% in final analysis	Withdrawals – Reasons stated	Intention to treat	Other outcomes
Chen (2004)	NS	NS	✓	✓	✓	✓	✓	NS	NS	NS	NS	✓	✓	✓	✗
Chen (2007)	NS	✓	✓	✓	✓	✓	✓	NS	NS	NS	NS	✓	✓	✓	✗
Douillard (2005)	NS	NS	✓	✓✗	NS	✓	✓	NS	NS	NS	NS	✓	✓	✓	✓
Fossella (2003)	NS	✓	✓	✓	✓	✓	✓	✗	✗	✗	NA	✓	✓	✓	✗
Gebbia (2003)	NS	✓	✓	✓	NS	✓	✓	NS	NS	NS	NS	✓	✓	✓	✗
Gridelli (2003)	✓	✓	✓	✓	NS	✓	✓	NS	NS	NS	NS	✓	✓	✗	✗
Helbekkmo (2007)	✓	✓	✓	✓	✓	✓	✓	NS	NS	NS	NS	✓	✓	✓	✓
Kelly (2001)	NS	NS	✓	✓✗	NS	✓	NS	NS	NS	NS	NS	✓	✓	✓	✗
Langer (2007)	✓	NS	✓	✓	NS	✓	NS	NS	NS	NS	NS	✓	✓	✗	✗
Martoni (2005)	NS	NS	✓	✓	NS	✓	✓	NS	NS	NS	NS	✓	✓	✗	✗
Ohe (2007)	✓	✓	✓	✓	NS	✓	✓	NS	NS	NS	NS	✓	✓	✗	✗
Scagliotti (2002)	✓	✓	✓	✓	NS	✓	✓	NS	NS	NS	NS	✓	✓	✓	✗
Schiller (2002)	NS	NS	✓	✓✗	NS	✓	✓✗	NS	NS	NS	NS	✓	✓	✗	✗
Smit (2003)	✓	NS	✓	✓	NS	✓	✓	NS	NS	NS	NS	✓	✓	✗	✗
Thomas (2006)	NS	NS	✓	✓	✓✗	✓	NS	✗	✗	✗	NA	✓	✓	✗	✗

✓ Yes (item adequately addressed); ✗ no (item not adequately addressed); ✓✗ partially (item partially addressed); NS not stated; NA not applicable impact on the credibility of the overall results of your systematic review. Irrespective of which tool you use to assess your studies, you need to summarize the findings in your thesis. You could use previous reviews in the topic area to guide you when you come to write up your quality assessment exercise. To help you, look for any guidance notes that accompany the quality assessment tool that you have used. Think about what you, as a reader, might want to know about the results of the quality assessment. Does the summary of your quality assessment exercise allow readers to reach an informed conclusion about the quality of the studies included in your review? Remember, you should only present the results of your quality assessment exercise in the 'Results' section; save discussion of these findings for the 'Discussion' section of your thesis (Chapter 13).

Quality assessing your own systematic review

There are specific quality assessment tools that you can use to quality assess your own systematic review. It may be useful to apply one of these tools to your work as a final check of your review. Your supervisor(s) and/or examiner(s) might also use a tool for this purpose. Table 8.6 shows the second edition of **Assessing the Methodological Quality of Systematic Reviews (AMSTAR 2)** quality assessment tool, which is designed for use with systematic reviews (Shea et al., 2017). The AMSTAR 2 checklist and guidance notes are available at https://amstar.ca/Amstar-2.php. The online version of AMSTAR 2 will even allow you to generate a quality rating for your systematic review.

There are also tools which you can use to assess the quality of the reporting of your systematic review. These include the:

- PRISMA (Preferred Reporting of Items for Systematic Reviews and Meta-Analyses) checklist (http://prisma-statement.org/PRISMAStatement/Checklist)
- **Meta-Analysis of Observational Studies in Epidemiology (MOOSE)** guidelines (Stroup et al., 2000)

There may be reporting guidelines specific to your review methodology. For example, there are guidelines for reporting meta-epidemiological methodology research (Murad & Wang, 2017) and there is a checklist for reviews of life cycle assessment data (Zumsteg et al., 2012).

Although the process of quality assessing your own systematic review can be time-consuming, it will be time well spent. It will help you to identify any areas of weakness in the conduct or reporting of your systematic review prior to submitting your thesis. It may also be beneficial if you are planning to later publish your systematic review in a peer-reviewed academic journal (see Chapter 14) as most peer-reviewed academic journals will require your manuscript to adhere to the principles set out in the PRISMA statement (or similar).

TABLE 8.6   The AMSTAR 2 tool for the quality assessment of systematic reviews

---

Reviewer name:

Author name/Study ID:

Response: Yes/No. (Some items may have additional options)

1. Did the research questions and inclusion criteria for the review include the components of PICO (Participants, Intervention, Comparator, Outcome)?
2. Did the report of the review contain an explicit statement that the review methods were established prior to the conduct of the review and did the report justify any significant deviations from the protocol?
3. Did the review authors explain their selection of the study designs for inclusion in the review?
4. Did the review authors use a comprehensive literature search strategy?
5. Did the review authors perform study selection in duplicate?
6. Did the review authors perform data extraction in duplicate?
7. Did the review authors provide a list of excluded studies and justify the exclusions?
8. Did the review authors describe the included studies in adequate detail?
9. Did the review authors use a satisfactory technique for assessing the Risk of Bias (RoB) in individual studies that were included in the review?
10. Did the review authors report on the sources of funding for the studies included in the review?
11. If meta-analysis was performed, did the review authors use appropriate methods for statistical combination of results?
12. If meta-analysis was performed, did the review authors assess the potential impact of RoB in individual studies on the results of the meta-analysis or other evidence synthesis?
13. Did the review authors account for RoB in individual studies when interpreting/discussing the results of the review?
14. Did the review authors provide a satisfactory explanation for, and discussion of, any heterogeneity observed in the results of the review?
15. If they performed quantitative synthesis, did the review authors carry out an adequate investigation of publication bias (small study bias) and discuss its likely impact on the results of the review?
16. Did the review authors report any potential sources of conflict of interest, including any funding they received for conducting the review?

Final thoughts

We have summarized the key points from this chapter in Box 8.3 and encourage you to think more broadly about quality assessment in context in Box 8.4. We think that you should save discussion of your results for the 'Discussion' section of your thesis (see Chapter 13). However, we considered it appropriate to finish this chapter with a few questions that may be helpful to reflect upon when writing your 'Methods' and 'Results' section and formulating your discussion:

- Were you surprised by the results of the quality assessment exercise? Did you find any elements of the exercise noteworthy?
- Did any of the results from individual studies appear to differ from the others? Were there any specific quality issues associated with these studies?
- How should the study results be synthesized? Is it reasonable to lump similar study interventions together if quality differs markedly between studies? If most studies included in your systematic review are assessed as being of poor quality,

you need to consider whether to carry out a meta-analysis. If you are planning to meta-analyse study results, should a sensitivity analysis of study results based on quality also be undertaken (see Chapter 10)? For example, excluding poor quality studies may change outliers and effect size and/or confidence intervals around the effect size.

- Did you find any patterns across studies? Can you offer recommendations for future research? For example, did most of your included studies fail to describe how participants were selected? A recommendation for future research could then include a statement that any future studies relevant to the topic of your review must improve the reporting of participant selection as this would enable reviewers to assess the generalizability of the study results to the target population.

For other ideas on how to integrate and discuss your quality assessment findings in your review, look at other reviews in your topic area and read Chapter 13.

Box 8.3

'Top tips' for quality assessment

- Quality assessment can be a time-consuming process and should not be left until the last minute.
- Carefully document where in the study you found information relating to each quality assessment question. This can save time later on and prevent you from having to rely on memory if you have to go back and check your reasoning.
- Use footnotes beneath the quality assessment table to clarify your responses where necessary. For example, if the participant characteristics were partially comparable between the groups, you might want to say in a footnote that this was because there were more males in one group than in another. As well as guiding the reader, this will help you when writing up the results.
- Make notes of anything that stands out as 'interesting' or 'quirky' when you quality assess a study, as this can help jog your memory of the study characteristics and help you to make sense of the study results.
- Quality assessing a paper appears to be a straightforward matter of answering a list of questions. However, the task is rarely so black and white. Whatever tool you use, some degree of judgement will be required to enable you to answer some of the questions. This is why it is useful to have a second reviewer to quality assess your studies.
- Reviewer experience, in terms of the topic being studied and familiarity with study type, can influence an individual's ability to quality assess studies. Ideally each included study should be quality assessed by two reviewers independently.

- Keep records of how you came to make your decisions, especially when you were unable to give a clear 'yes' or 'no' response to a question.
- Sometimes it may not be clear to you what a quality assessment question is really asking, even when there is a guide to help you use the tool. If this is the case, discuss your concerns with your peers or supervisor(s).

Box 8.4

Quality assessment in context

When thinking about how the results of your quality assessment exercise may shape your discussion and conclusions, it's important to think about your studies in context. For example, it's not sufficient to say that collectively the studies included participants similar to the wider target population – you must also reflect on whose voices are missing from your included studies. Often, research findings reflect the views of a comparatively advantaged majority – is this the case for your studies? What impact might this have on the results of your review, or the conclusions that can be drawn from the currently available evidence? Did findings differ between studies that used PROMs to assess outcomes and those that used clinician-reported outcome measures, for instance? What does that tell you about how services can and should integrate PROMs into routine clinical practice? What are the characteristics of the people who dropped out or discontinued a study? Are they in any way similar in terms of gender identity, ethnicity, socio-economic background, and so on? Can we learn anything about the intervention from the people who were unable to complete the study? We discuss these considerations further in Chapter 13, but we strongly encourage you to think about what is *not* reported in your included studies, and to critically reflect on equality, diversity, inclusion and PPIE in each of your included studies, together with the potential combined influence on the findings of your review. The **Grading of Recommendations, Assessment, Development and Evaluations (GRADE)** working group have developed a framework for appraising and summarizing clinical evidence to inform clinical practice recommendations (Schünemann et al., 2022). Used by the NIHR and Cochrane, one of the five elements (domains) of the framework is risk of bias. The GRADE framework may therefore be a helpful tool to use when thinking about how representative the populations included in individual studies are, and wider equality, diversity and inclusion (EDI) considerations.

Key points to think about when writing your protocol

- Types of studies (e.g. randomized or non-randomized) that you intend to include in your review
- Quality assessment strategy (e.g. what tool will you use, when will you use it and will anyone help you?)
- Length of time you plan to spend on the quality assessment exercise

---

What an examiner is looking for in your thesis

- Appropriate use of quality assessment tool(s) and consideration of their associated strengths and weaknesses
- Summary and tabulation of the results of your quality assessment exercise
- Detailed reporting of your quality assessment findings
- Clear discussion of how the quality assessment results might link to the review conclusions

---

Frequently Asked Questions

Question 1: What should I do if I can't find the right quality assessment tool for my review?

Sometimes formal tools need modifying to suit the purpose of a specific review. Rather than develop a completely new tool, it is probably easier to find validated tool(s) that best match the studies in your review and modify or add items to those tool(s). Please note that any changes may limit the validity of the tool, and the pros and cons of adapting the tool to a specific review should be discussed in your write-up.

Question 2: How long does quality assessment take?

Key steps include reading the publication(s), reading through the appropriate quality assessment tool, completing the tool, writing up the results in the review and synthesizing your results with quantitative and/or qualitative data. Usually, it will take *at least* 45 minutes to complete a quality assessment tool for one study publication. Quality assessment is not a quick task. You need to allow sufficient time to carry it out properly.

Question 3: How do I quality assess a study that is reported in more than one paper?

If a study is reported in more than one paper, then you should treat the paper with the key study data as the 'core' paper, using the other papers as supplements. The 'core' paper would be used in the quality assessment exercise. It is advisable for you to read all the papers relating to the study, especially if you are unclear about any of the study methods. If, for example, you can only answer a question about study quality using data presented in a supplement, then you will need to add a footnote to your quality assessment table to explain the source of this information. If, for reasons of time (or finances), you cannot obtain all the papers, you should acknowledge this as a limitation of your review.

Question 4: How do I (and should I) assess the quality of a study that is only reported in an abstract?

If you have included abstracts in your review (e.g. from a conference, or from a non-English-language paper with an English abstract), they should be quality assessed as far as possible. It should be made clear in the quality assessment table (using a footnote), and in the summary text, that the study data were only available from an abstract. If there is missing or unclear information, the reader will then be aware that the study information was limited rather than assume that it came from a poor-quality study.

Question 5: My systematic review is on a non-health topic. Can I still use this chapter as a guide?

Yes. The components of quality assessment are essentially similar across health and non-health topics. Have a look at other systematic reviews in the same topic area as your review and discuss potentially suitable quality assessment tools with your supervisor(s).

Question 6: Is identification of study type part of quality assessment?

As we note in Chapter 3 of this book, when setting inclusion criteria for a systematic review, researchers often include or exclude studies based on specific study types or designs. For example, often systematic reviews of the clinical effectiveness of healthcare interventions stipulate that only evidence from RCTs may be considered for inclusion. However, limiting inclusion criteria to specific study types or designs is not part of quality assessment. Quality assessment goes beyond this; it allows you to evaluate the validity, **reliability** and generalizability of the results of each included study.

Question 7: What should I do if I identify relevant systematic reviews in my topic area – should I quality assess them?

The short answer is that it depends on the focus of your review. If you are conducting an umbrella review (see Chapter 1) then you would only include systematic reviews in your systematic review, so of course you would include these in your review and quality assess them accordingly. If you plan only to critically appraise and synthesize empirical data but your searches have identified published systematic reviews in your topic area, you may want to use them as a reference tool. First, their reference lists make it easy for you to check that you haven't missed any potentially relevant studies. Second, reading the background and conclusion sections means that you can very quickly identify any important potential issues that you might also wish to consider in your review. In our systematic review of clopidogrel and modified-release dipyridamole for the prevention of occlusive vascular events (Greenhalgh et al., 2011), we found several existing systematic reviews; however, none addressed the specific question of interest in our review. In this case, we used the existing reviews to check for potentially relevant papers and summarized the quality of each systematic review in the appendix to our report, to demonstrate that we were aware of their existence.

Question 8: I have included RCTs, cohort studies and non-randomized intervention studies in my review. Should I use a generic quality assessment tool for all studies, or should I choose three different tools?

We think that the best option is to use three specific tools. You can then be sure that you are appraising elements that are specific and important to each of the study types and designs of interest. The purpose of quality assessment is to appraise the strength of the evidence you have presented. One of those strengths is inherent in the type and design of the study. It is not wrong to use a generic tool; however, you should be aware that using a generic tool might mask key strengths and limitations associated with studies.

Question 9: Is assessment of risk of bias the same as quality assessment?

Not quite. Although these terms are often used interchangeably, they have distinct meanings. Cochrane suggests that quality assessment refers to the extent to which researchers take steps to avoid systematic errors in the design, conduct, analysis and reporting of study. By contrast, risk of bias relates to the extent to which study findings are affected by flaws in the design, conduct and analysis of a study (Banzi et al., 2018).

Further Reading and Resources

Centre for Reviews and Dissemination. (2010). *Systematic reviews: CRD's guidance for undertaking reviews in health care.* www.york.ac.uk/inst/crd/SysRev/!SSL!/WebHelp/SysRev3.htm

Deeks, J.J., Dinnes, J., D'amico, R., Sowden, A.J., Sakarovitch, C., Song, F., Petticrew, M., Altman, D.G., & International Stroke Trial Intervention Group and European Carotid Surgery Trial Collaborative Group. (2003). Evaluating non-randomised intervention studies. *Health Technology Assessment, 7*(27), 1–173.

Greenhalgh, T. (2019). *How to read a paper: The basics of evidence-based medicine* (6th ed.). Wiley-Blackwell/BMJ Books.

Schünemann, H.J., Higgins, J.P.T., Vist, G.E., Glasziou, P., Akl, E.A., Skoetz, N., & Guyatt, G.H. (2022). Chapter 14: Completing 'Summary of findings' tables and grading the certainty of the evidence. In Higgins, J.P.T., Thomas, J., Chandler, J., Cumpston, M., Li, T., Page, M.J., & Welch, V.A. (Eds) (2022). *Cochrane handbook for systematic reviews of interventions* (version 6.3, updated February 2022). https://training.cochrane.org/handbook/current

9

Understanding and Critically Appraising Data from Experimental and Correlational Studies

Paul Christiansen and Andrew Jones

This chapter will help you to...

- Understand the different designs that you might come across in experimental and **correlational studies**

- Recognise the different analysis techniques commonly reported in experimental and correlational studies, and their strengths and limitations

- Interpret statistical outputs from *t*-tests, **analysis of variance (ANOVA)**, **correlation** analyses and **regression** models, and extract relevant effect sizes

- Identify the limitations of experimental and correlational study designs and associated statistical analyses

Introduction

This chapter is an addition to the previous edition of this book and may be particularly useful if your field of study is psychology or social sciences (although the content also broadly applies to other fields). It was borne out of the recognition that many students conduct systematic reviews of experimental and correlational studies that look at relationships or differences among or within groups of people, rather than studies that evaluate the effectiveness of interventions using randomized controlled designs. Therefore, this chapter is designed to help you to understand and critically appraise data from a range of experimental and correlational study designs but only briefly touches upon statistical *synthesis* of data (e.g. through meta-analysis). If you plan to meta-analyse data from experimental and/or correlational studies, also read Chapter 10 (which is designed to help you to understand and synthesize data from more 'typical' experimental intervention studies such as randomized controlled trials [RCTs] but whose principles also broadly apply to the meta-analysis of data from other types of study). Don't forget to also check out the recommended reading at the end of this chapter.

We found this chapter difficult to write because there are many different types of experimental and correlational studies, study designs and methods of analysis. To complicate matters further, researchers often use terms interchangeably (e.g. 'study type' and 'study design'; **'between-subjects design'** and **'independent groups design'**, and so on). Throughout this chapter, we include alternative methodological terms, but inevitably we can't include every term you may come across in the literature. Treat this chapter as an introduction to understanding and working with data from experimental and correlational studies, and, where appropriate, consult a statistician or do some further reading (including of the Glossary) if you feel unsure of anything.

In this chapter, we first discuss 'true' experimental and **'quasi-experimental'** studies to demonstrate how multifactorial **experimental study designs** can differ. We then illustrate how to identify and extract data that are relevant to your review question and outline the key limitations common to such study designs (e.g. arbitrary **dichotomization** of data). We then introduce correlational studies by describing their common methods and analyses, including **linear, logistic, multinomial** and **Poisson regression, mediation** and **moderation** and **structural equation modelling** (SEM). We hope that this gives you the confidence and knowledge that you need to extract, understand and critically appraise data from experimental and correlational studies, no matter what the design. A word of caution, though – this chapter is technical and covers a range of statistical methods, equations and assumptions. We don't expect you to routinely re-analyse data from included studies using any of these methods (although this information may come in handy if you go on to conduct any empirical experimental or correlational research yourself); the authors of the published studies should have already done this for you. We provide details about each method purely to help you to understand the data that you may come across in your included studies.

Experimental study designs

The first part of this chapter focuses on studies that use experimental designs, that is, studies that compare outcomes within or between two or more groups and/or conditions. Whilst this background may not immediately seem relevant to systematic reviews, it is important for you to understand the ways that groups and/or conditions can be formed before you start to critically appraise these study designs, the statistics used to analyse the resulting data and the conclusions which you can draw from them.

Box 9.1 outlines the two ways that conditions can be formed – **within-subjects** and between-subjects – and Figure 9.1 depicts the overlap between different experimental study designs.

Box 9.1

Ways of forming conditions

Within-subjects designs (also called repeated measures designs)

The term 'within-subjects design' (also called a **repeated measures design**) describes a study in which the same outcome (**dependent variable: DV**) is measured multiple times in the same individual(s). In intervention studies, the independent variable (IV) is usually time – for example, someone's level of anxiety (DV) before and after an intervention (i.e. Time 1 versus Time 2). However, a within-subjects design does not always use time as the IV. Imagine that researchers want to examine anxiety in individuals with arachnophobia. They could show individuals spiders and ask them to rate their anxiety, and then show the same individuals snakes and ask them to rate their anxiety. In this case, the outcome of interest (DV) is anxiety ratings, and the IV is the creature shown (spiders vs snakes).

There are pros and cons to using within-subjects designs, and they are important to keep in mind when evaluating any study as part of a systematic review. The results of studies that have within-subjects designs may be influenced by **practice effects** as individuals are assessed in the same way (DV) on multiple occasions. If the same memory test is administered multiple times to the same

(Continued)

individual, improvements in scores over time would be expected. Also, if a study takes multiple measures of a DV, **fatigue effects** are commonly observed (this may be particularly evident if the DV is measured using complex and/or taxing questionnaires or criteria). Well-designed studies have protocols in place to attenuate these effects – for example, washout periods (long periods of time between assessments) and/or counterbalancing of measurements so that not all individuals provide the measurements in the same order. When carrying out quality assessment as part of your review, these issues should be considered.

Between-subjects designs (also called independent groups designs)

You might see the terms 'between-subjects' or 'independent groups' designs used interchangeably. These terms refer to studies in which individuals who self-select to be in one group/level vs another (e.g. Everton or Liverpool Football Club fans) are compared. Alternatively, groups/levels might be experimenter generated (e.g. one group is shown pictures of food and the other is shown pictures of stationery). Importantly, each individual provides only *one* measure of the DV. Whilst the results of studies that use between-subjects designs are therefore less likely to be influenced by practice or fatigue effects than those that use within-subjects designs, they are generally less sensitive and data from more participants are required to detect effects due to increased error variance resulting from individual differences (DV). Remember this when quality assessing your included studies (particularly if the authors do not report a sample size calculation).

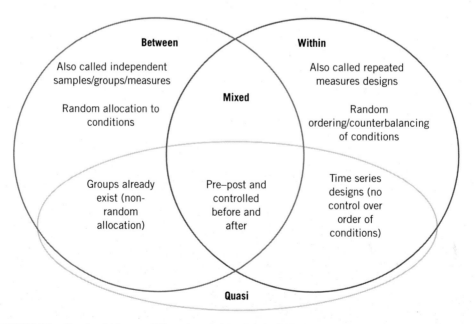

FIGURE 9.1   Overlap between different experimental designs

True experimental designs

A **true experiment** is an intervention study that involves more than one group, where groups are purposely created and participants are randomly assigned to those groups. Unlike in quasi-experimental designs (discussed below), groups are usually created for the purpose of the study (e.g. a treatment/exposure and control group) rather than being pre-existing (e.g. smoker vs non-smoker). There is debate around the difference between true experiments and RCTs, particularly within psychology (Donnon, 2012; Wiers et al., 2018). For example, many psychology or social sciences researchers randomize participants to purposely created groups but do not use the phrase 'RCT', and this can lead to confusion when searching for or synthesizing evidence. However, given their similarity with RCTs, true experiments can be useful for exploring causal relationships. If you plan to conduct a systematic review of true experiments and/or RCTs, we recommend that you read Chapter 10 so that you know how to interpret data from these types of study.

Quasi-experimental designs

A quasi-experimental design estimates the effect of a treatment or phenomenon (sometimes termed 'exposure') on an outcome. Whilst sharing many features with RCTs, the nature of these studies means that *individuals are not randomly allocated to groups*. For example, researchers may have limited control over the delivery of an intervention, or who receives it, but may still wish to test its effects. Alternatively, randomization may not always be feasible or ethical; for example, we cannot randomize individuals to be alcohol dependent, nor can we randomize individuals to live in specific parts of the country, or to have different socio-economic backgrounds. A study with a quasi-experimental design can also have a correlational design as there is no direct manipulation of the IV; instead, associations between variables are examined. Although this type of study allows you to establish whether an association exists, it does *not* allow you to establish whether the association is causal. Chapter 10 is useful if you plan to synthesize data from quasi-experimental studies.

Pre–post designs (also called uncontrolled before-and-after studies)

A **pre–post design** (also called an **uncontrolled before-and-after study**) uses a within-subjects design and is one of the most common forms of quasi-experimental design, in which behaviour, attitudes or knowledge are examined before and after some kind of change (e.g. in policy or practice). This design is superior to a study with a simple correlational design. However, it has two key limitations, mainly due to a lack of an **active control group** (Boot et al., 2013). First, it is impossible to account for natural trends, or sudden unplanned changes in outcome(s) that are not associated with the policy change under investigation. Second, if there is **regression to the mean** (which occurs when any sample measure is extreme and a subsequent measure is more moderate – i.e. closer to a true average), this may cause problems for data interpretation.

To illustrate, researchers might be interested in what happens to alcohol consumption after a policy to increase the price-per-unit of alcohol is implemented on a small island. Researchers might find a massive reduction in alcohol consumption after the policy is implemented. However, if the researchers did not know that there had been a fire in the only brewery on the island the day after the policy was introduced, which substantially limited the amount of alcohol available for consumption, they might erroneously claim that the policy effectively reduced alcohol consumption instead of taking account of the lack of alcohol available. Now, let's imagine the brewery re-opens a few days later. If the alcohol policy was implemented on 1 January and the researchers compared alcohol consumption in December with January, they might find individuals with extreme values of consumption in December (due to festive holidays) which might return to average in January. Again, here the researchers might erroneously attribute this reduction to successful policy implementation. These issues can influence the conclusions drawn about the effect of interventions and should be taken into account when interpreting and synthesizing quantitative data from studies using pre–post designs.

Controlled before-and-after studies

In a **controlled before-and-after study**, the population of interest is matched to a control population. This 'matching' is often carried out using demographic characteristics (e.g. similar ages and sex distribution; see Austin [2011] for more information on methods for matching). The DV is then measured before (Time 1) and after (Time 2) an intervention or phenomenon of interest. However, the analysis is usually based only on Time 2 data or by using a change score (Time 2 data minus Time 1 data). In this case, it is different from the uncontrolled before-and-after design described previously. This study design is more effective than an uncontrolled before-and-after study at determining the effects of changes in an outcome not related to the intervention due to the presence of a control population. However, it is often difficult to adequately match groups, and pre-existing differences between groups may mean different responses to natural trends or changes. The success (or otherwise) of the matching process should be taken into account when quality assessing included studies and synthesizing data.

Analysing and synthesizing quantitative data from experimental study designs

Within-subjects *t*-test

Simple within-subjects designs with only two levels of IV typically use what is known as a 'paired-samples *t*-test' (often used interchangeably with paired *t*-test), if data are **normally distributed**, to compare the variation in means between each level. Authors commonly report a **test statistic** (*t*), which is:

t = mean of the differences/**standard error** (SE) of mean of the differences

as well as the associated **degrees of freedom** (df) of the test,

df = number of paired measurements - 1.

The test statistic (*t*) and degrees of freedom (df) allow for a **p-value** to be calculated to determine statistical significance. If you plan to quantitatively synthesize the result (e.g. via meta-analysis), an effect size can be computed if the means and standard deviations (SDs) or SEs are provided (see Figure 9.2).

Between-subjects *t*-test

Data from between-subjects designs with only two groups/levels are typically analysed using a between-subjects *t*-test (often used interchangeably with independent samples *t*-test) assuming data are normally distributed. Similar to the within-subjects *t*-test, a test statistic (*t*), degrees of freedom (df) and associated *p*-value should be reported.

If you plan to quantitatively synthesize the result using meta-analysis, you can use the **standardized mean difference/Cohen's *d*** formula (see Chapter 10 or Figure 9.2). However, if the data that you need are unavailable and the number of participants in each group is similar, then a variation of Cohen's *d* can be calculated from the *t*-test statistic and degrees of freedom (df) using the formula:

Cohen's $d = t * 2 / \sqrt{(df)}$

If the numbers in each group are different then:

Cohen's $d = t * (\sqrt{(1/n1 + 1/n2)})$

Rules of thumb for interpreting the results of this formula are: Cohen's $d = 0.2$ is a small effect, Cohen's $d = 0.5$ is a moderate effect and Cohen's $d = 0.8$ is a large effect. The effect size can be interpreted as the difference between the two groups in terms

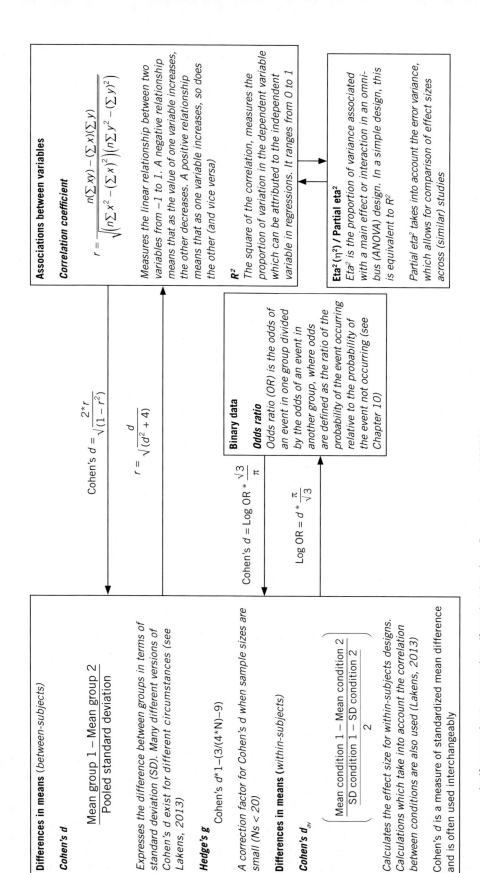

Differences in means (*between-subjects*)

Cohen's d

$$\text{Cohen's } d = \frac{\text{Mean group 1} - \text{Mean group 2}}{\text{Pooled standard deviation}}$$

Expresses the difference between groups in terms of standard deviation (SD). Many different versions of Cohen's d exist for different circumstances (see Lakens, 2013)

Hedge's g

$$\text{Cohen's } d * 1 - (3/((4*N) - 9)$$

A correction factor for Cohen's d when sample sizes are small (Ns < 20)

Differences in means (*within-subjects*)

Cohen's d_{av}

$$\left(\frac{\text{Mean condition 1} - \text{Mean condition 2}}{\frac{\text{SD condition 1} - \text{SD condition 2}}{2}} \right)$$

Calculates the effect size for within-subjects designs. Calculations which take into account the correlation between conditions are also used (Lakens, 2013)

Cohen's d is a measure of standardized mean difference and is often used interchangeably

$$\text{Cohen's } d = \sqrt{\frac{2*r}{(1 - r^2)}}$$

$$r = \sqrt{\frac{d}{(d^2 + 4)}}$$

Associations between variables

Correlation coefficient

$$r = \frac{n(\sum xy) - (\sum x)(\sum y)}{\sqrt{(n\sum x^2 - (\sum x)^2)(n\sum y^2 - (\sum y)^2)}}$$

Measures the linear relationship between two variables from −1 to 1. A negative relationship means that as the value of one variable increases, the other decreases. A positive relationship means that as one variable increases, so does the other (and vice versa)

R^2

The square of the correlation, measures the proportion of variation in the dependent variable which can be attributed to the independent variable in regressions. It ranges from 0 to 1

Binary data

Odds ratio

Odds ratio (OR) is the odds of an event in one group divided by the odds of an event in another group, where odds are defined as the ratio of the probability of the event occurring relative to the probability of the event not occurring (see Chapter 10)

$$\text{Cohen's } d = \text{Log OR} * \frac{\sqrt{3}}{\pi}$$

$$\text{Log OR} = d * \frac{\pi}{\sqrt{3}}$$

Eta² (η²) / Partial eta²

Eta² is the proportion of variance associated with a main effect or interaction in an omnibus (ANOVA) design. In a simple design, this is equivalent to R^2

Partial eta² takes into account the error variance, which allows for comparison of effect sizes across (similar) studies

⟶ signify approximate conversions (formula taken from Borenstein et al. (2009)

FIGURE 9.2 Common effect sizes and their relationships

of their pooled SD. However, without context, these interpretations should be used cautiously. For example, an effect size indicating individual differences in wellbeing (Cohen's $d = 0.2$) might be considered small at one time point. However, consider the accumulation of many small improvements in wellbeing over time (which may lead to a much larger effect over a longer period) or even a small effect in *everybody* in a population (which may lead to improvement in the public health of a nation). For an excellent discussion of the interpretation of effect sizes, see Funder and Ozer (2019).

Estimating the SE of Cohen's d is useful for generic **inverse variance** meta-analysis and can be performed using the following formula:

SE $d = \sqrt{(((n1 + n2)/(n1*n2))+(d2/2(n1 + n2)))}$

One-sample *t*-tests

You may come across *t*-tests that compare the mean of a sample to a specific (fixed) value. For example, researchers might investigate whether the average number of calories consumed per woman per day is greater or smaller than the average suggested by the Public Health England Guidelines (1600 calories per day). The same principles apply; the test produces a test statistic (*t*), degrees of freedom (df) and an associated *p*-value. One-sample *t*-tests are less common than other types of *t*-test but if there are established benchmarks or cut-off values of interest that relate to your specific research question, you may still come across them in your included studies.

An effect size for a one-sample *t*-test can be calculated as follows:

Cohen's d = (sample mean of variable of interest – specific fixed value) / SD of sample mean

Taking the above example of 1600 calories per day for women, a sample mean of 1350 calories and SD of 400 calories would result in the following effect size:

Cohen's $d = (1350 - 1600) / 400 = -0.625$

Analysis of Variance (ANOVA)

Not all experiments are limited to two groups or individuals that provide two measures of the DV. There can be multiple levels within a condition, whether the study uses a within- or between-subjects design. For example, researchers might be interested in the mental health of individuals who keep different pets (dogs vs cats vs goldfish). They could compare these self-selecting groups using a questionnaire which gives a continuous outcome score. In this case, they would have three independent groups. How could they find out whether these groups differ from each other? If they were to simply conduct multiple between-subject t-tests, they would have to conduct three tests (dogs vs cats; dogs vs goldfish; cats vs goldfish). Alternatively, they could look at this using a within-subjects design by letting people look after a dog for a week, a cat for another week and then a goldfish for another week. Again, if they were to conduct multiple within-subjects t-tests, they would have to conduct three t-tests. Regardless of whether their design is within- or between-subjects, conducting multiple t-tests is potentially problematic because multiple comparisons increase the chance of rejecting the **null hypothesis** (which states that there is no difference in the mental health of individuals who keep different pets).

The probability of making a **Type I error** (see Box 9.2) is .05 (or 5 per cent) for one hypothesis test (the inverse of the probability of not making the error, which is .95 (1 – .05)). However, the researchers in question have three hypothesis tests and therefore have to multiply these probabilities (.95 × .95 × .95 = .857). Therefore, the probability of the researchers making at least one Type I error is approximately 14 per cent (1 – .857 = .143). Now imagine they have five groups (dogs vs cats vs goldfish vs hamsters vs rabbits). There are now ten comparisons (dogs vs cats; dogs vs goldfish; dogs vs hamsters; dogs vs rabbits; cats vs goldfish... and so on). The chances of making a Type I error are now greater than 40 per cent (1 – $(.95)^{10}$ = .408).

Analysis of Variance (ANOVA) is an omnibus test which protects against inflation of Type I error rates when examining differences between more than two conditions. The results of an ANOVA will indicate if there is a statistically significant result overall (i.e. there is a difference between at least two of the conditions) but does not identify which conditions are different. Only after a statistically significant ANOVA result should individual condition differences be interpreted. In your included studies, you may see a statistically significant ANOVA result followed up with between-subjects t-tests contrasting each condition, or with post-hoc tests. These tests are sometimes corrected to account for the number of tests (e.g. **Bonferroni correction**, in which the threshold for statistical significance [e.g. p = .05] is divided by the number of tests) to further reduce the likelihood of Type I error (e.g. if conducting ten post-hoc tests, the threshold for significance would become p = .005, equivalent to p = .05/10). When quality assessing your included studies and synthesizing data, be wary of papers that: i) report individual condition contrasts without reporting a statistically significant ANOVA test; ii) report a non-statistically significant ANOVA but still interpret individual condition differences; or iii) do not report corrections for multiple comparisons. Indeed, in studies with the former two issues, the results should be treated with extreme caution. You may wish to place less weight on these results when interpreting and synthesizing findings (or excluding them from a meta-analysis, if you perform one, as a sensitivity analysis, to see if their exclusion changes the overall conclusions of your review; see Chapter 10).

An ANOVA should be reported with a test statistic (an *F* value – roughly interpreted as the ratio variance in the model explained by the conditions) and two separate degrees of freedom (df), one for the numerator (the model) and one for the denominator (the error or residual). From this test statistic and accompanying degrees of freedom (df), we can obtain a *p*-value – for example:

$$F(1,62) = 4.50, p = .0379$$

An ANOVA may also be reported with an effect size, usually called 'partial eta squared' (written as η_p^2). This is the ratio of variance in the model associated with the effect. For example, if $\eta_p^2 = .12$, it can be interpreted as 12 per cent of variance can be explained by the model (similar to measures of R^2 in regression – ANOVA is simply an extension of **linear regression**). ANOVA is not limited to between-subjects designs. If you find an experiment with multiple measures within individuals (within-subjects design), a repeated measures ANOVA will work in the same way (i.e. by controlling for the inflated Type I error rates).

Box 9.2

Statistical power

Ensuring appropriate **statistical power** is critical to the design and interpretation of experimental and correlational studies. Many research areas are gripped by a 'replication crisis', with lack of statistical power being cited as a potential explanation for why many studies fail to replicate statistically significant findings.

What do we mean by statistical power? The aim of null-hypothesis statistical testing is to examine whether, based on a sample of data, the null hypothesis can be rejected in favour of an alternative explanation. The null hypothesis is usually (but not always) interpreted as: there is no effect of X on Y or no association between X and Y. In null-hypothesis testing, there are two types of errors: Type I error (also known as a false positive), and **Type II error** (also known as a false negative). Type I error is a failure to reject a true null hypothesis and Type II error is a failure to reject a false null hypothesis. Many researchers (including us) still have difficulty remembering the difference between these errors, so a useful way to think about them is through the boy who cried wolf. First, he cried wolf and everybody believed there was a wolf when there was not (a false positive). The second time he cried wolf, nobody believed there was a wolf, but there actually was (a false negative).

(Continued)

Statistical power is the power to detect an effect size of interest (typically 80 per cent), taking into account the sample size and controlling for Type I error rate (typically $\alpha = .05$, i.e. the typical level of statistical significance). Power increases when any of these increases (e.g. detecting an effect that exists is more likely with more participants, and/or if the effect is large, and/or if we have a less stringent threshold for rejecting the absence of this effect). Statistical power can also be used to inform (a priori) sample sizes. For example, if a researcher knows the effect size they expect to find and can control for the probability of making Type I and Type II errors, they can estimate the minimum number of participants they need to detect this effect (known as a sample size calculation). It is important for researchers to routinely report effect sizes to allow future researchers to estimate accurate sample sizes and determine the feasibility of recruiting the correct number of participants. We hope you can see the importance of considering statistical power when assessing study quality and synthesizing data from included studies. Studies with low statistical power are less likely to detect an effect (if one exists), which means they will fail to reject the null hypothesis if false. This introduces bias into the study and, if you are not careful, your review.

Multifactorial ANOVAs

Often researchers are interested in complex phenomena and design studies with more than one IV. For example, researchers might be interested in both the effects of different treatment doses of aspirin (placebo vs low dose vs high dose) and biological sex (male vs female) on blood pressure. In this case, researchers often use a multifactorial ANOVA, also called a complex (or mixed) ANOVA. Complex ANOVAs usually break down the factors and levels of the IVs (e.g. a complex 3 [dose: placebo vs low vs high] × 2 [sex: male vs female] ANOVA was conducted on blood pressure). Importantly, these factors can be within-subjects or between-subjects and are not limited to two IVs.

A key difference between simple and complex ANOVAs is the ability of complex ANOVAs to examine potential *interactions* between the IVs. Interaction effects are the combined effects of IVs on the DV. This means that the impact of one IV is dependent on another (using the blood pressure example, dose might interact with sex, so that stronger aspirin might only reduce blood pressure in females). Importantly, without a complex ANOVA, it is not possible to calculate these interactions, so be wary of studies that don't examine potential interactions (or don't report the interaction) and head straight for pairwise comparisons tests.

ANCOVA

Analysis of Covariance or **ANCOVA** is an extension of ANOVA which includes a covariate. A covariate is an uncontrolled variable which is related to the DV but not the IV (e.g. you might be interested in looking at how plants tolerate drought, taking into account the size of the plant [covariate], the level of drought [IV] and how quickly the plant dies [DV]). Adding a covariate into an ANOVA reduces variation in the DV which is unattributed to the IV in the analyses. This 'noise reduction' technique then improves the power of the main test of the IV by removing extraneous variables as a possible explanation for the variation in the DV (see Miller & Chapman, 2001). When used correctly, ANCOVA is a powerful tool, which increases the robustness of predictions or reduces the number of participants required to adequately test the hypothesis. However, this technique may be used incorrectly, so look carefully at your included studies before you interpret the data.

Correlational designs

To answer your review question, you may need to include studies that use a correlational design. We therefore focus the second half of this chapter on this type of study design. We begin by describing correlational designs and then discuss statistical methods for examining the association between two (or more) variables.

A correlational design allows researchers to examine the association (or correlation) between variables. Correlational studies can be cross-sectional (i.e. variables are measured at the same time point), or longitudinal (i.e. measures are taken over time, either **prospectively** or **retrospectively**, and temporal relationships are examined). A correlational study design is used to determine the strength and direction of relationship(s) between variables and identify any potential confounding variables that influence these relationship(s). Longitudinal correlational studies also allow for causal or temporal relationships between variables to be examined.

For example, if your research question is, 'What is the association between the personality trait of extraversion and income in adults with long-term mental health difficulties?' you will likely include studies that use a correlational design because experimental manipulation of these variables is not possible. You *could* include studies that split individuals into groups based on their income and then conduct an ANOVA with extraversion as the DV, but this approach has limitations (as outlined previously). It's preferable to include studies that treat the two variables as continuous and explore the strength of the association between them. Synthesizing data from studies that use the latter approach allows you to establish whether an association exists between extraversion and income, but it does *not* allow you to establish whether this association is causal. To determine this, you need to include studies that have tracked people over time to establish a time–order relationship – that is, does one variable increase before the other variable? Synthesis of data from longitudinal correlational design studies gives an indication of a possible causal relationship but, because data are observational, a third variable being responsible for this effect (e.g. the state of the economy) cannot be ruled out.

There are many ways that correlational data can be analysed, and these largely depend on how the DV (or outcome variable) is measured.

Correlations

A correlation is the simplest way of looking at the linear association between two variables. In a correlational analysis, neither variable is the IV or the DV and no other information from additional variables is taken into account when calculating this association. Correlation coefficients range from −1 (perfect negative correlation: as values of one variable increase, values of the other decrease) to 1 (perfect positive correlation: as values of one variable increase, values of the other increase), with 0 meaning no association. Correlation coefficients are used, in conjunction with sample size, to derive a p-value for the association between two variables. In addition, they can be used as an effect size (see Figure 9.3). Two variables can have a strong association with each other but if this association is non-linear, then the resulting correlation will be weak.

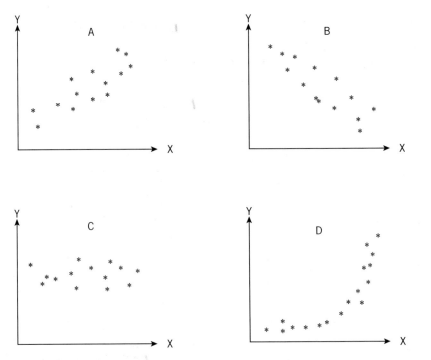

FIGURE 9.3   Examples of positive correlation (A), negative correlation (B), no correlation (C) and non-linear association (D)

The most common forms of correlation are Pearson's correlation and Spearman's rank correlation. The formula for a Pearson correlation is:

$$r = \frac{n(\Sigma xy) - (\Sigma x)(\Sigma y)}{\sqrt{\left(n\Sigma x^2 - (\Sigma x)^2\right)\left(n\Sigma y^2 - (\Sigma y)^2\right)}}$$

Pearson's correlation is used for **continuous data** (**interval data** or **ratio data**) that are normally distributed and, although Spearman's rank correlation is more suited to **ordinal data**, you may see Pearson's correlation used for ordinal data too. When sample sizes are moderate to large, the distribution of the data has little effect on this correlation (or, indeed, on the results of many statistical analyses). Remember, smaller samples are sensitive to outliers.

The formula for Spearman's rank correlation is:

$$r_s = 1 - \frac{6\Sigma d^2}{n(n^2 - 1)}$$

Spearman's rank correlation coefficient is generally reported for ordinal data or non-normally distributed data and is useful when samples are small with influential outliers. As previously described, you might see this correlation used when data do not follow a normal distribution. There are other related correlations, such as Kendall's Tau. Kendall's Tau is useful when you have a small sample and tied ranks (e.g. lots of people have the same rank score on a Likert scale) but is rarely used so you are unlikely to come across it when conducting your review.

Correlation coefficients are standardized effect sizes which can be entered directly into a meta-analysis (see Chapter 10) to generate a pooled correlation coefficient for a set of correlations. Sometimes a transformation is used to improve the distribution of coefficients, known as Fisher's Z:

Fisher's Z = 0.5 * Log((1 + correlation) / (1 − correlation))

To obtain the standard error of a correlation coefficient, the following formula can be used:

SE r = $1/\sqrt{(n - 3)}$

Correlation matrices

In multivariate studies (studies with more than two variables), you may come across a correlation matrix which reports correlations between multiple variables (one or more of which may be relevant to your review question). Don't read too much into statistically significant correlations taken from a matrix unless the authors have corrected the p-value (e.g. a Bonferroni correction) as the number of correlations in a large matrix increases the chance of Type I error. Furthermore, any simple correlation tells you only about the association between two variables in isolation; this represents an overly simplistic view of how variables might co-vary, especially if the authors have measured multiple variables (regressions, as discussed below, help in this regard).

Regression analysis

The term 'regression analysis' refers to statistical processes that estimate the association between one or more IVs (predictors) and a DV (outcome). There are many types of regression analysis; measurement of the DV is one of the key factors that informs the decision about choice of regression. To help you to understand, interpret and synthesize data from regression analyses, we provide an overview of common types of regression analysis that you may find in your included studies: linear, logistic, Poisson, ordinal and multinomial regression analyses. We go on to discuss extensions to the regression framework: moderation, mediation and SEM.

Linear regression and ANOVA are essentially the same thing. A regression analysis tests whether predictor variables (IVs) predict a significant amount of variance in the DV. In ANOVA, the critical ratio (F) tests the ratio of variance explained in the model by groups or conditions. If you conduct an ANOVA in a regression format, you will obtain broadly the same results (in probabilistic terms).

Linear regression
Model fit

Linear regression is normally used when there is a continuous DV (although you may see it used for ordinal DVs too). In a simple linear regression, there is only one predictor variable (which is essentially the same as a correlation), whilst a multiple regression has several predictor variables (IVs). A well-reported regression provides information on model fit – that is, the overall amount of variance that the model (the predictor variables) predict in the DV, which is evaluated with a coefficient of determination, usually an R^2 statistic which indicates the amount of variance the IVs predict in the DV:

$$R^2 = 1 - \frac{SS_{residual}}{SS_{Total}}$$

Dividing the residual variance (the unexplained variance – the sum of the squared [SS] distance each data point is from the line of fit) by the total variance in the model gives the proportion of unexplained variance. Subtracting the proportion of unexplained variance from 1 gives the explained variance.

Adjusted R^2 is interpreted in the same way as R^2 and represents an adjustment based on the number of predictors in the model, which means that adjusted R^2 will invariably be lower than R^2. Adjusted R^2 is useful; by adding new predictors, R^2 will increase even if the new predictors have no real impact on the predictive utility of the model. The adjusted R^2 will decrease substantially if variables with little predictive utility are added to the model. Therefore, if a regression has many predictor variables, you should look for an adjusted R^2, rather than R^2.

$$R^2_{adj} = 1 - (\frac{(1-R^2)(n-1)}{n-k-1})$$

n = number of observations, k = number of predictors

These coefficients of determination (R^2 and adjusted R^2) indicate the proportion of variance in the DV that is accounted for by the predictor(s). An associated p-value derived through an ANOVA (which, as discussed, is a linear model) indicates if the proportion of variance explained is statistically significant. This ANOVA is reported like any other ANOVA (F(df) =, p =), and is the same regardless of whether R^2 or adjusted R^2 is reported. Taken together, this model evaluation explains the amount of variance in the DV that the IVs predict, and whether this amount is statistically significant.

Regression coefficients

The overall regression model does not provide information about specific predictors. Imagine a statistically significant regression model (with three predictors) that accounts for 21 per cent of the variance in your DV. This information only has limited use. Do all three predictors account for 7 per cent of variance each? Or maybe one predictor accounts for 21 per cent of the variance? Furthermore, we do not know the direction of the association between variables (positive or negative association). To understand individual predictors, it is necessary to look at the individual **regression coefficients**.

A regression coefficient, B, is the number of units the DV changes for each one unit increase in the IV. A regression coefficient of 2.00 means that for each unit increase of the IV, the DV increases by two units (if it was –2.00, this means for each one unit increase of the IV, the DV decreases by two units). In isolation, this value has limited use, and must be interpreted alongside its SE which is an estimation of how much the regression coefficient deviates across cases. Ideally, the SE should be small, meaning the regression coefficient is precise. It is the ratio of the SE to the regression coefficient that allows the calculation of the alpha level through the t statistic:

$$t = \frac{B}{SE}$$

The larger the regression coefficient is compared to the SE, the larger the t statistic will be and the smaller the p-value will be for the association. These statistics allow researchers to understand which regression coefficients are associated with the DV, and the direction of this association. Unlike simple correlations, if there are multiple IVs in the regression, the regression coefficient indicates the relationship between the IV and the DV, whilst holding the other predictors constant.

Standardized regression coefficients

Standardized regression coefficients, often called beta (β) values, are also reported and explain the association between each IV and DV in terms of SD changes. A beta value of .50 means that for every 1 SD increase in the IV, there is a .50 SD increase in the DV (a beta of −.50 means that for every 1 SD increase in the IV, there is a .50 SD decrease in the DV). The beta value allows a simple comparison of the strength of the association between our IVs and DV – that is, the higher the beta, the stronger the association. However, when it comes to categorical predictors, beta values become a bit illogical. If a researcher had a two-level predictor (e.g. people who voted for Brexit vs those who voted Remain), expressing this in terms of SD changes is problematic (as a nominal variable does not have an SD). It is notable that a standardized regression coefficient is just a different way of expressing the same information as an unstandardized regression coefficient so they have exactly the same p-value.

Hierarchical linear regression

There is no difference between a multiple linear regression and a hierarchical regression except that in multiple linear regression, variables are added into the regression equation in blocks rather than all together. For example, researchers interested in predicting variance in alcohol units consumed in an average week may measure age, sex and impulsivity using the Barrett Impulsivity Scale (Patton et al., 1995). A normal multiple regression analysis would explain how much variance in alcohol units these variables predict and give regression coefficients for each variable. Alternatively, the researchers could use hierarchical regression and enter basic demographic variables into the first block followed by impulsivity into the second block. This approach has one major advantage over multiple linear regression as it also gives the R^2 change (and associated F-change statistic). This means that the model's output indicates the amount of variance in alcohol consumption explained by basic demographics, and then the *additional* variance explained by impulsivity (i.e. the sum of the R^2 changes gives the model's R^2). The F-change statistic indicates whether the change in R^2 is statistically significant for each block.

As shown in Table 9.1, the basic demographics in block one predict 2.9 per cent of the variance in alcohol units consumed, while impulsivity predicts an *additional* 3.2 per cent of variance, meaning the model predicts 6.1 per cent of variance.

TABLE 9.1   Hierarchical regression example

Variable	R^2 change	(df) F-change	β	p
Block1	.029	(2,227)3.51*		
Age			−.15	.015
Sex			−.07	.291
Block2	.032	(1,226)7.78**		
Impulsivity			.19	.006

*$p < .05$; **$p < .01$

Hierarchical linear regression is a useful method to parse out the amount of variance accounted for by different predictors and can have more than two blocks with any number of individual predictors in them (sample size permitting).

Does hierarchical regression change individual coefficients? Not really, although it depends on how the coefficients are reported. In Table 9.1, the (standardized) regression coefficients all come from the simultaneous model, i.e. all the predictors considered together (as in a standard multiple regression). This is the most common way of reporting the results of hierarchical regression. However, sometimes results are presented as shown in Table 9.2.

TABLE 9.2   Alternative way to present hierarchical regression results

Variable	R^2 change	(df) F-change	β	p
Block1	.029	(2,227)3.51*		
Age			−.16	.016
Sex			−.06	.294
Block2	.032	(1,226)7.78**		
Sex			−.07	.291
Impulsivity			.19	.006

*$p < .05$; **$p < .01$

The regression coefficients for age and sex are given for each block and change marginally when impulsivity is added to the model. Generally, you should be extracting the coefficients from the final model (i.e. the model that includes all variables) because extracting data for any single association and ignoring the wider context can be misleading.

This example also illustrates why it is problematic to use regression coefficients in meta-analyses. In multiple regression, the association between the IV and DV is influenced by the other variables in the model (and the more the IVs are correlated, the greater the influence). This means that the regression coefficients are 'adjusted' because the presence of the other IVs changes them.

Stepwise regression

Previous examples are 'forced entry' regressions where the researcher chooses the variables in the models. These are by far the most common. There is another way of conducting a multiple regression analysis whereby the variables included in the model are selected by an automatic statistical procedure. There are different methods for this: forwards (start with a null model and add the most significant variable and continue until the remaining variables meet pre-specified criteria); backwards (start with all variables in the model and remove the least significant one, continuing until all remaining variables meet pre-specified criteria) and stepwise (alternate between forwards and backwards, continuing until you reach a specified endpoint). Box 9.3 outlines some challenges associated with stepwise regression analyses.

Box 9.3

Step (un)wise regression?

Stepwise models are often mistakenly interpreted in the same way as forced entry models but should be interpreted through the lens of Harrell's (2001) critique:

1   They inflate R^2
2   The F-test statistic does not have the claimed distribution
3   The SEs of the regression coefficients are too small (resulting in overly narrow confidence intervals)
4   Regression coefficients are biased (away from zero)
5   Due to 3 and 4, the p-values are too low and are also difficult to correct for multiple comparisons

In essence, stepwise models make results look better than they probably are and should be treated with caution.

Logistic regression

Logistic regression, often referred to as binary logistic regression, is used when we have a two-level (binary) dependent variable (e.g. no relapse [0] or relapse [1]). Other than this, the terminology used to describe a logistic regression is similar to other forms of regression analysis, although the statistics underpinning the method are different.

Model fit

Unlike linear regression, logistic regression cannot produce an R^2 statistic. However, there are a series of pseudo R^2 statistics that are reported with logistic regression; the most common are Nagelkerke R^2, Cox and Snell R^2, or McFadden R^2. These statistics are interpreted in the same way, but some researchers avoid reporting them because they can produce very different estimates. For example, Nagelkerke R^2 tends to be much higher than the others. Logistic regression also reports a classification rate (usually as a percentage) – the number of people in the sample that the model correctly classified as 0 and 1 (i.e. the percentage of true positives and true negatives). The actual model fit in probabilistic terms is assessed using a chi-squared test.

Regression coefficients

As per linear regression, logistic regression produces both a regression coefficient and an SE, although in logistic regression, the coefficient represents log-odds. For example, imagine we have a model using impulsivity (IV) to predict a diagnosis of alcohol use disorder (DV) which has a regression coefficient of 1.2. This means that, for each unit increase in impulsivity, the log-odds of being diagnosed with alcohol use disorder increase by 1.2. The SE of the coefficient is the variability in the estimate. Similar to linear regression, the coefficient divided by its SE gives the critical ratio (Z in logistic regression) and the p-value is derived from this.

Odds ratios (regression)

The **odds ratio** is derived from the regression coefficient and is simply the exponentiation of the regression coefficient, which can be referred to as exp(B). See Chapter 10 for more information on odds ratios.

Other types of regression

You may come across different types of regression in your included studies, each of which generally has a model fit index and reports individual associations using regression coefficients and SEs.

Poisson regression

Poisson regression is used for count variables (e.g. number of relapses). As data also need to fit a Poisson distribution, we often see dispersion of data reported as a check of this (if the dispersion is greater than 1 then negative binomial regressions are often run instead; we don't cover these in this chapter, so we recommend some further reading, or consultation with a statistician, if you anticipate including studies that report this type of regression analysis). Poisson (and indeed negative binomial) regression models generate a goodness-of-fit statistic (i.e. is the model significant?) and sometimes a pseudo R^2 value. The regression coefficient in a Poisson regression represents the change in log-odds of the expected 'count' that a one unit change in the IV produces. You may also see an exponentiated value which can be easier to interpret.

Ordinal regression

People often fit ordinal outcomes using linear regression; however, **ordinal regressions** can be used. In an ordinal regression, the model fit is usually reported with a chi-squared statistic and p-value along with a pseudo R^2 value. Regression coefficients can be interpreted as follows: with each unit increase of the predictor, the ordered log-odds of moving to a higher level of the ordinal DV increase by the value of the regression coefficient.

Multinomial regression

Multinomial regression is similar to ordinal and logistic regression but is used when the DV contains three or more categories that cannot be put in a logical ascending order (e.g. predicting whether someone chooses to study medicine, psychology or mathematics at university). The model fit is usually reported with a likelihood ratio chi-squared statistic, p-value and a pseudo R^2. As with all regressions, individual associations are estimated with a regression coefficient and SE; however, with multinomial regression, odds ratios are also often reported. One of the categories in the DV is the reference category, so there are multiple effects for each IV. For example, if medicine is the reference category in the example above, then the model produces a regression coefficient for the likelihood of studying psychology vs medicine and another one for the likelihood of studying mathematics vs medicine.

It is important to note that, because the regression coefficients from different types of regression analysis mean something different, they cannot simply be compared to each other, whether in narrative terms or in a meta-analysis.

Extending the regression framework

Moderation

Moderation analysis explores the extent to which the strength of the association between an IV and a DV is influenced by a third variable (the moderator; see Figure 9.4). To illustrate, you may come across a study that looks at whether the relationship between years of work experience (IV) and salary (DV) differs according to gender (moderator). To conduct a moderation analysis, the proposed IV and moderator are entered into a regression model, then the product of the normalized (e.g. by mean centring) IV and the moderator (i.e. an interaction variable) is entered. If this interaction variable is statistically significantly associated with the DV, this indicates moderation. Individually, the IV and the moderator do not have to be associated with the DV, what is key is that the interaction predicts variance above and beyond those variables in isolation.

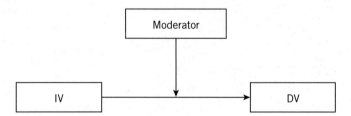

FIGURE 9.4   Visual representation of moderation analysis

Often, this analysis is followed up with a simple slopes analysis which shows the association between the IV and DV at different levels of the moderator (often –1 SD, mean, and +1 SD). However, there are other methods that can be used to explore these effects that are less commonly reported, for example, a Johnson–Neyman plot (see Lin, 2020).

Mediation

Mediation analysis is an exploration of the mechanism through which an IV influences a DV. In a simple mediation analysis (Figure 9.5), it is proposed that the total effect – the association between the IV and the DV (c) – is, at least partly, accounted for by the association between the IV and mediator (a) and the association between the mediator and DV (b). When accounting for this indirect effect, the direct effect (c') should be smaller than the total effect. For example, the relationship between food intake (IV) and obesity (DV) may be mediated by exercise frequency (mediator).

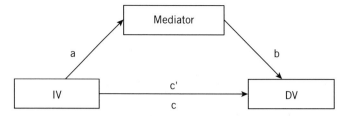

FIGURE 9.5   Visual representation of simple mediation

Although there are many different mediation tests, most are not commonly used (e.g. the Sobel test and causal steps approach) because they require lots of participants to detect effects and/or have assumptions that are erroneous or are rarely met in practice. As such, bootstrapping of the indirect effects has become increasingly common and gives a regression coefficient and SE for the estimated indirect effect.

There are some important considerations with mediation analysis. First, in correlational research, mediation analysis does not show causality (despite data being analysed as a chain of events [IV to mediator to DV]); if you come across studies that make claims of causality, they should be interpreted with caution. Second, to show mediation, you do not need to show an IV–DV association (i.e. 'c' does not need to be statistically significant). Indeed, the direct effect could be negative and the indirect effect could be positive. These two effects cancel each other out making the total effect (simple IV–DV association) zero. This is known as suppression (see Krause et al., 2010).

Structural equation modelling (SEM)

As you can see from Figure 9.6, SEM can look daunting. However, if you understand the principles of regression, you can understand SEM (because they're largely the same thing).

There are some terms that appear frequently in the SEM literature that may be unfamiliar to you. From bitter experience, there's nothing worse than staring at a statistical model that may as well be written in another language for all of the sense you can make of it. With this in mind, we've introduced some of the most commonly used terms below so that you feel able to extract, interpret and synthesize data from studies that report SEM analyses (regardless of how complex they may seem).

Latent variable (a)

Latent variables are the product of a factor analysis. For example, a six-item scale measuring consumption of slightly different aspects of unhealthy foods may be used as a latent variable whereby the items are used to create an underlying (and unmeasured)

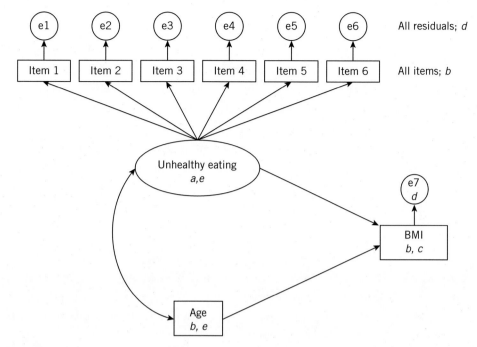

FIGURE 9.6   Example structural equation model

overall 'unhealthy food consumption' latent variable. The advantage of using latent variables is that a latent variable contains no error; the error resides in the residuals (*d*). Latent variables are always represented by ovals. This latent variable is then used in the model as either an endogenous variable or an exogenous variable.

Observed variable (b)

An observed variable is a standard variable (essentially something directly measured), is represented by a rectangle and can be either endogenous or exogenous.

Endogenous variable (c)

An endogenous variable is something that is being predicted, i.e. has an arrow going into it, so the model is predicting variance in this variable. These always have errors/residuals (*d*).

Exogenous variable (e)

An exogenous variable is something that is used as a predictor only (the exogenous variables in the model should be uncorrelated with each other).

Model fit

One of the differences between SEM and regression analyses is that SEM conceptualizes model fit. In SEM, the model (i.e. the hypothesized relationships between variables)
needs to fit the data. Whilst there are numerous ways to do this, some methods have
fundamental flaws. There are specific statistics (outlined below) that you should expect
to see when the model fit is evaluated. All fit measures have cut-off values for 'good' fit,
although sometimes this is circumstance dependent; indeed, some would argue that fit
should be calculated on a model-by-model basis and not by using universal cut-off values.

Most common measures of fit and their cut-off values

Chi-squared test (χ^2)

This test assesses the magnitude of the difference between the sample and the
covariance matrices of the fitted model. The null hypothesis is that the model fits
perfectly, so, to show the model fits, we want this to be non-statistically significant. However, this measure is invariably going to be statistically significant in
large samples, so it is not often used.

Normed chi-squared (χ^2/df)

This is simply the χ^2 divided by its degrees of freedom (df). There are several different cut-offs for good or adequate fit in the literature. McIver and Carmines
(1981) suggested <2 is a good fit, although <5 has been argued to be acceptable
(Schumacker & Lomax, 2016).

Baseline comparison measures of model fit

Tucker–Lewis index (TLI)

The TLI ranges from 0 to 1, with values closer to 1 indicating better fit. The most
commonly used threshold is .95 or above, although it has been argued that values
above .90 are also acceptable (Schumacker & Lomax, 2016).

Comparative fit index (CFI)

The CFI is closely related to the TLI and uses the same criteria for what constitutes a good or adequate fit. This is one of the most commonly reported measures
because it is less influenced by sample size than other measures of fit.

Normed fit index (NFI)

The NFI uses the same criteria for fit as the TLI and the CFI. It is, however, less commonly reported because it does not penalize the model for complexity (its calculation is based on χ^2 only, without the degrees of freedom [df] which the other two
measures use in different ways). This means that the more parameters there are in
the model, the higher the NFI (so this tends to make the model fit look better than
it is in larger models).

Absolute fit measures of model fit

Root mean square error of approximation (RMSEA)

One of the most commonly reported measures, RMSEA penalizes the model for complexity. The nearer to 0 the RMSEA is, the better the fit. Notably, several different cut-offs for fit are widely used (e.g. <.06 [Hu & Bentler, 1999] and <.08 [MacCallum et al., 1996]). The RMSEA measure is often reported with 90 per cent confidence intervals which give an indication of the precision of the estimate.

Standardized root mean residual (SRMR)

Another frequently reported measure of fit, the SRMR is based on the (square root) of the difference between the hypothesized and sample covariance matrix. It ranges from 0 to 1 with lower values indicating better fit; Hu and Bentler (1999) suggested an upper limit for good fit of .08.

Model comparisons

Akaike information criterion (AIC) and/or Bayesian information criterion (BIC) are reported when authors wish to see which of two or more models has the best fit. Lower values are indicative of better fit. In isolation, AIC and BIC do not tell us anything useful.

To accurately interpret SEM results, it is important to consider (and extract) a range of fit indices. As a minimum, you should expect to see a CFI (and/or TLI), an RMSEA and an SRMR and authors usually report a χ^2 statistic as well (although this may not be used to evaluate model fit in models with large samples). If just one fit index is reported, you cannot draw firm conclusions about model fit. Indeed, it is not uncommon to see badly fitted models inappropriately reported to be acceptable on the basis of a single fit index (e.g. 'NFI = 0.56, indicating a reasonable fit').

Individual predictors

Model fit indices indicate whether the findings of an SEM can be trusted, but do not tell us about associations between variables. When doing a systematic review, it is likely that you will be interested in a very specific relationship within a model and must extract only those data that allow you to answer your review question. Regardless of whether variables are observed or latent, associations between variables are reported as regression coefficients. SEM is identical to a standard regression analysis, and you should expect to see a regression coefficient and its SE reported, either in a table or in text. Sometimes standardized regression coefficients will be reported and, in figures, standardized regression coefficients are almost always used to label associations (as they take up less space). If you know how to interpret the results of a regression analysis, then you know how to interpret the results of an SEM – they are the same.

To meta-analyse or not to meta-analyse data from experimental and correlational studies?

Students often ask us if they need to (or indeed, can) meta-analyse data from experimental and correlational studies. We advise any student considering meta-analysis to seek the advice of a statistician (or experienced supervisor) early on to determine the feasibility of this approach, and the specific data needed to satisfy the assumptions of meta-analysis (more on this in Chapter 10). Often, narrative synthesis is sufficient when working with data from experimental and correlational studies but equally, if it is appropriate to meta-analyse your data, we would encourage you to do so. If you plan to narratively synthesize your data, re-read Chapter 7.

Final thoughts

This chapter has focused on understanding and synthesizing data from experimental and correlational studies. As you know, there is a range of different analyses that can be used depending on study design and data type, although many of the statistical assumptions and approaches underpinning these analyses are actually the same (e.g. ANOVA, linear regression and SEM). There are also some common data pitfalls and errors that you need to be aware of when extracting, interpreting, critically appraising and synthesizing findings from your included studies. We summarize them in Box 9.4.

Box 9.4

Common pitfalls and errors when interpreting data from experimental and correlational studies

- *Dichotomization of data.* Often, researchers split a continuous variable into categories. This is rarely a good idea – yet, despite the vast literature on the subject, it is still common practice. This approach is particularly problematic when a normative reference is used (e.g. median split). Using a normative reference to dichotomize data means that the resultant groups only represent that specific dataset; other datasets will likely have different median values making comparisons between datasets challenging. Doing this will also dramatically decrease statistical power. It's important to be aware of the risks associated with this approach when quality assessing and interpreting your included studies.

- *Adding covariates to control for group differences in **confounder variables***. It is common to see authors conduct ANCOVA because they have identified a variable that differs across their conditions so they add it as a covariate. Phrases such as 'Owing to there being a significant difference in age across conditions, we added it as a covariate in the subsequent analysis' are common. This is a violation of the assumptions of the test which is independence of the IV and the covariate and must be taken into account when interpreting findings from your included studies.

- *Confusing a p-value with a magnitude of effect size*. With larger sample sizes, small effects with limited practical or theoretical significance can still be statistically significant. Larger sample sizes mean that sample estimates, such as means, will usually be more precise and better representative of true (population) estimates. This increased precision allows for detection of smaller differences between groups. As such, *p*-values should always be accompanied by an effect size. Of course, larger effect sizes can be detected using data from a smaller number of participants (see Box 9.2). When writing up your results, it's important to consider an effect size alongside a *p*-value, rather than merely reporting significance level.

- *Confusing statistical significance with clinical significance*. Finding a statistically significant result does not mean that the result has real world relevance. In large samples, very small effects can be statistically significant but may not be noticeable or meaningful; conversely even non-significant effects may be clinically important. It's important to take context into account when interpreting findings of your included studies and making recommendations for practice or further research.

- *p-hacking (analysing data until a statistically significant result is obtained)*. Be careful with studies that seem to carry out unhypothesized or post-hoc testing (e.g. breaking up samples into subgroups or performing further tests on non-significant ANOVAs). It is believed that this has contributed to the 'replication crisis'. Pay close attention to the number of statistical tests reported in your included studies and take this into account when analysing your data and assessing the quality of your included studies.

Key points to think about when writing your protocol

- Think about the type of studies that you are likely to include in your review (e.g. pre–post design, cross-sectional studies)
- How will you determine whether your included studies report appropriate statistical analyses when assessing their quality?
- How do you plan to synthesize the results of different analyses reliably and informatively?
- How do you plan to assess whether the reported findings are reliable (e.g. is the model fit appropriate, were studies underpowered, was there arbitrary dichotomization of data)?

What an examiner is looking for in your thesis

- Critical appraisal of the study designs and statistical analyses within your included studies
- Correct interpretation of the findings from the individual studies included in your review
- Appropriate effect size computations and conversions (where they do not exist)
- Clear rationale for undertaking (or not) meta-analysis
- Valid approach used to perform a meta-analysis (see Chapter 10), including appropriate assessment of heterogeneity

Frequently Asked Questions

Question 1: What if I identify a serious flaw in the analysis of a study – for example, pairwise comparisons following a non-statistically significant ANOVA?

This is, unfortunately, common and can indicate a low-quality study (at least in analytic terms). It does not mean that the study findings should be ignored but, when describing the study, this limitation should be considered. If you plan to conduct a meta-analysis, you may wish to carry out a sensitivity analysis whereby low-quality studies are excluded and both sets of results are compared.

Question 2: What if the studies I find calculate effect sizes in different ways?

First, you could extract the data reported by the authors and make broad comparisons across studies (e.g. comment on the direction, magnitude and significance of the effect whilst recognising that the direct comparison of these results may not be meaningful). Second, you can use relevant statistics (e.g. means and standard errors) from the published studies to calculate the effect size that you are interested in. Third, you can convert some effect sizes directly (see Figure 9.2).

Question 3: The study contains the measurements I am interested in, but their associations have not been reported. Can I do anything?

The only solution to this problem is to contact the authors directly. They may be willing to share the data or run the analysis for you. The older the publication, the less likely you will be able to get hold of the information that you need, so ensure that you state this as a limitation in your write-up.

Question 4: The studies I have looked at all have regression coefficients. Can I use these in a meta-analysis?

It depends. First, is the same form of regression analysis reported in all studies? For example, linear and ordinal regression models give you regression coefficients but they mean something different (in terms of the influence of the IV on the DV). Even if all the coefficients you have found come from linear regression models, you may still be unable to use them in a meta-analysis. This is because regression models usually contain other IVs (unless it's a simple regression). The presence of these other IVs adjusts the association between the IV you are interested in and the DV. Correlation coefficients (i.e. associations between two measures in isolation) can be used in meta-analysis. Attempts have been made to extract effects from regressions, but they are statistically complex (see Aloe & Becker, 2012; Aloe et al., 2021).

Question 5: A study reports poor model fit indices (either regression or SEM) but statistically significant individual predictors. How should I interpret this?

Overall, if the statistical model is not a good fit to the data, then the relationship between the variables within the model cannot be trusted. Many factors might influence model fit (e.g. outliers, measurement error and/or distributions) and without a model that fits the structure of the data, 'parameter estimates obtained in the poor fitting model cannot be interpreted as reasonably summarizing the relationships between the variables' (Ryu, 2014, p. 2).

Question 6: What statistical data should I extract from my included studies?

It is likely that your included studies will include *irrelevant* data. Students often find it difficult to decide which data to extract and can fall into the trap of over-extracting data. Our advice is to first consult your protocol and remind yourself of what data you said you would extract to help you to answer your review question. For example, if you are interested in the association between variable X and variable Y, then you will probably want to extract relevant correlational data (i.e. correlation coefficients for X and Y and associated *p*-values) and data from regression models where Y is the DV and X is one of several IVs (i.e. relevant regression coefficients, covariates, overall model fit, etc.). However, you don't need to extract data regarding the relationship between variables A to C *unless they help you to answer your review question*. In an ideal world, authors would synthesize data using the same methods (e.g. including the same variables in the same type of regression model). However, this rarely happens. It can therefore be difficult to synthesize results from studies that analyse data using different regression models, or that report the results of their regression models in different ways, so we recommend that you consult a statistician or experienced supervisor if you plan to do this or if you get stuck when extracting and synthesizing data.

Further Reading and Resources

Austin, P.C. (2011). An introduction to propensity score methods for reducing the effects of confounding in observational studies. *Multivariate Behavioral Research*, *46*(3), 399–424.

Borenstein, M., Hedges, L.V., Higgins, J.P.T., & Rothstein, H.R. (2009). *Introduction to meta-analysis*. John Wiley & Sons.

Field, A. (2017). *Discovering statistics using IBM SPSS Statistics*. SAGE Publications.

Funder, D., & Ozer, D.J. (2019). Evaluating effect size in psychological research: sense and nonsense. *Advances in Methods and Practices in Psychological Science, 2*, 156–68.

Harrell, F.E. (2001). *Regression modeling strategies: With applications to linear models, logistic regression, and survival analysis*. Springer-Verlag.

Krause, M.R., Serlin, R.C., Ward, S.E., Rony, R.Y.Z., Ezenwa, M.O., & Naab, F. (2010). Testing mediation in nursing research: beyond Baron and Kenny. *Nursing Research, 59*(4), 288.

Lipsey, M.W., & Wilson, D.B. (2001). *Practical meta-analysis*. SAGE Publications.

Schumacker, E., & Lomax, G. (2016). *A beginner's guide to structural equation modelling*. Taylor & Francis.

10

Understanding and Synthesizing Numerical Data from Intervention Studies

Michaela Brown and Marty Chaplin

This chapter will help you to...

- Present and interpret the numerical results of your included intervention studies

- Recognize whether it is appropriate to combine your studies in a meta-analysis

- Understand the basic principles of meta-analysis

- Recognize heterogeneity and learn appropriate methods to deal with it

- Present and interpret the results of a meta-analysis

Introduction

This chapter outlines how to present and summarize numerical data from intervention studies. We start by discussing how to present the results of individual intervention studies and the best way to interpret them. We then explore the circumstances under which it is appropriate to combine data in a meta-analysis and explain what is involved in this process. We consider the importance of heterogeneity and how to deal with it. We finish by suggesting how you can present the results of your meta-analysis and interpret your findings.

Points to note

Throughout this chapter, we use the term 'intervention study' to refer to any study in which an intervention is evaluated. Many, but not all, intervention studies include a randomization process. Most of our examples include data from randomized controlled trials (RCTs) because they are considered to be the 'gold standard' of intervention studies. However, the principles discussed in this chapter apply to most types of intervention studies, unless stated otherwise.

Although this chapter has been written to guide you through the data synthesis process and explain the basic principles involved in a meta-analysis, it will not equip you with the skills to perform your own meta-analysis. Knowledge of the data synthesis process will allow you to interpret intervention study results correctly, and knowledge of the principles of meta-analysis will help you decide whether using this technique is appropriate for your data. We recommend that you talk to a statistician at key stages during the review process if you have not performed a meta-analysis before. A statistician will be able to check that your decision about whether to perform a meta-analysis is sensible. They can advise you on the correct methods for performing a meta-analysis using the software packages you have available and can also help you to understand the results. The textbook by Egger and colleagues (2022) provides a useful overview of meta-analysis software packages. Don't forget, you can speak to your supervisor(s) if you think you need advice from a statistician but don't know how to find one.

Before reading any further, it is important to note that a meta-analysis is not a required element of a systematic review. Meta-analysis should only be carried out if data from included intervention studies are sufficiently similar and it is sensible to combine them. There are several conditions that must be met before deciding to meta-analyse your data; if these are not fulfilled, then it is inappropriate and misleading to statistically combine data. Don't worry though, we'll talk you through this.

The latter half of this chapter focuses solely on meta-analysing data from RCTs because most current statistical methods use data from this type of study. However, meta-analyses of data from other types of study design are becoming more common. For more information on the meta-analysis of non-randomized studies, refer to Chapter 9 of this book, and Chapter 13 of the *Cochrane Handbook* (Higgins et al., 2022). Even though the examples that follow are often taken from healthcare research, the methods are also applicable to other fields, so don't be put off if your review is non-healthcare focused.

Presenting and interpreting the results of individual intervention studies

Chapter 7 outlined how to use data tables to present key data about the included studies in your systematic review, such as study characteristics, participant characteristics and study results, and how to describe these data narratively in the text. Chapter 9 focused on interpreting the results of experimental and correlational study designs. Here, we will consider in more detail how to present and interpret the results of individual intervention studies. As in Chapter 9, because numerical data can vary widely from study to study, we will first look at different types of numerical data and the ways that these data can be presented. It is not your job to manipulate the data, as the authors of the published studies should have done this for you – use this chapter as a guide to help you to understand the information that is reported in the studies.

Binary data

Binary data are outcomes that can only be expressed as one of two possible responses – for example, dead or alive, success or failure. These data may be presented as:

- The number of individuals who experience the outcome of interest in each group and the number of patients randomized to each group (e.g. in group A, 44 of the 60 people experienced an event; in group B, 32 of the 61 people experienced an event)
- The percentage of people experiencing an event in each group and the number randomized to that group (e.g. of the 60 people in group A, 73 per cent experienced an event; of the 61 people in group B, 52 per cent experienced an event)
- **Effect estimates** (**relative risk**, odds ratio or **risk difference**)

An effect estimate is a point estimate that is the 'best guess' of the direction and size of the treatment effect; the direction tells us which treatment is better and the size tells us by how much. An associated confidence interval is usually reported along-side the point estimate and describes the uncertainty around the estimate by giving the range of values within which the true effect is strongly believed to lie. The most commonly reported confidence interval is the 95 per cent confidence interval, which can be interpreted as meaning that we are 95 per cent certain that the true effect lies within the range of the confidence interval. A standard 95 per cent confidence inter-val can be calculated as follows:

$$95\% \text{ confidence interval} = \textbf{effect estimate} \pm 1.96 \times \sqrt{\text{standard error of the effect estimate}}$$

Narrow confidence intervals indicate that the treatment estimate is relatively precise, whereas wide confidence intervals suggest a high degree of uncertainty. A confidence interval that includes the value of no difference between the groups indicates that the treatments are not statistically significantly different. However, lack of statistical significance does not always mean that there is 'no effect'. Often, small studies report non-statistically significant results even when there are important, real effects, which can only be detected by a much larger study.

Relative risk is the risk of an event in one group divided by the risk of an event in the other group, where risk is defined as the probability of the event occurring. If risks are equal in the two groups being compared, the relative risk is 1. Therefore, the value of no difference for the relative risk is 1. If the risk in group A is lower than the risk in group B, the relative risk of the event occurring in group A compared with group B is less than 1 and the relative risk of the event occurring in group B compared with group A is greater than 1. If the relative risk in group A compared with group B is 0.67, this can be interpreted as meaning that the risk of an event in group A is 67 per cent of the risk of an event in group B. Put another way, there is a 33 per cent reduction in risk in group A relative to the risk in group B.

The odds ratio is the odds of an event in one group divided by the odds of an event in another group, where odds are defined as the ratio of the probability of the event occurring relative to the probability of the event not occurring. This sounds a bit complicated, but these odds are the same as those used in gambling to work out your financial gain if you win. For example, odds of 3:1 mean that for every £1 you bet, you win £3. Similarly, odds are often used in medicine, where a chance of survival of 50:50 means that for every 50 patients who survive, 50 die. In the same way as relative risk, if the odds in two groups being compared are equal, the odds ratio is 1. Therefore, the value of no difference for the odds ratio is 1. If the odds in group A are lower than the odds in group B, then the odds ratio of A relative to B is less than 1 and the odds ratio of B relative to A is greater than 1. Odds ratios are much less intuitive to interpret than relative risks. For example, an odds ratio of 0.54 indicates that there is a 46 per cent reduction in odds but this does not really tell us very much in terms of the change in the number of events across groups. People often incorrectly assume that relative risks and odds ratios are the same. When events are rare, the value of these two measures will be approximately equal, but, as risks and odds increase, large differences in size may exist between the two statistics. Odds ratios are sometimes chosen over relative risks because odds ratios have strong mathematical properties, such as being able to take any value between zero and infinity.

The risk difference is the risk of an event in one group minus the risk of an event in another group, where risk is defined as the probability of the event occurring (the same definition of risk as used to calculate a relative risk). This describes the absolute change so that if two groups are equal in terms of risk, the risk difference is zero. Therefore, the value of no difference for the risk difference is zero. If the risk in group A is lower than the risk in group B, the risk difference of A relative to B is less than zero and the risk difference of B relative to A is greater than zero. For example, if the risk difference of group A relative to group B is –0.39, this indicates that the risk of an event is 39 per cent lower in group A than it is in group B.

How to calculate effect estimates for binary data if they are not presented in a published paper

Let's assume that Table 10.1 shows the outcomes reported in one of your included intervention studies. The number of people who experience the event (treated here as a failure) are denoted as F_A and F_B depending on whether the people are in group A or group B respectively, and similarly, patients who do not experience the event (treated here as a success) are denoted as S_A and S_B.

TABLE 10.1   Possible outcomes from an included study

Group	Event (failure)	No event (success)	Total
A	F_A	S_A	N_A
B	F_B	S_B	N_B

Relative risk

The relative risk is calculated by dividing the risk of an event in group A by the risk of an event in group B:

$$\text{Relative risk} = \frac{F_A / N_A}{F_B / N_B}$$

An alternative way of presenting this information is the relative risk reduction, which is calculated as follows: relative risk reduction = 100% × (1 − relative risk).

Odds ratio

The odds ratio is calculated by dividing the odds of an event in group A by the odds of an event in group B:

$$\text{Odds ratio} = \frac{F_A/S_A}{F_B/S_B}$$

Risk difference

The risk difference is calculated by subtracting the risk of an event in group B from the risk of an event in group A:

$$\text{Risk difference} = \frac{F_A}{N_A} - \frac{F_B}{N_B}$$

Table 10.2 shows outcome data from an RCT. The outcome is presented as the number (n) of patients experiencing an infection, the number of patients for whom there are data that can be analysed (N), and the percentage of those patients who have data that can be analysed and who experience an infection (%). These numbers can be used to calculate relative risks, odds ratios and risk differences.

TABLE 10.2   Example of events reported in an included study

	Treatment group			Control group		
Trial	**n**	**N**	**%**	**n**	**N**	**%**
Longworth et al. (2020)	2	32	6	3	40	8

First, we need to rearrange the data in Table 10.2 into a 2 × 2 table, as shown in Table 10.3.

TABLE 10.3   Example of trial outcomes reported in an included study

	Infection (failure)	No infection (success)	Total
Treatment group	2	30	32
Control group	3	37	40

$$\text{Relative risk} = \frac{2/32}{3/40} = 0.83$$

The relative risk can be interpreted as meaning that the risk of experiencing an infection in the treatment group is 83 per cent of the risk in the control group. Put another way, there is a 17 per cent (100% × [1 − 0.83]) reduction in risk for patients in the treatment group relative to patients in the control group.

$$\text{Odds ratio} = \frac{2/30}{3/37} = 0.82$$

Odds ratios are much less intuitive to interpret than relative risks. An odds ratio of 0.82 means that there is an 18 per cent reduction in odds for patients in the treatment group relative to patients in the control group, but this doesn't tell us anything about the change in the number of events for patients in the treatment group compared with the number of events for patients in the control group.

$$\text{Risk difference} = \frac{2}{32} - \frac{3}{40} = -0.0125$$

The risk difference can be interpreted as meaning that the risk of an infection is 1.25 per cent lower in the treatment group than it is in the control group.

Continuous data

Continuous data are outcomes measured on a continuous scale – for example, age or height. These data may be presented separately for each treatment (e.g. with a mean and standard deviation [SD]) or as an effect estimate that measures the difference between two treatments (e.g. **mean difference** or **standardized mean difference**). If an effect estimate is not presented, and you are able to, we suggest you calculate this yourself as it is more meaningful than presenting the results separately for each treatment group.

The two effect estimates described below assume that the outcomes you have extracted from your included studies have a normal distribution in each arm of each study (Figure 10.1 shows how the data look graphically if they are normally distributed). This means that the data tend to be distributed around a central point with no bias to the left or right. This assumption is not always met as data may be skewed (Figure 10.2 shows how the data look graphically if they are skewed). **Skewed data** are not evenly distributed around a central point; rather, they are clustered to either the left or right. Under such circumstances, the mean is no longer the measure of choice. If you have concerns that your data may be skewed, speak to a statistician about the best approach to take to calculate the effect estimate.

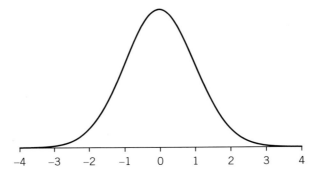

FIGURE 10.1   Example of normally distributed data

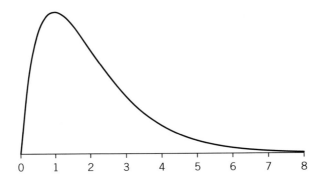

FIGURE 10.2   Example of skewed data

Mean difference

Mean difference is the absolute difference between the mean values of the outcomes in the two treatment groups. The mean difference is simple to interpret: a mean difference of 4.5 signifies that the outcome is 4.5 units bigger in one group than in the other.

Standardized mean difference

When studies assess the same outcome but measure it using different scales, the standardized mean difference is used instead of the mean difference, as it is necessary to standardize the results of the studies to a uniform scale. The standardized mean difference is a measure of the treatment effect that takes into account the variability observed across the participants. While standardized mean differences correct for different lengths of scales, they do not correct for differences in the direction of the scale (i.e. if one study uses a scale from 0 to 10 where 10 is good and another uses a scale from 0 to 10 where 10 is bad).

The standardized mean difference is more difficult to interpret than the mean difference as it is reported in units of standard deviation rather than in the units originally used to measure the outcome. The *Cochrane Handbook* (Higgins et al., 2022) discusses a 'rule of thumb' for interpreting this effect estimate as proposed by Cohen (1988) and discussed in the preceding chapter: 0.2 represents a small effect, 0.5 a moderate effect and 0.8 a large effect.

How to calculate effect estimates for continuous data if they are not presented in a published paper

The mean difference is calculated simply by subtracting one mean value from the other:

Mean difference = mean in group A – mean in group B

The standardized mean difference is calculated using the following equation:

$$\text{Standardized mean difference} = \frac{\text{mean in group A} - \text{mean in group B}}{\text{pooled standard deviation}}$$

For information on calculating a **pooled standard deviation** refer to *Practical Statistics for Medical Research* (Altman, 2020).

Example 1: Age

If you want to know the difference between two groups in terms of their mean age you can calculate the mean difference because the outcome is measured on the same scale in both groups (Table 10.4).

TABLE 10.4   Age of participants reported in a published paper

Group	Age of participants (years)										Mean age
A	56	62	57	55	59	57	58	55	54	58	57.1
B	58	61	64	62	63	61	59	63	60	62	61.3

Mean difference = 61.3 – 57.1 = 4.2 years

The mean difference indicates that on average, patients in group B are 4.2 years older than those in group A.

Example 2: Scores on tests

If you want to know the difference between two groups in terms of their test scores and the group A test was marked out of 60 and the group B test was marked out of 80 (as shown in Table 10.5), you couldn't use the mean difference as this wouldn't take into account the fact that the two tests were marked on different scales; instead, you would need to calculate the standardized mean difference as this adjusts for the difference between the two scales.

TABLE 10.5   Calculating standardized mean difference in two groups' scores

Group	Score										Mean	SD*	Pooled SD*
A	46	52	59	55	49	43	54	57	60	56	53.1	5.59	
B	73	77	64	59	78	66	75	74	67	69	70.2	6.20	8.34

*SD = standard deviation

$$\text{Standardized mean difference} = \frac{70.2 - 53.1}{8.34} = 2.05$$

According to Cohen's (1988) rule of thumb, discussed earlier, there is a large effect (as the standardized mean difference is greater than 0.8). This means that there is evidence of a difference between the two groups after allowing for the fact that the two tests had different maximum scores.

Ordinal data

Ordinal data fall into ordered categories – for example, mild, moderate and severe. It is common to analyse ordinal data with multiple categories as if the data were a continuous outcome, and ordinal data with few categories by grouping categories together and treating them as a binary outcome. It is possible to produce effect estimates to summarize ordinal outcome data, although this approach may be complicated and unnecessary if data can be instead treated as binary or continuous.

Count data

Count data are expressed as the total number of events that each participant experiences – for example, the number of infections patients experience during a clinical trial. Count data can be split into two types: counts of rare events and counts of common events.

For rare events, analyses of counts are based on rates that quantify the number of events occurring over a given time period. The effect estimate used for rare events is known as the rate ratio, which is calculated by dividing the rate of the event occurring in one group by the rate of the event occurring in the other group. For example, if in group A there are 14 events in a 24-hour period and in group B there are 3 events in a 24-hour period, the rate ratio is calculated by dividing 14 by 3, giving an answer of 4.7. This can be interpreted as meaning that the event of interest occurs 4.7 times more frequently in group A than in group B over a 24-hour period.

For common events, the outcome can be thought of as the number of events experienced by each participant in a group and analysed as if it were continuous data.

Time-to-event data

Time-to-event data are outcomes that measure the time taken for each participant to experience an event from a specified starting point – for example, months of survival. For those who do not experience the event of interest during the time they are observed, the length of time that they are in the trial is still recorded and they are classed as 'censored'.

It is possible to analyse time-to-event data in the same way as binary data by splitting patients into those who have experienced an event and those who have not experienced an event at a specific time period, but this requires knowledge of whether all patients have experienced the event or not at a given time point. The most common approach is to use **survival analysis**. This quantifies the data in terms of hazards, which are similar to risks (as mentioned in the binary data section) but are more unstable as they may change substantially over time. Hazard ratios are interpreted in the same way as relative risks: a hazard ratio of 0.43 means that the risk of experiencing an event in one group is 43 per cent of the risk of experiencing an event in another group in a given time period.

Results tables

It is considered best practice to present the results of the included studies in a combined study results table. As discussed in Chapter 7, complementary text should describe any similarities and differences that you have identified across the studies rather than be focused on the results of individual trials. It is important that what you write in the text *exactly* matches what is shown in the table. Table 10.6 is a hypothetical results table showing the results of four educational research studies.

TABLE 10.6   Example results table (educational research study data)

| | Achieved 5 A*–C examination grades following educational interventions | | |
Trial	Group A n (%)	Group B n (%)	Odds ratio (95% confidence interval)
Furnival (2018)	72 (29.9)	105 (43.2)	0.56 (–1.59, 2.72)
Price (2020)	152 (29.7)	244 (48.0)	0.46 (0.22, 2.55)
Quraishy (2018)	62 (27.4)	94 (40.9)	0.55 (–1.62, 2.72)
Smith (2012)	98 (32.6)	136 (45.9)	0.58 (–1.55, 2.71)

The following is an example of the text that might go alongside Table 10.6.

Four publications reported data on students' GCSE results following two different educational interventions designed to improve examination performance (Furnival, 2018; Price, 2020; Quraishy, 2018; Smith, 2012). The proportion of students achieving 5 A*–C grades at GCSE ranged from 27.4 per cent to 32.6 per cent in group A and from 40.9 per cent to 48.0 per cent in group B. The odds ratios from the four publications all indicated that the odds of achieving 5 A*–C grades at GCSE were lower in group A than in group B.

Meta-analysis of data from RCTs

First things first: what is a meta-analysis and why might you want to carry one out? A meta-analysis is a statistical method that allows results from individual studies to be combined to give an overall measure of the effect of one intervention compared with another (Glass, 1976). Meta-analysis allows the results from several RCTs to be combined; such analyses (usually) include a large number of patients, and therefore may be more likely to detect smaller (but still clinically significant) differences than an analysis of results from a single RCT. This means that the results of meta-analyses can be particularly useful when analysing subgroups – for example, when there are too few patients in the subgroups of individual RCTs to allow any differences to be detected. In addition to being able to detect smaller differences, any estimates detected by a meta-analysis will be more precise (i.e. have narrower confidence intervals) because the variability between patients is reduced as the number of patients increases.

The main assumption underlying a meta-analysis is that the RCTs are sufficiently similar for the results to be combined – that is, they are homogeneous. However, it is inevitable that RCTs will differ in some way or another. So, before using this method, you need to be confident that the studies you are interested in are not too different and can be grouped together, and that it is sensible to combine the results of these studies to get an overall measure of effect. The following sections outline the key steps involved in understanding *if* and *how* you might perform a meta-analysis (see Box 10.1).

Box 10.1

Key steps to consider when synthesizing data using meta-analysis

Step 1: Assess whether it is appropriate to combine your studies in a meta-analysis (i.e. check that the assumption of **homogeneity** is satisfied)

Step 2: Justify your decision to conduct (or not conduct) a meta-analysis in your write-up

Step 3: Choose an appropriate meta-analysis method

Step 4: Identify and discuss any heterogeneity in the meta-analysis results

Step 5: Present and interpret the results of your meta-analysis

---

Step 1: Assess whether it is appropriate to combine your studies in a meta-analysis (i.e. check that the assumption of homogeneity is satisfied)

Once you have presented the results of your included RCTs, the next task is to decide whether it is appropriate to combine the results of the studies in a meta-analysis. It is appropriate to combine study data in a meta-analysis only if the assumption of homogeneity is satisfied. Before being able to satisfy the assumption of homogeneity, four aspects need to be assessed. The first is that RCTs should be similar in terms of the patients they recruit; this can be checked by examining participant eligibility criteria and baseline characteristics across RCTs. This is a subjective approach as there is no quantitative measure of similarity.

The second aspect for consideration is that the RCTs should compare the same interventions and comparators; trial publications should provide detailed descriptions of each. It is important to check that these are consistent across the RCTs as, if they differ substantially, you will not be comparing like with like. For example, if you are looking at drug RCTs, it is important to check for details of treatment doses, duration of treatment and any supplementary care given alongside the investigational treatments.

The third aspect is that RCTs should report the same outcomes. It is OK if one RCT has the outcome of interest as a primary outcome, while another RCT has it as a secondary outcome – data from these RCTs can still be combined. Not only should the outcomes reported be the same, but the time frame over which they are measured should also be comparable. If the outcome of interest happens gradually over time and some RCTs are only measuring the outcome at 24 hours while others are looking at the outcome at seven days, the event rate in the shorter RCTs will be different from the event rate in the longer trials.

The fourth aspect is that the results of the RCTs should describe broadly similar effects and that the corresponding confidence intervals overlap. For example, if different studies show strong effects favouring different interventions, pooling data from these studies would be inappropriate. A good way to check this is by producing a **forest plot** using a statistical package; an example forest plot is shown in Figure 10.3.

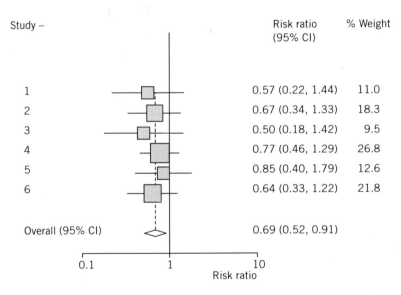

FIGURE 10.3   Example of a forest plot showing that it would be appropriate to perform a meta-analysis

The square in the centre of each horizontal line shows the point estimate of the effect recorded in each study. The size of the square is proportionate to the size of the study, so larger studies have a larger square. The short horizontal line shows the corresponding confidence interval. The length of the line is proportional to the width of the confidence interval, so longer lines indicate wider confidence intervals and therefore less accurate treatment effect estimates.

It is important to ensure that you enter the RCT results into the statistical software package in a consistent manner; comparative group results are generated, so it is important to make sure that in each case the same group is used as the reference group (i.e. ensure that all RCT results are always presented as group A relative to group B). If RCT data are entered inconsistently, it might look like the RCTs' results differ greatly, when in actual fact they are similar.

When the individual study estimates of effect are relatively consistent and have confidence intervals that overlap (Figure 10.3), it is appropriate to pool results in a meta-analysis. The diamond at the bottom of the plot shows the overall estimate of the treatment effect and the corresponding confidence interval obtained by performing the meta-analysis. The centre of the diamond indicates the point estimate of the effect, and the width of the diamond represents the width of the confidence interval. When estimates vary widely and confidence intervals do not overlap (Figure 10.4), this suggests that the RCTs are too dissimilar and that it may be inappropriate to pool the results in a meta-analysis.

If your data satisfy all of the four criteria related to homogeneity, you are ready to obtain an overall measure of effect by performing a meta-analysis. However, before we move on to discussing how to obtain the **pooled measure of effect**, let's think about what to do if your data don't satisfy all the criteria.

If only some of your included RCTs meet all the criteria related to homogeneity, then it may be sensible to perform a meta-analysis using data from only those RCTs

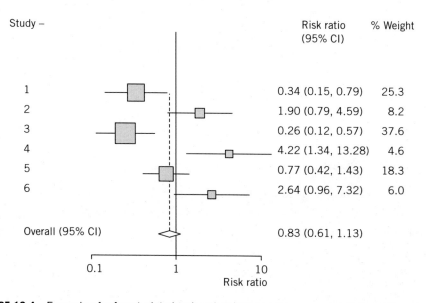

FIGURE 10.4   Example of a forest plot showing that it may not be appropriate to perform a meta-analysis

that do meet these criteria (the base case). If so, you should also carry out a sensitivity analysis by adding in the remaining studies, and re-running your meta-analysis to test the robustness of the results. Similarly, if all your included trials meet most of the criteria, then it may still be sensible to combine them in a meta-analysis. In both cases you must make it clear in your report that all criteria were not met by all the included RCTs and you must fully explain the implications that this may have on your results. If none of your RCTs fulfils any of the criteria (and this is highly probable), performing a meta-analysis would be inappropriate. In this case, combining your data would not be sensible as the overall measure of the effect would be misleading. Under these circumstances the data should be synthesized narratively (see Chapter 7).

Step 2: Justify your decision to conduct (or not conduct) a meta-analysis in your write-up

Whether you decide to perform a meta-analysis or not, it is important that you can justify your decision in your thesis. As previously mentioned, if your data satisfy all four criteria, then you can perform a meta-analysis and obtain an overall measure of effect. However, a meta-analysis is not a required element of a systematic review and, if you choose not to perform one, it is advisable to clearly set out the reasons for this decision. So, what might you write to explain why you have not performed a meta-analysis and how might you describe what you have done instead? The following text provides an example:

> A meta-analysis was not performed. Only a narrative synthesis of the data is presented. The differences across the RCTs, including differences in eligibility criteria, treatment regimens and follow-up times precluded statistical synthesis of the included trial results.

Step 3: Choose an appropriate meta-analysis method

The first mistake people make when conducting a meta-analysis is to simply pool all the data from the individual studies as if they were from one study. If you do this, you fail to preserve the randomization employed in each of the individual studies and you introduce bias and confounding (these concepts are discussed in Chapter 8). When randomized intervention studies are being designed, investigators put considerable effort into ensuring that the two (or more) treatment groups are similar in terms of the participants who will be enrolled. By lumping participants from different RCTs together, you may no longer be comparing like with like; it is therefore important to maintain randomization when combining data from your included studies.

Another common mistake is to simply calculate an arithmetic mean of the treatment effects of the different studies. This approach is inappropriate as it gives all studies equal influence over the size of the overall effect. The results of small studies are generally deemed to be less accurate than results from larger ones; the confidence intervals around the results are usually wider so results are less precise, and smaller studies are also more likely to detect a difference when it does not actually exist. For these reasons, smaller studies are given less weight in a meta-analysis. A meta-analysis needs to include a **weighted average** of the treatment effects whereby the results from larger RCTs take precedence over the results from smaller ones.

A meta-analysis can be performed in two steps. The first is to identify or calculate an effect estimate (relative risk, odds ratio or risk difference for binary data; differences in means for continuous data) for each study. The second step is to calculate the weighted average for this statistic. There are various techniques for calculating the weighted average depending on the effect estimate that is being analysed and the choice of weighting method. The techniques available all take a similar approach and are all derived from the following formula:

$$\text{Weighted average} = \frac{\text{Sum of } (\text{estimate} \times \text{weight of individual study})}{\text{Sum of weights}}$$

There are a number of different methods available for performing a meta-analysis (see Table 10.7 for some of them) and they can be classified into two main models – 'fixed effects' and 'random effects'. The fixed effects model assumes that there is one true effect observed across all studies and that any variability between study results is due simply to chance. In comparison, the random effects model assumes that the true effect varies from study to study but that it is centred on some overall average effect; this approach should not be used when there is assumed to be one true effect observed across all studies, but when there are believed to be some differences between study results that are not due to chance alone.

TABLE 10.7   Different approaches to meta-analysis

Outcome measure	Fixed effects analysis	Random effects analysis
Binary		
Relative risk	Mantel–Haenszel; inverse variance	DerSimonian Laird
Risk difference	Mantel–Haenszel; inverse variance	DerSimonian Laird
Odds ratio	Mantel–Haenszel; inverse variance; Peto	DerSimonian Laird
Continuous		
Mean difference	Inverse variance	Inverse variance
Standardized mean difference	Inverse variance	Inverse variance
Count		
Rate ratio	Inverse variance	Inverse variance
Survival		
Hazard ratio	Inverse variance	Inverse variance

Meta-analysis can be performed using one of a number of computer software packages. One of the most popular software packages for this is RevMan (Review Manager, 2020), the Cochrane software package for preparing and maintaining Cochrane reviews, which is freely available (www.training.cochrane.org/online-learning/core-software-cochrane-reviews/revman). Another widely used statistical software package is STATA, which is not free to download, but may be available through your academic institution. You will be able to perform a meta-analysis using STATA but, unlike when using RevMan, you will not be able to complete all aspects of your systematic review within it.

Step 4: Identify and discuss any heterogeneity in the meta-analysis results

Meta-analyses rely on the fact that the trials included in them are sufficiently similar to allow outcome data to be combined. However, we know that it is inevitable that trials differ in some way or another. In meta-analysis, heterogeneity is a measure of the variability between studies. There are three types of heterogeneity: **clinical heterogeneity**, which is the variability in participants, interventions and outcomes; **methodological heterogeneity**, which is the variability in trial design and quality; and **statistical heterogeneity**, which is the variability between the study results that is more than would be expected due to chance alone. Statistical heterogeneity can occur because of clinical heterogeneity, methodological heterogeneity or both. Throughout the remainder of this chapter, we will refer to statistical heterogeneity simply as heterogeneity.

First of all, you need to examine your forest plot to identify whether there is substantial heterogeneity between studies. If the studies are estimating the same true intervention effect, you would expect their confidence intervals to overlap; if there is poor overlap, this indicates that heterogeneity is present. This eyeballing approach is very subjective and is simply used to give you an initial overview of the level of heterogeneity present. Next, you could use the chi-squared test for heterogeneity to carry out a more formal assessment of heterogeneity. If you are using the RevMan software package (Review Manager, 2020) to undertake your meta-analysis, it will perform this chi-squared test for you. A chi-squared test allows you to assess whether the observed differences in treatment effects are due to chance alone; a low p-value indicates that heterogeneity is present. This test should be used with caution when there are only a few studies being assessed, or when the number of patients recruited to each study is small; under these circumstances, the test is unlikely to detect heterogeneity even if a moderate amount is present. For this reason, a p-value of .1 is often used for determining statistical significance, rather than the typical level of .05. It should also be noted that a non-statistically significant result cannot be taken as evidence of homogeneity. The use of the chi-squared test is also problematic when there are many trials; under these circumstances the test may detect clinically unimportant levels of heterogeneity.

After establishing that heterogeneity is present, you may want to calculate the degree of heterogeneity. This can be measured using the **I^2 statistic** (this can also be calculated in RevMan [Review Manager, 2020]). The I^2 statistic describes the percentage of the total variation across study results that is due to differences between study characteristics rather than chance, and results lie between 0 and 100 per cent. A value of 0 per cent would indicate that no heterogeneity was observed and, as the value increases, the level of heterogeneity increases. As a rough guide, 25 per cent represents low heterogeneity, 50 per cent represents moderate heterogeneity and 75 per cent represents high heterogeneity.

If you identify a large amount of heterogeneity, one way to deal with it is simply to acknowledge the problem and *not* report the results of the meta-analysis. Alternatively, you could present the forest plot but without the pooled effect (i.e. remove the diamond from the plot) to illustrate the different effects across the included intervention studies. However, it is important to ensure that you make it clear to the reader (e.g. your examiner(s)) that you think it is inappropriate to combine the results as they vary considerably and you consider that combining them would result in an invalid overall estimate of the effect.

A third approach may be to report your pooled results but to include a caveat to let the reader know that you have concerns about the reliability of your results. If you decide to do this, note that when there is a large amount of heterogeneity we do not recommend using a **fixed effects meta-analysis** as this invalidates the main assumption of the fixed effects meta-analysis – that is, that there is one underlying true effect measured across all trials. A **random effects meta-analysis** takes account of any unexplained heterogeneity between your studies, but it cannot explain the reasons for heterogeneity. For this reason, a full investigation of heterogeneity is still required.

Subgroups and sensitivity analysis

Heterogeneity is commonly investigated using **subgroup analysis**. Subgroup analyses determine whether different effects are observed in different subgroups of participants. For example, a larger effect may be observed in younger participants compared with the effect observed in older participants. If this is true, and there are substantial differences in the ages of participants in different trials, then this could be one reason for heterogeneity. If authors present subgroup data, you may want to meta-analyse the data for each of the subgroups to examine how the overall effect compares across the different subgroups.

Another, more advanced, way to investigate heterogeneity is to use a statistical technique known as **meta-regression**. This technique adjusts the meta-analysis to take into account factors that are considered to influence the effect, such as age (Cooper, 2010). Alternatively, you may wish to perform sensitivity analyses, including and excluding certain trials from the meta-analysis to test the robustness of the results.

You should think in advance about the specific factors that you will consider when exploring heterogeneity and discuss these factors in your review protocol. If you identify that heterogeneity is present, your results may be criticized because you are looking for reasons to explain the heterogeneity without an a priori rationale.

Step 5: Present and interpret the results of your meta-analysis

The best way to present the results of a meta-analysis is by using a forest plot and you can produce one easily using RevMan (Review Manager, 2020). A forest plot presents the separate results of individual studies and the overall combined estimate of the effect. It is important to label each study (e.g. with author and date). It is also useful to present the percentage weights that have been assigned to each study.

As well as presenting the results visually in a forest plot, you need to provide explanatory text, which summarizes and discusses the results. The overall effect can be interpreted as if it was from an individual study. If the meta-analysis combined binary data, the overall effect could be presented as an odds ratio, risk difference or relative risk; if continuous data were combined, the effect could be presented as a mean difference or standardized mean difference; if time-to-event data were combined, then a hazard ratio could be presented. The case study in Box 10.2 includes further details on presenting and interpreting the results of a forest plot from a meta-analysis.

Box 10.2

Case study: How to present and interpret a forest plot

The plot in Figure 10.5 shows an advantage for group A over group B; the point estimates are all to the left of the vertical axis indicating that all studies favoured group A over group B, and the diamond representing the pooled effect is also to the left of the axis. This advantage can also be seen in the risk ratios reported on the right, which are all less than 1. The pooled result reinforces this (risk ratio = 0.69), and the associated 95 per cent confidence interval suggests a statistically significant advantage for group A over group B as it doesn't contain 1 (95% confidence interval = 0.52 to 0.91). The relative risk of 0.69 means that participants' risk of experiencing an event is reduced by 31 per cent if they are in group A compared with the risk of experiencing an event if they are in group B. The 95 per cent confidence intervals all overlap, suggesting that the degree of heterogeneity is small, but this should be assessed more formally by using a chi-squared test.

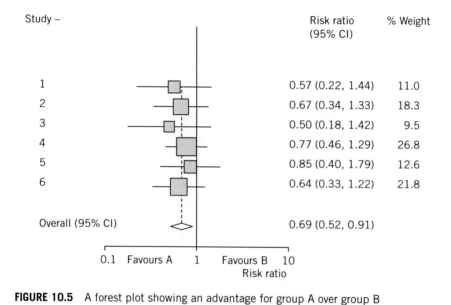

FIGURE 10.5   A forest plot showing an advantage for group A over group B

Alternative routes

This chapter focuses on standard aggregate data meta-analysis methods which can be used to perform pairwise comparisons of data reported in intervention studies. If you are a student who has a keen interest in meta-analysis, we have outlined below some of the more complex methods that you might find in the literature. If you wish to use these methods in your systematic review, we recommend that you seek input from a knowledgeable statistician and/or a methodologist who has prior experience with these methods. You would not be expected to use these methods without support from an expert.

Individual participant data (IPD) meta-analysis

An individual participant data (IPD) meta-analysis is an alternative method to aggregate data meta-analysis. In an aggregate data meta-analysis, summary data obtained from study reports or communication with study authors are synthesized. In an IPD meta-analysis, individual participant-level data from each study are combined in a common dataset; this approach allows for more precise analysis and is considered the 'gold standard' of meta-analytic techniques. There are advantages to conducting an IPD meta-analysis, such as having the option to standardize definitions of outcomes across studies and to consider both the clinical significance of interventions and their statistical significance. An IPD meta-analysis offers more flexibility in terms of the analysis strategy. However, an IPD meta-analysis is substantially more resource intensive and complex than an aggregate data meta-analysis. Obtaining IPD can also be challenging and time-consuming; authors of original studies may be unwilling or unable to share data for the purposes of an IPD meta-analysis and additional data sharing or ethical considerations may apply. If you decide to carry out an IPD meta-analysis, speak to your supervisor(s) early on about the practicalities and relevance of this method to your review and whether you have enough time to complete it.

Network meta-analysis

As an extension to performing comparisons between pairs of interventions, **network meta-analysis** can be used to compare three or more interventions simultaneously. Network meta-analysis incorporates both direct evidence (where interventions are

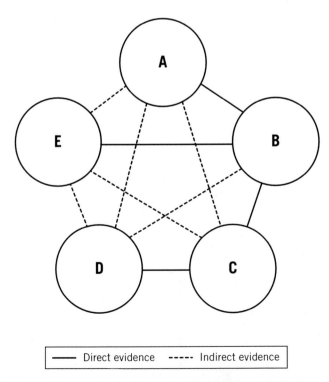

FIGURE 10.6   Example of a network of evidence for interventions A, B, C, D and E

compared within a study) and indirect evidence (where interventions are compared across studies based on a common comparator; see Figure 10.6). A key benefit of network meta-analysis is that it allows effect estimates to be generated for comparisons of interventions that have not been directly compared in existing studies. As with all meta-analyses, network meta-analysis requires the assumption that included studies are similar in terms of important study and participant characteristics that could impact the observed effect estimates.

Final thoughts

This chapter has focused on understanding numerical data from intervention studies and has introduced you to the basic principles of meta-analysis. Remember, a meta-analysis isn't mandatory for a systematic review of quantitative data. If your review includes data from studies other than RCTs, and you are thinking about performing a meta-analysis, then you really should also read Chapter 9 and speak to a statistician and/or your supervisor(s), as there is currently no gold-standard approach for synthesizing data from other study types.

Key points to think about when writing your protocol

- Whether you intend to perform a meta-analysis and how you will decide if it is appropriate to do so
- What kind of outcome data you are likely to find
- What type of effect estimate you will use in your meta-analysis (if appropriate)
- How you will identify and deal with heterogeneity in your meta-analysis (if appropriate)
- Whether you will perform any subgroup analyses or meta-regression and what factors you might adjust for in these analyses (if appropriate)

What an examiner is looking for in your thesis

- Clear interpretation of the results from your included studies
- Full description of whether your included studies meet the criteria for conducting a meta-analysis
- Rationale for undertaking or not undertaking a meta-analysis
- Valid approach used to perform a meta-analysis (if meta-analysis was undertaken)
- Appropriate assessment of heterogeneity (if meta-analysis was undertaken)

Frequently Asked Questions

Question 1: What if my included studies measure the same outcome but not at the same time point?

If your studies measure the same outcome but at different time points, you might want to contact the authors of the studies to ask for more information on a common time point and then use these data in a meta-analysis. If it is not possible to obtain data collected at broadly the same time point for all studies, it would not be appropriate to combine the data in a meta-analysis; you should only combine the data that are measured at broadly the same time point.

Question 2: What if the outcomes are defined differently across the studies (e.g. different definitions of a common primary study outcome)?

If outcomes are defined differently across studies, it is advisable to perform sensitivity analyses whereby studies that define outcomes differently are removed and/or replaced to test the robustness of the overall results.

Question 3: What if the studies I have included in my meta-analysis are of varying quality?

If the studies vary greatly in quality, you might wish to perform a sensitivity analysis. A sensitivity analysis may involve, for example, excluding lower quality results and re-running the meta-analysis. This will test the robustness of the overall results of your original meta-analysis.

Question 4: What if I only found one study?

If you have only identified one suitable study for inclusion in the review, then it will not be possible for you to synthesize your data in a meta-analysis; instead, you should simply present a narrative description of the results of the single study.

Question 5: If I have only two included studies, is it worth conducting a meta-analysis?

A minimum of two studies is required to perform a meta-analysis. However, the accuracy of the meta-analysis results increases with the number of included studies.

So, if you only identify two studies that are appropriate for inclusion, although you can still perform a meta-analysis you will need to explain the resulting limitations when you write up your review.

Question 6: What if the studies report the same outcome but use different effect measures?

If some studies present the outcome using a relative risk and others present the same outcome but using an odds ratio, check the data that are reported and, if possible, calculate the appropriate effect measure yourself. If the study does not provide sufficient data for you to do this, contact the authors and ask for them. Once you have the same effect measure for each study, you can include all of them in a single meta-analysis.

Further Reading and Resources

Borenstein, M., Hedges, L.V., Higgins, J.P.T., & Rothstein, H.R. (2009). *Introduction to meta-analysis*. John Wiley & Sons.

Crombie, I.K., & Davies, H.T. (2009). *What is meta-analysis?* Hayward Medical Communications.

Higgins, J.P.T., Thomas, J., Chandler, J., Cumpston, M., Li, T., Page, M.J., & Welch, V.A. (Eds) (2022). *Cochrane handbook for systematic reviews of interventions* (version 6.3, updated February 2022). https://training.cochrane.org/handbook/current

Lipsey, M.W., & Wilson, D.B. (2001). *Practical meta-analysis*. SAGE Publications.

Moore, R.A., & McQuay, H.J. (2006). *Bandolier's little book of making sense of the medical evidence*. Oxford University Press.

Review Manager (RevMan) Version 5.4 (2020). [Computer program]. Cochrane.

Whitehead, A. (2002). *Meta-analysis of controlled clinical trials* (7th ed.). John Wiley & Sons.

Understanding and Synthesizing Qualitative Data

M. Gemma Cherry, Helen Smith, Elizabeth Perkins
and Angela Boland

This chapter will help you to...

- Understand the principles of qualitative evidence synthesis and how these differ from the principles of quantitative evidence synthesis

- Define a review question for a qualitative evidence synthesis

- Understand the different approaches to synthesizing qualitative data

- Recognize challenges specific to qualitative evidence synthesis

Introduction

Since you are reading this chapter, you are likely thinking about conducting a system-atic review of qualitative evidence. Here, we revisit the principles outlined in some of the previous chapters but place emphasis on systematically reviewing qualitative evidence. As such, it's important that you've scanned the other chapters so that you understand the principles of systematic reviewing. First, we outline why we think **qualitative evidence synthesis** is important and discuss how the steps can differ from those involved in **quantitative evidence synthesis**. We discuss different methods of qualitative evidence synthesis before outlining some of their challenges, rewards and pitfalls. We conclude with frequently asked questions.

Why should I carry out a systematic review of qualitative evidence?

Historically, systematic reviews of the effectiveness of healthcare interventions have dominated (e.g. see reviews produced by Cochrane), largely because decision mak-ers need to know what works so that they can allocate scarce resources effectively. However, as interventions become more complex, and evidence-based policy making becomes the 'norm', the demand for systematic reviews of other types of evidence has grown. While systematic reviews of quantitative evidence generally determine whether something works (or not), systematic reviews of qualitative evidence allow *how* something works to be explored and allow researchers to better understand the lived experiences of participants. Qualitative evidence syntheses typically ask ques-tions that go beyond 'Does this intervention work?' by, for example, asking, 'Why and how does this intervention or policy work?', 'How acceptable is this intervention to end users?' or 'What are the barriers and facilitators to implementation of an inter-vention?' (Lavis, 2009). This can lead to a greater understanding of the sensitive issues that researchers frequently address and can provide rich data relating to the impact of a condition, intervention or policy on the lived experiences and feelings of those involved in research studies. Qualitative evidence synthesis can also allow for gaps in the literature base to be identified, and meta-level **themes**, theories, explanations, insights and/or conclusions to be developed.

There are several reasons why we encourage students to carry out a systematic review of qualitative evidence, not least because it provides an excellent opportunity for students to learn and then apply the principles of systematic reviewing. If your topic area of interest lends itself to qualitative evidence synthesis, we encourage you to go ahead. It will be an excellent learning experience for you, both as a student and as a researcher.

Differences between qualitative and quantitative evidence synthesis

Systematic reviews of quantitative evidence generally follow a series of distinct steps which we discuss in detail throughout this book. These steps are clear and well tested and are recognized as the gold standard for systematic reviews of quantitative evidence. However, these steps leave little room for interpretation and are mainly used in reviews of clinical effectiveness where the conclusions often take the form of 'A is better at treating X than B but isn't as good as C'.

Researchers conducting systematic reviews of qualitative evidence also follow a series of distinct steps, but these steps are less prescriptive than those required for systematic reviews of quantitative evidence, particularly with respect to quality assessment, analysis and synthesis of data. This is, in part, reflective of the breadth of qualitative philosophies, methodologies and methods currently available, which we have briefly summarized in Table 11.1.

There has been considerable debate about the feasibility and acceptability of synthesizing qualitative evidence derived from different theoretical perspectives and

TABLE 11.1   Common qualitative philosophies, methodologies and methods of analysis

Term	Definition
Phenomenological studies	Phenomenology is sometimes considered both a philosophical perspective and a research approach. It focuses on people's subjective experiences and interpretations of the world. These experiences are called lived experiences. The goal of phenomenological studies is to describe the meaning that these experiences hold for each person. In phenomenological research, people are asked to describe their experiences as they perceive them, most commonly either through an interview or through written accounts. To understand someone's lived experience, the researcher is required to identify what they expect to discover and then deliberately put aside their ideas; this process is called bracketing. Only when the researcher puts aside their own ideas about the phenomenon is it possible to see the experience from the eyes of the person who lived the experience.
Ethnographic studies	Ethnography has been the most common research approach used by anthropologists to study people all over the world. Ethnographic studies involve the collection and analysis of data about different groups or cultures. Ethnography can be defined as the systematic process of observing, detailing, describing, documenting and analysing particular patterns of a culture (or subculture). In ethnographic research, the researcher frequently lives with the people or groups being studied and becomes a part of their culture. This is called participant observation. Data are also collected through formal and informal interviews. Data collection and analysis occur simultaneously. As understanding of the data occurs, new questions emerge. The end purpose of ethnography is the development of cultural theories.

(Continued)

TABLE 11.1   (Continued)

Term	Definition
Grounded theory studies	Grounded theory is a qualitative research approach developed by two sociologists, Glaser and Strauss (1967). Grounded theory involves the generation of theory through the collection and analysis of data. Data are gathered in naturalistic settings and primarily involve observation and interviews. Data collection and data analysis occur simultaneously using a process called constant comparison. This means that as data are gathered, they are compared with the data previously gathered. Grounded theory involves the coding of data using concepts. These codes and concepts are reviewed and refined as data collection progresses. As data are gathered, adjustments are made to the theory to allow for the interpretation of new data that are obtained. There are a number of key theorists who are associated with grounded theory but they adopt different approaches to doing grounded theory.
Action research studies	Action research became popular in the 1940s because of the work of Kurt Lewin (1946). Action research aims to improve practice and involves studying the effects of the action that was taken. Solutions are sought to practice problems. Action research does not aim to generalize the findings of the study. In action research, the implementation of solutions occurs as an integral part of the research process.
Discourse analysis	Discourse analysis is a research approach used across a range of disciplines in the humanities and social sciences, including linguistics, education, sociology, psychology, social policy and geography. Discourse analysis encompasses a number of approaches to analysing different forms of communication, including written, spoken, visual or sign language. All approaches to discourse analysis look beyond the sentence and are primarily, although not exclusively, concerned with naturally occurring language use. Within discourse analysis, the different approaches reflect different theoretical perspectives on the nature of language. In some approaches, language plays a key role in creating and shaping identities and social relations; it is not seen as neutral. Discourse analysis draws on perspectives such as applied linguistics, conversation analysis, pragmatics, rhetoric, stylistics and text linguistics.

analytical approaches (Dixon-Woods et al., 2005). Some authors argue that when synthesizing data, the original studies should share similar methodologies, while others take the more pragmatic view that even data from diverse studies can be combined (Dixon-Woods et al., 2005). The main take-home message is that there is no standard approach for synthesizing qualitative research. This means you have the freedom to decide on how best to analyse your data. On the flip side, this also means you have to defend your chosen analysis technique and make it very clear in your write-up why you've chosen one method over another. Five researchers setting out to synthesize qualitative research on the same topic could potentially ask five different questions of the evidence, and therefore derive five different sets of conclusions depending on each researcher's choice of question, analysis, synthesis method and **theoretical standpoint**. Reviews of qualitative evidence may provide richer conclusions than reviews of quantitative data due to the potentially greater depth of analysis and/or depth of meaning and understanding contained within qualitative data; but be warned, this type of synthesis requires the researcher to be reflective and flexible in their approach.

Do I follow the same steps as in a quantitative review?

If you're thinking, 'Hang on, I've just trawled through the whole book and now you're telling me the principles differ between reviews of qualitative and quantitative evidence!', then don't worry, you haven't wasted your time. There are several common key steps involved in conducting a systematic review, be it of quantitative or qualitative evidence, which we have outlined in detail in the other chapters of this book. The key differences lie in data extraction, quality assessment and data synthesis. However, if you have just picked up this book and flipped to this chapter without reading the previous chapters, then *stop*! Make yourself a drink, get comfy on the sofa and read the book from the beginning. You'll understand more about what's covered in this chapter if you already know the general principles of systematic reviewing.

The main principles of systematically reviewing qualitative evidence map onto those of reviewing quantitative evidence and are outlined in Box 11.1.

Box 11.1

Main principles of qualitative and quantitative evidence synthesis

Step	Review of qualitative evidence	Review of quantitative evidence
1	Plan review	
2	Perform scoping searches, define review question and inclusion and exclusion criteria, and write protocol	
3	Literature searching	
4	Screening titles and abstracts	
5	Obtaining papers	
6	Selecting full-text papers	
7	Theoretical standpoint and synthesis plan	Data extraction

(Continued)

Step	Review of qualitative evidence	Review of quantitative evidence
8	Data extraction and quality assessment	Quality assessment
9	Analysis and synthesis (qualitative)	Analysis and synthesis (quantitative)
10	Writing up, editing and disseminating	

As outlined in Box 11.1, there are ten key steps in a systematic review of qualitative evidence. Most of these steps will be the same regardless of whether you're reviewing qualitative or quantitative data. However, some will require additional consideration, and so we'll discuss each step from a qualitative evidence synthesis perspective, highlighting where the steps differ from those involved in a systematic review of quantitative evidence.

Ten key steps in a systematic review of qualitative evidence

Step 1: Planning your review

The first step is to consider the time, resources and tools available to you. Chapter 2 provides a comprehensive guide to this step – we recommend that you (re-)read this chapter before going any further. It's worth bearing in mind that some stages in a qualitative evidence synthesis may take longer than if you were conducting a systematic review of quantitative evidence, so don't forget to factor this into your timelines.

Step 2: Performing scoping searches, defining your review question and inclusion and exclusion criteria, and writing your protocol

Chapter 3 discusses the importance of establishing a clear review question and lays out a number of steps for you to follow. The main additional points that you need to consider when conducting a systematic review of qualitative evidence are:

- Can my review question be answered using qualitative data?
- Have I developed a set of inclusion and exclusion criteria applicable to qualitative evidence synthesis?

You may begin your review with what you believe is a clear question. For instance, you may want to know about the experiences of older adults living in France who identify as homeless. Or you may want to find out more about the views of parents on the proposed government changes to pre-school funding in England. They may seem quite straightforward questions, but very few qualitative research studies will have asked these exact questions. This is where scoping searches prove useful. Scoping studies can be used to help you understand the current state of the literature and evaluate the suitability of your question. Alternatively, as you carry out your scoping searches, you may identify that there are other, more important, issues within each of these topics, and you may decide that you want to modify your question and follow where the research leads. This is a very acceptable qualitative approach but, be aware, it can often take up a great deal of time.

The second task is the development of your inclusion and exclusion criteria. While systematic reviews of quantitative evidence clearly define inclusion and exclusion criteria, often by using mnemonics such as PICOSS (Participants, Intervention, Comparison, Outcomes, Study Design and Setting), these inclusion criteria are not all relevant to systematic reviews of qualitative evidence. Rather than trying to devise a PICOSS table, we recommend that you think of your inclusion criteria in terms of **PICo: P**opulation, phenomena of **I**nterest (which may be either a condition or an intervention) and the **Co**ntext (Aromataris et al., 2020).

Conceptualizing the components of a review idea or topic area in terms of PICo helps you to plan what kind of studies you intend to include in your review without being so specific that you risk excluding a potentially relevant publication. This approach also provides your supervisor(s), examiner(s) and/or other readers with a significant amount of information about the focus, scope and applicability of your review. Table 11.2 provides two examples of PICo tables for qualitative evidence synthesis.

TABLE 11.2   Example PICo tables

Review question	What are the experiences of older adults living in France who identify as homeless?	What are the views of parents on the proposed government changes to pre-school funding in England?
P	Adults aged 60 years or older who have experienced homelessness within the last two years	Parents with infants (younger than compulsory school age)
I	Experiences and challenges of homelessness	Views on governmental policy changes designed to increase '30 free hour's provision
Co	France	England

Several alternatives to PICo exist and include **ECLIPS(E)**, developed to address questions relating to health policy and management; **SPICE**, developed specifically for questions in the field of library and information services (Wildrige & Bell, 2002); and **SPIDER**, developed specifically for qualitative evidence synthesis (Cooke et al., 2012). These three common approaches are summarized in Table 11.3. A paper by Booth includes a more comprehensive review of question formulation frameworks for qualitative evidence synthesis (Booth et al., 2019).

TABLE 11.3   Alternatives to PICo

ECLIPS(E)		SPICE		SPIDER	
E	Expectation: What do you want to find out?	S	Setting	S	Sample
C	Client group: Who are you interested in?	P	Perspective: Whose views are you interested in?	P I	Phenomenon of Interest
L	Location	I	Intervention: What is the phenomenon of interest?		
I	Impact: What's changed as a result of the policy/management change?	C	Comparison: What are you comparing the intervention with?	D	Design
P	Professionals	E	Evaluation: What was the result?	E	Evaluation
S	SErvice			R	Research type

When developing and refining your review question, we recommend that you follow the principles set out in Chapter 3 and modify your inclusion and exclusion criteria accordingly. However, be aware that it can take longer to develop a review question for a systematic review of qualitative evidence than for a systematic review of quantitative evidence. Amend your timelines accordingly and begin this process with patience and curiosity. A final word of advice – setting out your plans in a protocol is a great way to organize your thoughts (and your time). We discuss how to write and structure a protocol in Chapter 4, so we recommend that you revisit that chapter and follow the structure outlined in Table 4.1 when writing your protocol.

Step 3: Literature searching

Chapter 5 talks you through how to search for evidence. The general principles are the same when searching for qualitative studies. However, you need to think carefully about how you will find studies that have addressed your review question. A specific, detailed and complex search strategy may not be as helpful here as in a review of quantitative evidence. It might be better to consider combining a number of free-text words relating to your PICo, ECLIPS(E), SPICE or SPIDER table, using AND, OR and NOT. Using a broader and less precise search strategy may yield more titles and abstracts for you to examine during screening. This, in turn, means that you may have to look at more full-text papers than if you were conducting a review of quantitative evidence with very narrow and tightly defined parameters. However, this broader approach allows you to identify papers that you might not otherwise have found. It's also worth searching several databases. For health and social care reviews, we recommend that you start by searching CINAHL (Cumulative Index to Nursing and Allied Health Literature), as this database has indexed qualitative studies more completely and for longer than other databases (Booth, 2016; Flemming & Briggs, 2007). Other databases to consider, depending on your topic area, are MEDLINE (medicine-related disciplines), PsycINFO (psychology-related disciplines), Education Resources Information Center (ERIC; education-related disciplines), Social Sciences Abstracts, Sociological Abstracts and Web of Science (which includes the Social Sciences Citation Index). Have a look at Table 5.2 for more ideas. Sometimes qualitative researchers can be creative with the keywords they use in publication titles, so you might wish to spend time, before you start searching, familiarizing yourself with key subject headings and index terms that are relevant to your review question.

When formulating your search strategy, we recommend that, in addition to including terms that reflect your topic, you add generic terms (such as 'qualitative' or 'findings'); these can be organized under the abbreviation ESCAPADE (see Table 11.4). Don't forget to supplement your enquiries with searches of the reference lists of retrieved papers, hand searches of specific journals and use of Internet search engines (e.g. Google Scholar). As with all searches, there will be trial and error, but it is worth investing time to ensure that your searches have the appropriate balance of sensitivity and specificity (as mentioned in Chapter 5).

TABLE 11.4 ESCAPADE

E	Exploratory methods – Include methodological search terms, such as 'focus group', 'grounded theory' or 'action research'
S	Software – Include search terms related to the software researchers may have used to analyse their data, such as 'NVivo' or 'Nudist' or 'MaxQDA'
C	Citations – Include key references, both in your specific research area and more globally in the qualitative research arena
A	Application – Consider searching terms related to the wider application of potentially relevant studies, such as 'ethnography' or 'psychology'
P	Phenomenon – Include search terms related to the phenomenon of interest, such as 'perceptions', 'attitudes', 'viewpoints', 'standpoints'
A	Approaches – Consider searching for different methodological approaches, such as ethnography
D	Data – Think how researchers may have 'labelled' their data in their paper, and include terms such as 'stories', 'narratives', 'themes'
E	Experiences – Similarly, consider how researchers may have conceptualized participants' experiences, using search terms such as 'encounters'

Reproduced with permission from Andrew Booth, ScHARR, University of Sheffield, UK

This is a good time to discuss how many studies you might need to include in a systematic review of qualitative evidence. One approach is to draw upon methods from primary qualitative research – search only until you have retrieved sufficient studies to demonstrate that any additional studies do not provide any new information (i.e. you have, in qualitative terms, reached saturation). Another approach would be to take the standard systematic review approach – that is, to carry out a comprehensive and exhaustive search of the literature to identify all relevant evidence pertaining to your review question. Neither approach can be considered the 'right way', although purposive or **theoretical sampling** are increasingly recognized as appropriate and feasible approaches when undertaking qualitative evidence synthesis, provided that the included studies portray all likely insights into the topic (Hannes & Macaitis, 2012). It is important to decide on your approach to searching, describe it clearly and, in the 'Discussion' section of your thesis where you discuss the limitations of your review, explain how your approach to searching might have impacted on the conduct of the research and, importantly, on your findings and your conclusions. It is worth thinking about how you might deal with this issue before you start your review. Discuss your plans with your supervisor(s) and include a section in your protocol about how you will search for and include studies in your final review.

Step 4: Screening titles and abstracts

If your approach to searching for qualitative evidence is broad and inclusive, then you will likely have lots of studies to sift through at this stage. As discussed in Chapter 6, creating and piloting your screening and selection tool, and applying your inclusion and exclusion criteria, can take time so factor this into your plans. Compared with a review of quantitative evidence, it is likely to be more difficult to spot potentially relevant papers at this stage because some of the titles of qualitative papers may be conceptual and/or relevant findings may be housed within broad qualitative or mixed-methods studies. It's important to pay close attention to the abstracts and titles of potentially relevant studies and be inclusive rather than exclusive to maximize your chances of obtaining relevant full-text papers.

Step 5: Obtaining papers

It is likely that you will obtain more papers than your peers who are conducting reviews of quantitative evidence. Don't worry. There isn't a limit on the number of full-text papers that you can obtain. Just make sure that your institution has sufficient budget to pay for your inter-library loans and that you have allowed sufficient time for this part of your review.

Step 6: Selecting full-text papers

If you are being inclusive during screening, you may have more full-text papers to read through than your peers who are conducting reviews of quantitative evidence. Take your time. Read each paper carefully to identify all relevant data and, using your inclusion and exclusion criteria, make a decision about its applicability to your review question. Factor in an appropriate amount of time for this key task. Usually, this step is carried out by two people independently to bring rigour to the process. If your institution permits co-working, then you may find that it's possible to work with another student who is also conducting qualitative evidence synthesis. Ideally, the two of you should sift through the full-text papers that have made it through the title/abstract screening process. You should each decide which full-text papers meet your inclusion criteria, noting the reasons for excluding any studies as you go along (more on this in Chapter 6). You should meet to compare your decisions and discuss any disagreements, seeking arbitration from your supervisor(s) if you are unable to reach a consensus on whether a study should be included in or excluded from your review.

Step 7: Determining your theoretical standpoint and synthesis plan

Now you've got a final list of your included studies, it's important to consider your theoretical standpoint and your synthesis plan. Your theoretical standpoint reflects the prior conceptual frameworks and ideas that you bring to the synthesis process and the particular 'lens' you will apply when examining and synthesizing data. Your approach must be articulated before you start quality assessing studies, extracting data or producing data tables, because synthesis of qualitative data needs to be based on a defined philosophical stance (Estabrooks et al., 1994). Ring and colleagues (2011) discuss this in detail but essentially, in qualitative evidence synthesis, you have to choose your analysis method before you start because it will influence the data you extract, how you look at your data and how you draw conclusions from your data.

Insomuch as there are many ways to analyse primary data (see Table 11.1), there are also many methods to synthesize qualitative evidence. If you search the Internet using the term 'qualitative evidence synthesis', you'll likely find the terms **'qualitative meta-narrative'**, **'qualitative meta-aggregation'** and **'qualitative meta-summary'**, amongst others. There are about 20 different approaches to qualitative evidence synthesis (see Barnett-Page & Thomas, 2009; Dixon-Woods et al., 2005; Flemming & Noyes, 2021), each of which refers to a slightly different approach. The plethora of terms masks the fact that there are some basic similarities across the different approaches. In fact, many synthesis methods draw on established approaches used in primary qualitative data analysis, such as **constant comparison, thematic**

analysis and descriptive and explanatory accounts. In contrast to quantitative data synthesis, qualitative synthesis can appear to be very complex and confusing. In fact, students often ask us how they should synthesize their qualitative data. Broadly speaking, methods of qualitative evidence synthesis can be categorized into **integrative approaches** (also known as aggregative approaches) and **interpretative approaches**. When conducting integrative syntheses, data from primary studies are considered comparable and therefore suitable for aggregation. Integrative syntheses summarize data where the concepts and themes are already quite well defined or specified. For example, in our review of health system barriers and facilitators to the uptake of interventions to prevent malaria among pregnant women (Hill et al., 2013), the key concepts (health system barriers and facilitators, interventions to prevent malaria and pregnant women) had already been clearly defined up front. As such, we weren't concerned with developing these concepts and categories but rather used these existing concepts and categories to extract, describe and summarize data from multiple studies. As you can see from this example, integrative syntheses are therefore **deductive** in their approach – that is, they make use of a predetermined framework designed to organize data.

In contrast, interpretative syntheses are concerned with generating concepts and then developing theories that link together concepts and are grounded in the findings of the included qualitative studies. When conducting interpretative syntheses, concepts and categories are not fixed in advance; instead, it is the purpose of the review to identify them. In this way, interpretative syntheses take an **inductive approach**, where the structure or framework for organizing the data develops as the synthesis progresses.

Table 11.5 displays the most common types of integrative and interpretative qualitative synthesis methods, many of which are adaptations of methods used to analyse primary qualitative data. There is considerable overlap in the methods, so they are not completely distinct approaches. For example, most integrative syntheses include some interpretation, and most interpretative syntheses include an element of integration. Along this spectrum from integrative to interpretative, methods that are more integrative include **framework synthesis, thematic synthesis**, meta-aggregation and meta-summary while those that are more interpretative include **critical interpretative synthesis**, grounded theory, **meta-ethnography** and **meta-study**.

When deciding on a method for synthesizing qualitative evidence, it is important to keep in mind that there is no single correct approach. In many published syntheses, reviewers often appear to choose the method based solely on familiarity and fit with their theoretical standpoint (Lockwood et al., 2015). This is not ideal, as the method is driving the question rather than the other way around. Rather than choosing your method of synthesis on the basis of your familiarity or that of your supervisor(s) with the method, it is better to make an informed decision based on: a) your review question; b) the time, resources and expertise available to you; c) the type and availability of data that you will be reviewing; and d) the anticipated output or synthesis and what it will be used for.

TABLE 11.5   Methods of qualitative evidence synthesis

Method	Outline	Type of synthesis	Seminal references
Framework synthesis	Originates from framework analysis – a structured and transparent method of analysing primary qualitative data. Consists of five stages: *familiarization* with ideas about the topic; *selection of an initial framework* of concepts and themes (e.g. established theory, conceptual framework or logic model); *indexing* – extracting data using the framework; *charting* – constructing charts to map the features of each theme or topic area identified; *mapping and interpretation* – further interrogation of the data.	Integrative	Brunton et al. (2020); Oliver et al. (2008)
Grounded theory synthesis	Based on the well-established primary research method of grounded theory, where theory is inductively derived through the concurrent collection and analysis of data. Constant comparison is the most widely used element of grounded theory and, in a synthesis, it is used to compare new categories with existing ones and relate them to the emerging theory. Grounded theory synthesis takes primary research to a higher-order, more abstract level.	Interpretative	Eaves (2001); Kearney (1988)
Meta-ethnography	A method for combining participant findings and author interpretations from primary ethnographic studies to produce new meaning or theoretical understanding. A meta-ethnography produces a 'higher-order' interpretation and often produces explanatory theory. It is one of the most widely adopted methods of qualitative data synthesis.	Interpretative	Britten et al. (2002); Noblit and Hare (1988)
Meta-study	Meta-study comprises three components – meta-data analysis (analysis of findings), meta-method (analysis of methods) and meta-theory (analysis of theory). The idea behind this approach is to scrutinize the findings and methods and explore the theoretical assumptions across the included studies. The synthesis aims to develop a new interpretation and/or new or overarching theory based on the three components.	Interpretative	Paterson et al. (2001)

(Continued)

TABLE 11.5   (Continued)

Method	Outline	Type of synthesis	Seminal references
Qualitative meta-aggregation	A pragmatic and process-driven approach that avoids re-interpretation and instead presents the findings of included studies accurately and as intended by the original authors. Meta-aggregation assembles the conclusions of primary studies (however reported) and pools them on the basis of similarity in meaning; it is analogous and predicated on meta-analysis. The output tends to be generalizable recommendations for policy and practice.	Integrative	Lockwood et al. (2015)
Qualitative meta-narrative	An interpretative approach to qualitative data synthesis, which allows for synthesis of findings from research containing many different theories arising from many different disciplines and study designs. Often used to explore a topic by highlighting the contrasting and complementary ways in which researchers have studied the same or a similar topic.	Integrative and interpretative	Greenhalgh et al. (2005)
Qualitative meta-summary	A relatively new approach to qualitative evidence synthesis, qualitative meta-summary is an aggregative method whereby findings from individual studies are accumulated and summarized rather than transformed into a higher-order theory or interpretation. The approach produces a 'map' of the content of included qualitative studies and attempts to 'quantify' the frequency of each finding, even going as far as calculating 'effect sizes'.	Integrative	Sandelowski et al. (2007)
Textual narrative synthesis	An approach to qualitative evidence synthesis that can be used to combine different types of evidence. Rather than identifying concepts or themes, textual narrative synthesis prepares narrative summaries of included studies. Typically the study characteristics, design, methods and findings are reported in a standardized way in tables so that commonalities and differences among studies can be identified.	Integrative	Lucas et al. (2007)
Thematic synthesis	An approach to qualitative evidence synthesis that borrows from methods used to analyse primary research. Developed by reviewers at the Institute of Education in London, thematic synthesis has been applied to reviews of acceptability and appropriateness of health interventions. In thematic synthesis, codes are identified inductively, and constantly compared and regrouped into themes. Descriptive themes are further developed into analytical themes, similarly to higher-order interpretation in meta-ethnography.	Integrative and interpretative	Thomas and Harden (2008)

How do I choose my qualitative synthesis method?

Considering the type of question you wish to answer is a good place to start. As you can see from the information in Table 11.6, within the field of healthcare, some reviews of qualitative evidence ask questions about health-related behaviours or experiences of illness. To answer these questions, it may be important to identify concepts and metaphors relating to behaviours and experiences of ill health. As such, meta-ethnography is commonly used as it allows for the development of theories or hypotheses of health behaviour for further testing. Other qualitative reviews ask questions relating to the appropriateness or acceptability of interventions. Such reviews generally include studies of people's views or perspectives and tend to use thematic synthesis to identify descriptive (and sometimes analytical) themes across multiple studies. Some review questions are concerned with the implementation of interventions or policies. For example, if a lot is already known about the types of barriers and facilitators to implementation, framework synthesis could be used, which permits reviewers to extract and synthesize data in line with existing concepts or themes.

TABLE 11.6   Examples of different types of synthesis according to the review question

Review aim	Example review question	Synthesis or analysis method
To understand health-related behaviours or experiences, or responses to illness	What factors are considered important by patients, caregivers and healthcare providers in contributing to antiretroviral medication adherence? What factors underpin recognition and response to symptoms of meningitis in children aged under five years?	Meta-ethnography
To explore the need, appropriateness or acceptability of interventions or policies	What are menstruators' views of oral contraceptives? What are primary school children's perspectives of interventions to promote school attendance?	Thematic synthesis
To identify factors influencing implementation of interventions or policies	What barriers and facilitators affect implementation of educational interventions to promote engagement with climate change initiatives?	Framework synthesis

Second, you might wish to consider the time, resources and expertise available. Some interpretative methods (such as meta-ethnography) are time-consuming as they involve moving from description to re-interpretation of data across multiple studies; these methods also require expertise or at least familiarity with ethnographic research methods, and/or knowledge of the topic area. Thematic synthesis, framework synthesis and meta-aggregation are more integrative and can be less time-consuming.

Third, consider the type of data that you will be reviewing. Rich or thick accounts of findings (often derived from anthropological or ethnographic studies) will generally sustain interpretative synthesis using meta-ethnography or grounded theory, whereas studies that report thin or largely descriptive data may be more suited to aggregative approaches such as thematic synthesis, framework synthesis or meta-aggregation.

Finally, think about the output you expect to produce and how you anticipate it being used. For example, the output of some **integrative reviews** (thematic synthesis, framework synthesis) is more relevant to policy makers or those developing and implementing interventions than more interpretative reviews, which produce more complex and conceptual outputs (e.g. meta-ethnography, grounded theory, critical interpretative synthesis; Barnett-Page & Thomas, 2009; Thomas & Harden, 2008) that require practitioners to interpret relevance to their own context. This is unlikely to be the deciding factor for you as a postgraduate student, but it's worth considering, especially if you plan to publish your systematic review in a peer-reviewed academic journal (see Chapter 14).

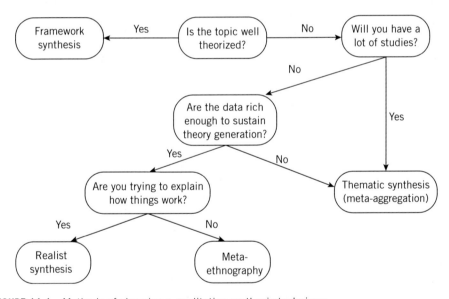

FIGURE 11.1   Methods of choosing a qualitative synthesis technique

Adapted with permission from a resource by Andrew Booth, University of Sheffield

Whatever approach to synthesis you decide to use, you need to ensure that you provide the reader with a clear overview of the method and your reasons for choosing it. You must take care not to break the first 'golden rule' of qualitative evidence synthesis: never violate the philosophical foundations (i.e. paradigm) of the primary research included in your review (Sandelowski & Barroso, 2007). We won't go into detail about the different approaches available as there are many excellent books and sources about each qualitative synthesis method; see the 'Further Reading and Resources' section at the end of this chapter. Consult Figure 11.1 and read up on your chosen approach *before* you attempt to carry out any form of data extraction or synthesis. Speak to your supervisor(s) and make sure that you don't make decisions about your method of analysis for the wrong reasons. Examples of poorly thought-out reasons for choosing a synthesis method are displayed in Box 11.2.

Box 11.2

Poorly thought-out reasons for choosing a qualitative synthesis method

- Assuming a technique is correct because it was the one used most frequently in the literature you have read
- Deciding on the technique used by a former student because they had experienced few problems and had passed their degree
- Choosing a method that was widely discussed at a conference you attended
- Deciding against one method because you know someone who had a bad experience using it
- Choosing a particular technique because your supervisor(s) or peers told you to

Step 8: Data extraction, data presentation and quality assessment

The next step is to extract and present data from your included studies. You also need to assess and tabulate the methodological quality of your included studies.

Data extraction and presentation

There are commonalities between data extraction for qualitative and quantitative evidence syntheses; namely, you must ensure that you provide the reader with a clear overview of the studies that you have included, their similarities and differences, and your view of their findings. We recommend that you revisit Chapter 7 and re-familiarize yourself with the principles of data extraction. There are some additional considerations with respect to data extraction from qualitative studies, which we summarize here. You must always ensure that your data extraction is tailored to your synthesis approach, theoretical standpoint and the aim of your review.

Irrespective of your synthesis approach, you must identify and present key descriptive information from each study. Some simple headings to use in your 'Study Characteristics' table are:

- Author(s)
- Date of publication
- Country
- Study setting
- Sampling approach
- Data collection methods

Extracting this information in a standardized way allows you to write a short paragraph (usually at the beginning of the 'Results' section of your thesis) describing any important overall trends or patterns identified from the studies included in your review.

Next, you need to decide which data to extract to help you answer your review question. For integrative reviews, it is usual to extract data (or themes) reported in the 'Results' section of your included studies and which are supported by direct participant quotes. Interpretative reviews tend to take a more inclusive approach, and reviewers extract any and all data that help to address the question, including author interpretations located in the 'Discussion' section.

How you extract and collate data from the included studies will differ depending on your approach to synthesis. For aggregative reviews (e.g. framework synthesis, **textual narrative synthesis** or thematic synthesis), key concepts and themes may already be quite well defined, so you should identify these within each study and summarize them as a whole. Specifically, in framework synthesis, you may begin with a highly structured table containing the concepts, issues and themes that are known to relate to your question. For example, in a review of barriers and facilitators to community distribution of misoprostol (Smith et al., 2016), barriers were generally well known and were documented within an existing framework of possible factors affecting implementation of health system interventions. The reviewers therefore used this framework to systematically extract findings relating to knowledge, skills and attitudes of healthcare providers, acceptability among recipients of care, health service delivery factors and factors relating to the health system and political context. For other types of integrative review, you may begin with a small number of known concepts and themes, which you can then add to as you become familiar with the studies and identify additional concepts, themes, ideas or findings.

Conversely, an interpretative approach will require a greater level of immersion in the findings of included studies. For example, when conducting a meta-ethnography, begin as if you were analysing primary data – that is, by familiarizing yourself with the findings sections of the studies, reading and re-reading and making notes about possible themes and concepts as you go. Continuously and iteratively revise this initial list of inductively derived themes as you read through your included studies. This is analogous to constant comparison in primary data analysis – where themes and concepts in one paper are compared to those in other papers. Ideally, you want to reach a point where all the studies have been included in the analysis and no new themes arise. This list of themes can then be used as a framework against which to extract data from each study. In meta-ethnography, sometimes a distinction is made between first-order themes (findings usually reported in the 'Results' section) and second-order themes (derived from authors' interpretations, and often found in the 'Discussion' or 'Conclusions' sections). However, increasingly, this distinction is seen to be less important as all reported findings are a product of authors' interpretations.

Irrespective of synthesis approach, there are key data extraction challenges which you would be wise to consider:

- *Transparency*. However you decide to extract and collate data, it must be systematic and transparent, and you should be able to describe the process in detail in your final write-up. You need to maintain an audit trail between the included studies, data extraction and synthesis of the findings.
- *Contextual information*. Extract and preserve information about contextual factors from the included studies to help explain differences between studies. This information is most useful when comparing studies against each other to detect patterns within themes. You can look for explicit differences between studies in relation to, for example, geographical location, socio-economic conditions, participant groups or type of intervention (if relevant).
- *Sufficient data*. There is an assumption that you will be able to find sufficient data to extract from the studies included in your review. However, poor quality reporting (e.g. lack of supporting quotes and/or thin description of themes and data) may limit the contribution of data from individual studies.
- *Internal consistency*. Pay attention, just as you would in primary analysis, to whether the extracted data actually relate to your review question, and make sure that the data you extract clearly illustrate the theme and contribute to some aspect of your review question. It is quite easy to become distracted by interesting but less relevant findings in the included studies. For this reason, consider having another reviewer independently extract or cross-check some or all your extracted data.
- *Authenticity*. It is important, especially for more interpretative reviews where concepts and themes are arrived at inductively, that you check that the themes you identify and decide to report on in your synthesis are actually developed from data in the included studies and not from your own armchair theorizing.

- *Iteration.* Data extraction is a necessary part of the synthesis process but extracted data do not constitute the final product of the synthesis. Rather, data provide the basis for summarizing, interpreting, reshaping and theorizing (i.e. the creative part of making meaning out of the data). In interpretative reviews, this process is likely to be iterative, as you move from initial themes and extracted data into a more distilled version that considers how the themes are interrelated. It is likely you will move back and forth between the individual studies, extracted data and the emerging model or theory. Do not do this in isolation; perhaps discuss this with your supervisor(s) and/or peers before you choose any final overarching model or hypothesis.

We have provided you with the basics to help you get going with data extraction, but you'll find more insight into the data extraction process for different types of review in the 'Further Reading and Resources' section at the end of this chapter. Similarly, how you choose to present these data is, to some extent, up to you; we recommend that you have a read around your chosen approach, take a look at other systematic reviews that have analysed qualitative data using your chosen synthesis method and explore how other authors have presented their data.

Quality assessment

The data extraction process, and therefore the overall synthesis, is dependent on the quality of the reporting in your included studies. Often, through quality assessment, you will identify weaknesses in how sampling, data analysis and the methods used to enhance trustworthiness were reported. You need to assess the quality of your included studies, but whether you do this before or after data extraction is up to you. You might decide to exclude 'low-quality' studies from your review, or you may choose to include all studies but report details of their quality as a narrative. Again, this depends on your synthesis approach; integrative and interpretative analyses may differ in their inclusivity. If you're planning to exclude low-quality studies from your review, then you should carry out quality assessment *before* data extraction, so that you don't waste your time extracting data from some papers. However, poor reporting is not synonymous with poor study quality. For this reason, many reviewers prefer to include studies assessed as poor quality because they can still make valuable contributions to the synthesis. Whatever you decide, we recommend that you seek advice from your supervisor(s) and make your decision making process explicit in your protocol before you start to search for evidence.

There are many ways to assess the quality of qualitative evidence. Flexibility is required when carrying out quality assessment, as the included studies will almost certainly be based on different qualitative research approaches; there isn't a hierarchy of evidence like there is with quantitative study designs. Majid and Vanstone (2018) offer a useful compendium of quality appraisal tools and Ring et al. (2011) provide an excellent overview of quality assessment options for qualitative studies. Many reviews of qualitative evidence employ the critical appraisal checklist for qualitative studies developed by the **Critical Appraisal Skills Programme** (CASP, 2018).

There are some basic quality assessment considerations that you may want to apply to qualitative studies. These include:

- Was the research guided by a clear question?
- Was the research conducted in an ethical and rigorous manner?
- Was there clear information about the methods that were used to collect and analyse the data?
- Did the research provide information that indicates the perspective of the researcher(s)?
- Did the researchers state that the findings had been verified (i.e. had a resonance or had been sense checked with the kind of people who participated)?

Additionally, when quality assessing qualitative research, it is important to consider a number of issues that are not relevant when quality assessing quantitative research. These include the congruity between the stated philosophical perspective and the research methods, whether the theoretical standpoint of the researcher(s) was considered and/or addressed, whether participants' voices were adequately represented and whether there was a statement of the theoretical or cultural location of the researcher(s). As there is no accepted gold-standard quality assessment tool, it is important to clearly present the quality assessment that you carried out, the reasons you chose that specific approach and the impact your approach had on the findings of your review. It is usual to report on study quality, drawing out broad strengths and weaknesses across the studies when describing the characteristics of the included studies at the beginning of the 'Results' section.

Step 9: Analysis and synthesis of qualitative data

Arguably, this section outlines the most important but challenging step when conducting qualitative evidence syntheses. As we have already highlighted, qualitative evidence synthesis takes a more iterative approach to sampling and data extraction than the linear steps taken in a review of quantitative data. This iteration continues into the analysis and/or synthesis phase of a review. Here we describe the basic principles and steps you can follow to bring together and make sense of the data from across your included studies.

If your review is integrative and aims to aggregate data across studies (e.g. meta-aggregation, framework synthesis or textual narrative synthesis), you should focus on summarizing data according to the concepts and themes found in the studies that are already well specified. Make sure that you define and list key concepts and themes prior to data extraction because you will need to extract and synthesize your data in line with them to arrive at a final list of categories (a **category** is a collection of similar data grouped together and is also commonly called a final theme). Commonly, the process of arriving at the final categories involves a degree of iteration between the individual studies, the emerging list of preliminary concepts and themes, and the final distilled list of categories. The synthesis output tends to be written descriptions of each theme, usually with illustrative quotes from included studies, an indication of which studies contributed data to the theme and some degree of contextualization of the findings (e.g. noting any distinct patterns in the findings per theme).

Interpretative reviews, which aim to integrate the concepts and themes from included studies into a higher-order interpretation, naturally take a more inductive and iterative approach to synthesis than integrative reviews and require deeper engagement with the findings of individual studies. Concepts and themes are identified during data extraction and analysis. This may involve moving to and from the included studies to refine and regroup the concepts into the final product, usually a theory or a model that is grounded in the data from included studies. For example, the synthesis process for a meta-ethnography of care-seeking for childhood illness (Colvin et al., 2013) involved the following steps: three reviewers discussed the initial findings extracted from studies and drafted a thematic framework to organize these findings. Each reviewer re-reviewed a subset of studies to identify findings that contributed to the thematic framework. The reviewers then compared notes, revised the framework and elaborated on the meaning of the themes. The findings that were relevant to each theme were compiled into one data table, which made it easy for the reviewers to look across all of the data per theme. From further interrogation of the contents of the data table, the reviewers identified three overarching themes that were reported in the synthesis, which formed the basis of a conceptual model for understanding pathways to care and decision making.

A final word on synthesis. Computer-assisted qualitative data analysis software (CAQDAS) packages designed for use in the analysis of primary qualitative data can also be used to help you to synthesize your data. Some reviewers use NVivo to organize extracted data, and JBI has developed a software package called **Qualitative Assessment and Review Instrument (QARI)** for meta-aggregation. **EPPI-Reviewer** is another software package developed by EPPI (the Evidence for Policy & Practice Information) Centre at University College London, specifically to support qualitative data synthesis. Software packages can help you to retrieve, organize and manage your extracted data, but will not do the hard work of synthesizing data for you. You may have to pay to use these software packages, so check with your supervisor(s) as they might already have access to them. Space constraints do not allow us to provide extensive detail relating to the various ways in which you might use software packages to aid synthesis but looking on the Internet and reading around this topic will help you get started.

Synthesis of qualitative data is not straightforward and may require you to use different techniques and tools concurrently. It is often hard to describe exactly what you have done, but you must confidently put into words how you synthesized your data and finalized your results, whether these take the form of a summary of findings under thematic headings or a more elaborate conceptual model or theory that explains the data found within multiple studies. We suggest that you look at the 'Further Reading and Resources' section at the end of this chapter. Choose an appropriate text relating to your preferred synthesis approach and spend some time familiarizing yourself with the requirements or recommendations associated with that approach.

Step 10: Writing up, editing and disseminating

When writing up a quantitative systematic review, reviewers generally focus on the transparency of the review process and the explicit methods that have been followed, with an emphasis on minimizing bias. The same principles apply when writing up a review of qualitative evidence. Keep your target audience – in your case, your examiner(s) – in mind and be explicit about your theoretical standpoint and the limitations of your review in your write-up. Qualitative evidence synthesis gives you freedom in your approach to analysis and synthesis but it also means that when you write up your review you have to be very clear about why you made your decisions, and how your decisions have impacted on your results and conclusions. The write-up is your chance to demonstrate that you have carefully considered every component of your review. It may be useful to consult the **ENTREQ** (Enhancing Transparency in Reporting the Synthesis of Qualitative Research) statement to help you to write up the searching, screening and selection, quality assessment, data extraction and data synthesis parts of your 'Methods' section (Tong et al., 2012). It may also be helpful to consult the **CERQual** (Confidence in the Evidence from Reviews of Qualitative Research) website (www.cerqual.org) for guidance on how to transparently assess and report the confidence you have in your review's findings. Don't forget to also make a plan for disseminating your review – we consider this to be an essential part of the review process. Chapter 14 provides more information about dissemination.

Final thoughts

We hope that this chapter has provided you with a useful introduction to the (sometimes complex) world of qualitative evidence synthesis. As a student, it's worth knowing that there is currently an ongoing debate about the appropriateness of conducting systematic reviews of qualitative data. Some researchers find drawing conclusions from qualitative data at a population level, rather than at the level of individual research studies, to be a difficult, if not impossible, task. Each qualitative research project is different, and each researcher brings their own perspective and theoretical standpoint to the analysis. Interpretation and reporting of data are therefore subjective; it's not as easy as saying, 'Ten people lived for an extra three years because they had drug X.' Because qualitative research starts with a view that phenomena are created and shaped within the social and historical context in which they are experienced, it becomes quite tricky to make comparisons among phenomena located in very different times and contexts, and you need to be aware of these contextual factors when interpreting and synthesizing the findings of your included studies. In addition, a successful synthesis of findings relies on the reviewers' ability to identify the ideological, philosophical and methodological similarities between studies to allow the findings to be compared in a robust way.

Qualitative research synthesis allows reviewers to construct greater meaning from the results of primary qualitative studies and aids translation of research findings into policy. Methods for synthesizing data from qualitative studies are evolving and make the process both challenging and rewarding and so we applaud you for choosing this path for your thesis.

Key points to think about when writing your protocol

- Clearly define your review question and inclusion and exclusion criteria
- Acknowledge that a variety of qualitative research approaches might mean that evidence synthesis is difficult
- Make explicit your preferred methods for data extraction, quality assessment and data synthesis

What an examiner is looking for in your thesis

- Critical in-depth analysis of your findings
- Critical appraisal of the review process and data analysis approach adopted

- Reflection on your methodological and analytical choices and explanation of how they may have influenced your conclusions
- Where appropriate, drawing alternative conclusions from the available data

Alternative routes

Text mining and qualitative evidence synthesis

Machine learning is an exciting methodological advance. Spearheaded by the EPPI Centre, it includes automated techniques for study identification (O'Mara-Eves et al., 2015) and semi-automated text mining to facilitate data familiarization and coding in qualitative syntheses (Haynes et al., 2019). Text mining can be used to retrieve information from unstructured text and may offer an efficient solution to the complex and time-consuming process of identifying relevant studies for inclusion in a review. One application is to automatically prioritize the items most likely to be relevant for manual screening; another is to use machine learning to automatically apply inclusion and exclusion criteria during the screening process. Whilst text mining methods are evolving and offer the potential to speed up the screening process, we recommend you don't rely solely on these approaches to identify relevant titles and abstracts; it's also important to manually screen identified citations to ensure none has been missed.

Text mining has also been used to analyse large amounts of text-based data, as are often generated in qualitative synthesis, more efficiently. Synthesizing textual data from multiple pooled sources is probably the most time- and resource-consuming part of a qualitative synthesis. Using machine learning to automatically code large textual datasets looks promising and could make the process more efficient and even uncover patterns in the data that may not be identified in researcher-driven analysis. To date, researchers have predominantly used a text mining software package called **Leximancer**, which comes with its own advantages and limitations, but seems capable of generating initial and fresh analytical lines of enquiry from large qualitative datasets. Although there has been incremental progress in this field lately, watch this space as software becomes more sophisticated and the opportunities open up.

Reporting guidance for qualitative evidence syntheses

Reporting standards designed for systematic reviews and meta-analyses (Page et al., 2021a; 2021b) or the PRISMA (Preferred Reporting Items for Systematic Reviews and

Meta-Analyses) extensions for scoping reviews (Tricco et al., 2018) or rapid reviews (Stevens et al., 2018) are not always appropriate for reporting complex qualitative evidence syntheses. Flemming et al. (2018) provide an overview of contemporary methods for presenting and reporting qualitative and other types of syntheses, including a decision flowchart to help decide on the most appropriate one. One of the first reporting guidelines specific to qualitative reviews is the ENTREQ tool, which is generic and applies to the most frequently used methods of qualitative evidence synthesis (Flemming et al., 2018; Tong et al., 2012). A recent development in this area is the eMERGe (Improving Reporting for Meta-Ethnography) guidance, developed specifically for improving completeness and clarity of meta-ethnography reporting (France et al., 2019). Meta-ethnography is one of the most used approaches in qualitative evidence synthesis, but one of the least well reported. This new guidance can help researchers to better report aspects of the methodology, but importantly may also help at the design phase when planning a meta-ethnography (and writing your protocol), and can be used as a checklist when conducting the review to ensure rigour in analysis, interpretation and synthesis.

Frequently Asked Questions

Question 1: Can I undertake a systematic review of qualitative studies on any topic?

In short, yes. If qualitative research has been undertaken, you can conduct a systematic review. Methods for conducting qualitative evidence syntheses have been developed largely within the fields of health and social care, including psychology, but there is no reason why the methods cannot be applied to other domains including education, environmental science and agriculture.

Question 2: Can I only review qualitative studies that adopt the same methodological approach?

No. Currently there are differing views among those involved in conducting qualitative evidence synthesis. Some researchers believe that only studies using the same methodology and analysis approach should be combined, while others take a more pragmatic view and suggest that any type of qualitative evidence can be summarized to answer a specific question. You should decide where you place yourself in this debate and be prepared to justify your stance.

Question 3: How many papers should I include in a qualitative evidence synthesis?

There is no set answer to this, as it largely depends on the number of studies identified by your comprehensive search of the literature. Sometimes the number of studies that meet your inclusion criteria is simply too large to work with. In this case, you may decide to limit the number of included studies. You can do this in several ways. You may revisit your review question and eligibility criteria and narrow them further or you may adopt **purposive sampling**, whereby papers are selected for inclusion based on specific criteria such as rich description or conceptual clarity. We encourage you to refer to Finfgeld-Connett (2008) and Dixon-Woods et al. (2006) for examples of qualitative evidence synthesis using purposive sampling. Finally, theoretical sampling can be used, i.e. papers are randomly sampled and included in your review until **data saturation** is reached.

Question 4: Do I have to use a computer-assisted qualitative data analysis software package to synthesize my findings?

No. Just as in primary qualitative research, CAQDAS such as NVivo or MaxQDA can help you to manage and organize qualitative data, but their use is not mandatory. The key to producing a rigorous and comprehensive synthesis of qualitative evidence is to be organized, and to have a clear plan for data extraction and synthesis. Data can be extracted from included studies into a table using a word-processing package or into a spreadsheet just as easily as it can be compiled in a CAQDAS project file. Further sorting and categorization of data extracts can also be done using computer software packages. The choice is yours, but your decision should be influenced by how familiar you are with the various software packages available to you.

Question 5: Should I exclude studies that I've assessed as being of poor quality?

There is considerable debate about this and various different viewpoints. Some reviewers think the assessment of methodological quality is not essential as poorer quality studies tend to contribute less to the synthesis anyway. Some reviewers, particularly those who use more integrative methods of synthesis, advocate that all studies should be quality assessed, and poor-quality studies should be excluded from analysis. Other reviewers, particularly those using meta-ethnography, do not advocate excluding studies based solely on quality because even studies that do not describe data collection or analysis methods clearly can still make a valuable contribution to the synthesis. Your decision to include or exclude poor-quality studies from your analysis will depend on the type of synthesis you are conducting and whether you judge that the poor-quality studies still have something to add. We recommend that you seek advice from your supervisor(s) before excluding studies based solely on quality.

Question 6: Do I extract data from the 'Discussion' and 'Conclusions' sections of a paper or just from the 'Results' section?

Data extraction for qualitative evidence syntheses is not as straightforward as it is for syntheses of quantitative data. Qualitative evidence can be presented in many formats, usually as themes, but often as diagrams, tables or other mapping of data. You must decide what you plan to class as 'evidence'. For some reviewers, only data (or themes) that are illustrated with direct quotes constitute evidence. Others take a more inclusive approach, whereby all data and/or themes are extracted regardless of supporting quotes. In meta-ethnography, all relevant data, including author interpretations (found in the 'Discussion' section) are extracted, whereas when adopting a more integrative approach, only research findings substantiated with excerpts or quotes (usually found in the 'Results' section) are extracted for synthesis.

Question 7: Where can I find out more about qualitative evidence synthesis?

Many international organizations support and promote qualitative evidence synthesis. These include:

- The Cochrane Qualitative & Implementation Methods Group (formerly the Cochrane Qualitative Research Methods Group; https://methods.cochrane.org/qi). This group supports the inclusion of qualitative systematic reviews in the Cochrane Database of Systematic Reviews and guides methodological work on qualitative evidence synthesis approaches.
- The EPPI Centre, based at University College London, which is at the forefront of methods development and training for research synthesis (https://eppi.ioe.ac.uk/cms). The Centre produces systematic reviews of research across diverse disciplines including health, education, finance and economics, social care and international development.

- The JBI, which is an international not-for-profit research and development organization based at the University of Adelaide, South Australia, that promotes and supports the synthesis, transfer and utilization of qualitative evidence.

Further Reading and Resources

Aromataris, E., & Munn, Z. (Eds) (2020). *JBI manual for evidence synthesis.* https://synthesismanual.jbi.global

Bearman, M., & Dawson, P. (2013). Qualitative synthesis and systematic review in health professions education. *Medical Education, 47*(3), 252–60.

Booth, A., Sutton, A., Clowes, M., & Martyn-St James, M. (Eds) (2021). *Systematic approaches to a successful literature review* (3rd ed.). SAGE Publications.

Centre for Reviews and Dissemination. (2010). *Systematic reviews: CRD's guidance for undertaking reviews in health care.* www.york.ac.uk/inst/crd/SysRev/!SSL!/WebHelp/SysRev3.htm

Gough, D., Oliver, S., & Thomas, J. (2013). *Learning from research: Systematic reviews for informing policy decisions: a quick guide.* A paper for the Alliance for Useful Evidence. Nesta.

Gülmezoglu, A., Chandler, J., & Shepperd, S. (2013). Reviews of qualitative evidence: a new milestone for Cochrane. *Cochrane Database of Systematic Reviews, 8*(11). https://doi.org/10.1002/14651858.ED000073

Hannes, K., & Lockwood, C. (2012). *Synthesising qualitative research: Choosing the right approach.* BMJ Books/Wiley-Blackwell.

Lewin, S., Booth, A., Glenton, C., Munthe-Kaas, H., Rashidian, A., Wainwright, M., Bohren, M.A., Tuncalp, O., Colvin, C.J., Carlsen, B., Lenglois, E.V., & Noyes. J. (2018). Applying GRADE-CERQual to qualitative evidence synthesis findings: introduction to the series. *Implementation Science, 13*(2). https://doi.org/10.1186/s13012-017-0688-3

Morgan, R.L., Whaley, P., Thayer, K.A., & Schünemann, H.J. (2018). Identifying the PECO: a framework for formulating good questions to explore the association of environmental and other exposures with health outcomes. *Environment International, 121*(1), 1027.

Noblit, G., & Hare, R. (1988). *Meta-ethnography: Synthesizing qualitative studies.* SAGE Publications.

Noyes, J., Booth, A., Cargo, M., Fleming, K., Harden, A., Harris, J., Garside, R., Hannes, K., Pantoja, T., & Thomas, J. (2022). Chapter 21: Qualitative evidence. In Higgins, J.P.T., Thomas, J., Chandler, J., Cumpston, M., Li, T., Page, M.J., & Welch, V.A. (Eds) (2022). *Cochrane handbook for systematic reviews of interventions* (version 6.3, updated February 2022). https://training.cochrane.org/handbook/current

Ring, N., Ritchie, K., Mandava, L., & Jepson, R. (2011). *A guide to synthesising qualitative research for researchers undertaking health technology assessments and systematic reviews.* https://dspace.stir.ac.uk/handle/1893/3205#.ZE1Q5C8w2Zw

Sandelowski, M., & Barroso, J. (2007). *Handbook for synthesizing qualitative research.* Springer Publishing Company.

Toye, F., Seers, K., & Allcock, N. (2014). Meta-ethnography 25 years on: challenges and insights for synthesising a large number of qualitative studies. *BMC Medical Research Methodology, 14*(1), 80.

12

Reviewing Economic Evaluations

Angela Boland, Sophie Beale and M. Gemma Cherry

This chapter will help you to...

- Develop your economic systematic review question

- Search for economic evidence

- Critically appraise economic evaluations

- Draw conclusions from economic data

Introduction

This chapter is written specifically to guide you as you undertake a systematic review of economic evaluations. First, we outline the purpose of a systematic review of economic studies. Second, we describe the types of economic studies you are likely to identify when searching for economic evidence. We also guide you through the key steps you are likely to take when reviewing economic evidence, highlighting where the process differs from other systematic review processes.

Points to note

We feel that we must make several points clear about this chapter. Economic reviews are important, but most students are not equipped to conduct them unless economics is their main area of study. We encourage these students to read on. This chapter focuses on economic evaluations of healthcare interventions – our area of expertise. However, we are confident that the universal principles described in this chapter will also be useful if you are reviewing economic evaluations from any other field of study.

This chapter is designed to help you to complete your systematic review of economic evaluations on time and without too many problems along the way. We've assumed that you have studied, are studying or at least understand the basic principles of economic evaluation. If you are interested in learning how to carry out an economic evaluation or how to build an economic model then you might find it helpful to consult the health economics textbooks and journal articles recommended in the 'Further Reading and Resources' section.

Reviews of economic evaluations fall into two types – reviews *of* economic evaluations and reviews *for* economic evaluations (Anderson, 2010). This chapter is written to help you complete a review *of* economic evaluations. The most frequently asked question in reviews of economic evaluations in the field of healthcare is, 'For a specific group of people, is intervention X cost-effective when compared with intervention Y?' This chapter has been written with this question in mind.

Undertaking a review of economic evaluations is just like undertaking a quantitative review. This chapter can be read as a stand-alone chapter, but you will find it more useful if you have already read Chapters 2 to 11 and 13 and 14. Each of these chapters contains information that will improve the content and quality of your thesis. In this chapter we offer you *additional* information that is specific to a review of economic evaluations.

What is a systematic review of economic evaluations?

A systematic review of economic evaluations is similar to any other kind of systematic review in that it aims to bring together all of the available relevant evidence to answer a specific question. As with other types of review, a systematic review of economic evaluations might be designed to answer a specific question to inform decision making; it might be conducted to summarize methodological arguments with a view to reaching consensus; or it might be carried out to search for data to inform an economic model or an economic evaluation. Some reasons for conducting economic reviews are shown in Table 12.1.

TABLE 12.1   Reasons for carrying out a review of economic evaluations in healthcare

Why might you carry out a review of economic evaluations in healthcare?	Example
To find out which of two drugs offers value for money for a specific group of patients.	Is pemetrexed cost-effective compared with gemcitabine for patients with non-squamous non-small cell lung cancer?
To identify the different types of economic models used in economic evaluations within a specific topic area.	What is the best way to model the costs of cardiac care in patients with multi-vessel disease?
To identify the available health-related quality of life evidence for a specific group of patients so that you can then use this information in your own economic evaluation.	What is the best source of quality-adjusted life year values for patients with breast cancer in the UK?

What type of studies might I find in a review of economic evaluations?

There are many sources of economic evidence, and these include economic evaluations, economic reviews, **cost analyses**, commentaries, editorials and letters. You can find economic evidence explicitly stated in the title or abstract of economic studies or lurking in the depths of a wide range of publication types. For the purposes of this chapter, we focus primarily on economic evaluations and there are four main types: **cost-minimization analysis** (CMA), **cost-effectiveness analysis** (CEA), **cost–utility analysis** (CUA) and **cost–benefit analysis** (CBA). These four types are usually grouped together and called **full economic evaluations** as they consider both the costs and benefits of healthcare interventions or programmes. **Partial economic evaluations** either do not involve a comparison between alternatives or do not relate costs to benefits; this type of study includes **burden-of-illness/cost-of-illness studies** (BOI/COI), **cost–consequence analyses** (CCA) or simply cost analyses.

In general, economic evaluations describe the costs *and* benefits of alternative courses of action, usually comparing innovative interventions with interventions that are gold standard or best practice. As shown in Table 12.2, the four types of full economic evaluation identify, measure and value the costs of interventions and comparators in the same way; they only differ in the way they identify, measure and value the benefits arising from the interventions and comparators. In healthcare, the most used methods of economic evaluation are CEA and CUA. Both approaches use **incremental cost-effectiveness ratios** (ICERs) to summarize their results. For example, CEAs often report results in terms of **incremental cost per life year gained** (cost per LYG) and CUAs often report results in terms of **incremental cost per quality-adjusted life year** (QALY) gained (cost per QALY).

TABLE 12.2 Types of economic evaluation studies

Full economic evaluations	Characteristics
Cost-minimization analysis	Benefits are proven to be equivalent. Focus is on costs. Costs are measured in currency (e.g. £ or $).
Cost-effectiveness analysis	Benefits are unidimensional and measured in natural units (e.g. cost per LYG). Costs are measured in currency (e.g. £ or $).
Cost–utility analysis	Benefits are multidimensional (e.g. quality and quantity of life) and typically measured in QALYs gained. Costs are measured in currency (e.g. £ or $).
Cost–benefit analysis	Both benefits and costs are measured in currency (e.g. £ or $).
Partial economic evaluations	**Characteristics**
Burden-of-illness/cost-of-illness studies	Economic burden of a disease is measured and the maximum amount of money that could potentially be saved, or gained, if a disease or condition no longer existed is estimated.
Cost–consequence analysis	Different costs and benefits of the interventions being compared are not aggregated. Benefits are measured in natural units (e.g. number of people cured) and costs are measured in currency (e.g. £ or $).
Cost analysis	No mention of outcomes; focus is solely on costs.

LYG = life year gained; QALYs = quality-adjusted life years

What are the key terms used in economic evaluations of healthcare interventions?

Some of the key terms used in economic evaluations of healthcare interventions and programmes are listed in Table 12.3. If you are planning to undertake a systematic review of economic evaluations then you need to be, at the very least, familiar with these terms as you won't be able to carry out your review successfully if you don't understand the terminology that is being used.

TABLE 12.3 Key terms used in economic evaluations of healthcare interventions and programmes

Key term	Definition
Cost-effectiveness	Extent to which costs and health effects of an intervention or programme can be regarded as providing value for money
Discounting	Technique used to enable comparison of costs and/or benefits occurring in different years
Incremental cost-effectiveness ratio (ICER)	Summary of all changes in costs and benefits between the different interventions or programmes
Perspective	Viewpoint adopted in the economic evaluation. Examples include patient, health service and society
Quality-adjusted life year (QALY)	Outcome measure that captures both length of life and quality of life
Sensitivity analysis	Technique used to test the robustness of economic results to uncertainty in parameters or methodologies
Utility	Measure of wellbeing or benefit gained from a healthcare intervention or programme

Box 12.1

Key steps to consider in the systematic review process

Step 1: Planning and managing your review

Step 2: Performing scoping searches, identifying the review question and writing your protocol

Step 3: Literature searching

Step 4: Screening titles and abstracts

Step 5: Obtaining papers

Step 6: Selecting full-text papers

Step 7: Data extraction

Step 8: Quality assessment

Step 9: Analysis and synthesis

Step 10: Writing up and editing

Ten key steps in the systematic review process

Box 12.1 outlines ten key steps in the systematic review process that we recommend you follow when doing a review as a postgraduate thesis. Most of these steps are exactly the same regardless of whether you are reviewing economic, clinical, educational or environmental papers. However, some steps do require additional considerations and we'll discuss each step from the perspective of an economist conducting a review of economic evaluations. We also highlight where the steps differ from those commonly used in other types of evidence synthesis.

Step 1: Planning and managing your review

Before you rush off to work on your review, you need to take time to think about how you are going to plan your review activities from now until the day that you submit your thesis. A successful systematic reviewer learns to multitask and works to deadlines. During the review process, you will ask yourself several questions: Do I have the full-text papers of all my included studies? What quality assessment checklist am I going to use? What software package shall I use to store my data? What is the submission date for my thesis? Do I have sufficient time to really think about the data I've extracted before I write my 'Discussion' and 'Conclusions' sections? Has my systematic review answered the research question? There are many different elements to manage during the review process, and these are discussed in Chapter 2. In Chapter 2, you will also find useful information that will help you to make sure that your review progresses smoothly – so don't forget to read, and then re-read, this chapter.

Step 2: Performing scoping searches, identifying the review question and writing your protocol

Scoping searches

One of the first tasks we recommend that you carry out is your scoping searches. Scoping searches are the searches that you undertake when you are still pondering the precise wording of your review question – you use simple search terms and search only a selection of relevant sources of information. The results give you an idea of the quantity of economic evidence available to you before you carry out your main search. Chapters 3 and 5 provide detailed advice on how to carry out scoping searches.

The results of your scoping searches may be disappointing – you might think that you have identified too many, or perhaps too few, relevant studies. If this is the case, we suggest that you meet with your supervisor(s) and agree a plan of action so that you know exactly what to do if your definitive search strategy leads to the identification of too many or too few relevant studies. Unfortunately, it is not unusual to identify only one or two (or even zero) relevant economic studies when looking for healthcare-related economic evidence, especially if the focus of your search is a drug or device that has only recently been introduced to market. Your supervisor(s) might think that not finding any studies is a valid result in itself or might suggest that you broaden the scope of your review question so that additional economic studies can be included. Just remember, however, that to get good marks for your thesis, you need to demonstrate that you have critical appraisal skills – this is difficult to do if you don't have any studies to critique. In contrast, identifying what you and your supervisor(s) consider as too many studies likely means that your review question is too broad and, if this is the case, you need to think about the best way to narrow the focus of your review question (e.g. by limiting your definition of population or choice of economic evaluation method).

Identifying the review question

Whatever the reason for conducting a review of economic evaluations, you need to be certain that you are asking a question that can be answered. For example, you may be interested in whether the cancer drug pemetrexed offers value for money to the health service. Unfortunately, the question 'Is pemetrexed cost-effective?' is too broad and therefore not easy to answer. Working through the population, intervention, comparator and outcome (PICO) and PICO plus study design and setting (PICOSS) headings described in Chapter 3 will help you to formulate a review question that you can answer (see Box 12.2).

Box 12.2

Developing an answerable review question

What is the cost-effectiveness of pemetrexed (*intervention*) versus gemcitabine (*comparator*) in the first-line treatment of patients with non-squamous disease in non-small cell lung cancer (*population*) in the UK NHS (*setting*) using data from cost–utility studies (*outcomes/study design*) published between 2010 and 2022 (*time frame*)?

Developing your review question can be a lengthy process and one that always benefits from discussion with others. As the review question that you want to answer becomes clear, your inclusion criteria will also become clear. As discussed in Chapter 3, your inclusion criteria describe the key characteristics that a study must have if it is to be included in your review – think carefully about population, intervention, comparator and outcomes. In addition, you might want to address issues of study design (e.g. by choosing only full economic evaluations), language (e.g. only searching for studies published in English) and time frame (e.g. including only papers published after 2010). In systematic reviews of economic evaluations, reviewers often specify the method of the economic studies to be included in the review (e.g. only include CEAs, or only include full economic evaluations). However, this is not always the case. Where the quantity of economic evidence available is limited, reviewers are less likely to restrict inclusion by economic evaluation method. Whether you do, or don't, apply any restrictions, you need to fully justify this decision in the 'Methods' section of your thesis.

It is good practice to state each of your inclusion criteria explicitly in your write-up; you could list them in a table alongside any exclusion criteria. Table 12.4 shows two very different sets of inclusion and exclusion criteria for use in two different reviews of economic evaluations.

TABLE 12.4   Examples of inclusion and exclusion criteria

	Inclusion criteria	Exclusion criteria
Review question: Is pemetrexed cost-effective compared with gemcitabine in the treatment of patients with non-squamous, non-small cell lung cancer in the first-line setting using data from cost–utility analyses from 2010 to 2022?		
Population	Chemotherapy naïve, first-line, non-small cell lung cancer, non-squamous disease	
Intervention	Pemetrexed or gemcitabine	
Comparator	Any chemotherapy	
Outcomes	Cost per QALY gained	
Study design	Cost–utility analysis	Cost-minimization analysis, cost–benefit analysis, cost-effectiveness analysis, editorial, letter, poster, abstract, methodological paper, partial economic evaluations
Setting	United Kingdom National Health Service	Non-United Kingdom
Language	English language	
Time frame	2010–2022	

	Inclusion criteria	Exclusion criteria
Review question: Are public health interventions aimed at low socio-economic groups a cost-effective use of resources?		
Population	Focus on people with low socio-economic status and/or health inequalities	
Intervention	Public health interventions	Pharmacological interventions
Comparator	Any	
Outcomes	Cost per LYG, cost per natural unit of effectiveness	
Study design	Full economic evaluations	Editorial, letter, poster, abstract, methodological paper, partial economic evaluations
Setting	Any	
Language	English language	
Time frame	2010–2022	

LYG = life year gained; QALY = quality-adjusted life year

If you are finding it difficult to define your review question, read Chapter 3 again and make sure that you follow the key steps that are discussed in the chapter: namely, identify a topic that interests you, carry out scoping searches, focus your ideas to define the scope of your review and finalize your review question. Unless your deadline is fast approaching, there's no real rush; time spent developing your review question is always time well spent.

Protocol

We always encourage students to write a review protocol (see Chapter 4), no matter what the topic area under review. A protocol doesn't have to be complicated or lengthy, but it should outline how you plan to search for evidence, screen and select studies, and report and critically appraise findings. It must also describe any planned data analyses. The time that you spend thinking about and writing your protocol will not be wasted. At times during the review process, you may feel as though you are not making much progress, or you may feel uncertain about which task to do next. Having a protocol that is clear and well thought out means that, on such occasions, you can simply refer to it and take your own good advice.

Step 3: Literature searching

Let's assume that you have carried out your scoping searches, refined your review question and written your protocol. You now need to think about your search strategy – that is, how you are going to search for economic evidence.

There are two key questions to consider:

- What bibliographic databases do you want to search for economic evidence?
- What key search terms do you want to use?

Databases

Most of the commonly searched health and social sciences bibliographic databases also index economics studies. Useful bibliographic databases for the identification of economic evaluation papers relating to health and social sciences include: MEDLINE, EMBASE, NHS Economic Evaluation Database (NHS EED), Health Economics Evaluation Database (HEED), Health Management Information Consortium (HMIC) and PsycINFO. Other useful databases that include economic studies are: Economics and Social Data Service, EconLit, Social Care Online, Educational Resources Information Centre (ERIC), Education-line, Current Education and Children's Services Research (CERUK) and Association of Public Health Observatories (APHO). See Table 5.2 for a list of useful web addresses.

Large numbers of papers containing economic evidence are published each year and are indexed in different databases and on Internet websites. Depending on the focus of your review, you will need to choose your databases and websites carefully. For example, economic evaluations of healthcare interventions are found primarily in established medicine-related databases (e.g. MEDLINE and EMBASE), whereas economic evaluations of public health interventions are more likely to be found on governmental and public sector websites (e.g. National Institute for Health and Care Excellence [NICE] and APHO). If you have doubts about this part of your review, we recommend that you turn to a librarian or information specialist for assistance.

Search terms

To make sure that you identify all the economic evidence that is relevant to your review question, you should think about using a broad search strategy. The economic data that you are interested in may be hidden in the depths of the text rather than being easy to spot in the title or abstract. Your objective is to identify all relevant economic evidence so that you can be sure that you are capturing the cost and benefit information that you need to answer your review question. Don't be too specific. We believe that it pays to be inclusive rather than exclusive when it comes to choosing economic search terms to identify studies. Performing a broad search means you'll find more papers than you would if you were to carry out a narrow search. So, for example, use the terms 'cost' or 'economic' rather than 'economic evaluation' and you will find more studies (as shown in Table 12.5). The extra time it takes you to look through the titles and abstracts of your retrieved papers is worthwhile, even if you find only one additional relevant economic study.

TABLE 12.5   Table of costing studies identified using different search terms

Bibliographic databases searched: 2018–2022	Number of hits (Nov. 2022) – using 'cost' as a keyword	Number of hits (Nov. 2022) – using 'economic evaluation' as a keyword
MEDLINE with Full Text (health)	244,085	24,242
EconLit (economics)	38,339	5,870
PsycINFO (psychology)	27,726	4,061
ERIC (education)	4,185	676

If you can, it is a good idea to ask a librarian or information specialist to double-check that the search terms you are planning to use will pick up all relevant studies. If you can't do this, then just check that your search terms are picking up the key economic studies that you have already identified from your scoping search results and through discussions with your supervisor(s). If your main search strategy is not picking up all of these studies, it is time to rethink your search terms and re-run your searches. See Chapter 5 for further explanation regarding how to develop your search strategy and improve the accuracy of your searching.

Step 4: Screening titles and abstracts

The fourth step in the review process is to use your inclusion and exclusion criteria to screen the titles and abstracts of the papers identified from your main searches. You need to refer to your criteria as you read through the titles and abstracts to identify the papers that are potentially eligible for inclusion in your review based on your specific criteria. Remember, you don't need to have the full-text papers in front of you at this stage as you are only reading through titles and abstracts.

Step 5: Obtaining papers

For some students, obtaining full-text papers can be a welcome distraction but for others it is the most boring task in the world. You must try to obtain the full-text papers of all the economic papers that you included in Step 4. If you are unable to obtain a paper, you need to let your supervisor(s) know and acknowledge this problem when writing up the limitations of your review.

Step 6: Selecting full-text papers

When selecting full-text papers for inclusion in your review, you follow the same process as you do when screening titles and abstracts. However, this time you have the full-text papers in front of you (in paper or in electronic format). Full-text papers give you the information you need to decide whether a study should be included in your review. You must check through the full-text paper of each study carefully to ensure that you don't miss any relevant information using your explicitly stated inclusion and exclusion criteria. Only after having done this will you be able to confidently include or exclude a paper from your review.

Step 7: Data extraction

The next step in your systematic review is to carry out data extraction. However, before you can begin to extract data from your economic evaluations you need to design a data extraction form. We suggest that you turn to Chapter 7 and read the sections on designing and piloting data extraction forms. Chapter 7 also includes useful advice on how to efficiently extract data from studies and provides examples of data extraction tables that have been well thought out.

The type of data that you extract from economic evaluations of healthcare interventions differs substantially from the data that you extract from other types of studies. However, the structure of most published reviews of health economic evaluations is straightforward and we suggest that you consider including the following data in your data extraction tables:

- *Table 1: Study characteristics*. Study reference, identify whether full-text paper or abstract, type of study, intervention, study population, country, time period, industry affiliation
- *Table 2: Economic costs and outcomes*. Study reference, type of model (if used), perspective, assumptions relating to costs, assumptions relating to outcomes
- *Table 3: Cost items and data sources*. Study reference, cost items and cost data sources, price year, currency, discount rate
- *Table 4: Efficacy and outcomes sources*. Study reference, efficacy data, efficacy data sources, outcomes, outcome data sources, discount rate
- *Table 5: Cost-effectiveness results and conclusions*. Study reference, total costs, total outcomes, ICERs, authors' conclusions
- *Table 6: Sensitivity analysis*. Study reference, summary of sensitivity analyses and results

As a student, you will probably be working independently. However, it is worth trying to find someone (suitably able) to check your extracted data for inaccuracies and/or transcription errors. This is especially important if your included studies contain large, complex data tables. This systematic review is your project and therefore your responsibility, and you are accountable for all decisions made and tasks undertaken. One benefit of working alone is that you can be sure you have adopted the same approach to data extraction across all studies. As mentioned in Chapter 2, check with your supervisor(s) regarding your institution's policy on working independently.

Step 8: Quality assessment

Let's assume that you have just completed your data extraction exercise. You are now getting to know your included studies and probably feel in control of your economic review. The next stage in the systematic review process is the critical appraisal (or quality assessment) of your included studies. Not all reviewers of economic evidence quality assess their included studies. However, if you are aiming to produce the best review that you are capable of writing, then this is a step that you cannot afford to skip.

The quality of economic evaluations varies. Most economic evaluations are carried out by individuals with expertise in economics, but some are conducted by, for example, clinicians or social scientists who are interested in exploring cost-effectiveness questions but do not always have the necessary skill base to do this well. It is, therefore, important that you are able to identify research that has been conducted and reported to a high standard so that you do not give equal weight to studies of variable quality.

Whether you carry out quality assessment before, after or during data extraction is a personal choice. Everyone has a preference – go ahead with the approach that suits your style of working. Remember, you need to quality assess each included study and it is up to you whether you do this on paper or electronically.

There are many different quality assessment tools available for the critical appraisal of economic evaluations and some are easier to use than others. Most of the available tools ask the same pertinent and probing questions. We suggest that you use a short version of a checklist by Drummond and colleagues (Drummond et al., 1997). The short version of the checklist has stood the test of time and is shown in Table 12.6. For a student writing a thesis, we consider that this ten-point checklist is the most appropriate tool for you to use. If you are feeling very enthusiastic, you could use the full 35-point version of the checklist (Drummond & Jefferson, 1996; Drummond et al., 1997). The questions posed in the Drummond checklist are generic and so can be used in the quality assessment of any economic evaluation, no matter what the field of study. The questions will lead you to consider the elements of the economic study that are most important. If you want to use a more contemporaneous checklist, we recommend the CHEERS 2022 statement (Husereau et al., 2022).

Remember to allow yourself sufficient time to think through your answers.

TABLE 12.6   Short checklist for assessing economic evaluations

Drummond et al. (1997) checklist questions

1	Was a well-defined question posed in answerable form?
2	Was a comprehensive description of the competing alternatives given (i.e. can you tell who did what to whom, where and how often)?
3	Was the effectiveness of the programmes or services established?
4	Were all of the important and relevant costs and consequences for each alternative identified?
5	Were costs and consequences measured accurately in appropriate physical units?
6	Were costs and consequences valued credibly?
7	Were costs and consequences adjusted for differential timing?
8	Was an incremental analysis of costs and consequences performed?
9	Was allowance made for uncertainty in the estimates of costs and consequences?
10	Did the presentation and discussion of study results include issues of concern to users?

Source: Box 3.1, *Methods for the Economic Evaluation of Health Care Programmes* by Drummond et al. (1997). By permission of Oxford University Press

There are also tools for assessing the quality of health economics models. The report by Philips et al. (2004) presents a useful review of guidelines for good practice in decision-analytic modelling in health technology assessment.

In an ideal world, you would be able to ask someone with sufficient time and suitable qualifications to read through the results of your quality assessment exercise to check the consistency of your judgements across your included studies. However, if you don't live in an ideal world (and who does?), make sure you mention this issue when writing up the limitations of your review.

Finally, don't forget that there are also tools for assessing the quality of systematic reviews and it is always a good idea to review the quality of your own systematic review (see Chapter 8).

Step 9: Analysis and synthesis

When it comes to the systematic review of economic evaluations there are no established methods for data synthesis other than narrative synthesis (see Chapter 7). So don't worry, it is probably not appropriate for you to perform a meta-analysis. How you write up your narrative synthesis will depend on the information you have reported in your data tables. Your data tables often reveal that the results of your included studies are different: some studies may demonstrate that 'Intervention X is cost-effective compared with intervention Y' while others may conclude that

'Intervention Y is cost-effective compared with intervention X'. If this is a feature of your review, then all that you can do in your narrative synthesis is report what you have found. You also need to acknowledge patterns (similarities and differences) in the data and in the magnitude of the reported ICERs.

There is no need to describe and then scrutinize each included study on its own merits; you need to spend your time thinking carefully about what the data are saying as a collective. Anderson (2010) argues that even trying to do this is a wasted effort as the individual papers included in systematic reviews of economic evaluations are often inherently different from each other, and attempting to compare studies with different perspectives, time frames and local settings is futile. However, we think that economic reviews, if carried out using systematic and rigorous methods, can be just as informative and useful for decision making and student learning as any other type of systematic review. We agree that reviews of economic evaluations usually comprise very different studies; however, we believe that this is an important observation. The information described and critiqued within a review of economic evaluations may serve many purposes, including summarizing what is currently known about a topic, helping to inform a policy decision, or identifying parameter values to use in an economic model or economic evaluation. Even if your review concludes that the results of the economic studies are too diverse to enable comparison, this can be a useful finding in itself.

Step 10: Writing up and editing

A successful review of economic evaluations (and any other type of review) is one that adds information to the existing knowledge base and answers the review question posed. This may sound obvious to you but believe us, not all reviewers manage to write 'Discussion' and 'Conclusions' sections that succinctly summarize the available data or meaningfully interpret the results of all the hard work that has been undertaken (see Chapter 13).

Reviewing the literature is mainly a technical exercise until this stage in the review process, and it is widely agreed that 'Discussion' and 'Conclusions' sections are the most difficult sections of any review to write. As a reviewer you need to think carefully about the information you have collected and decide whether there are enough data of sufficient quality to answer your review question. You really must take the time to match the extracted economic data with the results of your quality assessment exercise and then meaningfully interpret what you have found. There is no right or wrong way to do this. Planning your discussion and thinking through the key issues before putting pen to paper is always a good way to start. The questions raised in Table 12.7 might help you to clarify and organize your ideas.

TABLE 12.7   Writing the 'Discussion' section of an economic review

	Key questions/issues to think about when writing the 'Discussion'
Number of studies	Are there sufficient studies to answer your review question? If there are very few published economic evaluations included in your review, then you need to discuss the possible reasons for this. Perhaps your inclusion criteria are too strict or you didn't search enough databases, or maybe your topic is out of date or too new?
Quality	Economic evaluations are often inherently flawed. It is important that you acknowledge the link between study results and study quality in your 'Discussion' section. It is misleading to report that all included studies demonstrated that intervention A was cost-effective compared with intervention B if you don't mention that some of the studies didn't include all relevant costs, some overestimated benefits and others used limited perspectives.
Intervention and comparator	Do you have sufficient information about the intervention and comparator in each study to confidently compare them and draw conclusions? Do most of the studies in the review describe the same interventions and comparators with the same level of detail? Do any of the studies compare interventions with comparators that are no longer in use?
Perspective	Do all of the studies in the review adopt the same perspective? If not, is there a reason for this? Does the choice of perspective influence the results of the study? Narrow perspective/viewpoint: for example, patient. Wider perspective/viewpoint: for example, society.
Rate of discounting	No matter what discount rate is used in a study, it is helpful if the authors explore the impact of using different discount rates as part of their sensitivity analyses, including using a rate of 0 per cent. Watch out for studies that only discount costs *or* benefits, and studies that apply different rates to costs and benefits. What is the approach taken in most of the studies and why?
Price year and currency	Are all of the resource items used in the economic evaluations from the same price year and estimated in the same currency? Probably not. You need to be aware of how different price years and currencies might affect the size of the calculated ICERs and how this might influence decision making.
QALYs	Where do the QALY estimates come from? From the public or from a patient survey? What tools are used to derive utilities? Are the values used comparable across studies? Do you think there are better sources of utility values for this population?
ICERs	Are the estimated ICERs of a similar size? Are the results of the studies in agreement? If not, why not? What are the key drivers of the analyses? Are the drivers common to all studies? Can you make an overall judgement about whether the intervention is cost-effective compared with the comparator(s)?
Sensitivity analysis	Do the authors address uncertainty in their analyses? What are the main sources of uncertainty in the economic evaluations? How is this uncertainty explored?
Generalizability	Discussion of generalizability is paramount. Even if all of the evaluations in your review are expertly undertaken and assessed to be of excellent quality, if they are all inherently different in their approach to estimating cost-effectiveness, you need to think about whether the results of the studies can be used to answer the review question. When conducting an economic review, it is always possible that even studies that meet strict inclusion/exclusion criteria will fail on the test of generalizability. For example, some authors might include the costs of interventions that are not routinely used in all settings, others might employ a slightly wider definition of the patient population, while others might use published cost data from non-routine sources. Often this list is endless, and it is crucial to describe overall results in light of issues of generalizability so that the reader is clear about the circumstances under which the results of the review are valid.

QALYs = quality-adjusted life years; ICERs = incremental cost-effectiveness ratio

Final thoughts

Congratulations! You've made it – you have completed your review of economic evaluations. Is there a little voice in your head daring you to think about publishing your review? We hope so. Increasingly, reviews of economic evidence are being published in a wide variety of journals, not only specialist health economics journals. For example, you may come across a review of economic evaluations in a clinical journal or an economic review of housing alternatives in a health economics journal. You might also want to think about submitting an abstract of your review to a local, national or even international conference. We discuss these methods of dissemination further in Chapter 14 and we are confident that, if you have followed the advice in this book, your systematic review will pass even the highest of peer-review obstacles. Go on, put yourself (and your review) out there and get your results published.

Key points to think about when writing your protocol

- Present a clearly stated economic review question with as much detail as possible
- Be as comprehensive as possible when you outline your plans for searching for economic evidence
- Explain why you think that the quality assessment tool that you plan to use is appropriate

What an examiner is looking for in your thesis

- A clearly stated economic review question
- Appropriate search terms used and relevant databases searched for evidence
- Quality assessment of included studies
- Structured discussion showing how the quality of studies may influence the conclusions of the review
- Pertinent discussion of generalizability of results
- Statement relating to whether you were able to answer the review question

Frequently Asked Questions

Question 1: Can I do a review of economic evaluations that are unrelated to health?

Yes. Health economics is not the only branch of economics that employs methods of economic evaluation – environmental, housing and transport economics do too.

Question 2: What if the prices/currencies of the resources valued in my included studies are all from different years?

This is often the case. You must decide whether you need to compare the cost data from your included studies at a single point in time. You should think about whether this level of comparability is critical to the interpretation of the data and how converting prices/currencies to a **base year** might affect decision making. If you decide to convert your prices/currencies to a base year, then you can search the Internet for up-to-date and useful information on how to do this. Again, it is a good idea to discuss your planned approach with your supervisor(s).

Question 3: What do I do if the economic evaluations that I am interested in all adopt different viewpoints/ perspectives?

You need to make sure that the issue of viewpoint/perspective is intelligently discussed in your thesis. It is misleading to conclude that most of the results discussed in the included studies are sufficiently similar if the analyses have been conducted from widely different viewpoints. You need to think through your findings and comment on how choice of perspective can influence the magnitude of the estimated ICERs per QALY gained.

Question 4: How do I make sure that the conclusions of the review are generalizable to all users?

You can't. You can only write your conclusions based on the economic evidence that is described in your included studies. You need to think about the question that you set out to answer and make sure that you have attempted to do this to the best of your ability, based on the nature and quality of the data that are available to you.

Further Reading and Resources

Drummond, M., & Jefferson, T. (1996). Guidelines for authors and peer reviewers of economic submissions to the BMJ. *British Medical Journal, 313*(7052), 275–83.

Heslin, M., Forster, A., Healey, A., & Patel, A. (2016). A systematic review of the economic evidence for interventions for family carers of stroke patients. *Clinical Rehabilitation, 30*(2), 119–33.

Husereau, D., Drummond, M., Augustovski, F., de Bekker-Grob, E., Briggs, A., Carswell, C., Caulley, L., Chaiyakunapruk, N., Greenberg, D., Loder, E., Mauskopf, J., Mullins, C.D., Petrou, S., Pwu, R-F., & Staniszewska, S. (2022). Consolidated Health Economic Evaluation Reporting Standards 2022 (CHEERS 2022) statement: updated reporting guidance for health economic evaluations. *International Journal of Technology Assessment in Healthcare*, *38*(1), E13. https://doi.org/10.1017/S0266462321001732

Kobelt, G. (2002). *Health economics: An introduction to economic evaluation.* www.ohe.org/publications/health-economics-introduction-economic-evaluation-0

Petrou, S., & Gray, A. (2011). Economic evaluation alongside randomised controlled trials: design, conduct, analysis, and reporting. *British Medical Journal*, *342*, d1548.

Weise, A., Büchter, R.B., Pieper, D., & Mathes, T. (2022). Assessing transferability in systematic reviews of health economic evaluations – a review of methodological guidance. *BMC Medical Research Methodology*, *22*, 52. https://doi.org/10.1186/s12874-022-01536-6

13

Writing My Discussion and Conclusions

M. Gemma Cherry

This chapter will help you to...

- Understand the importance of taking adequate time to write up your review, especially the 'Discussion' and 'Conclusions' sections

- Gain an awareness of what to include in these sections, and why

- Recognize common pitfalls and learn how to avoid them

Introduction

Well done! You are nearing the end of your systematic review. In this chapter, we provide advice on how to write the final sections of your systematic review – your 'Discussion' and 'Conclusions' sections. In previous editions, we launched straight into outlining the purpose of these two sections and why they are important. Don't worry – we still cover this in the chapter, but we first want to discuss how to approach your write-up and what to include in your 'Introduction' section, so that you can situate your 'Discussion' and 'Conclusions' sections within the wider literature. We then discuss the general principles involved in writing your discussion and conclusions. Finally, we identify common pitfalls and how to avoid them.

How do I begin to write up my review, and what should I include in my 'Introduction' section?

By now, you will likely have already written up several sections of your review. We hope you will have written a protocol (as outlined in Chapter 4) and may have written up your 'Methods' and 'Results' sections, following the guidance provided in Chapters 5 to 12. You should be familiar with reference management software packages and have an idea of institutional requirements for presentation of your final work (Chapter 2). By now, most students feel confident that the end is in sight, but we are often asked how to begin or structure the write-up of a review, particularly the 'Introduction'. We begin this chapter with a few pointers to get you started.

First, remember that your introduction should act as a funnel to guide the reader to your review question. It should broadly discuss relevant concepts, policies and/or arguments that allow the reader to clearly understand how you have arrived at your review question, and where gaps exist in the literature. Think of this section as an inverted triangle – start broadly, by outlining the scope of the problem being addressed, before narrowing down to your specific topic area. Think carefully before referring to any of your included studies in the introduction though – the purpose of this section is to justify why your review is needed, so be wary of circuitous arguments.

It's difficult to think about writing your introduction out of context, so let's imagine your review question is, 'What are the clinical, psychological, demographic and social predictors of psychological distress in uveal melanoma survivors?' You might start your introduction by outlining the scope of the problem – so, what is uveal melanoma and how is it treated? How many patients are affected (referencing, for example, point-prevalence rates or population prevalence). How many patients go on to experience psychological distress and how is this defined (e.g. consider a definition followed by prevalence rates of anxiety and depression in survivorship)? Why is psychological distress problematic – what are the clinical, emotional or financial sequelae? Why do we need to understand what predicts distress in this population (what do clinical guidelines tell us about how best to treat distress; what existing interventions are there and how efficacious are they)? What clues do cross-sectional studies (*not* the prospective studies that will be examined in the review) tell us about factors that may be associated with distress? Why is the current review important, what is the review question and what are its aims?

Your introduction should always end with a clear statement of intent – your review question and associated objectives. Imagine telling someone who is new to the topic about your review. How would you explain your rationale to them? What key pieces of information would they need to know to be able to appreciate the importance and novelty of your work? Jot these thoughts down and use them to structure the paragraphs in your introduction.

What are the 'Discussion' and 'Conclusions' sections, and why are they important?

We now turn our attention to the 'Discussion' and 'Conclusions' sections of your write-up. The purpose of these sections is to provide a critical interpretation of the results of your review related to your review question. No matter how meticulously you conduct your review, if the discussion and conclusions do not reflect the nature and limitations of both the research process and the evidence you have presented, you have not appropriately addressed your research question. The discussion and conclusions are essential parts of your thesis and of any publications arising from it.

Mullins and Kiley (2002) wrote an informative and still-relevant paper looking at *how* examiners examine a thesis by surveying 30 experienced thesis examiners. While individual styles varied, examiners generally began by reading the abstract, introduction and conclusions of a thesis, and they then read the whole thesis in detail. When reading a thesis, they asked themselves, 'How would I have tackled the problem set out in the title and abstract?' and 'Do the conclusions follow on from the introduction?' In any document, the 'Conclusions' section represents the culmination of lots of work. It is important to remember that your examiner(s) may turn to this section first. If this section seems rushed then it is likely to influence how your examiner(s) perceives the rest of your thesis, so it's important to ensure that your conclusions are as good as they can be.

Students tend to spend most of their time writing the methodological aspects of their review, including data extraction and data synthesis and analysis; very few take adequate time to reflect on the possible interpretations of the data and the conclusions that can be drawn. It's important to leave sufficient time to think through the results of your review and their importance. Similarly, if you're planning to publish your review in a peer-reviewed academic journal (see Chapter 14), it's worth bearing in mind that readers often skim-read much of the paper and turn to the 'Discussion' and 'Conclusions' sections of a systematic review to find your review's take-home messages. As a student, academic and systematic reviewer, you have a responsibility to the readers to ensure that your discussion of findings and your conclusions are accurate, evidence based, appropriate and applicable to your review question.

How do I write my 'Discussion' and 'Conclusions' sections?

Your 'Discussion' and 'Conclusions' sections need to be clearly structured and make sense to the examiner(s). When writing your 'Discussion' and 'Conclusions' sections, remember that systematic reviews are designed to combine available data from a range of sources, so *there should be very limited discussion of individual studies*. Instead, most of the discussion needs to focus on what the research tells you when you consider the data overall. We recommend including the points set out in Box 13.1, although their exact order may vary.

Box 13.1

Main components of the 'Discussion' and 'Conclusions' sections

- First, start with a brief overview of the review question and methodology. Then, answer the following questions:
  - What were the main findings of my review?
  - How do my findings fit with previously published research?
  - What are the strengths and limitations of the included studies?
  - What are the strengths and limitations of the review process?
  - Can the findings be generalized?
  - What are the implications of the review?
  - What conclusions can be drawn from the review?

Brief overview of review question and methodology

By the time the reader arrives at your 'Discussion' section, they will have already taken in lots of information. As such, it's a good idea to first remind the reader of your review question and methodology to refresh their memory. This should be a clear and concise sentence or paragraph, which summarizes the aims of the review and your methodology.

Example:

This manuscript used systematic review methodology to investigate the association between expressed emotion and shame in family carers of adults with long-term mental health difficulties. (Cherry et al., 2017)

What were the main findings of my review?

Next should come a simple statement summarizing the main finding(s) of your review. If there isn't sufficient evidence from which to draw clear conclusions then you need to make this explicit. There is no need to repeat the 'Results' section here – the purpose is to remind the reader of the overall key findings so that they have a reference point when reading the rest of your discussion.

Example:

All studies assessing the efficacy of oral flecainide and propafenone reported favourable results in comparison to other treatment strategies. Oral sotalol was not found to be as efficacious as intravenous digoxin-quinidine. (Saborido et al., 2010)

How do my findings fit with previously published research?

At this stage, you may wish to consider outlining how your findings fit with the research that you outlined in the 'Introduction' to your review, and wider empirical and theoretical literature, where relevant. Do your findings contradict common practice or national policy? Do the data support existing theory? Are you surprised by your findings, or do they make sense when interpreted in light of the wider literature base? To answer these questions, you will likely have to do some additional reading, but it will be well worth it.

Example:

Collectively, these data are consistent with the notion that carers who experience shame within the context of their own, or service users', perceived characterological deficits, may engage in emotionally over-involved behaviours in an attempt to promote a positive self-image. (Cherry et al., 2017)

Students can find this process challenging, particularly if they don't properly understand the main findings of their included studies and/or what they mean as a collective. If this is true for you, then we recommend that you discuss with your supervisor(s) how best to link your findings to the wider literature base, while reflecting on *why* you think that this may be the case (i.e. could it be a reflection of the strengths and limitations of the included studies, or of the review process itself?).

What are the strengths and limitations of the included studies?

Consider the strengths and limitations of your included studies. If your included studies are of high quality, then you will have more confidence in their results and the conclusions of your review. Re-familiarize yourself with the results of your quality assessment exercise (Chapter 8). How consistent are the findings across different studies? How similar are the participants or outcome measures used? Whose voices are *not* represented? This is your chance to summarize your view on the extent to which data from the included studies allowed you to answer your review question.

Example:

Overall, the methodological quality of the included trials was poor. All stated that patients were randomly allocated to treatment groups; however only four studies described the method of randomization and only two of these noted how allocation was concealed. Most trials included either no post-treatment follow-up or less than 6 months' follow-up. There were 15 studies with post-treatment periods of 6 months up to a maximum of 12 months. (Greenhalgh et al., 2009)

What are the strengths and limitations of the review process?

It is important to discuss the strengths and limitations of the review process as this allows you to explain why you made the methodological decisions that you did, and to reflect on how these decisions may have influenced your review findings and the quality of your review. If you can correctly identify the strengths and limitations of your systematic review, this will help you to interpret your findings in the appropriate context, thus demonstrating insight and reflection on your part.

You may wish to reflect upon whether your inclusion and exclusion criteria were appropriate (Chapter 3) and that you have not ended up with such broad inclusion criteria that a number of your included studies did not address the question you were asking. If you invested time in the development of your review question (Chapter 3), this should not happen, but sometimes it does. Alternatively, you might also find that the participants were so different across studies that you ended up 'comparing apples with oranges' – again, this ideally shouldn't happen but if it does, you should reflect on it in your discussion.

You should discuss whether your search strategy was comprehensive and appropriate (Chapter 5). For example, did you include non-English-language papers or grey literature? Did you find an abundance of literature or was there very little? Was this because of what was available or because the search strategy was inappropriate? If you found a great deal of literature, you may have decided to limit your review question – this is where you can discuss that decision and the implications for the review findings.

This section can also be used as a platform to highlight the strengths of your research and to make it clear to the examiner(s) that you understand the review process and your findings. Don't forget to reflect upon the steps taken to increase the robustness of your review. For example, did anyone (a peer, or your supervisor(s)) help you with screening and selection (Chapter 6) or cross-check your extracted data (Chapter 7)? Did you assess the quality of your included studies (the answer should be yes and this is a strength of your review) and if so, did anyone help you with this (Chapter 8)? Did you perform appropriate analyses (Chapters 9, 10, 11 and 12) and, if so, did you seek the advice of others when conducting them? Make sure that you demonstrate that your review is clear, thorough, reproducible and transparent.

You should end this part of the discussion with a statement about whether you believe you have included all, or at least a representative sample, of the available evidence relating to your question. This gives the reader your view on whether the appropriate literature has been identified for consideration.

Example:

Application of the inclusion criteria to the results of the searches identified 15 papers for inclusion in this review, a surprisingly small number given the recent growth in editorials and review pieces advocating the application of attachment theory to the study of patient–doctor communication. Nonetheless, piloting of the search strategy and supplementation of the results of the electronic search with hand searching and searching of reference lists of included papers allows confidence in the conclusion that all relevant research was included in this systematic review and that conclusions arising from this review can be based on synthesis of all available evidence. (Cherry, 2013)

Can the findings be generalized?

This question can be answered by drawing together what has been explored in the previous sections. You need to focus this part of your discussion on the implications of the review and the generalizability or transferability of your findings to your review question and professional practice. When doing so, it's important to consider to whom the results apply and whether caution should be used when translating the results to specific populations.

Example:

> Studies also reported variations in the number of participants studied (...) Method of selection also varied, from self-selecting students to randomized groups. Self-selecting students may have different characteristics than students chosen randomly to participate. Given the nature of emotional intelligence, it is possible that self-selecting students may be more motivated to respond, more assertive, and generally may score higher on the intrapersonal dimension of emotional intelligence than those who may not respond to requests for participants. This may lead to a polarization of responses, thus jeopardizing the generalizability of findings. (Cherry et al., 2012)

What are the implications of the review?

Every systematic review has implications, be they clinical, educational, research or policy related. First, the implications of your review should be discussed in terms of the relevant client groups or stakeholders. For example, in healthcare reviews of effectiveness, implications are generally considered in terms of patient care or public health, and for educational reviews, the implications for students or educators are generally discussed.

Second, you should also discuss the need (if any) for future research. Avoid saying, 'More research is needed' and try to focus on the specific study (or studies) that you would like to see take place. Give clear direction about study design, choice of outcome measure, participant groups and so on. It often helps to base these implications on the findings of your quality assessment exercise by identifying where included studies were found to be lacking. It's also important to reflect on who were *not* represented, or under-represented, in your included studies (e.g. participants who do not speak English as a first language; participants who identify as belonging to minority groups; participants whose socio-economic circumstances limit participation in research for financial reasons) so that you don't inadvertently perpetuate inequalities when proposing recommendations for future research.

There is currently a vibrant debate regarding the role of systematic reviews in making recommendations for policy (Green & Allegrante, 2020). The emerging consensus is that the findings of one systematic review are not sufficient to allow policy makers to draw firm conclusions; the results of several systematic reviews may need to be considered, alongside risk, cost and patient preference.

Example:

Future research should consider and address the methodological and conceptual limitations of currently published findings. It should aim to assess the relationship between attachment style and objective, behavioural outcomes, transferable to the clinical setting, with the goal of establishing a theoretical, observable link between attachment style and communication. Such research should be adequately powered and should consider incorporating a longitudinal study design to ensure the most rigorous and conclusive findings. (Cherry, 2013)

What conclusions can be drawn from the review?

Your 'Conclusions' section should immediately follow the 'Discussion' section. There is no consensus on how much detail should be in the 'Conclusions' section. Reviews of effectiveness papers tend to have very short 'Conclusions' sections; the conclusions tend to be, 'Yes, the treatment works and we should be using it', 'No, it does not work and we should not be using it' or 'We don't know if it works because there isn't sufficient (high-quality) research available.' Social science researchers often use the 'Conclusions' section to explore the options relating to future action that is required as a result of the findings of the review. By contrast, the conclusions of qualitative reviews often explore the richness and context of the data that have been reviewed. We suggest that you take the lead from your supervisor(s) and consider how other academics in your topic area have approached this task.

Example:

Uncertainty in the available clinical data means there is insufficient evidence to support a recommendation for the use of the pill in the pocket strategy in patients with paroxysmal atrial fibrillation. (Saborido et al., 2010)

Common pitfalls to avoid when writing your 'Discussion' and 'Conclusions' sections

It is very frustrating to read an excellent thesis that falls apart towards the end because the student didn't take sufficient time to fully consider their findings when writing their discussion and conclusions. Box 13.2 summarizes some of the most common reasons that students write poor discussion and poor conclusions.

Box 13.2

Common reasons why students write poor 'Discussion' and 'Conclusions' sections

- Not answering or addressing the review question
- Not leaving sufficient time at the end of the project to adequately examine and reflect upon their data
- Not having enough confidence in themselves and their experience to draw firm conclusions from the data – too scared of 'getting it wrong'
- Having too much confidence in themselves and making grand, sweeping, over-generalized statements
- Including data that did not match the results they were hoping to get
- Not understanding their data or their analysis and so unable to adequately conclude anything from their review
- Not critically thinking about their work or its implications

Not answering the review question

The most important aspect of the 'Discussion' and 'Conclusions' sections is to make sure that you fully address your review question (see Chapter 3). This may sound obvious, but it is surprising how many students fail to adequately answer their review question. This most frequently happens when students don't clearly define their review question, or don't have a clear protocol to follow. The students who have made these mistakes often end up wandering their way through the evidence and are still wandering while writing their discussion because they didn't have a clear idea of their final destination, or they found something else that they thought was more interesting or important and lost sight of their original question.

Too little time

It is important to work backwards from your thesis submission date and set a realistic timetable to ensure that you meet your target deadlines (see Chapter 2). Unlike other research projects where you're encouraged to meet deadlines because of external commitments to others, when you're undertaking a systematic review as a student, you work primarily independently and therefore self-discipline is required. Sometimes the best-laid plans go awry due to unforeseen circumstances – you had to wait longer than you had planned for papers from the library, or your dog ate your hard drive midway through your data extraction! What's important is that you don't take that lost time from the time you've allocated to the write-up, especially the write-up of the 'Discussion' and 'Conclusions' sections. You'd be surprised how frequently this happens, particularly when the student isn't sure of their data or how to discuss them. Results need to be mulled over or considered during a walk in the park. This won't happen if you are writing up your discussion at midnight the night before submission. It is easy to spot these kinds of reviews – we have frequently seen well-conducted systematic reviews that have been carried out meticulously with very little text in the 'Discussion' and 'Conclusions' sections because the student spent all their time and energy on the description of what they did and far too little time writing up what it all meant.

Unsure of yourself and your opinions

If you choose a topic of genuine interest to you, then you are less likely to be unsure of your opinions than if your topic is unfamiliar to you, or worse, bores you from the very beginning. You've probably spent months reading around and summarizing the research on a topic that you already care about, and are likely to already hold – or at least want to develop – an opinion about. So be confident enough to say what you think. Others can disagree with your opinion but a well-formulated synthesis, interpretation and discussion of your data is what is expected of you at this level (see Chapters 9, 10, 11 and 12). What your examiner(s) want to see is evidence of the thought processes and critical thinking that brought you to your conclusions about the data. Your examiner(s) want you to show that you have explored the implications of your data and want to see how you think current practice, or your approach to your professional work, will benefit from the review that you have carried out. Your examiner(s) might not always agree with your conclusions but if you have presented a clear case as to why and how you came to those conclusions, you have succeeded in your work.

Too much confidence

Be careful not to be too confident or sweeping in your discussion or conclusions; both need to be firmly grounded in the context and limitations of the included data and the review process. If you didn't include grey literature, say so but don't then conclude that you've summarized all of the available evidence and go on to draw conclusions with a hundred per cent certainty. Every review and study has its limitations; it's important to recognize them and not to include broad statements without references or supporting data.

The data do not say what you want them to say

This happens far more frequently than most people admit. If you are conducting a review in a topic area that interests you, you probably already have an opinion about it. All too often, these opinions are not upheld by the data from your included studies. This can be a good finding and can provide you with a starting point for your discussion; it's often very interesting to read discussions that say, 'Current practice in the area is X but the research says Y' and to read the reviewer's take on the reason(s) for this finding. What you must not do, however, is to try to adapt your data to match your views. It can be frustrating to have mentally written your discussion before properly interpreting the data only to find that you have to re-formulate your arguments. It is far better to take the time to re-think your ideas during the review process rather than be challenged by an examiner or peer reviewer at a later date.

You do not understand your data

This is a real problem and usually happens when you don't leave sufficient time to explore your findings (see Chapters 9, 10, 11 and 12). It also often occurs when you're unfamiliar with your review methods, analysis strategy and/or what the results really mean (see Chapters 9 and 10). Equally, this can be a problem when all your included studies use different outcome measures, or research participants were recruited from very diverse settings. It's important to understand what your data mean before you attempt to discuss them or draw conclusions. This might mean you need to spend a bit more time considering your data, chatting to a statistician or your supervisor(s), doing some wider reading or simply taking a break from your review for a few days. Whatever you do, it's important to fully understand the implications of your findings. If the study outcome measures or participants are too diverse to statistically synthesize, say so. If you can't draw conclusions from the data due to the presence of heterogeneity, that's OK. You can recommend that future research focuses on a more homogeneous set of participants or outcomes.

Lack of critical thinking

Your examiner(s) will be checking whether you have critically engaged with the evidence and that you understand what the data mean. This is something that many students struggle with – they can describe the data that they have extracted but the majority fail to provide their reflection on what the data actually mean. Critical thinking is important because it shows that you understand the data and the limitations of the research. It's not sufficient to assess the quality of studies and report the findings in a table in the 'Results' section but not refer to the table again. Good and well-thought-out critical thinking is what separates exceptional students from average students, and it demonstrates an ability to not only discuss findings but to understand their broader (e.g. clinical, educational or policy) implications.

It can be frustrating for an examiner to read a thesis where the student follows all of the steps but doesn't think about what the findings mean; if one study reports a strong treatment effect for drug A but only tests it on two people, you need to develop the skills to interpret these findings in relation to the study that found no effect on a thousand people. A discussion should never be a list of 'Macrae said…', 'Gomez said…' and 'Ray said…'. It needs to examine and discuss the included studies as a group, highlighting where there are similarities and differences. Then you need to discuss what you think are the possible reasons for these similarities and differences. This is what critical thinking means and it is a vital part of every systematic review. Critical thinking skills can be difficult to develop but there are a number of excellent books and online educational materials to help you (see 'Further Reading and Resources').

Final thoughts

You're now coming towards the end of this book, which has focused on the practical elements involved in conducting and reporting a systematic review within the format of a postgraduate thesis. Throughout this book, the systematic review process has been likened to a journey. As with any journey, unless you know the route well, you would expect to consult your map numerous times along the way, particularly if you get lost. Treat this book as your map. Turn down page corners, highlight text and scribble notes to yourself in margins. Revisit chapters that discuss the concepts or methods that you are unsure about and skip through chapters discussing the aspects that you are most confident about. Most importantly, make sure that you keep this book with you throughout the review process as it can act as a handy guide, particularly when you feel lost. Don't close this book just yet though. The final chapter is essential reading for any student who is undertaking a systematic review as part of their thesis because it is dedicated solely to dissemination – after all, it would be a shame not to tell the world about your excellent systematic review after all this hard work, wouldn't it?

Key points to think about when writing your protocol

- A clear and concise introductory section that outlines the rationale and need for your review
- Most protocols don't require sections on discussion and conclusions because when you write your protocol you usually have no idea what you will find

What an examiner is looking for in your thesis

- An introductory section that brings together what's already known on the topic and sets the scene for your review
- Sensible discussion of study results based on intelligent critical interpretation of the data
- Orderly discussion of important points – keep discussion of similar points together
- Reflection on your methodological and analytical choices and explanation of how these choices may have influenced your conclusions
- Conclusions that come from critical consideration and are supported by evidence from included studies

Frequently Asked Questions

Question 1: What if I don't have any studies to discuss?

It would be unusual to carry out a systematic review that will be submitted for examination with no included studies, particularly given that your examiner(s) will consider your ability to quality assess the included studies, and to extract and synthesize relevant data from them. The exception to this would be if you chose to do a systematic review as part of your doctoral research to 'prove' that no empirical studies have been carried out, thus setting the scene for your unique empirical work.

If you choose to progress with no studies, then your 'Discussion' section is likely to be the most important part of your review, as it should contain a lengthy explanation of the reasons why you didn't find any studies and the research implications arising from your review. It would be important in such a case to explain that you carried out the review because you felt that there should be studies conducted in the topic area. The fact that you didn't find any studies implies either that the topic area should be highlighted as a research priority or that it isn't generally considered to be important. We recommend that you explore both interpretations. Be sure to include a discussion of the strengths and limitations of your review process too; even though you didn't find any studies, there will be adequate room to discuss your methodological approach and its pros and cons.

Question 2: What if I disagree with the findings of my review?

It can be frustrating when you have a mental picture of what you think you will find, but then the data suggest something entirely different. In this case, it is important to have an open mind and to try to interpret your findings with respect to the data. If you expected to find an effect or relationship but didn't, you might want to think about why you expected to find that result. Are there methodological considerations in the included papers that may have influenced the findings? For example, did the papers consider only participants aged over 65, whereas you based your hypothesis on working age adults? In cases such as this, it is often valuable to discuss your findings with your supervisor(s) or a peer; often we can't see the wood for the trees and find that getting other perspectives can really help us to reframe and reinterpret unexpected data.

Question 3: What if I discover that the way I have been doing things is wrong?

At this point, it is probably too late to redo your review. The best that you can do is make sure that you reflect on what went wrong, why it went wrong and how this may have influenced your findings. It might be something out of your control, such as you couldn't access any papers from a certain journal. It might be that you missed out a key search term, or your review question was far too broad. As long as you reflect on the potential implications of your (perceived) errors on the conclusions and the implications arising from your review, you are demonstrating awareness and reflection (although there is no guarantee that this will be sufficient from an examination point of view). It happens to the best of us, so don't beat yourself up too much. Discuss your concerns with your supervisor(s) and try to account for what has happened when writing your 'Discussion' and 'Conclusions' sections.

Question 4: What if there's no clear answer to my review question because my results are conflicting?

This often happens, so don't panic! We recommend that you discuss this with your supervisor(s) and think about potential reasons for any divergence. For example, did your included studies differ widely in their use of outcome measures, or their participant groups? Was there heterogeneity in study design? If so, then these points can all be reflected upon in your discussion and may form a solid basis for recommendations for future research or practice (e.g. it may be beneficial for researchers to focus upon standardizing their methodological approaches or reporting styles in future research).

However, don't assume that the fault lies solely with the available research; it's also important to pay careful attention to your review question and inclusion and exclusion criteria – were they too broad or too narrow? What might you have done differently, in hindsight, and how can you best reflect upon this in the discussion to demonstrate your learning? It's far better to demonstrate to the examiner(s) that you have noticed and reflected upon these limitations than to hope the examiner(s) won't notice – they probably will!

Question 5: Can I reference a study in my discussion that I haven't mentioned in my introduction?

In short, yes. The purpose of your discussion is to situate the results of your review within what is already known, and what remains to be known, about your review question and broader topic area. Whilst your scoping searches and wider reading may have given you a broad idea of what you would find in your review, your results will have nuance that you will need to consider. For example, you might end up finding differences in associations between variables across genders, or an unexpected result that you need to reflect on. It's fine (and indeed, expected) to reference literature, including perhaps drawing literature from parallel fields, or wider theoretical literature, to situate and discuss your findings.

Further Reading and Resources

Booth, A., Sutton, A., Clowes, M., & Martyn-St James, M. (Eds) (2021). *Systematic approaches to a successful literature review* (3rd ed.). SAGE Publications.

Bui, Y. (2019). *How to write a master's thesis*. SAGE Publications.

14

Disseminating My Review

M. Gemma Cherry and Gerlinde Pilkington

This chapter will help you to...

- Understand the importance of disseminating your systematic review

- Think about identifying and delivering to 'target audiences'

- Gain an awareness of the different ways in which your review can be disseminated

- Gain the confidence to disseminate your review widely and successfully

Introduction

Congratulations, the end is in sight! In this final chapter, we first discuss why we think it is important for you to take the final step and disseminate your systematic review. We then present tips for successful dissemination, before outlining some common avenues for dissemination. Finally, we conclude the chapter with frequently asked questions regarding dissemination. By doing so, we hope to give you the confidence to share your systematic review with different audiences in a variety of ways.

Why should I disseminate my research?

For some of you, submission and approval of your thesis may feel like the final destination. It is a significant achievement and you should be proud of attaining your new academic standing. However, we don't think that your journey should end here. We tell students that if we were in charge, all postgraduate students undertaking a systematic review would be required to at least think about disseminating their review to a wider audience than just their supervisor(s) and examiner(s). We would also ask students to include a **dissemination strategy** in an appendix and perhaps a draft manuscript for submission to a peer-reviewed academic journal. This mirrors practice across much of the research commissioned by funding bodies which, as part of the grant application, require a dissemination and communication strategy to be included that describes how findings will be disseminated to different audiences. Of course, students are very pleased that we do not have the power to enforce this.

However, we do think you should consider how the results of your review could be disseminated. If a team of experienced researchers conduct a review, there are often expectations for everyone to contribute to dissemination, with one person taking the lead. Unfortunately, we find that some postgraduate students are hesitant to take this next logical and, it might be said, ethical step – perhaps because they feel that their review is not good enough, or don't feel confident enough to lead on dissemination (or indeed, know where and/or how to start). We do not think there is any need for hesitancy. We have read many systematic reviews with the potential to make a valuable contribution to research and practice, but these were not seen by anyone other than the student and their supervisor(s) and examiner(s) or were sent to the funders as a report and then left on the shelf to gather dust. This frustrates us, because a systematic review is an important piece of research that deserves to be disseminated. Why? The answer is simple – your work can only advance your field of study and make a difference to others if people are aware of it. Sharing the results of your work can have an impact – transferring knowledge to academics and students, policy makers, practitioners and the public, and reducing unnecessary duplication of efforts.

Disseminating adds to your credibility as a researcher – making your final review available to others shows you are a committed researcher. Dissemination is also likely to have personal benefits. For example, it's likely to boost your job prospects (and self-esteem) while helping you to gain further experience of the research process. Dissemination can also be a powerful vehicle for networking, which can help you to develop valuable contacts in your field.

But surely no one would be interested in my work!

In our experience, we have found that most postgraduate students tend to underestimate the value of their research. In fact, the most common reasons given by students for not disseminating the results of their systematic reviews are that they do not consider their reviews to be of a sufficiently high standard, or that they do not feel qualified to disseminate the results. However, postgraduate students are frequently pleasantly surprised by the feedback when they do decide to share their research results.

Where do I start?

You may now be thinking, 'OK, I'm interested … but where do I start?' or perhaps you already began to think about dissemination when you were writing your protocol (if so, well done!). Box 14.1 contains some key tips and points that may help you when thinking about disseminating your work, regardless of your subject area, discipline or field.

Box 14.1

'Top tips' for successful dissemination

Tip 1: Act promptly

Tip 2: Decide on your target audience(s)

Tip 3: Think creatively about the best way to reach your target audience(s)

Tip 4: Devise a dissemination strategy

Tip 5: Keep your target audience in mind

Tip 6: Be mindful of copyright issues

Tip 1: Act promptly

Postgraduate students often think they must wait until the review process is over before dissemination begins. Although you can't share results and findings before you have completed your review (and in some cases, submitted it for academic qualification), you can consider getting ahead early. First, you can register your protocol on PROSPERO (an international prospective register of systematic reviews) or submit it for publication in a peer-reviewed academic journal as outlined in Chapter 4. This is a good way of building interest and support for your work from those in your field. Second, academic conferences tend to have fixed deadlines for abstract submission. This means you need to plan ahead and submit abstracts for posters and oral presentations quite a few months in advance if you want to present your review. You could consider presenting your protocol, or you could apply to present 'interim findings' based on where you think you'll be up to with your review at the time of the conference.

The best time to disseminate the main findings of your systematic review is probably just after you complete the write-up, as all your hard work is still fresh and clear in your mind. However, dissemination can be the last thing on your mind at this time. Once you have completed your review, it's important to get the ball rolling as soon as possible with your chosen dissemination approach(es), especially if you have reviewed a hot topic. If you delay disseminating your results, then you risk your results becoming out of date, thus reducing your systematic review's relevance. Inevitably, some methods of dissemination take longer to come to fruition than others, as we discuss later in the chapter. However, to ensure relevance and timeliness, our first tip for successful dissemination is to start as soon as possible.

Tip 2: Decide on your target audience(s)

The next step is to ask yourself, 'Who would benefit from knowing the results of my systematic review?' There are likely to be several different audiences that could benefit from, or be affected by, the results of your review. They are summarized in Table 14.1, together with the benefits of disseminating to each group.

TABLE 14.1   Potential target audiences for your review

Potential audience	Benefits of dissemination
Students	• Encourages their journey and instils hope • Provides reference points for own research • Encourages a culture of publication and dissemination • Prevents unnecessary duplication of research efforts

Potential audience	Benefits of dissemination
Researchers	• Informs future research by adding new perspectives or strengthening existing research findings • Helps ensure that research is not duplicated • Showcases you as an expert in the area
Academics	• Helps to promote and facilitate evidence-based teaching • Ensures academics draw from the most up-to-date knowledge base • May help when supervising future research projects or applying for grants
Policy makers and local government	• Can contribute to policy development • Generates interest and debate
Practitioners at different levels	• Informs decision making, even if findings are inconclusive • Helps when planning for change in practice or innovation • Encourages evaluative culture and evidence-based practice
Service users/individuals with lived experience of the phenomena that were studied	• Promotes empowerment and involvement in research • Informs decision making, even if findings are inconclusive • Facilitates meaning making or understanding
General public	• Raises or promotes awareness of the subject area and topic being studied • Promotes public engagement in research • Enhances research transparency • Facilitates knowledge transfer

Tip 3: Think creatively about the best way to reach your target audience(s)

Once you have decided on your target audience(s), it's important to think about how best to reach them. Insomuch as there is a range of target audiences who may benefit from your findings, there is also a variety of dissemination strategies available to you. We use the term 'traditional' methods of dissemination to refer to methods such as publication in peer-reviewed academic journals or academic books, presentation at local, national and international conferences, and **thesis archiving/indexing**. Traditional methods of dissemination are excellent choices if your primary target audience includes researchers, clinicians and/or academics (as they are the most common ways in which these groups engage with research).

There are also numerous alternative methods of dissemination. These methods may help to widen both the reach and the impact of your work. There are too many alternative methods of dissemination to list exhaustively here, but examples include academic social media, informal presentations to local services or groups, short reports in newsletters, summaries posted on online forums or websites, infographics, blog entries, podcasts or audio files, media sound bites, short animations … the list goes on. Don't forget the importance of word of mouth, too. A quick search of the Internet may reveal groups with a vested interest in your results, such as third sector organizations and stakeholder groups, which may value your research contributions and want to use them or share them with others. We summarize a few common methods of dissemination, together with their pros and cons, in Table 14.2.

TABLE 14.2   Common methods of dissemination, and their pros and cons

Dissemination method	Potential audience	Pros	Cons
Peer-reviewed academic journal article	Academic peers and researchers	Good addition to your curriculum vitae	Can be a lengthy and time-consuming process
	Practitioners	Academic 'currency'	Some journals may not publish systematic reviews
		Prestige – raises your profile	There may be a fee to publish
			It is hard on your ego when they reject your submission – so be thick-skinned
Conference proceedings	Academic peers and researchers	Abstracts are often published and searchable	May not feel comfortable presenting
	Practitioners	Good for networking with academic peers	Prohibitive costs of travel/accommodation
		Can choose method of dissemination (e.g. poster presentations are more informal than oral presentations)	Cost of printing, including mistakes (poster)
			May require time off work/study which can exclude certain people
Institutional repository	Academic peers and researchers	Institutional archiving requires little effort	Be careful to check copyright issues
		Online repository upload is a free way of disseminating your review	Might be important to choose indexed keywords carefully
		Can be found by search engines	Not all master's theses are archived, and not all institutions have accessible electronic repositories
Blogging	Academic peers and researchers	Free and inclusive way to share ideas	Takes effort and time to build a readership and provide content
	Service users	Adds to academic discourse	May have to pay for domain name/upkeep
	General public	Gives you good practice in writing for a variety of audiences	
Microblogging	Academic peers and researchers	Easily accessible	Takes effort and time to build a readership and provide content
	Policy makers	Can share other researchers' content	Not specifically for academic use – consider the impact of including social content on your professional profile
	Practitioners	Good for networking and keeping up to date with current research	
	Service users		
	General public		

Dissemination method	Potential audience	Pros	Cons
Academic social networking site(s)	Academic peers and researchers	Can upload documents and share research content Can network and make contact with academic peers Keeps you up to date with other research	Requires some effort to build a network and appropriate profile Regular upkeep may be required

When thinking about dissemination, remember that each systematic review is different, which means that each dissemination strategy is different. It's important to be creative and to remember that your colleagues, peers, or supervisor(s) are well placed to recognize the contribution that the results of your review might make to the professional practice of others. They may be able to offer you advice in the first instance on how to disseminate the findings of your systematic review. If your wider research involves PPIE (patient and public involvement and engagement) colleagues or you have links to a study advisory group, you have access to experts who can help you identify appropriate audiences, support you to write in plain English and co-develop your dissemination strategy.

Tip 4: Devise a dissemination strategy

We recommend that you devise a clear dissemination strategy and discuss and agree this strategy with your supervisor(s). When thinking about a dissemination strategy, it's helpful to think about:

- The most appropriate ways to reach your target audience(s)
- The audiences that you may *exclude* by selecting or prioritizing certain methods of dissemination over others
- The time that you (and your supervisor(s)) have available for dissemination
- Your motivation and enthusiasm for dissemination
- Your skill-set(s)
- The findings of your systematic review

A clear dissemination strategy can act as a guide or map for your dissemination journey, prevent you from losing focus and keep you motivated and on track. As mentioned previously, a dissemination strategy also makes an excellent addition to the appendix of your thesis, and demonstrates a commitment to good practice.

Tip 5: Keep your target audience in mind

Successful dissemination requires you to meet the needs of your target audience(s). For example, it would be unrealistic to expect your systematic review to be published in a newspaper or narrated as a podcast in its entirety – people would switch off almost immediately, irrespective of how well written it may be. Adapting your review to suit different target audiences may seem like an onerous task. To help with this, we include some prompts for writing for dissemination in Box 14.2.

Box 14.2

Prompts for writing for dissemination

Do:

- Keep the reader in mind; avoid assuming expert knowledge and use simple language
- Write concisely; avoid tangents and digressions
- Tell a story to your reader
- Emphasize the strengths and novelty of your work
- Seek feedback from others
- Look at examples, and stick to guidelines and word counts, where appropriate
- Structure your work carefully
- Highlight the relevance to your audience
- Explain why the audience should be interested in your findings

Don't:

- Feel as though you must include everything – key points are often enough
- Overuse jargon, unless appropriate for the audience
- Self-plagiarize, and think carefully about copyright
- Lose your work's fidelity or key messages along the way

Tip 6: Be mindful of copyright issues

Our final tip is to always check copyright law, particularly if you want to disseminate your review in several ways. So long as you have the copyright to your work, you are free to disseminate it however you see fit. But you *must* be sure of this to avoid difficulties further down the line.

Copyright applies to all manner of creative works, but especially intellectual property. Your thesis is your intellectual property, of which you are automatically the copyright owner. However, there may be issues with archiving/indexing your thesis if it contains third-party materials such as photographs or figures, or if you have borrowed extensive extracts from published or unpublished works (even when cited or attributed appropriately) and permission has not been sought from the copyright holder – in these instances check with your institution for clarification and assistance. Be aware that if you have signed agreements with government or funding bodies who have a stake in the intellectual property rights to your thesis, you may also need to check on your rights to publish or deposit your thesis electronically.

In addition, be mindful that most publishers require you to assign them the copyright to your work when your article is accepted for publication in one of their journals – in effect, many researchers do not have the copyright to their articles. This may have a bearing on whether you can deposit your thesis in a repository, as some publishers consider theses to be 'prior publications'. In these circumstances, it may be necessary to place restrictions on the deposited thesis, so that only an abridged or shortened version is available for a period of time, or only the record title is visible for a set period of time (i.e. the full text can't be accessed until an 'embargo' period has passed). Your institution should be able to provide you with further information and guidance. Also, be aware that some peer-reviewed academic journals may allow authors to distribute or make available different versions of their publications. For example, a researcher may be permitted to distribute an earlier version of the published article on a social networking site without contravening any copyright laws. If you have any doubts or queries about copyright, you must contact the publisher for guidance.

Serious about dissemination? Read on...

By now, we hope that you are starting to think seriously about disseminating your review. We now briefly discuss some key methods of dissemination in more depth: dissemination through publication in a peer-reviewed academic journal, dissemination in the form of conference proceedings, dissemination through thesis archiving/indexing and dissemination through academic social media.

Dissemination through publication in a peer-reviewed academic journal

By now, you will be familiar with peer-reviewed academic journals, as you will likely have sifted through hundreds, if not thousands, of journal articles while conducting your review. There's a good reason for this – peer-reviewed academic journal articles are often seen as currency in the research community and, as such, publication in a peer-reviewed academic journal is an excellent option if you want to reach research, academic and professional audiences. It is important to keep in mind that most journals publish only a small proportion of the submissions that they receive and therefore the process of publication can often be frustrating, time-consuming and difficult for would-be authors. We outline eight key steps involved in disseminating your review through publication in a peer-reviewed academic journal (see Box 14.3).

Box 14.3

Steps involved in disseminating through publication in a peer-reviewed academic journal

Step 1: Think very carefully about the suitability of your review for publication in a peer-reviewed academic journal

Step 2: Pick an appropriate journal

Step 3: Decide on authorship (and author order)

Step 4: Turn your review into a paper

Step 5: Write your covering letter

Step 6: Submit your paper

Step 7: Receive and respond to reviewers' and/or editors' comments

Step 8: Receive final decision

Step 1: Think very carefully about the suitability of your review for publication in a peer-reviewed academic journal

Before you start, it's important to carefully consider whether your review is suitable for publication in a peer-reviewed academic journal. Most academic journals apply stringent standards and checks to the papers that they publish, and therefore it's important to make sure that your work doesn't fall at the first hurdle. We recommend that you reflect upon the scientific rigour of your work, the importance of your findings and the conclusions that you were able to draw. How can the quality assurance of your work be communicated? You should apply a quality assessment tool to your review, as discussed in Chapter 8, to see whether it meets quality standards – you can be sure that the journal's peer reviewers will do this, so beat them to it and address any issues. Most issues do not preclude publication in a peer-reviewed academic journal but may require some careful phrasing or reframing in your submission (e.g. pointing out the limitations of the review and the potential implications for the review's conclusions). Alternatively, you may wish to consider repackaging the results of your systematic review by writing a discussion paper in which you reflect upon the lack of evidence. This may be of particular value in fields where evidence is lacking and direction and guidance for further research is needed.

At this stage, it's also essential to consider the timeliness of your review. How long has it been since you ran your searches or completed your review? Do your searches need updating to ensure that your review findings are current? If there's a time lag between searching and submission, this is likely to be picked up at the peer-review stage. Have you checked for any similar systematic reviews that may have been published *after* you completed your review? It might sound obvious, but it's an important step as there's no point trying to publish your work if someone has already beaten you to it (unless you can strongly argue that you have a unique angle). These considerations may take some time, but in our opinion it's time well spent, as it may potentially help you to avoid disappointment later on. Gauge others' opinions as to the suitability of your review for publication at this stage, including your supervisor(s). This may help you to view your work more objectively and spot potential limitations that may otherwise have passed you by.

Step 2: Pick an appropriate journal

Once you are satisfied that your review is eligible and suitable for publication in a peer-reviewed academic journal, it's important to carefully select the most appropriate one. When doing so, it's helpful to consider several factors.

The first is the subject area and readership of the journal. Which journals publish work in a similar topic area to yours? Do these journals accept systematic review articles or do they prioritize primary research? Have there been any calls for review articles lately from these journals? It may be helpful at this stage to consider where the included papers in your review were published, as this normally gives a good indication of the key journals in your field. A brief email or letter of enquiry to the journal's editor may help to answer some of your questions and to clarify the relevance and appropriateness (or otherwise) of your proposed submission.

The second is the prestige and quality of the journal. Prestige and quality are traditionally measured in terms of **impact factor** – a term used to refer to the average number of times an article in that journal has been cited (i.e. referenced) over the past year. Put more plainly, an impact factor of 1.0 indicates that you may expect your article to be cited once in the year post-publication, whereas an impact factor of 4.0 would indicate four citations over that same one-year period. Generally speaking, many academics would argue that the higher the journal's impact factor the better. However, impact factor isn't everything – you should also consider the context of the topic area and target audience for your work. For example, some fields of study are relatively small; although your review may have a significant impact and be cited widely within that field, articles published in journals in niche areas will probably be cited less than articles published in more mainstream journals, thereby leading to a lower impact factor for niche journals. Furthermore, if one of the goals of publication is to inform practice, reaching your audience through a journal with an appropriate readership has more impact than publishing in a more prestigious journal. It is also important to note that a journal needs to have been indexed in the Web of Science for at least three years before an impact factor can be calculated, which means that newer journals do not have an assigned impact factor. A journal's ranking within the field often gives a more balanced view of its prestige than impact factor alone. There are several websites dedicated to this, which can be easily found via an Internet search.

Third, consider cost. We are in the middle of a transition from print to online publishing, which is an exciting time for the research community. In light of this, many peer-reviewed academic journals now offer open-access publication, which means that anyone can view their publications as long as they have Internet access. This is in contrast to journals that require a subscription before articles can be viewed. There are obvious advantages to open-access publication, not least that it widens the readership beyond those who subscribe to a particular journal. However, there are also costs – literally. The fee to be published in an open-access journal can be substantial, so it's imperative to check at this stage whether your institution (or funding arrangement where applicable) is willing to cover the cost. If not, cross open-access journals off your list and start again.

Finally, think about structure and length. Often the length of your article determines your choice of journal; if you have a lot to say, then consider journals with more generous word limits, and remember that different types of articles are often allocated different word limits. If you wish to submit a concise summary, this may not be as much of a concern. Some journals will allow a certain number of supplementary materials (e.g. additional tables and figures, similar to what you might find in an appendix) which are accessible online, and this might help with word limits.

At this stage, you may find that you've narrowed your choice down to three or four potentially suitable journals. Remember, it is worth aiming high (i.e. choosing good-quality journals) to start with, even if you don't think you've got a shot at acceptance. You might be very pleasantly surprised, or, at the very least, you may receive useful reviewers' comments, which may help you to address any issues with your review prior to submitting to another journal.

Step 3: Decide on authorship (and author order)

The next step is to discuss and decide on authorship. The term 'authorship' refers to who is listed as an author on your submitted paper, together with the order of authors. Author position means different things in different disciplines but generally indicates an author's degree of involvement in, and contribution to, the paper. The first author should always be the person who has made the largest contribution to the final manuscript and would normally be either the principal investigator or the researcher who has conducted the research and written up the results (you!). Authors are then listed in terms of decreasing contribution to the manuscript. In some disciplines, being last author is seen to be almost as prestigious as first author – this position is normally reserved for the project manager or lead supervisor. However, this doesn't always carry across different disciplines, so it's important to check the degree of responsibility, contribution and prestige attached to each position in an authorship list. Ask your supervisor(s) if you are unsure.

Determining authorship sounds simple but in practice can be challenging. It may be that your academic institution has a policy on the publication of research findings from thesis projects, which may outline the inclusion of supervisors as authors on all publications. If your institution does not have a publication policy, and you have not had this discussion with your supervisor(s), then now is the time. You may automatically want to include your supervisor(s), which may indeed be appropriate, but it's important to consider their contribution to the final manuscript. Most peer-reviewed academic journals have guidelines on what constitutes inclusion as an author; the International Committee of Medical Journal Editors (ICMJE, www.icjme.org) suggests that to be eligible for authorship you must have made a 'substantial contribution' to the work and the drafting or revising of the manuscript in addition to approving the version for submission and agreeing to be accountable for the work published. These guidelines apply to any author and so, in addition to considering the contribution of your supervisor(s), you should also reflect upon your fellow students' contributions: did a friend help you with your screening or selection stages and if so, does this constitute a substantive scientific contribution? Probably not, but this needs to be clear and transparent from the start of their involvement to avoid any difficulties or conflict later on. Most journals allow you to include an acknowledgements section where you can name people who do not fulfil the explicit criteria for authorship but who have assisted you with your work. As a student, you may find that making good use of the acknowledgements section allows you to retain full ownership of your work whilst still giving recognition to people who have helped ensure the rigour of your review.

Step 4: Turn your review into a paper

This is another step that sounds deceptively easy – you've already done the hard work, right? However, transforming your review into a draft paper for submission to a journal requires skill, time and patience. You may have to update elements of your review, as previously discussed, which can feel like lots of additional work (which is why we suggest you write the paper as you are finishing writing your review). You'll also likely need to compress your work into a concise and readable article that tells a story to the reader. It can be heart breaking to delete paragraphs that you've spent hours getting just right but the key to writing a journal article is succinctness. You may wish to request the input of your co-authors at this stage, particularly if you're not able to view your work objectively.

When writing your manuscript, it's essential to conform to the journal's guidelines for authors; otherwise your paper will be immediately returned to you. This means adhering to the journal's preferred referencing style, formatting style (including font, spacing and language requirements) and word limit. Journals often also request that tables and figures be submitted separately to the final manuscript, so expect to put something like *Insert Table 1 here* in the final submission in place of the original table. Journals often send out anonymized manuscripts for peer review, and so they may ask you to anonymize your final submission or include a separate title page. They may also ask for additional requirements, such as short biographies, an explicit statement of author contributions, keywords or bullet points that summarize the key findings of your review, or a declaration of competing interests. These requirements should all be clearly stated in the author guidelines, which are usually available on the journal website, but this can take up valuable time and they often differ between journals, making formatting frustrating.

Step 5: Write your covering letter

When you submit your manuscript, you'll normally be expected to include a brief covering letter to the editor (see Box 14.4 for an example of a covering letter for a review that was later accepted for publication). This is a valuable opportunity for you to outline the unique contribution that your review makes, and one that should not

be underestimated. We recommend that you address your letter to the editor person-
ally (their name can usually be found on the journal's website) to demonstrate your
interest in that particular journal. It's often helpful to keep letters short by:

- outlining the title of your review and its main findings
- explicitly stating the novelty of your review and what it adds to the existing literature base
- explaining why it is likely to be of interest to the journal's readership and why it
  is specifically appropriate for this journal
- politely requesting that it be considered for publication in the journal

Box 14.4

Example covering letter to an editor of a peer-reviewed academic journal

Dear [insert editor's name here]

As you may recall, we were in correspondence last year regarding a systematic review that myself and my colleagues from the UK were conducting. We
have now finished the review, which is entitled 'The relationship between
perfectionism and exercise self-efficacy: a systematic review' and wish to
submit it for consideration by *Frontiers in Psychology*. The systematic review
narratively synthesizes the findings of 10 studies, reported in 15 papers,
which investigate the relationship between perfectionism and exercise self-
efficacy in adults aged 18 and over. This is an area which, to the best of our
knowledge, has not been systematically explored to date, yet which we feel
can add a valuable contribution to the literature base. We hope that the findings of the review may facilitate a greater understanding of the psychological
processes underpinning exercise self-efficacy. We feel that the submission is
timely in light of the recent governmental update to national physical activity
guidelines. We also feel that the paper would be of relevance and interest to
your readers and would fit well with the scope and remit of the journal. As
such, we hope that it will be considered for publication.

Thank you very much.

Sincerely,

[Callum Longworth]

Step 6: Submit your paper

Again, this step sounds like a simple process but it can take some time. Normally, papers are submitted to journals using an online system. This usually requires researchers to first create an account with their journal of choice by following the instructions on the journal's home page. Once this has been created, you'll be asked to add in your details such as positions and affiliation(s), contact details, and **ORCID ID** (Open Researcher and Contributor ID; a unique persistent digital identifier, which takes minutes to register for and allows you, and others, to view all of your scholarly activity in a single space). You will also be expected to fill in similar details for your co-authors, and you'll usually have to select areas of interest and keywords for the paper too. You will have to submit a PRISMA (Preferred Reporting of Items for Systematic Reviews and Meta-Analyses) checklist to show you are following the guidelines for reporting a systematic review, and you will probably have to fill out an ICMJE conflict of interest form. Finally, you'll be asked to submit each of your files electronically and in the correct file type (i.e. manuscript, figures, tables, cover letter, etc.) and then approve a PDF proof of the final submission. Ensure that you allow a few hours to make sure that you get this right; otherwise you may fall at the first hurdle (i.e. the manuscript never even gets considered). It's also important to check that you provide the correct contact details – this sounds self-explanatory, but you'd be surprised at the number of students who provide an institutional email address which may be about to expire.

Step 7: Receive and respond to reviewers' and/or editors' comments

Usually, members of the journal's editorial team are the first to evaluate submissions. The purpose is to ensure that submissions are of a suitable quality, relevance and format to be sent out for peer review. Sometimes you'll hear back from the editor immediately. They may request additional materials or edits, or merely reply with a thank you but no. The latter can be disheartening but we prefer to look at the positives – we would rather be told 'no' quickly than wait months for the same outcome, and it may not reflect the quality or focus of our work but the level of interest from other authors who have submitted papers to the journal.

Most of the time, articles are sent to a jury of peers (usually three or four academics, researchers or clinicians in the field) to be evaluated, normally against a standardized checklist or set of criteria. As you can imagine, this may take some time, as the submission first has to be sent out to potential reviewers, they respond, and then their comments have to be received, collated and sent back to you. Furthermore, most reviewers are not paid for their time but offer their services in a voluntary capacity.

As you can imagine, their paid work can often take precedence over reviewing papers, therefore leading to delays. Most journals' home pages contain information about how long you can expect to wait before you receive a response, so we recommend being patient and not contacting the journal unless you've been waiting longer than you might reasonably expect.

Occasionally, the editor may reply to say that they wish to accept the submission in its current form. If this happens to you, well done! It's a very rare occurrence, so you should be very proud of yourself. The most common outcomes, however, are either an outright 'no' or 'revise and resubmit'. If it's a 'no', try not to get disheartened. In 1937, Krebs' and Johnson's seminal paper, about (you guessed it) the Krebs cycle, was rejected by *Nature* before later being accepted by *Enzymologia* (Holmes, 1993), so you're in good company. We hope you will receive some constructive feedback alongside the 'no', which may be helpful when you submit to your second-choice journal. We suggest that you return to Step 4 and begin the process again. However, although it might be tempting to address all comments before submitting to your second-choice journal, only address comments if you're certain that, by doing so, you will improve the quality of the paper – it's often not worth the effort to tailor the paper to a single reviewer as you are likely to receive feedback from people with different opinions in your next peer review.

If the response is a 'revise and resubmit', well done. This is a good outcome, although it may feel disheartening to have to do even more work on your review. There are often no guarantees that your review will be accepted pending changes but it gives you an opportunity to demonstrate why your research is worthy of publication. It's important to note that you might be asked to revise and resubmit your paper several times to the same journal, so keep your spirits high each time. Box 14.5 contains some tips for revising and resubmitting; additional pointers can be found in an excellent article by Paltridge (2013).

Box 14.5

Tips for revising and resubmitting your manuscript

- Carefully consider the reviewers' and/or editors' comments
- Try to take emotion out of your interpretation; it's not a personal attack (having a thick skin can be helpful)

(Continued)

- Make amendments in line with suggestions, where appropriate
- Don't feel as though you have to address *all* comments; if you disagree, or the comments are contradictory, then clearly and politely outline your decision to disregard comments
- Track changes or note the location of your changes or edits in the text
- Outline your responses to the reviewers' and/or editors' comments in a point-by-point letter, addressed to the editor
  - Begin by thanking the reviewers for their good suggestions and their help in improving the manuscript; they generally aren't paid for the role, so it's important to express your appreciation
  - Respond to each point in turn, and don't forget to acknowledge positive comments. This is often a strategic move, as it reminds the editor of the novelty and worth of your paper, which they'll likely have forgotten by the time they receive your response
  - Indicate the location of changes in your paper (using page and line numbers)
  - Clearly outline the changes you've made to your paper, using direct quotations from the paper where appropriate – you could do this in a table or in prose form to reduce the burden on the reviewer
- Take the opportunity to check for errors in your original submission when responding to comments (and fix them)

Step 8: Receive final outcome

Congratulations, you're nearing the end. We hope you will receive a 'yes' from the journal, in which case we say a big 'well done' to you. Expect to receive proofs of your article some time after your paper has been accepted; these are often accompanied by queries from the copyediting team. Reply promptly and take the opportunity to check for additional errors in the manuscript – this is your last chance. Once published, celebrate by giving signed copies of your manuscript to everyone you know. If it's a 'no', don't worry. It's common to receive a negative response even after several cycles of revising and resubmitting. It can feel really disheartening but consider the reasons for rejection – might you need to revise your style before submitting to another journal? When you're ready, revisit Step 4 and begin again. Don't lose heart; plenty of papers are rejected from numerous journals before being accepted for publication.

Dissemination in the form of conference proceedings

Local, national and international conferences are also great places to disseminate your research, especially to clinical and academic audiences, as they often represent a snapshot of the most cutting-edge research around. There are many benefits to disseminating your work in the form of conference proceedings (i.e. oral or written communication). For example, you don't have to wait until you have finished your review; in fact, you can apply to present your work during almost all stages of the review process, from protocol through to completion. Not only does this give you the opportunity to hone your skills and learn how to succinctly communicate your work to others in the field, but you are also likely to receive valuable feedback from others and therefore you may be able to spot studies of relevance to your review even before they are published. Conference attendance also enables you to meet like-minded others, make valuable connections and contribute to advancing your own research profile and your field of study.

There are numerous ways in which you can find out about conferences in your topic area. For example, you could try searching the Internet, signing up to relevant mailing lists, looking for calls for applicants to conferences, speaking to your supervisor(s) or connections in your field or keeping an eye out for advertisements in relevant peer-reviewed academic journals. Our advice to you is to think small as well as big; local university-based or clinical conferences are as good a place to start as any and may help you to build your confidence before applying to a national or international conference. Institutions often organize conferences or events for postgraduate students or early career researchers to discuss their work – if you are offered this opportunity, do participate, you're likely to learn a lot.

When applying to present at conferences, there are a few things that we recommend you consider. First, think about funding. Often, local conferences charge a nominal fee, yet national or international conferences can be costly. As well as the conference attendance fee, which can vary between conferences, you also need to factor in travel and accommodation costs. It's worth having a funding strategy in place before agreeing to attend a specific conference, but don't worry if you can't afford to self-fund. Often, conferences offer reduced rates for students, and have a look to see whether your university has a conference budget that may cover you; you can also check for wider institutional or national grants that would cover costs.

Next, it's important to think about the type of contribution that you would like to make, and the time frame available to you. Would you like to do an oral presentation? This option is typically a short (10–30 minutes) presentation with slides in front of a group of conference delegates who then might ask a few questions about your work, or it could take the form of a shorter rapid-fire presentation of three to five minutes with limited time for questions afterwards. Perhaps you would feel more comfortable preparing a poster, which you then talk about? Usually, posters are displayed throughout the conference, and there are dedicated sessions in between oral presentation sessions when delegates have the chance to look at posters and ask questions about the research. In both cases, consider what the application process is like. Do you have time to prepare a poster (it will have to conform to certain size and format requirements, and will take time and cost money to print)? What is the deadline for applications? Who will be your co-authors? Usually, conferences require that you submit a short abstract of your work, which may take some time to prepare. It will be peer reviewed and the outcome fed back to you in due course, so it's also important to think about the deadline for abstract submissions in your planning process. Sometimes, you may apply for an oral presentation and instead be asked to give a poster presentation, so think carefully about whether you would accept this option if it was offered to you.

Finally, once you've been accepted as a delegate, it's important to be well prepared. There are lots of excellent resources available to help guide you through the conference process, from the design of a presentation or poster through to the day itself. Don't forget to include your conference proceedings on your curriculum vitae too; they are something to be very proud of.

Dissemination through archiving/indexing

We use the term 'archiving/indexing' to refer to the electronic or physical storage of a thesis within a repository or library. Thesis archiving/indexing is a relatively straightforward method of dissemination, and one that may be mandatory for postgraduate students upon award of their degree. Most universities have their own repositories whereby students can archive/index their work electronically (i.e. upload a final version of their thesis as a PDF or Word document). There are also online repositories that span institutions and countries, such as ProQuest (www.proquest.com), OpenThesis (https://library.queensu.ca/search/database/openthesis) and the British Library's e-theses online service (https://ethos.bl.uk). To give you an example of how wide-reaching these repositories can be, ProQuest is accessed by over 3000 institutions worldwide, and disseminates and archives over 90,000 graduate theses per year. Access and costs for other repositories vary (e.g. indexing is free in ProQuest but a subscription is required to access full-text copies of theses by other people).

Not all institutions offer postgraduate students the opportunity to archive/index their thesis, but we would strongly recommend that you archive your work if this option is available to you as it's an excellent way to expand the audience of your systematic review. Many indexes also allow postgraduate students to place a restriction on access rights (e.g. for a two-year period) so that they have time to publish or disseminate their findings. However, it's worth checking whether this option is available to you, together with the copyright agreements for online indexers, *before* you deposit your work, so as to avoid any nasty surprises later on.

Dissemination through academic social media

Although peer-reviewed academic journal articles still hold a great deal of currency in the world of academia (and probably always will), researchers are increasingly using more creative ways to share their ideas and findings to a much wider audience (including academics, peers, practitioners, politicians, stakeholders and the public), thus increasing both the potential impact of their work and their academic/professional profile. In particular, using social media for academic purposes (or using specific academic social media) is increasing in popularity. We use the term 'social media' to refer to platforms used for blogging, **microblogging**, networking and sharing content. Used appropriately, social media are an instantaneous way to publicly share your views or links to interesting articles, comment or share the work of peers, and establish connections and engage with others in your field. Different platforms can allow you to:

- Create a public profile with academic interests, specialisms
- Upload your own published/unpublished papers as PDFs or share links to your work or its key findings
- Establish a network of contacts who can send messages and engage with content
- Instantly receive feedback, encouragement and publicity from others
- Engage with current discourses and debates in your field, and discover new work
- Stay up to date with current research and practice – e.g. conferences often use searchable hashtags to help users identify specific content for events
- Gain experience of academic writing

Don't forget, social media aren't foolproof: you'll need to get used to conventions and norms, set up and manage accounts, and take time to explore how different social media sites operate and how to get the best from your chosen platform(s). Mark Carrigan's book *Social Media for Academics* (2019) provides an excellent introduction to the world of academic social media and is worth a read if you choose this method of dissemination. A word of caution though: as with any method of online dissemination, always be sure to read the terms of service before posting anything online and pay special attention to copyright issues. Furthermore, make sure that you are aware of institutional rules – for example, are you required to include a disclaimer that your posts reflect your views rather than those of your institution? You can normally find out more about specific policies from your institution but this is well worth checking before starting out.

Final thoughts

We hope that this chapter has encouraged you to consider how the results of your review could be disseminated to a range of audiences and we wish you well in your dissemination journey.

Frequently Asked Questions

Question 1: When should I disseminate my systematic review?

Obviously, it wouldn't be appropriate to focus all your efforts on disseminating your review before you've written it (and/or your thesis, depending on your level of study), as this must take priority. However, this doesn't mean that you can't take small steps towards disseminating your work early on. For example, as discussed in Chapter 4, it's an excellent idea to register your review on the PROSPERO database as soon as you can, provided that your review relates to health and social care, welfare, public health, education, crime, justice, and/or international development. The PROSPERO database includes basic protocol details for each registered review, so even if you don't take any further dissemination steps, at least your protocol is out there for all to see.

Many conferences have a closing date for submission of abstracts for consideration for oral or poster presentations, so it's also worth making sure that you don't miss these while writing your review. You don't need to have finished your review to submit an abstract (although it often helps if your abstract includes your results and conclusions); instead, you can say that your oral or poster presentation will include a discussion of the main findings of your review.

With respect to your completed review, if you don't want to be drafting an academic journal article while finalizing your review for submission, why not consider taking the time between submission and examination to prepare your manuscript for submission to a peer-reviewed academic journal, taking time to scope out the journals and begin the submission process?

Question 2: Do I need to list my supervisor(s) as co-authors even if they haven't helped me to prepare my review for submission to a peer-reviewed academic journal?

This is a common worry faced by students. If your institution does not have a policy for publication, we would advise you to refer back to the journal's guide for authors and/or the ICMJE guidelines and agree potential authors' contributions as early as possible. Having said that, the contributions made by a supervisor to a systematic review, and those made by a co-author, may differ. For example, a supervisor may not substantially rewrite a section of a discussion, whereas a co-author may. Transparency is the key: discuss how to manage this early on and keep returning to published guidance if it becomes blurry.

Question 3: My supervisor(s) haven't mentioned publication – what should I do?

If your supervisor(s) haven't mentioned publication, don't dismiss it out of hand. This does not mean that your work is unpublishable – they may not think you want to publish, or they may just be too busy to have given it any thought. Having said that, if they raise concerns about whether your work is of a publishable standard, listen to these concerns carefully and consider how best to proceed.

Question 4: I received permission from the author of a quality assessment tool to include it in the appendix of my thesis for examination purposes. What does this mean for dissemination?

This is a tricky one. If the measure is freely available in the public domain without copyright restrictions, you are free to disseminate it how you wish (e.g. by including it in the appendix of a journal article, or by posting it on academic social media). However, if it is not (e.g. if it has been published in a subscription-only peer-reviewed academic journal) you *must* check copyright before disseminating it in any way other than that permitted by its author (e.g. even by archiving/indexing your thesis with it in the appendix). You can't be too careful.

Further Reading and Resources

Beller, E., Glasziou, P., Altman, D., Hopewell, S., Bastian, H., Chalmers, I., Gøtzsche, P.C., Lasserson, T., Tovey, D., & the PRISMA for Abstracts Group. (2013). PRISMA for abstracts: reporting systematic reviews in journal and conference abstracts. *PLoS Med, 10*(4), e1001419.

Carrigan, M. (2019). *Social media for academics* (2nd ed.). SAGE Publications.

Kamler, B. (2008). Rethinking doctoral publication practices: writing from and beyond the thesis. *Studies in Higher Education, 33*(3), 283–94.

Paltridge, B. (2013). Referees' comments on submissions to peer-reviewed journals: when is a suggestion not a suggestion? *Studies in Higher Education, 40*(1), 106–22.

Piper, P. (2014). Writing your journal or conference abstract. *Journal of Pediatric Surgical Nursing, 3*(2), 47–50.

Thompson, B., & Kamler, P. (2012). *Writing for peer reviewed journals: Strategies for getting published*. Routledge.

Epilogue

First, we'd like to thank our loyal readers for their continued support and guidance. We'd also like to thank our authors who have worked tirelessly, under difficult circumstances, during and post-COVID-19, to hone their contributions – this book wouldn't be possible without them. Finally, we would like to thank our colleagues at Sage Publishing for their unwavering faith in our expertise and for keeping our dreams of literary success alive!

We finish this book at a very different time and place from where we began. Four years ago, we couldn't have imagined working predominantly remotely, choosing to work unsociable hours around other commitments or routinely video-calling colleagues and students in different places and time zones, but this has now become our new normal. For us as academics, this way of working has brought many positives (e.g. we've been able to continue collaborating with students and colleagues across the globe, including Rumona, who has moved back to Canada), but has also brought many challenges (e.g. the blurring of boundaries between our work and home lives). What's clear to us, however, is that hybrid and/or remote working is here to stay and we fully expect this shift to be influential in shaping future systematic review methodology and conduct. For researchers embedded within a supportive team, these changes will likely be beneficial. However, for postgraduate students new to reviewing and who may also be grappling with additional challenges, such as adjusting to a new academic programme, location and/or subject area, these changes may not be as welcome. Thinking ahead, we strongly encourage students and supervisors to reflect on the potential impact of these changes, take the necessary steps to mitigate any possible negative consequences, and optimize mental health, social connectedness and student experience wherever possible.

An epilogue is supposed to focus on the future and writing this epilogue has led us to an epiphany. We planned to write about advancements in review methodology and the future of systematic reviews but quickly realized that we may need to adapt our approach for subsequent editions to ensure that we meet the ever-changing needs of our readers. As much as we would like to pretend that we are still in our twenties, the reality is that our children are closer in age to the target audience of this book than we are (sob). This made us pause and reflect on *how* the current (and next) generation of students do (and will) learn, and how we can ensure that this resource is future-proofed and continues to meet postgraduate students' needs. We know how to do systematic reviews but technological advances mean that we have to work hard to keep up with the spiralling developments in how students access information and how review methodology will likely evolve. We are committed to continuing to author new editions of this book until it is no longer useful but recognize that students increasingly value instant access to information and that a textbook is not the only way to engage new learners. We therefore plan to spend more time engaging with students so that, by the time we edit the fourth edition, we can put into practice what we have learned and can adapt and improve our approach. Please continue to let us know how you use this book and how we might improve subsequent editions to continue to meet our readers' needs.

With best wishes

Gemma, Angela and Rumona

Glossary

Academic integrity software Software such as TurnItIn that encourages honest and moral behaviour in an academic setting and uses built-in systems that have been developed to ensure that appropriate credit is awarded to people whose ideas are being used by others, copyright is protected and plagiarism is minimized.

Academic social networking sites Commercial websites that enable and encourage academics to promote and share their work and engage with other users.

Action research (also known as: participatory action research) A study that is initiated to generate solutions to practical problems, typically conducted in the field of education. Often called 'participatory action research' because participants become involved in gathering information about the issue and implementing a solution, thus blurring the distinction between the 'researcher' and the 'researched'.

Active control group A comparator group in which participants believe they have received some kind of intervention.

Allocation bias Bias common to intervention studies, which occurs as a result of methods used to allocate participants to different intervention or treatment comparison groups.

Analysis of Variance (ANOVA) A statistical test comparing three or more groups.

Analytical data Qualitative or quantitative study results.

ANCOVA (also known as Analysis of Covariance) A statistical test comparing two or more groups whilst adjusting for an uncontrolled variable.

Assessing the Methodological Quality of Systematic Reviews (AMSTAR 2) An 11-item measurement tool for assessing the quality of systematic reviews.

Attrition bias Bias common to intervention studies, which occurs because of differences in participant withdrawal rates between intervention or treatment comparison groups.

Backward searching (also known as backward snowballing) The process of consulting the bibliography of a key reference to find other relevant research.

Base year (also known as base period) A term used in economic studies to refer to the year used as the beginning or reference year for comparison when calculating an economic index.

Between-subjects design (also known as independent groups design) A study design in which participants in a single group provide outcome data.

Bias Distorted or inaccurate study findings which occur because of systematic flaws in the conduct, reporting or design of the study.

Bibliography A full list of all the sources that were consulted or used when preparing a document.

Binary data (also known as dichotomous data) Data outcomes that can only be expressed as one of two possible responses – e.g. dead or alive, success or failure.

Blind assessment (also known as blinding of outcome assessment; blinded outcome assessment) An approach commonly used in clinical trials and empirical research to reduce detection bias. Assessors are 'blinded' to (unaware of) the treatment allocated to/received by a particular patient group.

Blog A website which comprises discrete text entries ('posts'), which are usually presented chronologically in reverse date order.

Bonferroni correction An adjustment (to the alpha level) that is used when multiple dependent or independent statistical tests are performed at the same time.

Boolean operators Words (AND, OR, NOT or AND NOT), which are used to combine or exclude keywords in a search, leading to increased focus and precision.

Burden-of-illness (also known as cost-of-illness study) A study in which the economic burden of a disease is measured and the maximum amount of money that could potentially be saved, or gained, if a disease or condition no longer existed, is estimated.

Campbell Collaboration   A non-profit international research organization that produces and disseminates systematic reviews of the effectiveness of interventions in the social and behavioural sciences.

Case–control study   A comparative study in which a group of participants with a particular condition are 'matched' (i.e. paired on the basis of specific characteristics) with a control group of participants who do not have the condition.

Case series   A study in which a person, or series of people, who have been given a similar treatment are followed for a specific time.

Category   A collection of similar data grouped together for the purposes of analysis or synthesis.

Centre for Reviews and Dissemination   (also known as CRD) A health services research centre based at the University of York, UK, which carries out systematic reviews and meta-analyses of healthcare interventions and disseminates these findings to decision makers in the National Health Service (NHS).

CERQual   (also known as Confidence in the Evidence from Reviews of Qualitative Research) A system, analogous to the GRADE system for quantitative evidence, for assessing the extent of uncertainty surrounding qualitative review findings.

Citation   A reference to a scholarly book, paper or author.

Citation chaining   (also known as snowballing; forward searching; forward snowballing; backward searching; backward snowballing) The practice of looking at the bibliography of one study to find other, related studies.

Clinical effectiveness   The extent to which an intervention or programme can be regarded as providing clinical or healthcare advantages.

Clinical heterogeneity   Differences in the participants, outcome measures and/or intervention characteristics of individual intervention studies.

CLUSTER approach   A sampling method in which the whole study population is divided into externally homogeneous but internally heterogeneous groups called clusters.

Cochrane   An independent, non-profit, non-governmental organization that produces systematic reviews of primary research in human healthcare and health policy. Reviews are internationally regarded as the highest (gold standard) in evidence-based healthcare resources.

Cochrane Handbook for Systematic Reviews of Interventions (also known as the *Cochrane Handbook*) A publication that provides guidance to authors preparing Cochrane systematic reviews of healthcare interventions.

Cohen's *d* An effect size which conceptualizes the difference in groups/conditions in relation to their pooled standard deviation (see also Standardized mean difference).

Cohort study A study in which a group of participants is identified and followed over time to assess specific outcomes. The study may, or may not, also have a concurrent control group.

Complex systematic review A systematic review which brings together multiple sources of data and uses advanced methods of evidence synthesis to answer an often multi-faceted and interdisciplinary review question.

Conference proceedings A collection of academic works (i.e. oral or written contributions) presented by delegates attending a conference. Conference proceedings are normally made available either electronically or in print format immediately prior to, or after, a conference.

Confidence interval A statistic, usually reported alongside the point estimate, used to describe the uncertainty around the estimate by giving the range of values within which the true effect is strongly believed to lie.

Confounder variable An extraneous variable that is related to a study's independent and/or dependent variable(s).

Constant comparison A method used in qualitative data analysis whereby themes and concepts reported in one study are compared to those reported in other studies.

Continuous data Data outcomes measured on a continuous scale – e.g. age or height.

Controlled before-and-after study A type of non-randomized study in which outcomes for two or more groups, matched on key characterisics, are compared before and after an intervention, exposure or treatment.

Correlation The association between two continuous variables.

Correlational study (also known as correlational study design) A study designed to allow researchers to examine the association (or correlation) between variables.

Cost analysis An economic study in which there is no mention of outcomes; focus is solely on costs.

Cost–benefit analysis   An economic evaluation study in which both benefits and costs are measured in currency (e.g. £ or $).

Cost–consequence analysis   An economic study in which the different costs and benefits of the interventions being compared are not aggregated. Benefits are measured in a range of natural units (e.g. number of people cured) and costs are measured in currency (e.g. £ or $).

Cost-effectiveness   The extent to which costs and health effects of an intervention or programme can be regarded as providing value for money.

Cost-effectiveness analysis   An economic evaluation study in which benefits are unidimensional and measured in natural units (e.g. cost per life year gained). Costs are measured in currency (e.g. £ or $).

Cost-minimization analysis   An economic evaluation study in which benefits are proven to be equivalent and the focus is on costs. Costs are measured in currency (e.g. £ or $).

Cost–utility analysis   An economic evaluation study in which benefits are multidimensional (e.g. quality and quantity of life) and typically measured in quality-adjusted life years. Costs are measured in currency (e.g. £ or $).

Count data   Data that are expressed as the total number of events experienced by each participant – e.g. the number of infections patients experience during a clinical trial.

Critical appraisal   The process by which evidence is carefully and systematically assessed to determine its relevance, validity, credibility and value.

Critical Appraisal Skills Programme (CASP)   An organization that develops and delivers critical appraisal training via tools and workshops (online and face to face).

Critical interpretative synthesis (CIS)   A technique, adapted from meta-ethnography, which incorporates principles of grounded theory and aims to generate theory. Critical interpretative synthesis differs from meta-ethnography in that it includes studies that use multiple methods (not just qualitative research) and offers a more in-depth critique of data included in the review.

Cross-checking   The process by which the accuracy of something (such as extracted data or selected studies) is verified by another person in an attempt to reduce bias and error.

Cross-sectional study   (also known as transverse study) An observational study in which data are collected at one point in time.

Data extraction   (also known as abstraction; coding; data abstraction; data coding) The process whereby relevant data are taken from included papers and stored in a single format – usually a data extraction form or data extraction table.

Data extraction form   A standardized form, usually developed or modified to fit each systematic review, in which relevant data for a particular study can be recorded.

Data extraction table   A means of tabulating extracted data from individual studies.

Data saturation   The point at which enough data have been collected and analyzed to draw necessary conclusions and new data are not deemed to significantly change the analysis or conclusions.

Data synthesis   (also known as data analysis) The process by which relevant data from individual studies are aggregated and synthesized with the goal of answering a review question.

Data tables   Tables that describe and summarize extracted data.

Deductive approach   Making use of a predetermined framework to organize data.

De-duplicate   The process of removing duplicate copies of identified references.

Degrees of freedom (df)   The maximum number of logically independent values that have the freedom to vary in a sample of data.

Dependent variable (DV)   An outcome which changes as a result of independent variable(s).

Descriptive data   Data that help to describe or summarize a population's or sample's characteristics in a meaningful way.

Detection bias   (also known as response bias; ascertainment bias; measurement bias) Bias that occurs when a phenomenon is more likely to be observed in one group than another (e.g. awareness of treatment allocation may distort the assessment of outcome measures).

Dichotomization   Act of splitting a continuous variable into two groups, often based on a median and almost always a bad idea.

Discounting   A technique used to enable comparison of costs and/or benefits occurring in different years.

Discourse analysis (also known as critical discourse analysis; empirical discourse analysis) A generic term that encompasses several approaches to studying and analysing the use of language. Discourse analysis can be performed on a wide range of data sources including written, spoken and visual or sign language.

Dissemination The process of tailoring and distributing information to an intended audience.

Dissemination strategy A written document that: a) identifies the target audience(s) for dissemination; b) clearly defines and prioritizes dissemination methods; and c) defines timelines for the planned dissemination strategies.

ECLIPS(E) A mnemonic used to guide the development of inclusion and exclusion criteria for qualitative evidence syntheses.

Economic evaluation An umbrella term that refers to a range of study designs that are used to compare the costs and benefits of different treatments or interventions.

Effect size (also known as effect estimate) A quantitative measure of the difference between two groups. Examples of effect sizes are the mean difference or the relative risk.

ENTREQ (also known as Enhancing transparency in reporting the synthesis of qualitative research) A set of guidelines designed to aid clear reporting of qualitative evidence syntheses.

Epidemiological survey A method used to collect data from specific population samples to identify causal disease factors. Findings are then used to inform the development of potential preventative interventions.

EPPI (Evidence for Policy & Practice Information Centre) EPPI uses a mixed-methods approach to synthesize qualitative and quantitative evidence.

EPPI-Reviewer Special software developed by the Evidence for Policy & Practice Information Centre (University College London) for conducting systematic reviews.

Ethics committee A panel of multidisciplinary experts who consider the ethical implications of research studies.

Ethnographic study (also known as ethnography) A qualitative study that uses ethnographic research methods to collect and analyse data about different groups or cultures. Researchers completely immerse themselves in the lives, culture or population that they are studying to observe society from the point of view of those being studied. Ethnographers typically study social interactions and behaviours among groups or communities through observation and informal interview methods.

Evidence-based   Informed by or derived from objective, current and best available evidence.

Evidence map   (also known as mapping study; mapping exercise; systematic map; evidence mapping; mapping review) A method of evidence synthesis in which the current state of an evidence base is mapped out, presented in a user-friendly format and used to inform future practice by identifying gaps in knowledge or research.

Evidence synthesis   An umbrella term for a series of research methods that allow researchers to combine evidence from more than one source to answer a specific review question.

Exclusion criteria   A list of characteristics that disqualify a piece of evidence from inclusion in a systematic review.

Experimental study design   Intervention and non-intervention studies that compare outcomes within or between two (or more) groups and/or conditions.

Fatigue effects   Decline in performance on a lengthy or challenging study task which is generally attributed to tiredness or boredom.

Filter   Features of many electronic bibliographic databases that allow searches to be narrowed (or filtered) – e.g. according to study design.

Fixed effects meta-analysis   A method of conducting meta-analysis in which it is assumed that there is one true effect observed across all studies and that any variability between the study results is due simply to chance.

Focus group   A qualitative research methodology in which the views, opinions or perceptions of a small group of people towards a product, experience or service are collectively solicited.

Forest plot   A graphical display of the results of a meta-analysis, which may be accompanied by a pooled estimate of the effect.

Forward searching   (also known as forward snowballing; citation chaining) The process of identifying articles that cite a key reference.

Framework synthesis (also known as framework-based synthesis; best-fit framework synthesis) An approach to qualitative evidence synthesis that applies framework analysis – a structured and transparent method of analysing primary qualitative data. Framework synthesis starts with an a priori framework of concepts and themes against which data are extracted and synthesized. Although more deductive than other approaches, new themes and topics can be added to the framework during synthesis.

Free-text words Single or multiple terms and phrases, such as 'cancer' or 'educational intervention', used when searching bibliographic databases.

Full economic evaluation A method of evaluation that identifies, measures and values both costs and benefits.

Funding bias (also known as sponsorship bias) Bias that may arise when authors of a study report data consistent with the interests of the study funder or industry sponsor.

Generalizability To extrapolate research findings from individual study samples to the entire target population of interest.

Gold standard The highest quality of its type.

Grading of Recommendations, Assessment, Development and Evaluations (GRADE) A transparent framework for developing and presenting summaries of evidence and making recommendations.

Grey literature (also known as unpublished literature) A term used to refer to the vast array of evidence not controlled by commercial publishers.

Grounded theory A qualitative research method characterized by simultaneous collection, coding and analysis of data that is repeated until a theory that explains the phenomenon being studied is developed. Constant comparison is used to compare new categories with existing ones and relate them to the emerging theory. When new data do not change the developing theory, this is known as 'data saturation' and data collection is usually stopped.

Grounded theory synthesis (also known as grounded formal theory) A method of qualitative data synthesis derived from grounded theory. The key principles of grounded theory are applied to the synthesis of a body of grounded research to a higher order and more abstract level.

Hand searching   Manual searching of potentially relevant information sources (e.g. conference proceedings) in an attempt to identify eligible studies for inclusion in a systematic review.

Harvard referencing style   (also known as the Harvard system) A style of referencing citations or sources in the text and reference list of academic work.

Hazard ratio   A measure of how often an event happens in one group compared to another group over time.

Health economics   A branch of economics concerned with the costs, benefits, efficiency, effectiveness, value and behaviour of healthcare systems.

Heterogeneity   Variability between studies included in a systematic review. There are three types of heterogeneity: clinical, methodological and statistical. In the literature, the term is commonly used to refer to statistical heterogeneity.

Homogeneity/homogeneous   Similarity between studies included in a systematic review.

I^2 statistic   A statistic that describes the percentage of the total variation across study results in a meta-analysis, due to differences between study characteristics rather than chance. Possible values range from 0 to 100 per cent.

Impact factor   A term used to refer to the average number of times an article in an academic peer-reviewed journal has been cited (i.e. referenced) over the past year.

INCLUDE framework   (also known as Innovations in Clinical Trial Design and Delivery for the Under-Served) A tool designed by the National Institute for Health and Care Research (NIHR) to help trials teams to think about how to make their research more inclusive.

Inclusion criteria   (also known as eligibility criteria) A list of characteristics that a piece of evidence must have to be included in a systematic review.

Incremental cost-effectiveness ratio   (also known as ICER) Summary of all changes in costs and benefits between the different interventions or programmes being compared.

Incremental cost per life year gained   An incremental cost-effectiveness ratio that represents the change in the cost of an intervention divided by the change in life years associated with the intervention.

Incremental cost per quality-adjusted life year   (also known as cost per quality-adjusted life year) An incremental cost-effectiveness ratio that represents the change in the cost of an intervention divided by the change in the quality-adjusted life years associated with the intervention.

Independent groups design   (also known as between-subjects design) A study in which participants are assigned or self-select to belong to one group or condition and provide only one measure of the dependent variable.

Independent variable   The variable that is modified or controlled in a scientific experiment.

Individual patient data   (also known as individual participant data) Raw data from individuals in a study.

Inductive approach   (also known as inductive reasoning) Reasoning often used in qualitative research, which allows for themes, patterns and categories to be identified from the data, rather than pre-existing categories or concepts being imposed (see Deductive approach). The researcher typically moves from observation to hypothesis- or theory-generation.

Information specialist   An individual with expert knowledge in bibliographic databases and information retrieval.

Institutional repository   A digital archive of the outputs from an institution (e.g. a university).

Integrative approach   (also known as aggregative approach) An approach to qualitative evidence synthesis in which emphasis is placed on previous analytical categories obtained from a theory, a conceptual framework, the researcher's own professional knowledge or a topic guide.

Integrative review   (also known as mixed-methods review) A literature review that includes both quantitative and qualitative evidence.

Interface   (also known as platform) The structure via which bibliographic databases are accessed.

Interpretative approach   An approach to qualitative evidence synthesis, which is concerned with generating concepts and developing theories that link together concepts and which are grounded in the findings of the included qualitative studies.

Interpretative phenomenological analysis   (also known as IPA) An experiential approach to qualitative research which attempts to provide a detailed account of the personal lived experience of participants by interpreting how they make sense of a given phenomenon.

310 Doing a Systematic Review

Interval data   Data that are measured along a scale and all values on the scale are the same distance apart (e.g. time).

Intervention study   (also known as effectiveness study) A study in which the impact of an intervention on a population or group is studied.

Inverse variance   (also known as inverse-variance weighting) A method of combining results from two or more intervention studies, commonly used in a meta-analysis to combine the results from individual studies.

JBI   (formerly known as the Joanna Briggs Institute) An international not-for-profit, research and development organization based at the University of Adelaide, South Australia, which promotes and supports the synthesis, transfer and utilization of evidence.

Keywords   A way of classifying and organizing digital content within bibliographic databases according to factors such as the topic being studied and the methodology adopted.

Language bias   Bias resulting from the exclusion from a systematic review of evidence written in certain languages (e.g. only considering English-language studies).

Latent variable   (also known as an unobserved variable) A variable that is not directly measured by a researcher but is the product of a mathematical model (factor analysis) of other variables.

Leximancer   A software package used for text mining.

Linear regression   A statistical modelling technique that shows the linear relationship between a dependent variable and one or more independent variables.

Literature review   A common catch-all term for any study that assimilates and synthesizes or describes the findings of more than one study and/or review.

Living review   A review that is updated at regular intervals to reflect the latest data available, thus making sure that the findings are always up to date.

Logistic regression   (also known as binary logistic regression) A regression model used to predict binary (two-level nominal) outcomes.

Main search   (also known as search; searches) A term used to refer to a global approach to searching (sometimes called the 'search plan'), which covers all of the activities involved in the main searches (e.g. specific bibliographic databases or other resources to be searched, key search terms and any date limits).

Mean difference   (also known as difference in means) The absolute difference between the mean values of the outcome in two treatment groups.

Mediation (statistical)   Exploration of the mechanism through which an independent variable influences a dependent variable whereby the association between the independent variable and the dependent variable is, at least in part, accounted for by the association between the independent variable and mediator and the association between the mediator and dependent variable.

Medical Subject Headings (MeSH) terms   A list of subject headings used for indexing articles for the bibliographic databases MEDLINE and PubMed.

Meta-analysis   A statistical technique that allows results from individual studies to be combined to give an overall measure of the effect of one intervention compared with another.

Meta-Analysis of Observational Studies in Epidemiology (MOOSE)   A checklist designed to aid clear reporting of meta-analyses and systematic reviews of observational data.

Meta-ethnography   A method of qualitative data synthesis developed as an alternative to meta-analysis, which brings together concepts, themes and metaphors from individual studies (ethnographies) into a 'whole' result, which is greater than the sum of the parts. A meta-ethnography produces a higher-order interpretation and often produces explanatory theory.

Meta-regression   A statistical method, often regarded as an extension to meta-analysis, which allows for further investigation of heterogeneity.

Meta-study   An interpretative approach to qualitative evidence synthesis, which comprises meta-data analysis, meta-method and meta-theory. The components can be conducted concurrently and aim to reveal similarities and differences in the data, scrutinize the methods and explore theoretical assumptions across the included studies. The synthesis brings together the three elements and provides a new interpretation and/or new or overarching theory of the phenomenon.

Methodological heterogeneity   Variability in the design and quality of intervention studies.

Methodological quality   (also known as study quality) The extent to which a study takes steps to minimize bias and error in its conduct, analysis and reporting.

Microblogging   (also known as tumblelogs) Blogging that allows users to exchange short messages (e.g. sentences, individual images or video links). Examples include Twitter, Tumblr, FriendFeed, Mastodon and Plurk.

Mind map   (also known as spider diagram) A hierarchical diagram that can be used to organize information and show relationships between ideas or constructs.

Mixed-methods review   A review that combines and synthesizes two or more types of data (e.g. quantitative and qualitative data) in a single primary synthesis.

Model fit indices   (in structural equation modelling) A range of statistical tools used to evaluate the extent to which a hypothesized model fits a dataset.

Moderation (statistical)   The extent to which the strength of the association between an independent variable and a dependent variable is influenced by a third variable.

Multinomial regression   A regression model used to predict multicategory nominal variables.

Narrative review   (also known as literature review) A study that assimilates and synthesizes or describes in words the findings of more than one study and/or review.

Narrative synthesis   (also known as qualitative synthesis) A term used to refer to any write-up of results using words only (with reference to data in tables).

National Institute for Health and Care Excellence (NICE)   A non-departmental public body that determines which drugs and treatments are available on the National Health Service (NHS) in England.

National Institute for Health and Care Research (NIHR)   A UK government agency, funded by the Department of Health and Social Care, that funds, enables and delivers world-leading health and social care research that improves people's health and well-being and promotes economic growth.

Network meta-analysis   A statistical method that can be used to quantitatively compare similar treatments at the same time in a single analysis by combing different sources of evidence.

Non-randomized study   A study in which participants are assigned to two or more treatment groups but randomization methods are not used in the allocation process.

Normally distributed data   Data that are symmetrically distributed with no skew (i.e. no unevenness).

Null hypothesis The hypothesis that there is no statistically significant difference between specific groups or populations.

NVivo Computer-assisted qualitative data analysis software (CAQDAS) which helps researchers to manage and organize qualitative data by using functions such as coding, searching, retrieving and grouping data. It is an aid to qualitative data analysis, helping the researcher to interrogate the data to discover connections and find insights.

Observational study A non-intervention study in which phenomena are observed rather than manipulated. The most common examples are cohort studies, case–control studies and cross-sectional studies.

Odds ratio The odds of an event occurring in one group divided by the odds of an event occurring in another group, where odds are defined as the ratio of the probability of the event occurring relative to the probability of the event not occurring.

ORCID ID A unique persistent digital identifier that connects with an ORCID record that contains links to an individual's research activities.

Ordinal data Data that fall into ordered categories (e.g. mild, moderate and severe).

Ordinal regression A regression model used to predict outcomes on an ordinal scale.

Partial economic evaluation A method of economic evaluation that addresses either costs or benefits (e.g. a cost analysis).

Patient and public involvement and engagement (PPIE) The process of considering key stakeholders' views in the research process.

Patient-reported outcome measure (PROM) Questionnaires measuring a patient's views of their own health status.

Peer-reviewed academic journal A publication containing journal articles that have been subjected to scholarly peer review (also known as refereeing).

Performance bias Bias that may arise as a result of differences in knowledge of intervention allocation in either the researcher or participant.

Perspective The viewpoint adopted in economic evaluations (e.g. patient, health service, society).

Phenomenological study (also known as phenomenology) A qualitative study that makes use of phenomenological theory to explore how individuals make sense of the world and to produce accounts of the lived experience of participants. Studies tend to use in-depth interviews and diaries to track individual stories and the way that participants make sense of their experiences. Phenomenological studies focus on providing accounts of individuals' experiences within a specific setting rather than being more widely generalizable.

PICo   A mnemonic used to guide the development of inclusion and exclusion criteria for qualitative evidence syntheses.

PICO   A mnemonic used to guide the development of inclusion and exclusion criteria for quantitative evidence syntheses.

PICOSS   A mnemonic used to guide the development of inclusion and exclusion criteria for quantitative evidence syntheses.

Poisson regression   A regression analysis used to fit data with a Poisson distribution, usually count data.

Pooled measure of effect   (also known as pooled effect size) Overall measure of the effect of one group compared with another, which is calculated by combining studies in a meta-analysis.

Pooled standard deviation   The weighted average of standard deviations for two or more groups.

Practice effects   The change in performance resulting from repeated testing or exposure to a study task.

Practitioner   Any person actively engaged in a discipline (e.g. healthcare professionals, teachers/educationalists, policy makers, criminologists and information technology consultants).

Preferred Reporting Items for Systematic Reviews and Meta-Analyses   (also known as the PRISMA Statement) A 27-item checklist and a four-phase flow diagram that outlines all aspects of the conduct of a systematic review.

Pre–post design   (also known as an uncontrolled before-and-after study) A study in which the dependent variable is measured before and after an intervention.

Primary data   (also known as primary research) Original research that results in first-hand data acquisition or theory development.

Primary research   Data collected directly by a researcher through observation, surveys, interviews, etc.

Prospective study   A longitudinal study that prospectively follows a group (or groups) of people over time.

PROSPERO   An international database of prospectively registered systematic review protocols relevant to a number of subject areas.

Protocol   (also known as study protocol; review protocol) A written document that clearly states the methods to be used in the systematic review.

Publication bias   Bias that occurs when published evidence is not representative of the entire body of evidence in an area. This arises because negative or null findings are less likely to be published by commercial publishers than positive findings.

Published evidence   Evidence from commercial publishers.

Purposive sampling   A sampling technique in which researchers select particular information-rich studies for inclusion in a qualitative evidence synthesis.

p-value   (also known as probability value) The probability of obtaining test results at least as extreme as the observed results of a statistical hypothesis test, assuming that the null hypothesis is correct.

Qualitative Assessment and Review Instrument (QARI)   Software developed by JBI specifically to support meta-aggregation of the findings of qualitative research.

Qualitative data/evidence   Data that approximate or characterize. These data are usually, but not always, non-numeric. Qualitative research generates large amounts of textual data, which may include verbatim transcripts of interviews or focus groups, notes or field observations, participant diaries and the researcher's own reflections on the research process. Transcripts and notes represent the raw data of qualitative research, which the researcher makes sense of using a specific analytical process of organizing, sifting and interpreting.

Qualitative evidence synthesis   (also known as QES; qualitative systematic review; qualitative meta-aggregation; qualitative meta-narrative; qualitative meta-ethnography; qualitative meta-summary; qualitative meta-synthesis; qualitative synthesis) A means of identifying, appraising and synthesizing qualitative data pertaining to a specific review question from a range of sources. Ultimately, the value of qualitative evidence synthesis lies in being able to produce new understandings of a topic or area from primary qualitative research.

Qualitative meta-aggregation   A pragmatic and process-driven approach to qualitative evidence synthesis that avoids reinterpretation and instead presents the findings of included studies accurately and as intended by the original authors. Meta-aggregation assembles the conclusions of primary studies (however reported) and pools them on the basis of similarity in meaning; it is analogous to and predicated on meta-analysis. The output tends to be generalizable recommendations for policy and practice.

Qualitative meta-narrative   An approach to qualitative evidence synthesis that involves interpretative synthesis, in which primary sources are read and narratives are used to summarize their key methods and findings. A meta-narrative review seeks to explore a topic area by highlighting the contrasting and complementary ways in which researchers have studied the same or a similar topic. As such, it's often considered to be a means of identifying 'storylines' across different qualitative research. This approach to the synthesis of qualitative data is traditionally used to inform policy making.

Qualitative meta-summary   An aggregative method of qualitative data synthesis in which findings from individual studies are accumulated and summarized rather than transformed into a higher-order theory or interpretation. The approach produces a map of the content of included qualitative studies and attempts to quantify the frequency of each finding, even going as far as calculating effect sizes.

Quality-adjusted life year (QALY)   Outcome measure that captures both length of life and quality of life.

Quality assessment   (also known as quality appraisal; risk of bias assessment) The process of determining the quality of the evidence included in a systematic review.

Quality assessment tool   (also known as quality appraisal tool; risk of bias assessment tool) A (normally) standardized measure of assessing the quality of the evidence included in a systematic review.

Quantitative data   Data that can be quantified, verified and manipulated using statistical techniques (e.g. height, distance, duration of survival).

Quantitative evidence synthesis   (also known as quantitative systematic review) A means of identifying, appraising and synthesizing quantitative data pertaining to a specific review question from a range of sources.

Quasi-experimental study design   A study design in which individuals are not randomly allocated to groups.

Random effects analysis   A method of conducting meta-analysis in which it is assumed that the true effect varies from study to study but is centred on some overall average effect.

Randomized controlled trial (RCT)   A study in which participants are randomized to two or more treatment groups using robust methods of randomization.

Rapid review   A systematic review in which researchers utilize time-saving shortcuts to deliver findings rapidly.

Ratio data   Data that are measured using a continuous scale with the same distance between adjacent values.

Realist review   (also known as realist synthesis; realist evidence synthesis) An evidence synthesis approach that focuses on identifying what works, for whom, in what circumstances, in what respects and how.

Reference list   A full list of all of the sources referenced within a document.

Reference management software   (also known as bibliographic database; database of bibliographic records; electronic database; electronic bibliographical database) A digital collection of references of published and grey literature, including journal articles, theses and dissertations, books, government and legal reports, newspaper articles, conference abstracts and patents.

Regression   A range of statistical processes that estimate the association between one or more independent variables (predictors) and a dependent variable (outcome). The form of regression used is based on how the dependent variable is measured and the type of association the researcher is interested in.

Regression coefficient   The effect of a one-unit change in an independent variable (predictor) on the dependent variable (outcome) accounting for the relationship between the independent variable and any other independent variables in the model.

Regression to the mean   A statistical phenomenon that happens when unusually large or small measurements are followed by measurements that are closer to the mean.

Relative risk   The risk of an event occurring in one group divided by the risk in the other group, where the risk is defined as the probability of the event occurring.

Reliability   The degree to which a measure or test provides similar results across consistent conditions.

Repeated measures design   (also known as within-subjects design) An experimental design in which the same participants take part in each condition of the experiment.

Reporting bias   (also known as outcome reporting bias) Bias that occurs as a result of selective reporting of data (either by participants themselves or by study authors).

Research question   (also known as review question) A formal statement of the intent of a piece of research.

Retrospective study   A study which looks backwards at a group (or groups) of people to examine whether a suspected risk or protection factor has had an influence on an outcome specified at the start of the study.

Review question   (also known as research question) A formal statement of the intent of a review.

Risk difference   The risk of an event in one group minus the risk in another group, where risk is defined as the probability of the event occurring.

Scoping review   (also known as scoping study; scoping project; scoping exercise, scoping report; scoping method; scoping exercise method) A literature review which follows a similar process to a systematic review but is performed to rapidly outline the breadth, depth and type of literature available on a certain topic and/or the key constructs underpinning it.

Scoping searches   Relatively brief searches that are performed to help determine whether a topic area is suitable for a review by providing a snapshot of the volume and type of evidence available for synthesis.

Screening   (also known as first and second stage screening; first and second level screening; Stage 1 and Stage 2 screening; title and abstract screening) The process by which potentially eligible studies are screened against inclusion and exclusion criteria to determine their eligibility for inclusion in a systematic review.

Screening and selection tool   (also known as study screening tool; study screening form; selection tool; selection form) An electronic or paper tool that enables studies to be easily screened against inclusion and exclusion criteria.

Search strategy   (also known as main search) An umbrella term that refers to all searching activities for a specific systematic review.

Search terms   (also known as keyword; key word; search query) Terms, words or phrases that can be used to electronically identify relevant data from bibliographic databases, Internet web pages or other information sources.

Searching   (also known as search process; literature searching; systematic review searching) An umbrella term to refer to the process by which relevant data or evidence sources are identified for inclusion in a systematic review.

Secondary data   (also known as secondary research) Summation, collation and/or synthesis of primary research findings.

Selection bias   (also known as selection effect) Bias arising because of unrepresentative sampling or selection of participants, groups or data.

Selective reporting bias   Bias that arises when not all results are fully or accurately reported to avoid or suppress negative, unwanted or null findings.

Sensitivity analysis   Additional analysis used to test the robustness of results to uncertainty in parameters or methodologies.

Skewed data   Data that are not evenly distributed around a central point but rather are clustered to either the left or right of a distribution curve.

SPICE   A mnemonic used to guide the development of inclusion and exclusion criteria for qualitative evidence syntheses.

SPIDER   A mnemonic used to guide the development of inclusion and exclusion criteria for qualitative evidence syntheses.

Standard deviation (SD)   A measure of the amount of dispersion within a dataset.

Standard error (SE)   An index of the accuracy of a given estimate.

Standardized mean difference   A measure of the treatment effect that takes into account the variability observed across the participants (i.e. when studies assess the same outcome but measure it using different scales).

Standardized systematic review checklist   A set of standards or quality criteria for the conduct and reporting of systematic reviews (and sometimes meta-analyses).

Statistical heterogeneity   Variability between intervention study results that is more than would be expected due to chance alone.

Statistical power   Ability to detect an effect size of interest, based on sample size, under predetermined Type I and Type II error control.

Structural equation modelling (SEM)   Statistical modelling that uses a set of techniques to examine the association between latent variables and/or observed variables.

Subgroup analysis   Analysis used to determine whether different effects are observed in different subgroups of participants.

Subject headings/index terms   (also known as medical education subject headings; MeSH terms) Words or phrases used to index the content of electronic bibliographic databases.

Survival analysis   A method for analysing time-to-event data.

Systematic review   A literature review that is designed to locate, critically appraise and synthesize the best available evidence relating to a specific research question to provide informative and evidence-based answers.

Systematic review software packages   Software packages that are designed to aid management of key aspects of the systematic review process.

t-test   A statistical test to compare two independent groups (between-subjects t-test), two related groups (paired-samples t-test) or one group against a reference value (one-sample t-test).

Test statistic   Outcome of a statistical test from which the p-value is generated.

Text mining   (also known as data mining) An automated method for retrieving information from unstructured text.

Textual narrative synthesis   An approach to synthesis that can be used to combine different types of evidence. Rather than identifying themes or concepts, narrative synthesis prepares narrative summaries of included studies. Typically, the study characteristics, design, methods and findings are reported in a standardized way in tables so that commonalities and differences can be identified.

Thematic analysis   One of the most common forms of primary qualitative data analysis. Themes or patterns of relevance to a particular review question are identified, examined and scrutinized across data sets.

Thematic synthesis   An approach to qualitative evidence synthesis that borrows from methods used to analyse primary research and has been applied to reviews of acceptability and appropriateness of health interventions. In thematic synthesis, codes are identified inductively, and constantly compared and regrouped into themes. Descriptive themes are further developed into analytical themes, similar to higher-order interpretation in meta-ethnography.

Theme   A basic topic that runs through the data and describes what it is about in qualitative analysis or synthesis.

Theoretical sampling   A sampling technique used to generate theory.

Theoretical standpoint   Prior conceptual frameworks and ideas that researchers bring to the synthesis process and the particular lens applied when examining and synthesizing data.

Thesaurus terms   Terms used in electronic databases to give consistent labels to studies which describe the same concepts but in different ways.

Thesis archiving/indexing   (also known as thesis indexing; thesis archiving) Electroni cally preserving and promoting a thesis in an online repository.

Time-to-event data   Data that are expressed as the time taken for each participant to experience an event from a specified starting point (e.g. months of survival).

Transferability   The extent to which research findings can be applied to other groups, contexts or settings.

True experiment   A research design in which groups are created purposely and individuals are randomly allocated to them (see also Randomized controlled trial).

Type I error   (also known as false positive) Rejection of the null hypothesis which is true.

Type II error   (also known as false negative) A failure to reject a null hypothesis which is false.

Umbrella review   (also known as a review of reviews) A systematic review of the findings of systematic reviews.

Uncontrolled before-and-after study   (also known as a pre–post design) A study in which the dependent variable is measured before and after an intervention.

Utility   A measure of wellbeing or benefit gained from a healthcare intervention or programme.

Validity   The degree to which a test measures what it claims to measure.

Vancouver referencing style   A style of referencing citations or sources in the text and reference list of academic work.

Weighted average   A method of computing an arithmetic mean whereby certain values in a dataset are given more influence than others according to some attribute of the data.

Within-subjects design   (also known as repeated measures design) A study design in which the same participants contribute outcome data under more than one condition.

References

Allers, K., Hoffmann, F., Mathes, T., & Pieper, D. (2018). Systematic reviews with published protocols compared to those without: more effort, older search. *Journal of Clinical Epidemiology, 95*, 102–10.

Aloe, A., & Becker, M. (2012). An effect size for regression predictors in meta-analysis. *Journal of Education and Behavioural Statistics, 37*, 278–97.

Aloe, A., Thompson, C.G., Lui, Z., & Lin, L. (2021). Estimating partial standardized mean differences from regression models. *The Journal of Experimental Education, 9*(4), 898–915.

Altman, D.G. (2020). *Practical statistics for medical research* (2nd ed.). Chapman and Hall/CRC Texts in Statistical Science Series.

Anderson, R. (2010). Systematic reviews of economic evaluations: utility or futility? *Health Economics, 19*(3), 350–64.

Arksey, S., & O'Malley, L. (2005). Scoping studies: towards a methodological framework. *International Journal of Social Research Methodology, 8*, 19–32.

Aromataris, E., & Munn, Z. (Eds) (2020). *JBI manual for evidence synthesis*. https://synthesismanual.jbi.global

Austin, P.C. (2011). An introduction to propensity score methods for reducing the effects of confounding in observational studies. *Multivariate Behavioral Research, 46*(3), 399–424.

Banzi, R., Cinquini, M., Gonzalez-Lorenzo, M., Pecoraro, V., Capjobussi, M., & Minozzi, S. (2018). Quality assessment versus risk of bias in systematic reviews: AMSTAR and ROBIS had similar reliability but differed in their construct and applicability. *Journal of Clinical Epidemiology, 99*, 24–32.

Barnett-Page, E., & Thomas, J. (2009). Methods for the synthesis of qualitative research: a critical review. *BMC Medical Research Methodology, 9*, 59.

Boot, W.R, Simons, D.J, Stothart, C., & Stutts, C. (2013). The persuasive problem with placebos in psychology: why active control groups are not sufficient to rule out placebo effects. *Perspectives on Psychological Science, 8*(4), 445–54.

Booth, A. (2016). Searching for qualitative research for inclusion in systematic reviews: a structured methodological review. *Systematic Reviews, 5*, 74.

Booth, A., Harris, J., Croot, E., Springett, J., Campbell, F., & Wilkins, E. (2013). Towards a methodology for cluster searching to provide conceptual and contextual 'richness' for systematic reviews of complex interventions: case study (CLUSTER). *BMC Medical Research Methodology*, *13*, 118.

Booth, A., Noyes, J., Flemming, K., Moore, G., Tunçalp, Ö., & Shakibazadeh, E. (2019). Formulating questions to explore complex interventions within qualitative evidence synthesis. *BMJ Global Health*, *4*(Suppl 1).

Borenstein, M., Hedges, L.V., Higgins, J.P.T., & Rothstein, H.R. (2009). *Introduction to meta-analysis*. John Wiley & Sons.

British Library Archives. (2013). *The British newspaper archive*. www.britishnewspaperarchive.co.uk

Britten, N., Campbell, R., Pope, C., Donovan, J., Morgan, M., & Pill, R. (2002). Using meta-ethnography to synthesise qualitative research: a worked example. *Journal of Health Service Research*, *7*, 209–15.

Brown, T., Pilkington, G., Bagust, A., Boland, A., Oyee, J., Tudur-Smith, C., Blundell, M., Lai, M., Martin Saborido, C., Greenhalgh, J., Dundar, Y., & Dickson R. (2013). Clinical effectiveness and cost-effectiveness of first-line chemotherapy for adult patients with locally advanced or metastatic non-small cell lung cancer: a systematic review and economic evaluation. *Health Technology Assessment*, *17*(31), 1–278.

Brown, T., Platt, S., & Amos, A. (2014). Equity impact of population-level interventions and policies to reduce smoking in adults: a systematic review. *Drug and Alcohol Dependence*, *138*, 7–16.

Brunton, G., Oliver, S., & Thomas, J. (2020). Innovations in framework synthesis as a systematic review method. *Research Synthesis Methods*, *11*, 316–30.

Campbell Collaboration. (2012). www.campbellcollaboration.org

Carrigan, M. (2019). *Social media for academics* (2nd ed.). SAGE Publications.

Centre for Reviews and Dissemination (CRD). (2010). *Systematic reviews: CRD's guidance for undertaking reviews in health care*. www.york.ac.uk/crd/SysRev/!SSL!/WebHelp/SysRev3.htm

Centre for Reviews and Dissemination, University of York. (2016). *Guidance notes for registering a systematic review protocol with PROSPERO*. www.crd.york.ac.uk/prospero/documents/Registering%20a%20review%20on%20PROSPERO.pdf

Chalmers, I., Enkin, M., & Keirse, M. (Eds) (1989). *Effective care in pregnancy and childbirth*. Oxford University Press.

Chalmers, I., Hedges, L.V., & Cooper, H. (2002). A brief history of research synthesis. *Evaluation and the Health Professions*, *25*(1), 12–37.

Chalmers, I., Hetherington, J., Newdick, M., Mutch, L., Grant, A., Enkin, M., Enkin, E., & Dickersin, K. (1986). The Oxford Database of Perinatal Trials: developing a register of published reports of controlled trials. *Journal of Controlled Clinical Trials*, *7*(4), 306–24.

Cherry, M.G. (2013). *Exploring the relationships between attachment style, emotional intelligence and patient–provider communication*. PhD thesis, University of Liverpool.

Cherry, M.G., Fletcher, I., O'Sullivan, H., & Shaw, N. (2012). What impact do structured educational interventions to increase emotional intelligence have on medical students? BEME Guide No. 17. *Medical Teacher*, *34*, 11–19.

Cherry, M.G., Taylor, P.J., Brown, S.L., Rigby, J.W., & Sellwood, W. (2017). Guilt, shame and expressed emotion in carers of people with long-term mental health difficulties: a systematic review. *Psychiatry Research, 249*, 137–51.

Cochrane, A.L. (1972). *Effectiveness and efficiency: Random reflections on health services.* Nuffield Provincial Hospitals Trust.

Cochrane, A.L. (1979). *1931–1971: A critical review. Medicines for the year 2000.* Office of Health Economics.

Cochrane. (2019). *Guidance for the production and publication of Cochrane living systematic reviews: Cochrane Reviews in Living mode.* https://community.cochrane.org/sites/default/files/uploads/inline-files/Transform/201912_LSR_Revised_Guidance.pdf

Cohen, J. (1988) *Statistical power analysis in the behavioral sciences* (2nd ed.). Lawrence Erlbaum Associates.

Colvin, C.J., Smith, H.J., Swartz, A., Ahs, J.W., de Heer, J., Opiyo, N., Kim, J.C., Marraccini, T., & George, A. (2013). Understanding careseeking for child illness in sub-Saharan Africa: a systematic review and conceptual framework based on qualitative research of household recognition and response to child diarrhoea, pneumonia and malaria. *Social Science and Medicine, 86*, 66–78.

Cooke, A., Smith, D., & Booth, A. (2012). Beyond PICO: the SPIDER tool for qualitative evidence synthesis. *Qualitative Health Research, 22*(10), 1435–43.

Cooper, H. (2010). *Research synthesis and meta-analysis: A step-by-step approach.* SAGE Publications.

Cowley, D.E. (1995). Prostheses for primary total hip replacement: a critical appraisal of the literature. *International Journal of Technology Assessment in Health Care, 11*, 770–8.

Critical Appraisal Skills Programme (CASP). (2018). *10 questions to help you make sense of qualitative research.* https://casp-uk.net/images/checklist/documents/CASP-Qualitative-Studies-Checklist/CASP-Qualitative-Checklist-2018_fillable_form.pdf

Deeks, J.J., Dinnes, J., D'amico, R., Sowden, A.J., Sakarovitch, C., Song, F., Petticrew, M., Altman, D.G., & International Stroke Trial Intervention Group and European Carotid Surgery Trial Collaborative Group. (2003). Evaluating non-randomised intervention studies. *Health Technology Assessment, 7*(27), 1–173.

Department for International Development (DfID). (2012). *Systematic reviews in international development: An initiative to strengthen evidence-informed policy making.* www.gov.uk/government/publications/systematic-reviews-in-international-development/systematic-reviews-in-international-development

Dixon-Woods, M., Agarwal, S., Jones, D., Young, B., & Sutton, A. (2005). Synthesising qualitative and quantitative evidence: a review of possible methods. *Journal of Health Services Research and Policy, 10*(1), 45–53.

Dixon-Woods, M., Cavers, D., Agarwal, S., Annandale, E., Arthur, A., Harvey, J., Hsu, R., Katbamna, S., Olsen, R., Smith, L., Riley, R., & Sutton, A.J. (2006). Conducting a critical interpretive synthesis of the literature on access to healthcare by vulnerable groups. *BMC Medical Research Methodology, 6*, 35.

Donnon, T. (2012). Experimental or RCT research designs: a crisis of nomenclature in medical education. *Canadian Medical Education Journal, 3*(2), e82.

Downs, S.H., & Black, N. (1998). The feasibility of creating a checklist for the assessment of the methodological quality of both randomised and non-randomised studies of health care interventions. *Journal of Epidemiology and Community Health, 52,* 337–84.

Drummond, M., & Jefferson, T. (1996). Guidelines for authors and peer reviewers of economic submissions to the BMJ: The BMJ Economic Evaluation Working Party. *British Medical Journal, 313*(7052), 275–83.

Drummond, M., O'Brien, B., Stoddart, G., & Torrance, G. (1997). *Methods for the economic evaluation of health care programmes.* Oxford University Press.

Eaves, Y. (2001). A synthesis technique for grounded theory data analysis. *Journal of Advanced Nursing, 35*(3), 654–63.

Egger, M., Higgins, J.P.T., & Smith, G.D. (2022). *Systematic reviews in health research: Meta-analysis in context* (3rd ed.). John Wiley & Sons.

EQUATOR. (2017). EQUATOR Network website. www.equator-network.org/home

Estabrooks, C., Field, P., & Morse, J. (1994). Aggregating qualitative findings: an approach to theory development. *Qualitative Health Research, 4,* 503–11.

Finfgeld-Connett, D. (2008). Meta-synthesis of caring in nursing. *Journal of Clinical Nursing, 17,* 196–204.

Flemming, K., Booth, A., Hannes, K., Cargo, M., & Noyes, J. (2018). Cochrane Qualitative and Implementation Methods Group guidance series – paper 6: reporting guidelines for qualitative, implementation, and process evaluation evidence syntheses. *Journal of Clinical Epidemiology, 97,* 79–85.

Flemming, K., & Briggs, M. (2007). Electronic searching to locate qualitative research: evaluation of three strategies. *Journal of Advanced Nursing, 57,* 95–100.

Flemming, K., & Noyes, J. (2021). Qualitative evidence synthesis: where are we at? *International Journal of Qualitative Methods.* https://doi.org/10.1177/1609406921993276

France, E.F., Cunningham, M., Ring, N., Uny, I., Duncan, E.A.S., Jepson, R.G., Maxwell, M., Roberts, R.J., Turley, R.L., Booth, A., Britten, N., Flemming, K., Gallagher, I., Garside, R., Hannes, K., Lewin, S., Noblit, G.W., Pope, C., Thomas, J., ... Noyes, J. (2019). Improving reporting of meta-ethnography: the eMERGe reporting guidance. *BMC Medical Research Methodology, 19,* 25.

Funder, D., & Ozer, D.J. (2019). Evaluating effect size in psychological research: sense and nonsense. *Advances in Methods and Practices in Psychological Science, 2,* 156–68.

Fusar-Poli, P., & Radua, J. (2018). Ten simple rules for conducting umbrella reviews. *Statistics in Practice, 21*(3), 95–100.

Glaser, B., & Strauss, A. (1967). *The discovery of grounded theory.* Aldine Publishing Company.

Glass, G.V. (1976). Primary, secondary, and meta-analysis of research. *Educational Researcher, 5*(10), 3–8.

Green, L.W., & Allegrante, J.P. (2020). Practice-based evidence and the need for more diverse methods and sources in epidemiology, public health and health promotion. *American Journal of Health Promotion, 34*(8), 946–8.

Greenhalgh, J., Bagust, A., Boland, A., Martin Saborido, C., Oyee, J., Blundell, M., Dundar, Y., Dickson, R., Proudlove, C., & Fisher, M. (2011). Clopidogrel and modified-release dipyridamole for the prevention of occlusive vascular events (review of Technology Appraisal No. 90): a systematic review and economic analysis. *Health Technology Assessment, 15*(31), 1–178.

Greenhalgh, J., Dickson, R., & Dundar, Y. (2009). The effects of biofeedback for the treatment of essential hypertension: a systematic review. *Health Technology Assessment, 13*(46), 1–104.

Greenhalgh, T., Kristjansson, E., & Robinson, V. (2007). Realist review to understand the efficacy of school feeding programmes. *British Medical Journal, 335*, 858.

Greenhalgh, T., Robert, G., Macfarlane, F., Bate, P., Kyriakidou, O., & Peacock, R. (2005). Storylines of research in diffusion of innovation: a meta-narrative approach to systematic review. *Social Science & Medicine, 61*, 417–430.

Hannes, K., & Macaitis, K. (2012). A move to more systematic and transparent approaches in qualitative evidence synthesis: update on a review of published papers. *Qualitative Research, 12*, 402.

Harden, A., Thomas, J., Cargo, M., Harris, J., Pantoja, T., Flemming, K., Booth, A., Garside, R., Hannes, K., & Noyes, J. (2018). Cochrane Qualitative and Implementation Methods Group guidance series – paper 5: methods for integrating qualitative and implementation evidence within intervention effectiveness reviews. *Journal of Clinical Epidemiology, 97*, 70–8.

Harrell, F.E. (2001). *Regression modeling strategies: with applications to linear models, logistic regression, and survival analysis.* Springer–Verlag.

Haynes, E., Garside, R., Green, J., Kelly, M.P., Thomas, J., & Guell, C. (2019). Semiautomated text analytics for qualitative data synthesis. *Research Synthesis Methods, 10*(3), 452–64.

Higgins, J.P.T., Thomas, J., Chandler, J., Cumpston, M., Li, T., Page, M.J., & Welch, V.A. (Eds) (2022). *Cochrane handbook for systematic reviews of interventions* (version 6.3, updated February 2022). https://training.cochrane.org/handbook/current

Hill, J., Hoyt, J., van Eijk, A.M., D'Mello-Guyett, L., ter Kuile, F.O., Steketee, R., Smith, H., & Webster, J. (2013). Factors affecting the delivery, access and use of interventions to prevent malaria in pregnancy in sub-Saharan Africa: a systematic review and meta-analysis. *PLoS Medicine, 10*(7), e1001488.

Holmes, F.L. (1993). *Hans Krebs: Volume 2: Architect of intermediary metabolism 1933–1937.* Oxford University Press.

Hong, Q.N., Rees, R., Sutcliffe, K., & Thomas, J. (2020). Variations of mixed methods reviews approaches: a case study. *Research Synthesis Methods, 11*(6), 795–811.

Hu, L.T., & Bentler, P.M. (1999). Cut-off criteria for fit indexes in covariance structure analysis: conventional criteria versus new alternatives. *Structural Equation Modelling: A Multidisciplinary Journal, 6*(1), 1–55.

Husereau, D., Drummond, M., Augustovski, F., de Bekker-Grob, E., Briggs, A., Carswell, C., Caulley, L., Chaiyakunapruk, N., Greenberg, D., Loder, E., Mauskopf, J., Mullins, C.D., Petrou, S., Pwu, R-F., & Staniszewska, S. (2022). Consolidated Health Economic Evaluation Reporting Standards 2022 (CHEERS 2022) statement: updated reporting guidance for health economic evaluations. *International Journal of Technology Assessment in Healthcare, 38*(1), E13. https://doi.org/10.1017/S0266462321001732

Kearney, M. (1988). Ready-to-wear: discovering grounded formal theory. *Research on Nursing and Health, 21*, 179–86.

Khan, K., Kunz, R., Kleijnen, J., & Antes, G. (2003). *Systematic reviews to support evidence-based medicine: How to review and apply findings of healthcare research.* Royal Society of Medicine Press.

Krause, M.R., Serlin, R.C., Ward, S.E., Rony, R.Y.Z., Ezenwa, M.O., & Naab, F. (2010). Testing mediation in nursing research: beyond Baron and Kenny. *Nursing Research, 59*(4), 288.

Kristjansson, B., Petticrew, M., MacDonald, B., Krasevec, J., Janzen, L, Greenhalgh, T., Wells, G.A., MacGowan, J., Farmer, A.P, Shea, B.J., Mayhew, A., & Tugwell, P. (2007). School feeding for improving the physical and psychosocial health of disadvantaged students. *Cochrane Database of Systematic Reviews, 2*(1), 1–189.

Lakens, D. (2013). Calculating and reporting effect sizes to facilitate cumulative science: a practical primer for *t*-tests and ANOVAs. *Frontiers in Psychology, 4.* https://doi.org/10.3389/fpsyg.2013.00863

Lavis, J. (2009). How can we support the use of systematic reviews in policymaking? *PLoS Med, 6*(11), e1000141. https://journals.plos.org/plosmedicine/article?id=10.1371/journal.pmed.1000141

Levac, D., Colquhoun, H., & O'Brien, K. (2010). Scoping studies: advancing the methodology. *Implementation Science, 5*, 69. https://doi.org/10.1186/1748-5908-5-69

Lewin, K. (1946). Action research and minority problems. *Journal of Social Issues, 2*(4), 34–46.

Liberati, A., Altman, D.G., Tetzlaff, J., Mulrow, C., Gøtzsche, P.C., Ioannidis, J.P.A., Clarke, M., Devereaux, P.J, Kleijnen, J., & Moher, D. (2009). The PRISMA statement for reporting systematic reviews and meta-analyses of studies that evaluate healthcare interventions: explanation and elaboration. *British Medical Journal, 339*, b2700.

Library of Congress. (2013). *Chronicling America – historic American newspapers.* https://chroniclingamerica.loc.gov

Lin, H. (2020). Probing two-way moderation effects: a review of software to easily plot Johnson-Neyman figures. *Structural Equation Modelling: A Multidisciplinary Journal, 27*(3), 495–502.

Lockwood, C., Munn, Z., & Porritt, K. (2015). Qualitative research synthesis: methodological guidance for systematic reviews utilizing meta-aggregation. *International Journal of Evidence Based Healthcare, 13*, 179–87.

Lucas, P., Baird, J., Arai, L., Law, C., & Roberts, H. (2007). Worked examples of alternative methods for the synthesis of qualitative and quantitative research in systematic reviews. *BMC Medical Research Methodology, 7*(4). https://bmcmedresmethodol.biomed-central.com/articles/10.1186/1471-2288-7-4

MacCallum, R.C., Browne, M.W., & Sugawara, H.M. (1996). Power analysis and determination of sample size for covariance structure modeling. *Psychological Methods, 1*(2), 130.

Majid, U., & Vaenstone, M. (2018). Appraising qualitative research for evidence synthesis: a compendium of quality appraisal tools. *Qualitative Health Research, 28*(13), 2115–31.

McIver, J., & Carmines, E.G. (1981). *Unidimensional scaling* (No. 24). SAGE Publications.

Miake-Lye, I., Hempel, S., Shanman, R., & Shekelle, P. (2016). What is an evidence map? A systematic review of published evidence maps and their definitions, methods, and products. *Systematic Reviews*, *5*(28). https://systematicreviewsjournal.biomedcentral.com/articles/10.1186/s13643-016-0204-x

Miller, G.A., & Chapman, J.P. (2001). Misunderstanding analysis of covariance. *Journal of Abnormal Psychology*, *110*(1), 40–8.

Moher, D., Liberati, A., Tetzlaff, J., & Altman, D.G. (2009). Preferred reporting items for systematic reviews and meta-analyses: the PRISMA statement. *British Medical Journal*, *339*, b2535.

Moher, D., Shamseer, L., Clarke, M., Ghersi, D., Liberati, A., Petticrew, M., Shekelle, P., Stewart, L.A., & the PRISMA-P Group. (2015). Preferred reporting items for systematic review and meta-analysis protocols (PRISMA-P) 2015 statement. *Systematic Reviews*, *4*(1), 1.

Mullins, G., & Kiley, M. (2002). 'It's a PhD, not a Nobel Prize': how experienced examiners assess research theses. *Studies in Higher Education*, *27*(4), 369–86.

Munn, Z., Peters, M.D., Stern, C., Tufanaru, C., McArthur, A., & Aromataris, E. (2018). Systematic review or scoping review? Guidance for authors when choosing between a systematic or scoping review approach. *BMC Medical Research Methodology*, *18*(1), 143.

Murad, M.H., & Wang, Z. (2017). Guidelines for reporting meta-epidemiological methodology research. *Evidence Based Medicine*, *22*(4), 139–42.

National Heart, Lung and Blood Institute (NHLBI). (2021). *Study quality assessment tools.* www.nhlbi.nih.gov/health-topics/study-quality-assessment-tools

National Institute for Health and Care Excellence (NICE). (2012). *Methods for the development of NICE public health guidance: Appendix E, Algorithm for classifying quantitative (experimental and observational) study designs.* www.nice.org.uk/process/pmg4/chapter/appendix-e-algorithm-for-classifying-quantitative-experimental-and-observational-study-designs

National Institute for Health and Care Excellence (NICE). (2023). *Developing NICE guidelines: the manual.* https://www.nice.org.uk/process/pmg20/chapter/introduction

Noblit, G., & Hare, R. (1988). *Meta-ethnography: Synthesizing qualitative studies.* SAGE Publications.

Oliver, S., Rees, R., Clarke-Jones, L., Milne, R., Oakley, A., Gabbay, J., Stein, K., Buchanan, P., & Gyte, G. (2008). A multidimensional conceptual framework for analysing public involvement in health services research. *Health Expectations*, *11*, 72–84.

O'Mara-Eves, A., Thomas, J., McNaught, J., Miwa, M., & Ananiadou, S. (2015). Using text mining for study identification in systematic reviews: a systematic review of current approaches. *Systematic Reviews*, *4*(1), 5.

Page, M.J., McKenzie, J.E., Bossuyt, P.M., Boutron, I., Hoffmann, T.C., Mulrow, C.D., Shamseer, L., Tetzlaff, J.M., Aki, E.A., Brennan, S.E., Chou, R., Glanville, J., Grimshaw, J.M., Hróbjartsson, A., Lalu, M.M., Tianjing, L., Loder, E.W., Mayo-Wilson, E., McDonald, S., … Moher, D. (2021a). The PRISMA 2020 statement: an updated guideline for reporting systematic reviews. *British Medical Journal*, *372*, n71.

Page, M.J., Moher, D., Bossuyt, P.M., Boutron, I., Hoffmann, T.C., Mulrow, C.D., Shamseer, L., Tetzlaff, J.M., Aki, E.A., Brennan, S.E., Chou, R., Glanville, J., Grimshaw, J.M., Hróbjartsson, A., Lalu, M.M., Tianjing, L., Loder, E.W., Mayo-Wilson, E., McDonald, S., … McKenzie, J.E. (2021b). PRISMA 2020 explanation and elaboration: updated guidance and exemplars for reporting systematic reviews. *British Medical Journal, 372*, n160.

Paltridge, B. (2013). Referees' comments on submissions to peer-reviewed journals: when is a suggestion not a suggestion? *Studies in Higher Education, 40*(1), 106–22.

Paterson, B., Thorne, S., Canam, C., & Jillings, C. (2001). *Meta-study of qualitative health research: A practical guide to meta-analysis and meta-synthesis.* SAGE Publications.

Patton, J.H., Stanford, M.S., & Barratt, E.S. (1995). Factor structure of the Barratt impulsiveness scale. *Journal of Clinical Psychology, 51*(6), 768–74.

Pawson, R., Greenhalgh, T., Harvey, G., & Walshe, K. (2005). Realist review – a new method of systematic review designed for complex policy interventions. *Journal of Health Services Research and Policy, 10*(1), 21–34.

Philips, Z., Ginnelly, L., Sculpher, M., Claxton, K., Golder, S., Riemsma, R., Woolacott, N., & Glanville, J. (2004). Review of guidelines for good practice in decision-analytic modelling in health technology assessment. *Health Technology Assessment, 8*(36), 1–158.

Reisch, J., Tyson, J.E., & Mize, S.G. (1989). Aid to the evaluation of therapeutic studies. *Pediatrics, 84*, 815–27.

Rethlefsen, M., Kirtley, S., Waffenschmidt, S., Ayala, A.P., Moher, D., Page, M.J., Koffel, J.B., & PRISMA-S Group. (2021). PRISMA-S: an extension to the PRISMA Statement for Reporting Literature Searches in Systematic Reviews. *Systematic Reviews, 10*(1), 39.

Review Manager (RevMan) Version 5.4 (2020). [Computer program]. Cochrane.

Ring, N., Ritchie, K., Mandava, L., & Jepson, R. (2011). *A guide to synthesising qualitative research for researchers undertaking health technology assessments and systematic reviews.* https://dspace.stir.ac.uk/handle/1893/3205#.ZE1Q5C8w2Zw

Rombey, T., Allers, K., Mathes, T., Hoffman, F., & Pieper, D. (2019). A descriptive analysis of the characteristics and the peer review process of systematic review protocols published in an open peer review journal from 2012 to 2017. *BMC Medical Research Methodology, 19*, 57. https://bmcmedresmethodol.biomedcentral.com/articles/10.1186/s12874-019-0698-8

Ryu, E. (2014). Model fit evaluation in multilevel structural equation models. *Frontiers in Psychology, 5*, 81. www.frontiersin.org/articles/10.3389/fpsyg.2014.00081/full

Saborido, C.M., Hockenhull, J., Bagust, A., Boland, A., & Dickson, R. (2010). Systematic review and cost-effectiveness evaluation of 'pill-in-the-pocket' strategy for paroxysmal atrial fibrillation compared to episodic in-hospital treatment or continuous anti-arrhythmic drug therapy. *Health Technology Assessment, 14*(31), 1–75.

Sandelowski, M., & Barroso, J. (2007). *Handbook for synthesizing qualitative research.* Springer Publishing Company.

Sandelowski, M., Barroso, J., & Voils, C. (2007). Using qualitative metasummary to synthesize qualitative and quantitative descriptive findings. *Research in Nursing and Health, 3*(1), 99–111.

Schumacker, E., & Lomax, G. (2016). *A beginner's guide to structural equation modelling* (4th ed.). Taylor & Francis.

Schünemann, H.J., Higgins, J.P.T., Vist, G.E., Glasziou, P., Akl, E.A., Skoetz, N., & Guyatt, G.H. (2022). Chapter 14: Completing 'Summary of findings' tables and grading the certainty of the evidence. In Higgins, J.P.T., Thomas, J., Chandler, J., Cumpston, M., Li, T., Page, M.J., & Welch, V.A. (Eds) (2022). *Cochrane handbook for systematic reviews of interventions* (version 6.3, updated February 2022). https://training.cochrane.org/handbook/current

Shamseer, L., Moher, D., Clarke, M., Ghersi, D., Liberati, A., Petticrew, M., Shekelle, P., Stewart, L.A., & the PRISMA-P Group. (2015). Preferred reporting items for systematic review and meta-analysis protocols (PRISMA-P) 2015: elaboration and explanation. *British Medical Journal, 349*, g7647.

Shea, B.J., Reeves, B.C., Wells, G., Thuku, M., Hamel, C., Moran, J. Moher, D., Tugwell, P, Welch, V., Kristjansson, E., & Henry, D.A. (2017). AMSTAR 2: a critical appraisal tool for systematic reviews that include randomised or non-randomised studies of healthcare interventions, or both. *British Medical Journal, 358*, j4008.

Smith, H., Colvin, C., Richards, E., Roberson, J., Sharma, G., Thapa, K., & Gulmezoglu, A. (2016). Programmes for advance distribution of misoprostol to prevent post-partum haemorrhage: a rapid literature review of factors affecting implementation. *Health Policy and Planning, 31*(1), 102–13.

Social Care Institute for Excellence. (2010). *SCIE systematic research reviews: guidelines*. www.scie.org.uk/publications/researchresources/rr01.pdf

Sterne, J.A.C., Hernan, M.A., Reeves, B.C., Savovic, J., Beckman, N.D., Viswananthan, M., Henry, D., Altman, D.G., Ansari, M.T., Boutron, I., Carpenter, J.R., Chan, A.W., Churchill, R., Deeks, J.J., Hróbjartsson, A., Kirkham, J., Jüni, P., Loke, Y.K., Pigott, T.D., … Higgins, J.P. (2016). ROBINS-1: A tool for assessing risk of bias in non-randomized studies of interventions. *British Medical Journal, 355*, i4919.

Stevens, A., Garritty, C., Hersi, M., & Moher, D. (2018). *Developing PRISMA-RR, a reporting guideline for rapid reviews of primary studies (protocol)*. www.equator-network.org/wp-content/uploads/2018/02/PRISMA-RR-protocol.pdf

Stroup, D., Berlin, J., Morton, S., Olkin, I., Williamson, G., Rennie, D., Moher, D., Becker, B., Sipe, T., & Thacker, S. (2000). Meta-analysis of observational studies in epidemiology: a proposal for reporting. *Journal of the American Medical Association, 283*(15), 2008–12.

Thomas, B.H., Ciliska, D., Dobbins, M., & Micucci, S. (2004). A process for systematically reviewing the literature: providing the research evidence for public health nursing interventions. *Worldviews Evidence Based Nursing, 1*(3), 176–84.

Thomas, J., & Harden, A. (2008). Methods for the thematic synthesis of qualitative research in systematic reviews. *BMC Medical Research Methodology, 8*, 45. https://bmcmedresmethodol.biomedcentral.com/articles/10.1186/1471-2288-8-45

Tong, A., Flemming, K., McInnes, E., Oliver, S., & Craig, J. (2012). Enhancing transparency in reporting the synthesis of qualitative research: ENTREQ. *BMC Medical Research Methodology, 12*, 181. https://bmcmedresmethodol.biomedcentral.com/articles/10.1186/1471-2288-12-181

Tricco, A.C., Lillie, E., Zarin, W., O'Brien, K.K., Colquhoun, H., Levac, D., Moher, D., Peters, M.D.J., Horsley, H., Weels, L., Hempel, S., Akl, E.A., Chang, C., McGowan, J., Steward, L., Hartling, L., ALdcroft, A., Wilson, M.G., Garritty, C., Lewin, S., ... Straus, S.E. (2018). PRISMA extension for scoping reviews (PRISMA-ScR): checklist and explanation. *Annals of Internal Medicine, 169*(7), 467–73.

Vergnes, J., Sixou, C., Nabet, C., Maret, D., & Hamel, O. (2010). Ethics in systematic reviews. *Journal of Medical Ethics, 36*, 771–4.

Wells, G., Shea, B., O'Connell, D., Peterson, J., Welch, V., Losos, M., & Tugwell, P. (2012). *The Newcastle–Ottawa Scale (NOS) for assessing the quality of nonrandomised studies in meta-analyses.* www.ohri.ca/programs/clinical_epidemiology/oxford.asp

Wiers, R.W., Boffo, M., & Field, M. (2018). What's in a trial? On the importance of distinguishing between experimental lab studies and randomized controlled trials: the case of cognitive bias modification and alcohol use disorders. *Journal of Studies on Alcohol and Drugs, 79*(3), 333–43.

Wildrige, V., & Bell, L. (2002). How CLIP became ECLIPSE: a mnemonic to assist in searching for health policy/management information. *Health Information and Libraries Journal, 2*, 113–15.

Williams, J.W., Plassman, B.L., Burke, J., & Benjamin, D. (2010). Preventing Alzheimer's disease and cognitive decline. *Evidence Report/Technology Assessment, 193*, 1–727.

Wilson, S.A., Byrne, P., Rodgers, S.E., & Maden, M. (2022). A systematic review of smartphone and tablet use by older adults with and without cognitive impairment. *Innovations in Aging, 6*(2). https://doi.org/10.1093/geroni/igac002

Zaza, S., Wright-de Aguero, L.K., Briss, P.A., Truman, B.I., Hopkins, D.P., Hennessy, M.H, Sosin, D.M., Anderson, L., Carande-Kulis, V.G., Teutsch, S.M., & Pappaioanou, M. (2000). Data collection instrument and procedure for systematic reviews in the Guide to Community Preventive Services. *American Journal of Preventative Medicine, 18*(1), 44–74.

Zumsteg, J.M., Cooper, J.S., & Noon, M.S. (2012). Systematic review checklist. *Journal of Industrial Ecology, 16*, S12–S21.

Index

Note: Page numbers in *italics* refer to figures and tables.

Made in United States
North Haven, CT
03 August 2024

55707134R00207